THE BRITISH ARCHAEOLOGICAL ASSOCIATION

CONFERENCE TRANSACTIONS
For the year 1984

X
MEDIEVAL ART, ARCHITECTURE AND ARCHAEOLOGY
in London

Edited by
Lindy Grant

1990

Previous volumes in the series

I.   Medieval Art and Architecture at Worcester Cathedral
II.   Medieval Art and Architecture at Ely Cathedral
III.   Medieval Art and Architecture at Durham Cathedral
IV.   Medieval Art and Architecture at Wells and Glastonbury
V.   Medieval Art and Architecture at Canterbury before 1220
VI.   Medieval Art and Architecture at Winchester Cathedral
VII.   Medieval Art and Architecture at Gloucester and Tewkesbury
VIII.   Medieval Art and Architecture at Lincoln Cathedral
IX.   Medieval Art and Architecture in the East Riding of Yorkshire

Copies of these may be obtained from W. S. Maney and Son Limited, Hudson Road, Leeds LS9 7DL
or from Oxbow Books, 10 St Cross Road, Oxford OX1 3TU

ISBN Hardbook 0 901286 25 7
Paperback 0 901286 24 9

PRINTED IN GREAT BRITAIN BY W. S. MANEY AND SON LIMITED
HUDSON ROAD, LEEDS LS9 7DL

CONTENTS

PAGE

Preface   v

The Contribution of Archaeology to our Understanding of Pre-Norman London, 1973–1988
by RALPH MERRIFIELD   1

Medieval and Tudor Domestic Buildings in the City of London
by JOHN SCHOFIELD   16

Shops and Shopping in Medieval London
by DEREK KEENE   29

The Romanesque Architecture of Old St Paul's Cathedral and its Late Eleventh-Century Context
by RICHARD GEM   47

The First Façade of Old St Paul's Cathedral: Did it Have Flanking Towers?
by J. PHILIP MCALEER   64

The New Work at Old St Paul's Cathedral and its Place in English Thirteenth-Century Architecture
by RICHARD K. MORRIS   74

Restorations of the Temple Church, London
by C. M. L. GARDAM   101

'Liber Horn', 'Liber Custumarum' and Other Manuscripts of the Queen Mary Psalter Workshops
by LYNDA DENNISON   118

London, Londoners and Opus Anglicanum
by PENELOPE WALLIS   135

Some New Types of Late Medieval Tombs in the London Area
by BRIDGET CHERRY   140

Abbreviations   155

References   159

Plates   at end

Preface

The publication of this volume has been aided by generous contributions from the Fishmonger's Company and from the Brewer's Company, for which the Association is most grateful.

In this volume, we have adopted the author/date system for footnotes, and full references will be found in the single large bibliography at the back of the volume. Where an author/date reference was bibliographically impossible, or misleading, shortened titles have been used. These, together with abbreviations, occupy the first section of the bibliography. The Association would like to thank Mrs F. M. Grant for her help in typing the bibliography.

LINDY GRANT
Editor

The Contribution of Archaeology to our Understanding of Pre-Norman London, 1973–1988

By Ralph Merrifield

The publication by Rescue of *The Future of London's Past* in 1973[1] marked a turning-point in the hitherto lamentable course of archaeological endeavour in London — a saga of heroic efforts by a few individuals, indifference and neglect by public authorities, and the tragic loss of a priceless heritage. Martin Biddle and Daphne Hudson with Carolyn Heighway produced a report setting out these circumstances in detail, supported by maps that demonstrated graphically the rate of destruction of archaeological evidence in the City of London. It had been forestalled a few months earlier by a simpler but equally effective report, *Archaeology in the City of London — an Opportunity*, presented to the Corporation of London by the newly-appointed Director of Guildhall Museum, Max Hebditch.[2] Both reports stressed the need for a team of full-time professional archaeologists to devote their attention to what is arguably the most important archaeological site in Britain, and before the end of 1973 such a team had already commenced work. Guildhall Museum, instead of a single field officer, suddenly found itself responsible for a new Department of Urban Archaeology that needed supporting services in conservation, photography and draughtsmanship. This responsibility was taken over by its successor, the Museum of London, two years later, but the new Museum was concerned with the whole of London, not merely with its historic core, the Roman and medieval walled city. Its other progenitor, the London Museum, already had a small Field Department, and it was impossible to ignore the claims of other areas of archaeological importance, such as north Southwark and west London, where important discoveries had been made, to say nothing of Westminster, which had always been neglected. By one means or another, mainly through Government grants administered by County Societies and independent Trusts, professional archaeological cover was extended through Greater London, but it was only in 1983 that a unified archaeological service for Greater London was set up under the administration of the Museum of London, in parallel with its service for the City.[3] In the City itself activity at the time of writing has reached unprecedented heights, with work proceeding concurrently on no fewer than six major sites. This is in part a direct result of the technological revolution in the financial world, for it has been necessary to rebuild extensively in the City to accommodate the necessary equipment, so that many buildings constructed after the war have already become obsolete. Fortunately in the changed climate of opinion developers are now mostly prepared to contribute generously towards the cost of investigating and recording the archaeological evidence that they will inevitably destroy. This may be a small proportion of the total cost of development, but is a considerable sum, for which archaeologists are duly grateful. After fifteen years of vastly increased endeavour, it is an appropriate time for a general survey of the achievements of that period. Sacrifices have been made, not least by archaeologists, who have devoted years of their lives to a profession that makes great demands, and to the great majority offers little reward. Most work under contract with minimal security and no adequate career prospects, for only a few can hope eventually to find permanent academic or museum posts for which their skill and experience will be an advantage. The justification for such sacrifices must be the contribution made by rescue archaeology to our understanding of London's past, but it is not easy to assess this. It would be unfair merely to list outstanding discoveries in the last fifteen years, for one generation of archaeologists must build on the work of its predecessors, and relatively minor additions to our knowledge may provide the solution to a long-standing problem, or may even change our views completely. A better test might be to compare the model we had constructed fifteen years ago with the one we now believe to be closer to reality. Yet even this is unfair, if it fails to take account of the importance of recent work that has confirmed many of our earlier ideas, and has given substance to what was previously a tenuous hypothesis. We must also consider the value of the immense work of research that has followed excavations, notably in the study of finds, which has also led to reassessment of the significance of earlier finds. Value judgements are always subjective, and a short paper must also be highly selective. The archaeological contributions discussed here are those that seem most significant to the writer.

PREHISTORY

In general the importance of archaeology as the source of our knowledge increases the farther we go back in time. In the recent periods where documentation abounds it can restore flesh to the bare bones of history, and can give invaluable new information to specialists, such as students of domestic buildings or ceramics, but is unlikely to modify our overall view of the period. In prehistory, however, we are totally dependent on it, and a single find can suddenly illuminate the darkness of millennia. This has recently happened with the discovery of an Upper Palaeolithic hunters' camp at Uxbridge, dating from the final stages of the last glaciation, where flint artefacts have been found associated with bones of reindeer and horse.[4] Provisionally dated about 8000 B.C., it appears to be 2000 years earlier than the oldest comparable camp of hunter-gatherers found in the lower Thames region — an early post-glacial (Boreal period) site at Broxbourne in the Upper Lea Valley. The Uxbridge find is of great importance since it demonstrates that the Thames basin was inhabited sooner after the severest phase of the last Ice Age than had been thought — and no unstratified artefacts that could be firmly dated to that period and culture had previously been identified in our Museum collections to prepare us for the discovery.

The reverse is true of other recent finds of the later prehistoric periods, which have rightly been acclaimed because for the first time Neolithic, Bronze Age and Early Iron Age structures have been found *in situ* in central London. These are important, if somewhat less significant as they are not unexpected, in view of the numerous artefacts of these periods that have in the past been found in the City, north Southwark, Westminster and north Lambeth, or in the adjacent river.[5] As I have pointed out elsewhere, however, some of these may have been brought to the older parts of London by later collectors, who since Roman times have valued antiquities of certain kinds, notably polished stone axes, as protective talismans.[6] There are also special problems about river finds, of which large quantities have been found by dredging in west London, where Bronze Age weapons are particularly common. The deposition of weapons in rivers at certain periods is a familiar phenomenon, by no means confined to the Thames, and most prehistorians would probably agree that a ritual motive underlies it, though it remains uncertain whether the ritual accompanied ceremonies to placate the gods, to honour the dead, or to gain social prestige by destroying valuables, as in some tribes of British Columbia.[7] Ritual, however, often involves a journey, as in pilgrimage, and may also take place at tribal boundaries, so a concentration of offerings at a river — a natural boundary — does not necessarily indicate the proximity of a settlement. We therefore need to build up a pattern of occupation from structures *in situ* at all periods. The commencement of this process — and it is no more — is therefore welcome. On the site of the Bricklayers Arms Railway Depot in Southwark we now have a platform of interlacing sections of wood, associated with two neolithic stone axes and flint flakes, and presumably neolithic in period; scientific dating by carbon 14 should in due course confirm this and give a fairly close date.[8] A ring-ditch 8 m (26 ft) in diameter found at Fennings Wharf, Southwark, is attributed to the Late Bronze Age or beginning of the Early Iron Age from pottery found in a central pit, but the structure was itself ritual — almost certainly funerary, for cremated human bone was found in the fill of the ditch. It does not therefore indicate occupation on this site, but it need not have been far away; and from more than one site in central London the intensive investigations of the last few years have brought to light pottery sherds of this period, indicating the close proximity of domestic life. The most important structural evidence of later prehistory in this area comes from Richmond Terrace, Westminster, where a timber platform and post, now dated by carbon 14 to 590 ± 70 bc, were found in 1983 by the Central Excavation Unit.[9] The significance of this find was its excellent preservation and the fact that it lay deep under a clay-like silt that would normally be described as 'natural soil' and would not be investigated. Now that archaeologists have been alerted by this discovery, we may hope for more finds of this nature.

Now it may reasonably be asked what all this has to do with London. Indeed the existence of small scattered communities of primitive farmers and fishermen along the banks of the Thames has no bearing on the history of London beyond demonstrating that the environment could support human life, at least at subsistence level. This is not always understood by the general public, as was recently demonstrated by a newspaper comment that the Neolithic structural finds at the Bricklayers Arms indicated that the beginnings of London were 'earlier and more extensive than had been thought'! In fact, as Merriman has pointed out, research into local prehistory 'has been bedevilled by the search for a nucleated Late Iron Age settlement in the area of the City which would have been a predecessor to Roman Londinium'.[10]

Yet prehistoric studies of the Lower and Middle Thames are not by any means irrelevant to our understanding of the special strength and occasional weakness of London, and may help to explain its vicissitudes. The prehistorians of an earlier generation had little information from excavation, but had an immense wealth of unstratified finds to study, mostly from the river. Specialists in Bronze Age metalwork, such as the late J. D. Cowan, were able to demonstrate that new inventions and improvements of foreign origin appeared in the Thames valley earlier than in any other part of Britain, but were then copied with small changes of design by British smiths. These British copies were concentrated like the imports in the Thames valley, in the general area of London, and there seems little doubt that they were made there. More remarkably, some of these copies have been found widely distributed on the Continent, strongly suggesting an export trade from the Thames valley. This can be demonstrated particularly clearly by the varieties of the bronze slashing sword with leaf-shaped blade.[11] The earliest imported types originated in Switzerland and the Upper Rhine Valley, and there is no doubt that the great Rhine-Thames water-route was already being exploited. The existence of Thames-side settlements that were concerned both with trading and manufacture, and could be regarded as forerunners (though not ancestors) of London was therefore postulated, and the most important prehistoric discovery of recent years in the area has been an extensive Late Bronze Age settlement in Egham, on the western fringe of suburban London, excavated by Surrey Archaeological Society between 1972 and 1978. A substantial wharf with pile-driven timbers was found at the southern end of Runnymede Bridge, and occupation levels of the same period 80 m to the south were associated with post-holes and spreads of daub from huts. Imported objects such as a vase-headed pin, a notched razor and amber beads suggested trade with north or central Europe. There were also indications of local bronze-working, including a miscast razor still partly encased in its clay mould. 300 m further south, evidence of somewhat later metal-working has been found, continuing to the 7th and 6th century B.C. It included a hoard of bronze scrap with fragments of swords, knives and spearheads, and more complete but damaged socketed axes, gouge and spear-head. A stone mould for casting socketed axes of a distinctive south Welsh type — also represented in the hoard — came from the same area.[12] A manufacturing tradition seems to have been transferred from a place near the source of at least one of its raw materials — copper — to a place remote from them all, because of its advantageous position on a trade route. This may reflect not only the need to trade manufactured products, but also the importance of the collection of scrap metal for recycling from broken or obsolete tools and weapons.

It has been suggested that the Runnymede Bridge settlement was more than a village and acted as a regional centre of power — a little 'London', in fact, defended by its site between two channels of the Thames, by a palisade along the river-front, and possibly a big ditch further south.[13] There may well be others, yet to be found, especially on the Thames between Kingston and Wandsworth where abundant finds from the river have suggested the possible proximity of similar trading and manufacturing centres from the Middle Bronze Age to the earlier part of the Iron Age — about 1200–300 B.C.[14] Throughout this period there are indications that innovations from the Continent were being adapted and copied by local smiths, and that the river was intensively used as a trade route.

It also served as a boundary, however, and a site actually on the river may under some circumstances have seemed too peripheral and vulnerable for a regional centre — a function no doubt fulfilled by the earliest hill-forts of the Late Bronze Age, such as Wimbledon Common and Carshalton. The great archaeological wealth of the Thames dwindles later in the Iron Age, probably as a result of the declining importance of long-distance trade. Bronze as scrap metal or as its ingredients of copper, tin and lead, had to be brought from afar, whereas iron ore could be found everywhere and was particularly abundant in south-east Britain. Rosamond Hanworth has noted that in the years before the Claudian invasion Surrey seems to have turned its back on the Thames valley and was finally facing south.[15] As we know from coins and the first glimmerings of history, the Thames was then the boundary between the powerful kingdoms of the Atrebates and Cantii to the south and the Catuvellauni and Trinovantes to the north — circumstances unfavourable to its commercial exploitation and probably to settlement on its banks. Yet objects of value, such as the Battersea Shield and the Waterloo Helmet, were being dropped into the Thames during this period, probably reflecting in the ritual not local prosperity but the power and wealth of the aristocracy of adjacent kingdoms and its concern to defend its territory. John Kent, however, has suggested that the distribution of coin-finds indicates there probably was an *oppidum* of considerable importance on or near the Thames in the west London area, during the earlier 1st century B.C. It may have been a settlement of Trinovantes, brought to an end by the expansion of Cassivellaunus' power, and it almost certainly no longer existed when Julius Caesar passed through this area in 54 B.C.[16] Archaeologists have as yet found no evidence of its site, however, and its existence remains hypothetical.

Prehistoric settlements on the Thames may have fulfilled certain functions that were later characteristic of London, but they lacked its permanence, for their landward communications gave no particular advantage to any one site. London was essentially a Roman creation, as dependent on the Roman road system centring on London Bridge as it was on the river itself. Moreover it could only achieve its proper purpose as a centre of communications under a strong government in firm control of both sides of the river.

ROMAN LONDON

It is particularly interesting to those of us who were concerned with the problems of Roman London twenty years ago to observe how some have since been solved while new ones have arisen. The model we constructed then has on the whole survived subsequent investigation reasonably well. By general consensus we still view Londinium as a new town created under Claudius by the provincial administration for its own purposes, totally destroyed by Boudica, but recovering and reaching the height of its prosperity and development in the late 1st-early 2nd century, the period in which its major public buildings were constructed. To the forum and basilica, the great public baths on Huggin Hill, the palatial building in Cannon Street that may well have been the governor's winter quarters, and the Cripplegate fort that housed his guards and staff, all of which have long been known, we now have to add another — an amphitheatre found in 1988 on a site where its existence had never been suspected. Its central arena lay beneath Guildhall Yard, which seems to have remained an open space and natural place of assembly in London's subsequent history. The first Guildhall was built in the 13th century over the centre of the northern half of its raised seating, the place imperial and civic dignitaries would have occupied in Roman London. The proximity of the south-east corner of the fort suggests that the amphitheatre served a dual purpose — as *ludus* or training-ground for the garrison as well as for entertainment.

In this period Londinium was undoubtedly the centre of provincial administration — in effect the capital city of Roman Britain,[17] as we knew in the 1960s from earlier finds. Our dating of two important events in the history of Londinium — the construction of its outstandingly large basilica and forum to about A.D. 100, and the building of its great landward city wall to about a century later — has survived subsequent work and reassessment. Several errors, for which I was responsible, have however now been corrected. The first was historical and at that time seemed logical. I argued then for the construction of London Bridge and the beginning of Londinium at an early phase of the Claudian conquest, immediately following the initial crossing of the river in A.D. 43.[18] Our present consensus is that London Bridge was not built (and Londinium born) until at least seven years later.[19] This is based on pottery-dating of the earliest occupation levels beside the roads leading to the bridge in Southwark, and also on a statistical analysis of the Claudian coin pattern of Southwark, which conforms more closely with sites considered to have been occupied after A.D. 50 (Exeter and Lea Mills) than with those known to have been occupied in A.D. 43 (Richborough, Hod Hill and Colchester).[20] Some reservations remain, however, since this date must imply the regular use by the Romans of another crossing-place of the Thames for at least seven years. It ought to be at Westminster, for the alignments of Watling Street north and south of the river should meet there, and an early road has been found in Southwark, apparently leading from London Bridge in the direction of this putative crossing in north Lambeth. The onus is now on the archaeologists to find evidence of the early military occupation that must be associated with such a crossing.

Another error was topographical, and although less important, it was also less excusable. On the large map of sites that accompanied my 1965 book,[21] I placed my conjectural Roman water-line near London Bridge just south of Thames Street, disregarding the wharf-like structures that had already been recorded on both sides of King William Street. I had not then seen any Roman wharf, but had seen Roman terracing with stone retaining walls in the western part of the City, and assumed that these massive wooden walls served a similar purpose in providing level ground for building at an earlier date. It is a measure of the increase of our knowledge in the last twenty-five years that I could not then believe that the Roman river-front ever extended 100 m north of the present river-edge. As a result of a series of important excavations that began in 1973 and continued until 1982, we now know that the waterfront in the City has repeatedly advanced to the south, at least three times in the Roman period and several more times in the Middle Ages and later. The great advantage given to archaeologists by the massive water-logged timbers of waterfronts is that they can now often be closely dated by dendrochronology, providing a series of fixed chronological points, not only for the structures of which they form part, but also for any artefacts these may contain. In Roman times waterfront construction or reconstruction took place in the late 1st, early 2nd, mid-late 2nd, and early 3rd centuries, but seems to have been a piecemeal process in which different parts of the waterfront had somewhat different histories. Nevertheless, the massive box-like wharfs have the appearance of public works carried out to a uniform standard, though with minor variations in construction. Each time one was constructed the shore-line was advanced, and the old wharf, usually still in good condition, was buried under the new embankment. It has been suggested that one purpose was to gain more space for warehouses and dockside activities, but a more important reason was probably the need to maintain a certain depth of water adjacent to the wharf, so that large ships could come alongside. Refuse and silt accumulated against the wharfs, and it may then have been easier to enclose this under a new extension than to remove it by dredging. Certainly warehouses were built near the bridge on land won by extensions of the water-front in the late 1st and early 2nd century, but, as we shall see, the need for more space probably does not account for the subsequent extension of the late 2nd-early 3rd century. All aspects of the port of Londinium have been discussed in a recent book by Gustav Milne, one of the leading investigators of these riverside sites, with contributions from his colleagues.[22] This is a major addition to the literature on Roman London. Interestingly, its conclusion is to minimise the importance of the port of Londinium, even in the earlier period when it developed rapidly, in contrast with the city's obvious importance as an administrative centre. Its varied imports, mostly luxuries, were primarily for local consumption, it is suggested, with a regional distribution no more extensive than that of many other Romano-British ports. This opinion is based mainly on the small scale of the warehouses in the central area that has been investigated. On this point we must reserve judgement. It is impossible to make any quantitative estimate of the overseas trade of Londinium on our present evidence. What port facilities were there on the other side of the river, where medieval erosion has removed almost the entire Roman waterfront? Certainly there were some, for a well-preserved wooden warehouse of the earlier Roman period was found in 1988 at the foot of a ramp beside the river on the Courage Brewery site, Park Street, Southwark. Here, well upstream of the Roman bridge, the southern river edge has been exceptionally preserved from erosion by a small inlet. What evidence have we lost further downstream in the area more accessible to sea-going ships, where the Roman riverside has gone completely?[23] Even on the City side, we know virtually nothing of the warehouses and other facilities that must have accompanied the waterfronts east of Botolph Lane — a stretch of more than 600 m. It cannot be assumed that they were all like those found near the bridgehead. These seem to have been 'primarily associated with the storage and selling of relatively small quantities of the kind of luxury goods for which we have evidence in the form of amphora sherds — wine, *garum*, olive oil, etc.'.[24] The luxury trade may in fact have been concentrated here precisely *because* of its central position, while bulk cargoes were unloaded in outlying parts of the waterfront, where they could more conveniently be transferred to road transport. If we were to judge from these excavations alone, we would have to accept that no port of Londinium existed before the Flavian period, and would be left wondering why Londinium was founded twenty years earlier, if not to take advantage of its maritime possibilities on or near the tidal part of the river. The earliest revetment on the foreshore is dated by dendrochronology 'after A.D. 59 but before A.D. 74, possibly A.D. 70',[25] and otherwise mid-1st century activity is limited to quarrying for sand and gravel, a flint and chalk spread and several rows of piles to strengthen a modest gravel embankment.[26] Yet even if we disregard the statement of Tacitus about the activity of *negotiatores* and the abundance of supplies in the Londinium destroyed by Boudica in A.D. 60,[27] we have archaeological evidence from sites in the centre of the city that not only luxury imports in amphorae were already reaching Londinium, together with fine imported pottery, but also bulk cargoes such as grain. A timber-framed building north of Fenchurch Street that was probably a corn chandler's shop, burnt in A.D. 60, contained a deposit of carbonised grain a metre thick, some of which has been identified as imported from the Mediterranean.[28] These goods must surely have reached London by ship at least ten years earlier than the first harbour installations recognised by Milne. It seems clear that excavation has not given us the full story of the port of Londinium, and now perhaps never can. Where so much remains unknown we should not attach too much importance to negative evidence.

The intensive investigation of the river-front by archaeologists in the last fourteen years has however corrected yet another misconception to which I have subscribed. In the 1960s we were well aware that Roach Smith and others had observed a great wall or walls under the middle of Upper Thames Street and under the north side of Lower Thames Street, and knew that these were close to the river-edge. As they were of varied builds, however, very different from the uniform landward defensive wall, we assumed that they were a series of river embankments and stone quays not unlike those of today.[29] This view was abandoned when a close investigation of levels in 1974–6 showed that the base of the wall stood well above the river level when it was constructed; in the part examined closely in the south-west corner of the city there was evidence of an internal bank, but not of the massive dumping that would have been necessary if the wall had merely been for terracing; moreover, for a long stretch the wall appeared to be continuous. All this was convincing evidence that its purpose was defensive, and the variations in structure were accounted for by differences in the sub-soil and the local availability of material from earlier buildings for re-use.[30] Where the underlying ground was gravel the wall was built on a chalk raft and wooden piles; where it was clay the piling and chalk were missing and the foundations were of large stones laid directly on the clay.[31] It was this portion of the wall that contained reused material, including architectural and sculptured blocks. These suggested that the wall was not earlier than the Christian 4th century, for they included pagan religious sculptures and altars from a demolished temple or temples, with an inscription indicating that the temple from which it came had been rebuilt in the joint reign of two emperors, most probably either Trebonianus Gallus and Valerian or Valerian and Gallienus (A.D. 251–9).[32] If this is the date when the altar was set up in the rebuilt temple, subsequently demolished and used as a source of building material for the wall, it is hard to believe that the latter was built earlier than a date well into the 4th century, when under Christian dominance such a demolition would have been acceptable. For the portions of wall built upon piles and chalk no archaeological indication of date was available, and there was recourse to a combination of C14 dating and dendrochronology of samples taken from the wooden piles. Unfortunately in the late 1970s the dendrochronology of Roman Britain was still 'floating', and not firmly anchored in chronological time by correlation with events of known date, like German dendrochronology, then still unpublished and inaccessible to British scholarship. One group of piles could be compared with another or with other wood from Roman Britain, but they could only be given a date by C14 with its large margin of error. On this basis they were then attributed to 'about A.D. 330–50 in radio-carbon terms', with corrective calibration bringing the wall's construction 'closer to A.D. 400'.[33] It was therefore then possible to believe that in spite of its diversity of structure the entire riverside wall had been built at one time, as part of the same late-4th century preoccupation with defence that had produced the bastions in the eastern part of the landward wall. These likewise were uncertainly dated, but with some coin evidence and the common use of reused material from monuments in the Roman cemetery pointing to a 4th-century origin.[34] Records of a long wall under Upper Thames Street, observed by Roach Smith in 1841, seemed in fact to give some confirmation of the contemporaneity of the two types of wall found in 1974–6, by combining their characteristics — a foundation of piles and chalk with reused architectural material from an impressive building or buildings.[35] Subsequent developments in dendrochronology, however, have led to a drastic revision of the views expressed in 1980. In the following year an absolute chronology of British timbers extending back to A.D. 404 was published, and at about the same time two independent chronologies of German timbers extending back into the first millennium B.C., as well as an Irish sequence going back to 13 B.C., all became available. By cross-matching these a revised date of A.D. 255 was given to the final ring of the riverside wall piles at Baynard's Castle, indicating a date in the third quarter of the 3rd century for the foundations of the wall.[36] These foundations are similar to those of the first phase of the riverside wall at the Tower of London, where a later wall just to the north *is* fairly securely dated by coin evidence to the late 4th century.[37] Clearly the history of the riverside wall is much more complex than we believed in 1980, with at least two phases of building or rebuilding, the first of which may not have completed its extension to the extreme west of the city. Interpretation of evidence is constantly being revised by new discoveries and new research, and we should not forget the possibility that the 3rd-century foundations might have been laid for another purpose altogether, although they were subsequently used for the defensive wall. They are very much like the pile and chalk foundations that supported the south and west walls of a massive structure, believed to be a temple, just to the east on Peter's Hill.[38] This whole area in the south-west corner of the city seems to have been a religious precinct in the 3rd century, and the dendrochronological date of the piles beneath the riverside wall is very close to the date of the rebuilding of the temple whose fragments are incorporated in it. From other architectural pieces it contains, it has been possible to reconstruct a monumental arch and a screen of deities in relief, which evidently formed part of the precinct.[39] As for the similar foundation of piles and chalk at the Tower of London, which may well be of equally early date, it must be remembered that this corner of the city's defences was particularly vulnerable, and the need for some sort of continuation from the landward wall along the river-front may have been felt as soon as the landward wall was built; it did not necessarily continue to enclose the entire river-front.

The discovery in 1976–7 of a Roman defensive riverside wall partly underlying the southern side of the Inner Curtain wall of the Tower of London, together with that of a hitherto unknown bastion of the city wall in 1979–80, has given new credibility to an old hypothesis. The newly-discovered bastion 4A lies exactly midway between the known bastions 4 and 5, and demonstrates that there was a series of four bastions regularly spaced south of Aldgate at intervals of about 180 ft, a spacing approximately comparable to that of the known bastions 6–9 north of Aldgate. John Maloney also demonstrated that the known bastions 2 and 1 (Wardrobe Tower) to the south could be fitted into the same regular series on the assumption that there were three more missing bastions, one at the junction of the landward and riverside walls, as would be expected, and a somewhat wider gap to accommodate a suspected Roman Postern Gate. If the same spacing were continued along the riverside wall, there would have been late Roman bastions on the sites of the medieval Lanthorn Tower, Wakefield Tower, Bell Tower and Middle Tower, all spaced 170–85 ft apart.[40] The suggestion that these towers were built on the sites of Roman bastions, with the Lanthorn Tower on the corner bastion at the junction of landward and riverside walls, was made as early as 1913,[41] based mainly on Fitzstephen's 12th-century account of the riverside wall, then long vanished, but remembered as 'towered like the landward wall'.[42] His view that it was undermined and destroyed by river action has been confirmed archaeologically, and there is no reason to doubt the tradition of its towers.

Whatever the importance of Londinium as a port in the 1st and 2nd centuries, it can hardly have survived even the partial enclosure of the waterfront by a defensive wall, constructed just behind it and effectively barring communication with the city itself, except at intervals where a gate might give restricted access. No doubt this was the reason that the riverside wall was never rebuilt in the Middle Ages, whereas the landward wall was repaired and strengthened on more than one occasion. There is in fact evidence that a surviving portion of riverside wall at Blackfriars was deliberately demolished by pulling it down to the landward side, probably not earlier than the late 12th century, when there are indications of a revival of waterfront activities in the area.

In earlier Roman times London was primarily an administrative and trading centre; in late Roman times, after the building of its great landward wall about A.D. 200, its most important role seems to have been that of strategic base, a place from which imperial authority could re-establish its control against the threat of anarchy. Albinus probably hoped to do so in 196; Severus did so in 208, but was able to move on at once to develop an advance base at York for a similar purpose; Carausius established his mint in Londinium and evidently made it his base in 287; to Constantius Chlorus in 296 the rescue of London meant the recovery of Britain; Lupicinus came to London as a trouble-shooter for Julian in 360; Theodosius reconstructed the army there in 368 after the worse troubles of 367, and marched from London to recover Britain for Valentinian the following year — a service that may have earned Londinium its new name of Augusta.[44] Against this historical background we can readily understand that London had become a very different kind of city, more concerned with defence than trade, but retaining an administrative role in the various reorganisations of Britain.[45]

There is not much archaeological evidence for life in late Roman London, but its very sparseness indicates the change. There is now little doubt that in spite of London's continuing historical importance, its population had shrunk. A valuable survey of Roman rubbish pits, published by Peter Marsden in 1980, demonstrated that more domestic rubbish was deposited in the first century of London's existence than in the following 250 years.[46] Those who were familiar with the collections of Roman London had always been aware that those of the earlier period were overwhelmingly predominant, but Marsden's study presented this fact to others in quantitative form. The same truth emerged from site after site in Southwark and in the western part of the walled city, indicating continued occupation until the second half of the 2nd century, followed by a period when the site remained open and was perhaps under cultivation of some kind, indicated by featureless 'dark earth'. The date of abandonment of the hitherto much frequented Walbrook valley in the centre of the city is shown by coin evidence to have been about A.D. 155–60.[47] Whether this was due to a visitation of plague, economic depression due to changes in trading patterns, the breakdown of order resulting from civil disturbance or hostile incursions, or some combination of these circumstances, remains obscure. Harvey Sheldon has pointed out that the decline was not confined to London but may have been widespread in southern

Britain.[48] There is evidence of reoccupation later in the 3rd century of some abandoned areas, both on the banks of the Walbrook and in Southwark, by the construction of substantial stone buildings. Even in the period of apparent decline, however, imperial patronage ensured that Londinium received the benefit of great public works — new wharfs built in the early 3rd century, its landward wall of *c.* 200, and a precinct of temples and sculptural monuments built in the late 2nd or (more probably) early 3rd century. Further contraction seems to have taken place in Southwark, however, perhaps because of its lack of defences, and the site of a succession of Roman buildings in Southwark Street was being used as a burial ground in the later 4th century.[49] Within the walled city itself there is evidence of very late Roman occupation near the river-front, on sites between Peter's Hill in the west and the Tower of London in the east. There is even evidence of a revival of activity at this time, with rebuilding east of Fish Street Hill after 375.[50] It is possible that this is another manifestation of the last flicker of life in the port of Londinium, that is demonstrated by the presence of amphorae of about this period from the eastern Mediterranean. A fragment of one of these underlay the ashes of the final fire of the furnace that supplied under-floor heating to a house overlooking the river near Billingsgate. This was occupied at least until the last years of the 4th century, as is shown by a scattered coin hoard found within it, and was subsequently quietly abandoned and left to become ruinous.[51] I have suggested that London's security, combined with its accessibility to shipping, may have made it a convenient entrepôt for trade in captives, the one commodity that became increasingly available at times of trouble. Eastern traders, however, are unlikely to have taken much part in this traffic before the disruption of western trade by barbarian invasion in the early 5th century.[52]

ANGLO-SAXON LONDON

Our understanding of Anglo-Saxon London has developed dramatically within the last decade, but this has been due less to the discovery of positive evidence by excavation than to the steady accumulation of negative evidence on site after site within the Roman city. The derelict late Roman building near Billingsgate had visitors in the second half of the 5th century, one of whom lost a brooch in the debris of its collapsed roof. It can be closely paralleled in the early Saxon cemetery at Mitcham in Surrey, and is one of only two or three portable objects of this period found in the City of London — the only one, in fact, from an archaeological context. It merely indicates that the ruins of the Roman city were sometimes visited, probably by foragers. To find evidence of actual occupation in the 5th and 6th centuries, in the form of burials or domestic refuse, such as pottery, we have to go further afield — to Mucking overlooking the Thames estuary, to Greenwich, Mitcham and Croydon, or to Clapham, where pits and pottery of the early Saxon period have been found.[53] Brian Hobley has pointed out that, according to Ammianus, Saxon invaders of Gaul had a horror of Roman cities and regarded their walls as a trap.[54] They had particularly good reason to do so in the case of London, with its circuit of more than 3 miles (5 km) of defences, that could only be guarded by a large standing garrison — an impossible requirement for anyone but a powerful ruler who could draw on great territorial resources. It was doubtless for this reason, as well as economic necessity, that the walled city was soon abandoned by the British refugees, who, according to the Anglo-Saxon Chronicle, took refuge there after the Battle of Crecganford, traditionally dated to 457. It was safer to be in open country, where there was a chance to run away and hide when danger approached. The Thames, in fact, now reverted to its pre-Roman role of a frontier, separating the kingdoms that were taking shape, between Essex and Kent, and subsequently between Mercia and Wessex.

In the absence of trade or any economic basis beyond mere subsistence, it is not surprising that our archaeological evidence of life in London is negative for the period 450–600. What has always been particularly disturbing, however, is that it continued to be so until a very much later date. In the City of London collections gathered over many years, Anglo-Saxon objects of all dates were much rarer even than those of the late Roman period. When Jean Cook, a specialist in Anglo-Saxon archaeology, joined the staff of Guildhall Museum in 1956, her first task was to search the collection for material of this period. Apart from two sculptured stones of the 11th century, one from St Paul's churchyard, with a few complete pots of dubious or unknown provenance, they could all be contained in just two of the Museum's standard storage boxes, a little longer than shoe-boxes. Structures of the period were practically unknown, apart from a single sunken hut-site attributed to a late Saxon date in Cannon Street, and a few portions of similar huts and pits on Wood Street. There was also a standing arch of ragstone and reused Roman brick, revealed by bombing in All Hallows Barking Church, near the Tower, attributed to the Middle Saxon period. This was all we had to show for the four centuries of history during which St Paul's was built and the Bishopric of London founded in 604: trade revived so that London could be described in the 730s by Bede as a trading centre of many nations, coming to it by land and sea: Alfred captured London in 886 and made it one of his strongholds, after which it successfully resisted the Danes in 994, 1009 and 1014. The sparseness of archaeological evidence from these four centuries was attributed by Martin Biddle in 1973 to the less conspicuous character of Anglo-Saxon buildings, and the tendency of archaeologists 'to concentrate upon the study of Roman London without an equal regard for the archaeology of the city's subsequent periods'.[55]

Thanks largely to the campaign led with such resolution by Martin Biddle, in the next ten years excavation in the City of London took place on a hitherto unprecedented scale, and the skilled archaeologists of the newly-established Department of Urban Archaeology of the Museum of London were determined to solve this long-standing problem. To this end all that was known of Anglo-Saxon pottery was closely studied, and a careful watch was maintained for all traces of vanished timber structures. Certainly more Anglo-Saxon wooden buildings were identified, ranging from small sunken-floored huts of 'Grubenhaus' type to large halls, on at least eight sites, but their number was still small in proportion to the vastly increased scale of excavation. Moreover, when these structures could be dated, they all belonged to the period between the late 9th and the 11th centuries, and it was to this late period that all evidence of Anglo-Saxon occupation within the city walls seemed to belong.[56] Ten years of controlled excavation on a large scale had not changed the overall picture of Anglo-Saxon London, worrying as it was, that had been presented by the earlier very small-scale excavations of W. F. Grimes and the unsatisfactory observations of building-sites that had extended over many years. Much important information had been acquired, including some of great topographical interest, such as the tendency to build houses in minor Roman roadways, and to establish new street-lines.[57] The outstanding question remained unanswered, however; where was the busy trading port of the 8th century that had been described by Bede? It seems to have been in existence as early as 672–4, when it is mentioned in Frithuwald's charter as 'the port of London where ships come to land'.[58] Yet the earliest post-Roman embankment yet discovered in an intensive investigation of the City waterfronts was one of the 10th century at New Fresh Wharf.[59]

In 1984, Martin Biddle and Alan Vince independently put forward the same answer, which has a ring of truth. Basing their conclusions on the distribution of earlier casual finds

B

and on the significance of place-names, both suggested that the Middle Saxon port was to be found not in the Roman city but west of it, along the riverside between the river Fleet and Whitehall, occupied by the modern street appropriately called the Strand. The name Aldwych is even more significant, as meaning 'the old *wic*', a name often given to mid-Saxon trading settlements. Now the name of a 20th-century street, it was formerly applied to an area at the eastern end of the Strand.[60] The walled city, it is suggested, was at this time partly under cultivation of some kind — hence the ubiquitous 'dark earth' — with a church and bishop's palace on the site of St Paul's, and possibly a royal palace with chapel within the former Roman fort.[61] The church of All Hallows Barking at the eastern end of the city may also have been built by the end of the 7th century as a dependency of Barking Abbey. Hobley has pointed out that there were two names for London in the 8th and 9th centuries — Lundenburh and Lundenwic — and suggests that the former referred to the walled city with its few residences of high status, and the latter to the open trading settlement to the west.[62]

Excavation took place in 1985 at Jubilee Hall, Covent Garden, and Anglo-Saxon deposits 0.75 m thick were found, representing a sequence of occupation throughout the mid-Saxon period, with evidence for timber buildings with clay floors, pits, wells, a hearth, and a burial. The pottery included imports from northern France and the lower Rhine, and spanned the period 650–850. Quite recently the river-front has been located south of the Strand, and no doubt future excavations in this area will in due course build up our knowledge of mid-Saxon London. As might be expected, there is no evidence of a considerable movement of population back into the walled city before it was reorganised and again made a stronghold by Alfred in the late 9th century.

One important question seems to have been overlooked in most discussions of mid-Saxon London. If its port developed west of the Roman city, London Bridge no longer existed. It would, in fact, be unlikely that it could have survived 150 years of neglect before A.D. 600 in a safe condition, but at some point sufficient clearance of its wreckage must have been made to allow safe passage for shipping at least through a wide gap, and it was this act that created the port of *Lundenwic*. It seems impossible that a sophisticated drawbridge could have been constructed and operated in the almost derelict city, as we must assume was the case in Roman times. If it had been, tolls would have been levied, disputes would have arisen, and some record or tradition of all this must surely have survived. Instead, we have a tradition that implies the bridge was no longer there. This, handed down through the Priory of Saint Mary Overie, is the legend that the first church on that site, now occupied by Southwark Cathedral, was built in the 7th century by the daughter of a ferryman, who inherited her father's wealth, and founded a religious house for women just upstream of the site of the Roman and medieval bridges.[63] Since the Roman roads still led to this point, in the absence of a bridge a ferryman would never have lacked trade.

Perhaps archaeology, aided by dendrochronology, will one day give us the date London Bridge was rebuilt. At present we can only discuss probabilities. We have no specific reference indicating the existence of the bridge before the late 10th century, when the laws of Aethelred fixed tolls for vessels bringing fish and wood to the bridge.[64] By this time it appears that the bridge was an important part of the defences of London, and could effectively block the movement upstream of hostile ships, as seems to have happened in 994, when a powerful Viking fleet was repulsed with heavy losses. An essential feature of this river defence must have been the fortification of Southwark, believed to have given Southwark its name of *Suthringe geweorch* as early as *c.* 910,[65] though archaeological evidence of this fortification has yet to be found. If the stirring account in the Olaf Sagas is to be believed, the defence of the bridge in 1014 could only be overcome by loosening its piles in a frontal assault from the river, in which the ships were protected by stout wooden roof-like screens — the historic occasion when a poet could claim 'London Bridge is broken down'.[66] Two years later, Cnut made no such attempt, but undertook the immense task of digging a great ditch south of the Southwark defences, no doubt linking many natural channels, so that his ships could be dragged upstream — another topographical feature that remains to be discovered by archaeologists. Yet ships *could* pass under the bridge if they were not opposed, as was shown in 1052, when the fleet of Earl Godwin was allowed to pass under it near the south shore, with the collaboration of Londoners, but it was only possible when the tide was flowing upstream.[67]

Dyson makes a strong case for the building of the bridge and fortification of Southwark being part of Alfred's programme of urban renewal of about A.D. 900, and points out that special attention was also being given elsewhere to important river-crossings and the control of river traffic in the years between 907 and 920.[68] How does this fit our archaeological and historical evidence from the City? We know something about the development of four areas of Anglo-Saxon waterfronts and their hinterland. The oldest is Queenhithe, then called *Aetheredeshyd*, first mentioned in 889, with grants of land behind it dated 889–99. There is no archaeological evidence. This waterfront is well upstream of the bridge, and if the latter was already being planned can only have been intended for upstream traffic. There is then a gap of forty years between this documentary date and the middle radio-carbon date of 940 for the New Fresh Wharf embankment just below the bridge, but we must remember the margin of error of ± 80 years, so the two waterfronts *could* be contemporary. On the other hand New Fresh Wharf could equally well be contemporary with the better-dated Billingsgate, further downstream from the bridge, first mentioned in documents of *c*. A.D. 1000. Occupation seems in fact to have begun at the north end of Botolph Lane and not reached the waterfront until the late 10th century. The dendrochronological dating of the first embankment is 1039–40, and a later embankment is dated 1050–70 by dendrochronology and after *c*. 1080 by a coin.[69] Waterside activity at Billingsgate therefore seems to have begun after A.D. 1000. A similar late date would be likely for Dowgate, above the bridge, where activity does not appear to be earlier than the 11th century. Queenhithe, therefore, seems to be the sole harbour within the city walls that is certainly of Alfred's time; it must originally have been as much concerned with downstream as with upstream traffic. If the development of Billingsgate as a more convenient site for the former was the direct result of building the bridge, it is unlikely to have been delayed for eighty years or so. On present evidence, therefore, the bridge should be of the *later* 10th century, and would have been a fairly new structure when it began to have a prominent role in London's history in 994. We do however need more evidence, particularly in view of the difficulty in close dating by purely archaeological means at this period. Dendrochronology clearly offers the best prospect, particularly in waterfront sites where timber usually survives in good condition.

Our knowledge of early London has made great strides thanks to the excavations and archaeological studies of the last fifteen years, and the archaeologists concerned are to be congratulated on their success in accomplishing such dramatic results. They were achieved by persistence in the face of many difficulties, which are unlikely to diminish in the next fifteen years. These will doubtless produce quite as many challenges and opportunities, and quite as much new knowledge if archaeologists are given a fair chance to rescue and record the remaining evidence before it is destroyed by development. As we have seen, there are still many unanswered questions, and many gaps to be filled.

REFERENCES

1. Biddle *et al.* (1973).
2. Hebditch (1973).
3. This does not include the boroughs east of the Lea, where the service is administered by the Passmore Edwards Museum, or the outer boroughs in Kent, administered by the Kent Archaeological Service.
4. Girardon and Heathcote (1988), 412.
5. Recently reassessed in Merriman (1987), 318 ff.
6. Merrifield (1987), 9–16.
7. Ibid., 23–30, 108ff; Bradley (1982), 108–22.
8. Girardon and Heathcote (1988), 414.
9. Merriman (1987), 320.
10. Ibid., 318.
11. Cowan (1951), 195–213; Cowan (1967), 377–454.
12. Longley and Needham (1980a); Longley and Needham (1980b), 397–436; Needham (1987), 116–23; O'Connell (1986), passim.
13. Needham (1987), 119.
14. Merrifield (1975), 30–8.
15. Hanworth (1987), 162.
16. Kent (1978), 53–8; Merrifield (1983), 9–12.
17. It has been pointed out that this status had no basis in any law or constitution. The same is, I believe, true of modern Britain and probably of most European states, but 'capital' remains a convenient term for the city where the principal instruments of central government are located — in Londinium the office of the procurator and the residence of the governor when he was not campaigning with the army. It had also probably become the meeting-place of the Provincial Council (Roman Britain's only representative body) and the headquarters of its staff, concerned mainly with administration of the State Cult of Emperor worship.
18. Merrifield (1965), 32–5; and (1969), 20–4.
19. Merrifield (1983), 23–36.
20. Bird *et al.* (1978), I, 22–7, 239–43; II, 588–93.
21. Merrifield (1965).
22. Milne (1985).
23. The river-front above the bridge was not necessarily concerned solely with upstream traffic, as was shown by the discovery of remains of a sea-going ship at County Hall, Westminster, and one that had brought ragstone from Kent at Blackfriars. There was a warehouse just above the bridge on the City side that was full of imported Gaulish pottery when it was destroyed by fire *c.* 130, see Milne (1985), 29. It is presumed that a draw-bridge allowed passage.
24. Milne (1985), 78.
25. Ibid., 37.
26. Ibid., 25–7.
27. Tacitus, XIV, 33, *Negotiatores* were merchants operating on a large scale, often engaged in import and export business.
28. Milne (1985), 77; Marsden (1980), 33, 208 n. 9.
29. Merrifield (1965), 108, 110–11.
30. Hill *et al.* (1980), 66–7.
31. Ibid., 30–1, 38, 45.
32. Ibid., 195–9.
33. Ibid., 93–4.
34. Ibid., 69.
35. Smith (1859), 18–19.
36. Sheldon and Tyers (1983), 355–61.
37. Parnell (1977), 97–9; Parnell (1978), 171–6.
38. Richardson (1982), 162.
39. Hill *et al.* (1980), 124–69.
40. Maloney (1980), 68–76.
41. Clapham and Godfrey (1913), 32–5.
42. William Fitzstephen in the prologue to a projected life of Becket, attributed to *c.* 1173: 'Similiterque ab Austro Londonia murata et turrita fuit; sed fluvius maximus piscosus Thamensis, mari influo refluoque, qui illac allabitur, moenia illa tractu temporis alluit, labefactavit, dejecit.'
43. Hill *et al.* (1980), 71–3.
44. For a full discussion of these events, see Merrifield (1983), chs 8 and 9.

45. Severus had divided Britain into two provinces, with London the capital of Britannia Superior and York that of Britannia Inferior. Under Diocletian it was further divided into four provinces, with London the capital of one, but also the seat of the *vicarius*, the link between the provincial governors and higher authority.

46. Marsden (1980), 148, 213 n. 27.

47. Merrifield (1962), 38–52.

48. Sheldon (1981), 363–82.

49. Beard and Cowan (1988), 375–81.

50. Milne (1985), 33.

51. Marsden (1980), 180–6.

52. Merrifield (1983), 250–1.

53. Densem and Seeley (1982), 177–84. Residual sherds of the late 6th-early 7th century have however been found in plough soil at 250 Euston Road, much closer to the Roman city, Whytehead and Blackmore (1983), 82–3.

54. Hobley (forthcoming).

55. Biddle *et al.* (1973), 16. In my own experience, however, all archaeologists concerned with the City of London between 1950 and 1973 were quite as interested in the problem of the missing Anglo-Saxons as any of their successors.

56. Hobley (1985), 22.

57. Ibid., 20.

58. Dyson (1980), 84. The identification of the land-grant with Southwark must now be questioned.

59. Schofield (1981), 24.

60. Biddle (1984), 23–7. Vince (1984), 310–12.

61. By tradition, recorded by Matthew Paris, the church of St Alban Wood Street was founded on the chapel of this palace and was contiguous with it.

62. Hobley (forthcoming).

63. Quoted by Stow, who had the story, directly or indirectly, from the last Prior, Stow (1615), 168.

64. A reference to the drowning of a witch at 'London bridge' about the middle of the 10th century has been doubted as evidence, since the crime took place at Ailsworth, Northants, and it is considered unlikely that the witch would have been brought eighty miles for punishment. The reference may be to a local bridge by which the London road passed over the river Welland. (Hill (1976), 303–4).

65. Dyson (1980), 91, citing the 'Burghal Hidage'.

66. Home (1931), 12–13, citing *The Olaf Sagas* with poem by Ottar Svarte.

67. Ibid., 10, 14–15.

68. Dyson (1980), 92–3.

69. Hobley (forthcoming).

Medieval and Tudor Domestic Buildings in the City of London

By John Schofield

INTRODUCTION

This paper is by way of an introduction to the complex subject of medieval London. The subject of this paper is itself so large that only a summary of current work and thoughts can be attempted. I therefore propose to maintain, where possible, an almost aerial viewpoint and describe some of the main features of the development of domestic buildings in London from the 13th to the 16th century. My paper divides into two parts: a brief survey of the most useful sources for study of medieval and Tudor London buildings, and then suggestions about some of the significant developments in domestic architecture and planning in these centuries.

MAIN SOURCES

The main sources for study of domestic building in this period are the surviving historic fragments, the results of archaeological excavation, and documentary evidence (especially building contracts, panoramas, drawn surveys and plans).

Surviving Buildings

The nineteen surviving fragments of secular medieval and Tudor buildings (including, for completeness, those of the early 17th century) in the City of London are a peculiar group, the product of chance survival through the Great Fire of London in 1666 and after three subsequent centuries of commercial redevelopment. At Guildhall (Pl. IIIA), traces of three successive stone buildings (two of which have left remains) have been recorded; there are also fragments of four other medieval undercrofts, a fifth undercroft below the medieval Merchant Taylors Hall, two timber buildings in the Tower of London, two timber buildings above gateways at Smithfield and in Fleet Street, and medieval or 16th-century halls and other buildings at five inns of lawyers. In Southwark the west gable of the hall of the Bishop of Winchester's town house can be seen, and to the north-west of the City a large part of a late 16th-century noble residence is preserved in the Charterhouse. To this group of survivals *in situ* should be added the hall of Crosby Place, removed to Chelsea, and the façade of Paul Pindar's house in Bishopsgate, now in the Victoria and Albert Museum.[1]

These are almost all fragments of well-built, high-class buildings, and almost all are late medieval or Tudor in date. It is axiomatic that only the better sort of building would have survived into early modern times even if the Great Fire of London had not taken place. The buildings which were recorded by 18th- and 19th-century antiquaries were also generally the more remarkable or durable structures, such as stone undercrofts, or the buildings of the late medieval and post-medieval period (Pl. I); a similar pattern can be found both in the region and in other medieval English towns where more has survived.[2] Though one or two London undercrofts date from the 13th century (most notably, the west undercroft of Guildhall), the majority of the standing remains date from the 15th or 16th centuries.

The surviving buildings are notable for the number of halls and hall roofs among them; for roofs, the surviving examples are a major source of information. The sheer bulk of Guildhall's walls has preserved enough evidence to make possible a reconstruction of its original roof.[3] Smaller roofs of the 15th century survive at Barnard's Hall and Lincoln's Inn; the ornamented ceiling of Crosby Hall presumably represents an otherwise lost genre. The halls at Gray's Inn (1560), Middle Temple (1572) and Staple Inn (1581) are useful for charting the introduction of Renaissance details into the woodwork of the medieval assembly-hall. Two Tudor gatehouses, similarly of a scale too large to be used in a study of domestic buildings except by way of analogy, survive at Lambeth Palace (1490) and Lincoln's Inn (1519); but Merchant Taylors Hall still retains (and keeps in use) its late 14th-century kitchen, rebuilt in the early 15th century, a valuable survivor of an originally widespread form of detached kitchen.

Several fragments of undercrofts, and four fairly complete examples, still survive inside modern buildings. Guildhall's two undercrofts, of c. 1270 and 1410–30, are both of three aisles, as befits a structure below a large public building; the domestic undercrofts, when known, were smaller structures of two aisles or, more commonly, one row of vaulted bays. These one-row undercrofts ran either at right angles to the street down the side of a property or under the street-range of a larger complex. In several prominent tenements of courtyard plan, the hall was raised on an undercroft which might be vaulted in stone; this practice continued into the late 15th century, when brick was employed to form vaulted cellars beneath the hall at Crosby Place (1466) and Lincoln's Inn (1489). The surviving buildings are also rich in details of windows, stairs, fireplaces, and building techniques (especially the introduction and spread of brick during the 15th century),[4] though all have suffered great damage and received much restoration.

Archaeological Excavation

Pre-Fire domestic buildings have been excavated on a number of sites, all since the War. The sites can be grouped into two zones: the waterfront area south of Thames Street, where the deposits are exceptionally deep due to the frequent raising of the ground level against the Thames, and the rest of the city inland, where medieval remains have been destroyed by later building to a far greater degree.[5] In the waterfront zone, where much redevelopment has taken place since the early 1970s, several excavations have recorded the process of land reclamation from the 10th to the 16th centuries. In the central stretches of Thames Street, such as between the bridge and Billingsgate, stone buildings were appearing on the reclaimed land during the 12th century, adapting the decayed Roman riverside city wall as their frontage and helping to define Thames Street itself. On most waterfront sites these buildings, rebuilt several times, displayed remains from the 12th or 13th centuries until their destruction in the Great Fire in 1666.[6]

The sites of several seigneurial town houses have been excavated, but the results have generally been meagre. Three have produced partial plans: Neville's Inn, Warwick Inn and the Inn of the Bishop of Bath in the Strand, where Hollar's engravings of 1647 and map evidence place the excavated undercroft and other walls in a recognisable context.[7] At Warwick Inn and Bath Inn courtyard houses of the 14th century are indicated. Fragments of more ordinary domestic buildings are commonly found on sites throughout the city, but on inland sites, apart from fortuitous survivals such as the undercroft supporting a post-Fire building at 7–8 Philpot Lane, the only remains are the deeper foundations, cesspits and wells. The waterfront zone provides fuller evidence, in the form of building and property plans from the 12th to the 15th centuries, constructional details and internal or external features.[8] Archaeological investigations, particularly the large-scale exercises since 1973, have also provided two further major sources of evidence: a series of well-preserved wooden revetments, with a corpus of timber carpentry which is otherwise largely absent from the city or its records;[9] and many objects, now under study, which represent house fittings such as locks, window and door fittings, candlesticks, window cames, glass and moulded stones.[10]

Documentary Evidence

Before 1250, historical sources such as charters, deeds, rentals and chronicles survive almost by accident, in the records of a small number of large religious institutions — St Paul's, Westminster Abbey, the Priory of Holy Trinity Aldgate, for example. After 1250 the city government attempted to record changes of property ownership and the wills of citizens more systematically. From these it is normally possible to reconstruct the ownership and layout of properties on archaeological sites. Occasionally, but rarely, measurements are supplied. One can normally tell how many, and what type of, properties existed in the medieval period; and perhaps some personal details about their owners and their families. More tends to be forthcoming from properties along the waterfront, which seem to have changed hands more often; or from sites which were additionally a matter of royal or civic concern, such as properties near the defences, or close to public buildings.[11]

The documentary evidence for domestic buildings in medieval and Tudor London is vast, and other students can better describe its potential. I wish to highlight two particular sources I have found useful — building contracts and drawn surveys.

Building Contracts

Sixteen building contracts or detailed building leases dating from 1308 to 1532 relate to domestic buildings in the City of London or Southwark; they deal mainly with the erection of blocks of shops, but also include a tavern, a garden gallery, and two complete domestic complexes.[12] The contracts are important for providing accurately dated examples of room sizes, plan form and constructional details of many kinds. They supply the earliest documented examples of developments, perhaps occurring earliest in London, of the first-floor kitchen by 1308, and second-floor privies by 1310. Later, by contrast, the lack of use of the term *solar* in contracts after 1373 may indicate that the term itself fell out of use, as buildings with more than two storeys became the norm in London streets. The contracts give dated examples of major rooms in better houses, and the size and position of a hall, parlour or kitchen can be reconstructed in outline. Six contracts are for blocks of shops, varying from three to twenty shops in size; and four of these six are from the period 1369-83. This might be an accident of survival, but it might also reflect a resurgence of building as the city recovered from the Black Death. As a group also the contracts complement the archaeological evidence for the disposition of privies and for timber sizes,[13] though generally the contracts are more concerned with the forms of future buildings than with building materials.

Panoramas, Drawn Surveys and Plans

Apart from a small number of crude sketches, the pictorial evidence for London begins in about 1480 with the view of London, including the Tower, in the poems of Charles, Duke of Orleans[14] and, a generation or so later, the panorama by van Wyngaerde of 1538–40 (see

Cover).[15] Several panoramas, all from the south, were drawn and engraved in subsequent years, the best and most useful being that of Hollar in 1647.[16] Pre-Fire Cheapside is also shown in the painting of the Coronation Procession of Edward VI (Pl. IV) and in an engraving of 1638.

Especially useful are two collections of house surveys by Ralph Treswell the elder, who surveyed property for two institutions, the Clothworkers' Company and Christ's Hospital, in 1611–12 (Pl. II). Together, the two collections feature forty-nine blocks of London property.[17] The majority are groundplans of individual buildings, or groups of contiguous buildings, with doorways, stairs and chimneys shown, along with yards and gardens. Timber-framed walls are ubiquitous, with the occasional stone or brick wall differently coloured or identifiable by its width. In the great majority of cases the plans are accompanied by a text of reference describing, with measurements, the upper chambers of each building. Thus the buildings can be reconstructed in three dimensions — though the height of each storey is lacking — and such detailed statistics as the size of rooms, the number of rooms in each tenancy, the proportion that were heated, and the proportions of groundspace covered by buildings or cellared can be calculated. These surveys provide much of the information concerning ground plan which is otherwise lacking in the archaeological record. They are, on the one hand, a sample or snap-shot view of contemporary housing in the opening years of the 17th century, a picture of a townscape made up from many elements of different dates. It has so far proved extremely difficult to identify the medieval cores, if they existed, of the buildings shown in the surveys. On the other hand, their value for providing a detailed picture of houses in 1612, without the centuries of subsequent alteration suffered by contemporary houses in other historic towns, has been widely appreciated.

HOUSES IN LONDON, c. 1200–1500

The development of housing in London, as in other medieval cities, was subject to many gradual developments and changes within a densely-populated urban topography which was already finely structured by the early medieval period. The processes of formation of property boundaries and streets, and the range of building styles in 10th/12th-century London, are currently the subject of archaeological studies based on the recent programme of excavations. Though the evidence is fragmentary, these studies will bring together a considerable body of material, especially in two areas of interest: the range of timber building types in late Saxon and Norman London,[18] and 12th/13th-century stone houses.[19] It is now the case that the majority of London's physical evidence for 12th- and 13th-century domestic buildings comes from excavation; the building forms can be compared with those of Romanesque houses elsewhere in Britain and abroad. The present paper takes up the theme about 1200.

In this brief survey I shall concentrate on two important groups: firstly the town houses of the religious and secular lords in the 13th and 14th centuries and secondly the proliferation of company halls in the later medieval period.

Ecclesiastics and Nobles

This group of houses, of which at least a hundred are known in some detail, is a rather arbitrary but pragmatic subdivision. It is based largely on the work of C. L. Kingsford, the editor of Stow's *Survey*, working mainly from records in the Public Record Office,[20] and later studies of the same and similar houses by Marjorie Honeybourne.[21] These houses belonged to those who moved in or on the periphery of royal circles or attended parliament, and included some prominent citizens whose houses were comparable. They fall into two kinds: the town houses of the religious, which as endowments of the institution (a distant abbey or see) tended to be kept in the institution's ownership until the Dissolution, and the secular town houses, which changed hands, and sometimes their character and function, quite often.

Both archbishops, eighteen bishops, at least twenty-two abbots and at least six priors established a town house in London or its suburbs during the medieval period. There were two purposes for such a house: the provision of accommodation for those engaged in the everyday affairs of the house or the see, such as the selling of produce or the buying of goods, and as the town house of the institution's head when in London, especially when in attendance on the king at Westminster. The first function can be seen to have a longer history than the second; until the second decade of the 13th century, when the organs of government and the meetings of parliament began to crystallise at Westminster, the documented town houses of the religious are to be found in the City or in Southwark, showing that when they first appear in 12th-century records, they were sited near the markets and the port. Several whose mother houses were south of London (e.g. Lewes, Bishop of Rochester), were erected in Southwark by the middle of the 12th century. The 13th century however saw a marked swing towards Westminster and the road to it (the Strand outside the city boundary, Fleet Street within it); first to settle here, before 1225, was probably Ralph Neville, Bishop of Chichester and Chancellor.[22] By 1253 five other bishops and the Archbishop of York had houses in the area; the Archbishop of Canterbury had settled on Lambeth in the last decade of the 12th century. Though details are largely lacking, it is fair to assume that the larger among these mansions were imbued with the court style, and were comparable in size and architecture to royal houses. The Bishop of Ely's house in Holborn, for example, built late in the sequence around 1290, included a private chapel on two floors (Pl. VA) which should be compared with royal chapels such as St Stephen's Chapel (with which it may have shared the same architect, Michael of Canterbury)[23] and the Sainte Chapelle in Paris.

The larger group of houses of secular lords, knights and prominent public servants are more difficult to characterise. Though often extensive, the immediately available documentary information on them is sketchy, being confined in the main to successions of title.[24] This must stem in part from the use of these urban inns or bases by the owners themselves. Often the owner of the property had a rural seat and used his London town house only when on business in the capital or as an outstation for the procuring of necessaries and luxuries: as illustrated, for example, by the household accounts of the stewards of Bogo de Clare in 1284–5.[25] The expenses of his wardrobe include robes, furs, drapery, carpets and banquaria (rugs for seats or benches), spices, plate (especially silver or silver-gilt cups), horses and lawsuits. The general dearth of information is offset by a small number of drawn surveys of the houses, when they were in changed circumstances in the late 16th or early 17th centuries, and their occasional but fragmentary appearance in the archaeological record.

The 14th-century grand residence was characterised by its large number of rooms, and the main chambers were often architecturally embellished. The presence of hall, parlour and chapel are sufficiently rare to suggest exceptional circumstances. As hinted above, the large hall of stone (and later, of brick) was a durable feature of several noble houses, surviving long after they had lost their high status; similarly undercrofts, often sited below the hall or other principal buildings, were sometimes vaulted in stone at some expense (Pl. IIIB). Secular towers are known at several 14th-century houses, in documentary record or in the panoramas (see Cover, middle left (Poultney's Inn)), though none has yet been excavated. It seems that seigneurial lords, despite the comparative absence of the clan-fighting which governed the domestic architecture of cities such as Siena or Genoa, still had sufficient influence and apparent need to build or maintain such towers. These were not truly fortified complexes, but they bear comparison with contemporary forms of accommodation such as Stokesay Castle or, within the Tower of London itself, the suite of rooms connected to the Bloody Tower, built in 1361.[26]

Parallels for these houses may be found in the Home Counties around London, for example in Kent, where there are three examples of mid-and late 13th-century rural houses of status: Nettlestead Place (c. 1250–60), Old Soar, Plaxtol (c. 1290), and Penshurst Place (late 13th century in parts);[27] or further afield, a good parallel is found at Little Wenham Hall, Suffolk (1270–90).[28] It is not unreasonable to transport the plan form and architectural detail of Little Wenham Hall into late 13th-century London.

These large houses are to be found throughout the city, but two particular concentrations, both on the west side, are noteworthy. Some suburban mansions around Fleet Street and Holborn became the legal inns during the 13th and early 14th centuries; and, nearby, the settling of the Blackfriars in the south-west corner of the city after 1275 seems to have encouraged high-status residences to colonise the waterfront below and next to the precinct, in the area later to accommodate the second Baynard's Castle.

Foreign Influences

London had been an international port since at least the end of the 10th century. It would be natural to expect traces of foreign affinities in the city's early medieval buildings. When archaeological study of London's Romanesque buildings has reached a suitable stage, such a comparative survey will be possible; and as the Jewish community may have had its origin in the years after the Norman invasion, as an offshoot of the community at Rouen,[29] the disposition of stone houses in the area north of Cheapside still commemorated by the street name Old Jewry will necessarily form part of such a survey. Presumably stone houses in London gradually assimilated accepted details of Gothic style during the 13th century; they would have been influenced by the almost constant large-scale building programmes in the monastic houses, especially the friaries, and the influx of native and foreign craftsmen to the royal works at Westminster Abbey and at the Palace.

North Italian cities such as Siena, Florence, San Gimignano and Lucca may already have sprung to mind when considering the occurrence of towers on 14th-century domestic sites.[30] Certainly the Italian influence on medieval architecture in London should be sought. Italian banking families were firmly established in London during the early part of the reign of Henry III.[31] Sienese merchants were used to further the king's business in the papal court; in 1239 a Burgundio Bacarelli is mentioned in this context.[32] In 1251 Matthew Paris noted that the merchants bought 'nobilissima palatia Londini' for themselves, and set up house in the manner of native citizens; so much so that during one of the periodic persecutions they decided to remain in England because of the losses, especially in their property, they would suffer if they escaped. In Edward I's reign a list of the home-towns of the bankers can be drawn up from his payments to them: Lucca, Siena, Pistoia and several families from Florence. Apart from the house of the Bardi of Florence in Lombard Street, however, first mentioned in 1318 and later the Pope's Head tavern, very little is known of the medieval appearance of these houses.[33]

There was probably a common European architectural style in the prominent secular buildings of the Gothic period as there had been in the Romanesque; the variety of their occupants can be illustrated by the history of Servat's Tower. William Servat, alderman and member of parliament, had licence to build a tower in Bucklersbury in the heart of the city in 1305, which had passed by 1317, via a Genoese merchant, to the king; lessees during the second half of the 14th century included two merchants from Lucca and prominent native drapers.[34]

Changes in the Fifteenth Century: Company Halls

The 15th century was a time of gradual and perhaps inevitable changes for the large town house in London. Information is at present sparse, but two tendencies can be noted: the passing of some former grand houses into corporate ownership of the livery companies to form company halls, and the transformation of others into taverns (for which their vaulted undercrofts were particularly suited). Against these changing and generally declining fortunes of the grand house, the building of Crosby Place in 1466 seems all the more exceptional and untypical.

Between three and five companies are known to have possessed halls before 1400: the Goldsmiths (1339), Merchant Taylors (1347), possibly the Skinners (?1380, certainly by 1408) Cordwainers (1393) and Saddlers (?shortly before 1400). Merchant Taylors' Hall (Fig. 1) survives to illustrate both the form and the problems of analysis. A large mansion with gates to Cornhill and Threadneedle Street (then called Broad Street) passed in 1347 from John Yakesley, tent-maker to the king, to a group of merchant tailors and linen-drapers. The existing hall can be dated only roughly to the 14th century, and thus it is not clear whether Yakesley or the company built it; two surviving bays of an undercroft, which extended at least one further bay to the north, at the east end of the building may well be a relic of the private house and precede the walls of the hall. The medieval kitchen, on its present site by 1388 and rebuilt in 1432–3, could also incorporate fragments of the previous mansion. This mixture of elements from both before and after acquisition by the company underlines two aspects of the gradual adaptation of private houses as company halls by the crafts. The process of acquiring the hall was almost always the same: a prominent member of the craft would bequeath his house, nearly always a courtyard house with a large hall suitable for the ceremonies and convivial meetings of the brethren, to a group of trustees, including members of the guild. Once in possession the company would generally adapt and expand the buildings, but not alter their arrangement. Typical additions were a parlour or the laying-out of a formal garden, two developments which were also taking place in larger houses still in private hands. The need for a central hall for feasting, working meetings and ceremony helped to prolong the life of the large, open-roofed hall as a building form into the early years of the 17th century.

A list of prominent buildings in the city which can be dated to c. 1475[35] mentions 27 halls belonging to 25 companies (the Fishmongers having three separate halls); and in 1532–3, at least 45 of the 60 companies who had places at the Mayor's feast at Guildhall[36] had their own hall. John Stow's *Survey* of 1598 mentions 46 halls, and three more are known to have existed in the city at this date. This suggests that the years of greatest proliferation of the company hall as a building form was in the period c. 1400–1530. The pre-1400 halls, with the possible exception of the Merchant Taylors, were in or near areas associated with their trades from 1300, as attested by the street-name evidence which seems to indicate trade groupings of the late 13th century.[37] After 1400, however, the tendency was to find a hall away from the central commercial districts, in the outer parts of the city. This tendency continued at the Dissolution, when several company halls were transferred to grander sites in the newly-acquired ex-monastic precincts (e.g. Drapers, Leathersellers). This may be

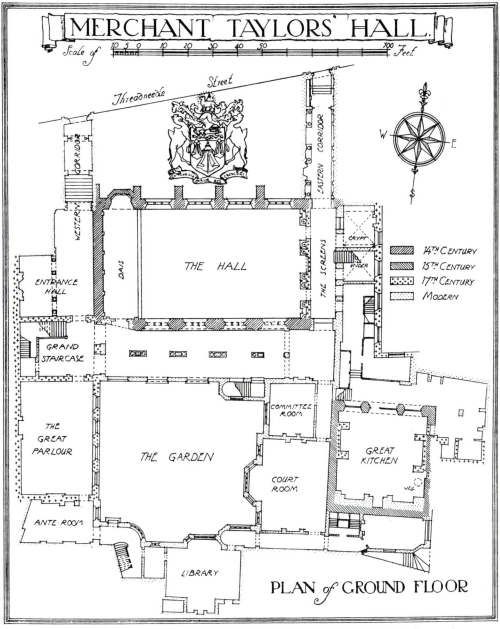

FIG. 1. Plan of Merchant Taylors Hall, Threadneedle Street, in 1929. War damage has altered some details
RCHM

because suitable buildings in the commercial centres were either too expensive or were already converted to other purposes such as taverns.

The wealth of surviving company accounts and deeds means that the company hall complex, so often repeated throughout the city, is one of the main sources of information about secular medieval building history in London. The company hall forms a link with the grander residence, which its plan and building details resembled, and the private houses of the more prominent citizens who formed the livery. The history of the hall, parlour, kitchen, service rooms and garden can be reconstructed in detail from company accounts. The company hall was also an estate office, and a centre for charitable functions. Certain of the companies built almshouses by the hall, or nearby. The Merchant Taylors in 1414, the Brewers in 1423, and the Carpenters in 1448 were the earliest; unfortunately no plans of these earliest almshouses have survived, and the known plans are of 16th-century date.[38]

Many other companies never had a hall of their own; some hired a hall from a company that had one, others met in taverns. The Weavers had a hall but dined in taverns. The Cheapside area was thick with taverns which must have had a frequent trade in company meetings and feasts, possibly in special chambers. Taverns were in addition used by parish councils conducting their business: to seal contracts on new building ventures, to settle local arbitrations, or for dinners for lawyers conducting litigation on the parish's behalf.[39]

The 15th century also saw public building on the grand scale, financed partly by a small number of rich city dignitaries such as Richard Whittington and Simon Eyre: the Guildhall was rebuilt by 1440, the great quadrangular market and granary of Leadenhall shortly after. The houses of these civic leaders are generally only known in outline, if at all. Thus Crosby Place, which has survived, is without detailed parallel; it was probably, as Stow thought, exceptional for its age. The house of John Crosby, a grocer and member of parliament who was knighted for his services to Edward IV, was removed to Chelsea in 1907. It illustrates the narrow gap between the house of a merchant who moved in royal circles and the palace of a real monarch. Crosby rebuilt the house in Bishopsgate in 1466–75.[40] He retained one wing of an already large mansion, which had once been occupied by a distinguished Italian merchant, to form the southern range of a courtyard entered from the street via a passage under six tenements. The hall and parlour block were of ashlar-fronted brick on brick undercrofts. A semi-octagonal oriel window at the dais end of the hall incorporated Crosby's crest in its stone vault. The hall and upper parlour had richly gilded and ornamented timber ceilings, and behind the main house lay gardens and a private gate to St Helen's church where Crosby and his wife lie in their own chapel, his merchant's mark in the stained glass of the windows. The hall resembles that of Eltham Palace (1479) and may have been built, like Eltham, by the king's mason, Thomas Jurdan. Just as the religious leaders were perhaps the means of diffusing architectural standards and styles from the milieu of royal palaces in the 13th century, so, though to a lesser extent because they were few in number, may have been the merchant princes of the 15th century. Much more needs to be known about the stratum of houses below the high-quality level of Crosby Place.

SIXTEENTH-CENTURY DEVELOPMENTS

Despite the increased abundance of documentary and, later, pictorial and survey evidence, the history of the London house in the 16th century has yet to be written. The conversion of larger private houses into company halls continued. Increasing pressure on space, a result of rapid increase in population, encouraged subdivision of properties and the erection of 'tenements' on former gardens and yards. Buildings rose higher; by the end of the century four or five storeys were common, and even six storeys in some principal streets. Stylistically there are traces of French and Italian Renaissance decoration in woodwork (chiefly panels and furniture) in the first quarter of the century, and much evidence of strapwork and grotesque ornament in the Flemish style from c. 1550 to c. 1600. Brick was now wide-spread, though almost totally as an infill in timber-framing; some, but very few prominent buildings were totally of brick (for example, Clothworkers' Hall of 1549), but at the vernacular level there are virtually no traces of buildings wholly of brick in this century except for almshouses. The availability of brick may, however, have contributed to an occasional display in larger houses in the form of a garden tower, of which there are several examples from the 1530s.

The Dissolution caused an immense upheaval in the appearance of London's buildings; chiefly the monastic precincts themselves, but also, in time, their substantial urban property holdings. Most of the precincts, sold off to courtiers or officials of the Court of Augmenta-tions, were turned into bizarre urban palaces where contemporary notions of domestic planning at the high level, such as the provision of several suites of rooms and a long gallery, were imposed in fashionable timberwork on hacked-about stone structures often of great age.[41] The three decades after 1536 must have seen a frenzy of building all over the city which has not yet been studied, and which cannot be covered here.

TRESWELL'S SURVEYS

The wave of recent rebuilding, subdivision and change is evident in the documents which two contemporary observers at the end of the century have left to us: Stow's *Survey* of 1598 and, much less well-known, the corpus of house-plans surveyed by Ralph Treswell in 1594–1613. The majority of the plans seem to date from c. 1612, the year in which Treswell was commissioned to survey the London property of the Clothworkers' Company and of Christ's Hospital, the two surveys which have survived.[42]

The Treswell surveys describe a range of house-forms, and serve as an end-point to this survey of the medieval and Tudor house in London. Here can be found examples of most of the historical elements and styles of the previous four centuries, from the stone walls of a house in the former Jewry to the most up-to-date timber-framed house erected by a prominent Clothworker. The fastidious detail of the surveyed plans and their accompany-ing texts describing the upper chambers puts the scattered or sometimes partial evidence of engravings, archaeological excavation or title deeds into context.

Four general types of house-form can be distinguished. The large courtyard house, still medieval in layout though adapted, rebuilt with more chambers and often divided into tenancies, could still be found off the smaller streets and lanes, behind a street range of shops (Fig. 2). In many larger houses galleries ran round the congested yards or served several superimposed storeys, as in galleried inns. Even in these large houses stone walls were now a rarity, though several had been partially rebuilt in brick. At a lower social level the Treswell surveys are the first fixed point for a comprehensive analysis of smaller house forms, which can be divided into a further three types in decreasing size of ground area and complexity of plan. Although there were some medium-sized properties where variety in planning was possible, the most numerous type was the house with two rooms on three or four floors (Fig. 2); the type is known from documentary and archaeological evidence from the early 14th century.[43] In these houses the ground floor was a shop and warehouse, sometimes thrown together to form one room, or occasionally a tavern. The hall of the tenant was on

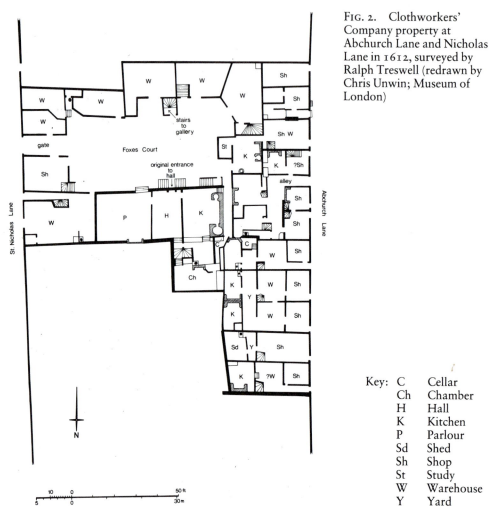

FIG. 2. Clothworkers'
Company property at
Abchurch Lane and Nicholas
Lane in 1612, surveyed by
Ralph Treswell (redrawn by
Chris Unwin; Museum of
London)

Key: C   Cellar
      Ch   Chamber
      H   Hall
      K   Kitchen
      P   Parlour
      Sd   Shed
      Sh   Shop
      St   Study
      W   Warehouse
      Y   Yard

the first floor at the front, overlooking the street. Where space allowed the kitchen might still
be a separate building across a small yard, but in the majority of cases surveyed by Treswell
the kitchen occupied the back room on the first floor. Apart from common yards and alleys
there was little private open space in the middle of the city; only larger houses and those
towards the periphery of the built-up area, or in the suburbs, had gardens. Houses only one
room in plan were found both on principal streets, where they formed a screen for the larger
houses behind, and in courtyards where they assumed awkward, angular shapes to take up
every inch of space. While apparently similar in plan, the individual houses in the rows on
the streets were often of differing heights, the product of rebuilding at different times. The
surveys also provide important examples of buildings with functions slightly outside the
domestic sphere: inns with extensive stables and guest chambers, cookshops, two company
halls (the Clothworkers' (Pl. II) and the otherwise unknown pre-1575 Woodmongers' Hall)
and two sets of almshouses.

CONCLUSIONS

In this brief survey I have outlined the potential of some of the sources for study of the domestic buildings of medieval and Tudor London, and described some of the principal groups of domestic buildings. It will be appreciated that much remains to be done. This paper has attempted to draw attention to the amount of work recently published or currently in progress. The combination of documentary study with the results of archaeological excavation, in particular, further enriched by London's exceptional legacy of pictorial evidence, should make possible the detailed reconstruction of many parts of the capital's medieval townscape. London's role in the development of domestic building traditions or decorative fashions at both a regional and a national level will then become clearer.

REFERENCES

1. For surviving buildings, see RCHM *London*, IV; B/E *London 1: The Cities of London and Westminster* (1957; 3rd ed. 1973); Schofield (1984).
2. The few timber-framed buildings still surviving in the Greater London area are well-built, middle-class examples, see B/E *London 2: South* (1983), 104; in Norwich, the 500 buildings still surviving from the 16th and 17th centuries are thought to represent the residences of only the most affluent 5–10% of the city's population, see Priestley and Corfield (1982), 94 and n. 5.
3. Barron (1974); Wilson (1976), 1–14.
4. Schofield (1984), 106–29.
5. On recent archaeological work in the City, see Grimes (1968); Hobley and Schofield (1977), 31–66; Dyson and Schofield (1981), 24–81. Several individual site reports and papers are cited in the following notes.
6. Schofield (1981), 24–31.
7. For archaeological evidence of these inns, see Grimes (1968), 164–7 (Neville's Inn); Hammerson (1975), 209–51.
8. Schofield (1977), 66–73; Dyson and Schofield (1981), 70–4.
9. Milne and Milne (1982).
10. For the house fittings, see *Med. House Fittings*. The moulded stones from excavated secular undercrofts have been studied by R. Lea, and archive reports on particular sites are in preparation. It is hoped that a corpus of moulding forms will shortly be available.
11. For the techniques and examples, see Schofield and Dyson (1980); Dyson (1982), 4–9; Harding (1980), 11–30.
12. Most are printed in Salzman (1952). In addition Salzman prints contracts dealing with waterfront structures in timber and stone in the City (ibid., 434–5, 469–70), the rebuilding of watermills in Southwark (ibid., 467–8) and the building of a brewhouse at St Martin-in-the-Fields (ibid., 552–3).
13. Three contracts provide detailed specifications for the timbers of the future building, enabling comparisons to be made between timber use in 1369, 1383 and 1532. These are all in Salzman (1952), 434–5, 469–70, 579–80.
14. BN MS Royal 16F, ii, f.73.
15. Reproduced by the Lond. TS, Publication 77 (1944); the original is in the Ashmolean Museum, Oxford.
16. Hollar's panorama has been published by the Lond. TS, Publication 19 (1906–7, repr. 1988).
17. Schofield (1987).
18. Horsman *et al.* (1988).
19. Schofield and Allen (in preparation).
20. Kingsford (1916; 1917; 1920).
21. Honeybourne (1965), 29–76 and separate map.
22. *Henry III: Letters*, 248, 298, 496–7.
23. Harvey (1954), 18. A good number of the architects traced by Harvey, mostly through their royal or ecclesiastical work, were based in London. Their work on secular London buildings has yet to be traced in detail.
24. This of course is not the case when thorough documentary study of individual sites or areas is undertaken. Several documentary historians are now working on areas of the city or individual sites, including the sites of current archaeological excavations. The Social and Economic Survey of Medieval London (SESML), under the direction of Dr D. Keene, has completed an in-depth study of five parishes around the east end of Cheapside: Keene and Harding (1987).

25. Giuseppi (1920), 1–56.
26. Probably from the 14th century, the Bloody Tower was in the corner of the garden of the Queen's House, about 25 yards away; it was formerly also known as the Garden Tower. It may thus have been attached as a separate tower to the residence of the Constable of the Tower in the medieval period (Curnow (1978), 59).
27. Wood (1965), 96–8.
28. Ibid., 22.
29. See Brooke and Keir (1975), 179–82, 222–7.
30. For Siena, see Balestracci and Piccinni (1977); for Florence, *Corinti*.
31. Bond (1840), 207–326.
32. Ibid., 261.
33. Ibid., 240.
34. Honeybourne (1965), 67–8. The site has been identified by SESML (site 156/14).
35. BM Harley MS 541.
36. Stow (1971), ii, 190–2.
37. Ekwall (1954).
38. Schofield (1987), Figs 38, 48.
39. Overall (1871), 16, 19, 93; *St Mary at Hill: Medieval records*, 70, 179, 203, 230, 274.
40. Norman (1907); Clapham and Godfrey (1913), 119–38.
41. Schofield (1984), 130–55, and Schofield (in preparation).
42. The planbook produced in 1612 for the Clothworkers' Company is still held at Clothworkers' Hall; the Christ's Hospital survey, probably of the same year, is Guildhall Library MS 12805.
43. Schofield (1981) and Schofield *et al.* (in preparation).

Shops and Shopping in Medieval London

By Derek Keene

Even in these days of the out-of-town superstore, shopping is a quintessentially urban activity. A notable, and perhaps to some unexpected, feature of the revitalisation of many town centres has been the proliferation of small-scale, retail shops. As in the past, they are often clustered according to the type of goods sold in them, reflecting their owners' desires to occupy a site which customers will recognise as one where these items will be available. For some social historians the permanent retail shop, by contrast with the market stall or the craftsman's workshop, did not come to be established in English county towns until the 17th century.[1] Undoubtedly, with the growth of consumption from the 17th century onwards, shops became a more widespread and more obvious urban phenomenon, but, equally certainly, shops, with a form and function which we would recognise today, were a well-established feature of the English urban scene by A.D. 1300, if not two hundred years earlier. London, by virtue of its size and wealth, contained the greatest number and the greatest concentration of shops in the kingdom, but there is sufficient evidence to show that the shopping activities which formed so large a part of life in the capital were replicated on a smaller scale in many other English towns. The written records of medieval London provide an unparalleled opportunity to study both the form and the use of an important type of small-scale urban building, of which today hardly any physical remains survive.[2]

In the context of the art and architecture of medieval London the shop occupies a special position. Some shops, like the corner grocery store of modern times, provided for daily household needs. Others, generally to be found in side streets, were manufacturing workshops rather than purely distributive establishments. There was probably a gradation of functions between these two extremes, so that many shops would have housed both manufacturing or finishing processes and retail activity. In the principal thoroughfares, however, especially towards the centre of the city, the shopping scene was dominated by distributive trade. In these streets the shop was the place where many of the finest products of the city's craftsmen, as well as imported goods, were sold. A place of display, fronting on to some of the most important spaces for public assembly in the city, the shop had a distinctive social role, both as the focus for special patterns of behaviour and as one of the most visible features of the landscape which expressed the city's identity. Some shops were in themselves striking works of elaborate or high-quality craftsmanship, or formed part of buildings which were notable works of architecture. This was one way in which medieval shopkeepers, like their successors in the 18th century and later,[3] attracted custom. We know relatively little of this aspect of medieval shopkeeping, but the very high values of shops and the sites they occupied suggest that their owners were prepared to invest in the decorative features which would make them attractive for trade.

This essay is based mainly on the results of a detailed reconstruction of the histories of all the houses and other properties in a group of parishes in the Cheapside area of London between the 12th and the 17th century (Fig. 1). Shops were to be found in virtually all the streets and in many of the lanes in the city, but throughout this period Cheapside was without rival as the principal shopping street in London. This intensive examination of a single area has made it possible to reconstruct both the character of shops and shopping during the medieval period and their wider social, economic and topographical setting. The discussion concentrates on the period before 1350, but concludes with a summary of the changes which took place in the later medieval period.

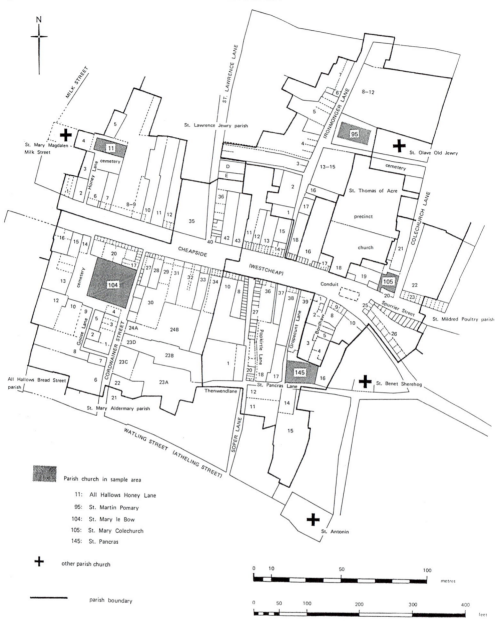

N

MILK STREET

ST. LAWRENCE LANE

IRONMONGER LANE

St. Lawrence Jewry parish

St. Mary Magdalen Milk Street

St. Olave Old Jewry

COLECHURCH LANE

cemetery

8–12

95

13–15

cemetery

St. Thomas of Acre

precinct

church

CHEAPSIDE

(WESTCHEAP)

Conduit

104

105

22

Spurrier Street

St. Mildred Poultry parish

CORDWAINER STREET

Goose Lane

Honey Lane

Poultrie Lane

Cropecunt Lane

Bordhaw

145

St. Benet Sherehog

All Hallows Bread Street parish

St. Mary Aldermary parish

Thenwendlane

St. Pancras Lane

SOPER LANE

WATLING STREET (ATHELING STREET)

St. Antonin

Parish church in sample area

11:   All Hallows Honey Lane
95:   St. Martin Pomary
104: St. Mary le Bow
105: St. Mary Colechurch
145: St. Pancras

+   other parish church

———   parish boundary

0   10   50   100
                              metres

0   50   100   200   300   400
                                    feet

FIG. 1.   The Cheapside study area *c.* 1300. The map shows property boundaries in the five parishes which covered the eastern half of Cheapside. Pecked lines indicate boundaries of which the approximate position is known. Frontages in Cheapside and in most of the side streets were lined with shops. It is not always known how many shops occupied the frontage of a given property, so that the boundaries of individual shops cannot always be shown. Nevertheless, it is clear that the Cheapside shops at this time were of a consistent size and character. The numbers identify the properties in Keene and Harding (1987)

Cheapside's national reputation as a shopping centre is nowhere better expressed than in the report of the seditious chatter overheard in Beverley market-place during the Northern Rebellion of 1536, when men talked of going to London and bringing home the goods of Cheapside and the South.[4] As a store and display of wealth it made no less of an impression on foreigners. About 1500 a Venetian visitor certainly had Cheapside in mind when he wrote of the riches of the London shops:

in a single street, called 'The Street' (la Strada) leading to St Paul's there are fifty-two goldsmiths' shops, so rich and full of silver vessels, great and small, that in all the shops in Milan, Rome, Venice, and Florence together it seems to me that you would not find so many of such magnificence as you would see in London.[5]

Whatever we may think of the comparison, the number of goldsmiths' shops was not exaggerated, for a list of the goldsmiths in Cheapside in 1558 contains sixty-three names.[6] At this time the goldsmiths' shops probably dominated the image of Cheapside in the minds of those who knew the street. They were certainly an essential part of the Cheapside scene which was depicted in a contemporary painting as the main setting for King Edward VI's coronation procession through the city in 1547 (Plate IV). This notable expression of Cheapside's role as a place of display, and as a focus of the city's power and wealth, clearly shows the goldsmiths' wares exhibited in shop frontages of some elaboration and splendour. This was a ceremonial occasion, when painted or woven hangings were also displayed, but John Stow's contemporary description of one of the buildings in which the goldsmiths' shops were housed shows that richly modelled and gilded work in wood and lead would have been seen every day by those who visited the shops or passed them by.[7]

The goldsmiths were just one of the groups of tradesmen who were to be found in distinctive clusters of Cheapside shops from at least as early as the 13th century onwards. The largest of these groups was probably that dealing in textiles, clothing, and personal adornments. Mercers and drapers, for example, congregated in very much the same parts of Cheapside on the eve of the Great Fire of 1666, and even in the early 19th century, as they had done in the 1240s when Mercers' Row (Merceria) and Drapers' Row (Draperia) were distinctive local landmarks.[8]

Other notable groupings of shopkeepers in medieval Cheapside included goldsmiths, spicers, saddlers, girdlers, chandlers, ironmongers, cutlers and spurriers. In the side streets nearby were the founders, wiredrawers, bucklemakers, pursemakers, buttonmakers, hosiers, hoodmakers and embroiderers who made or processed the goods sold in Cheapside itself. This, too, is a pattern as characteristic of the 17th century as of the 13th.[9]

The word 'shop' seems originally to have conveyed the notion of an open-sided stall or booth. It is striking to note, however, that a translator of the Gospels into Old English, used the term sceoppa to denote the temple treasury (gazophilacium) in Jerusalem, in a context which closely associates the word with the payment of money.[10] In the early 12th century there was a group of escheopes (the Old French version of the term) in Winchester High Street, where they appear to have stood next to the street in front of a larger house behind.[11] This was probably an already long-established arrangement, and is well attested as the common pattern in the many thousands of references to shops in English towns among the abundant records which survive from the early 13th century onwards. An early record of shops in London concerns the division, in 1212–13, of a large Cheapside property into two parts comprising, respectively, the twelve shops on the street frontage and the land and houses which lay behind them.[12] Within a decade or so of this division London deeds reveal the very active market which had developed in shops. Groups of shops, individual shops, parts of shops, rooms over shops and rents charged on any one of these were all bought and

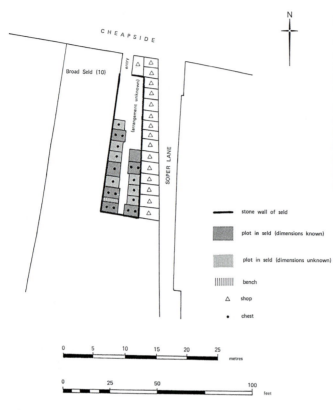

Fig. 2. St Martin's Seld *c.* 1250.
The plan shows the internal
arrangement of the seld (Keene
and Harding (1987), no. 145/8)
and the shops which adjoined it in
Soper Lane ('Shopkeepers' Lane').
The name of the seld is not
recorded until the late 13th
century. It was also known as
Girdlers' Seld and as Narrow Seld
by contrast with the adjoining
Broad Seld. For the location, see
Figure 1. For the same property in
the 1360s, see Figure 3

sold. The records generated by these transactions thus give us an exceptional insight into the physical arrangement of shops, their structure and fittings, and their dimensions.

The twelve shops sold in 1212–13 lay on the north side of the street, and were said to be opposite the shopkeepers (*sopparii*). Records of ten years later reveal that these shopkeepers occupied a row of small shops in Ironmongers' Row (*ferronaria*). That the earlier source should have referred to the shopkeepers rather than to the shops or to Ironmongers' Row on the south side of the street, suggests that contemporaries saw these shops, in one of the city's busiest streets, as places associated primarily with distributive or retail trade and only secondarily with a particular craft specialism. The occupation or profession of shopkeeper was thus already a well-established one. Indeed, two of the earliest named London tradesmen were shopkeepers. They seem to have been men of some wealth or standing, since in 1130 they were both in debt to the king.[13] The term 'shopkeeper' is rarely used as an occupational description or as a byname for medieval Londoners after *c.* 1250, presumably because in this later period occupational ascriptions tended to denote the civic status and craft affiliation of individuals rather than to be purely descriptive. Around 1200, however, the shopkeepers of London seem regularly to have been described as such. A new lane leading off Cheapside which came into existence at about this time soon came to be known as 'Shopkeepers' lane' or Soper Lane (*Sopereslane*) on account of the numerous small shops which lined its frontages (see Figs 1 and 2).[14]

Before we look more closely into the private space inside the shops, it is necessary to appreciate that a great deal of trading took place in the public space represented by the

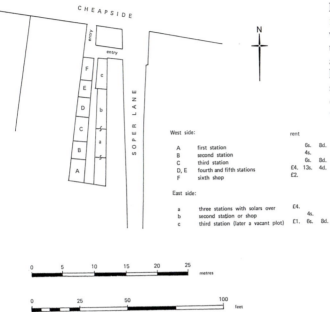

C H E A P S I D E

N

FIG. 3.   St Martin's Seld in the
1360s. The space inside the seld
was now much less intensively
used than *c.* 1250 (cf. Fig. 2),
although upper rooms appear to
have been erected over some plots
since then. The terms used to
describe the plots are based on
those in a contemporary rental

West side: rent

A	first station	6s.	8d.
B	second station	4s.	
C	third station	6s.	8d.
D, E	fourth and fifth stations	£4. 13s.	4d.
F	sixth shop	£2.	

East side:

a	three stations with solars over	£4.	
b	second station or shop	4s.	
c	third station (later a vacant plot)	£1. 6s.	8d.

0   5   10   15   20   25
metres

0   25   50   100
feet

street. Cheapside, known as *Chepe, forum, Westchepe,* or *vicus fori* in the Middle Ages,[15] was itself the city's greatest market-place, measuring some 450 yards long by 20 yards wide. By the mid-13th century traders had established permanent stalls and chests in the street from which they sold corn, bread, fish and meat, as well as leather goods and woollen and linen cloth. These probably occupied the middle of the street, but at an inquiry made in 1246 were not recognised as encroachments, presumably because they were generally approved and provided a regular rental income for the city authorities. In 1274, however, they were removed on the orders of the mayor, so as to make Cheapside into a clean and uncluttered highway suitable for welcoming the new king, who was expected shortly to arrive in England.[16] From this time onwards Cheapside was kept clear of permanent obstructions, except for the Great Conduit at the east end, the Little Conduit by the church of St Michael le Querne at the west end, the Great Cross commemorating Queen Eleanor, and the lesser structure known as The Standard. These monumental structures punctuated the street, serving as stations for the pageants staged during ceremonial processions for which it was often the setting.[17] They were also focal points for expressions of public authority in the form of proclamations, punishments and tournaments, and for challenges to that authority.[18] Street traders, principally those dealing in foodstuffs, congregated around them,[19] or were assigned to the various zones within Cheapside which were delimited by them. These traders, many of them women, were governed by a constantly changing pattern of regulations, defining where they were supposed to stand or to perambulate. A regulation of 1588 conveys something of the scene: the sellers of flowers, herbs, roots and seeds were to occupy the western part of Cheapside between the Little Conduit and the Cross, the flower-sellers standing to the south of the channel (i.e. the gutter in the middle of the street), and the others to the north; the out-of-town sellers of victuals were to occupy the street east of the Cross.[20] Congestion was the almost inevitable accompaniment to shopping in medieval London, and street traders tended to obstruct access to the shops.[21] Outbreaks of disorder were common. In 1297 the city authorities prohibited a fair established by out-of-town traders in Soper Lane since it encouraged thieves, cut-purses and wrongdoers in Cheapside ('the market') nearby. Crowds and the solicitations of importunate tradesmen dominate the street scene evoked in the 15th-century poem 'London Lyckpeny'.[22]

The most striking characteristics of the city's shops were their small size and their great number. The twelve shops sold in 1212–13, occupying a site which was not in the busiest part of Cheapside, would have had a mean frontage width of 11 ft 8 in. About 1220 eight shops in a row opposite, fronting on to the street now known as Poultry, had a mean width of 7 ft 4 in. In this row individual shops ranged in width from 6 ft 10 in. to 9 ft 2 in., and in depth from 12 ft 10 in. to 18 ft 9 in.[23] Before the third decade of the 14th century the typical Cheapside shop probably measured six or seven feet in front, and ten to twelve feet in depth. On and near corner sites they could be as small as four feet square.[24] So far as we can tell, both sides of Cheapside were lined with shops, so that in the 13th and early 14th centuries the street as a whole would have contained about 400 of them. This was the greatest concentration of shops in London, but probably only a small proportion of the total number of shops in the city. The principal thoroughfares were lined with shops, and in the side streets leading off Cheapside shops extended in continuous rows at least one hundred yards from the market-place. In most of these secondary locations, however, the shops in this period were larger than those in Cheapside. Thus c. 1300 in Poultry, along the Cheapside axis but at a point some 200 yards east of Cheapside itself, shops had frontages of about 13 ft 6 in., while 100 yards further east, in Broad Street and Cornhill, their frontages were generally between 15 ft and 20 ft.[25]

The narrow Cheapside shops probably each had a single window opening on to the street, with a doorway beside it. In a row of eight chandlers' shops, which in the 13th century occupied the frontage where Mercers' Hall now stands, the mean frontage width was 5 ft. Adjacent shops were then joined together, so that in 1336 the same site was occupied by a row of four shops, each of which was said to contain two windows, presumably with a door in between.[26] The space within which shopkeepers and their customers manoeuvred was extremely tight. Thus in Soper Lane a shop measuring 4 ft 9 in. next to the street, 4 ft 5 in. at the rear, and 10 ft 1½ in. in depth was acquired in 1279–80 by Hugh de Chelmeresford, an ironmonger, and his wife Alice. They sold the shop in 1293, reserving for Alice during her lifetime a place in the shop and a stall in front in the window where she could carry on her trade. This stall, which was presumably raised at night in order to close the window, extended 3 ft 7 in. in length from the shop entry on the south to the post of the window on the north. The doorway must therefore have been 1 ft 2½ in. wide.[27] That part of the cramped space inside which Alice did not occupy was presumably used for trading by the new owner (a mercer) or his servants. Crowded conditions such as these were common. In 1319 the shop next door, which seems to have been about the same size, contained two chests and three stalls inside, and there were two more stalls before the door. Three doors away, in 1299, a widow who sold her shop reserved for herself two stalls at the front where she could sit and sell her wares as before: they measured 3 ft by 4 ft.[28]

Many customers at shops like these presumably stood in the street (cf. Fig. 4), and may only rarely have entered the shop, the rear part of which would have been used for storing goods. On the other hand, traders at the rear of the shop would have needed to go in and out and may have attracted customers there. The frequent reference to chests, coffers, and even benches as fixtures in shops[29] suggests that several traders, perhaps sometimes servants or apprentices of the shopkeeper, could be accommodated within the shop, each possibly having charge of a chest or stall from which he or she did business with customers.

FIG. 4. Dinah meets the women of the region, and is then raped. Drawing by Nick Griffiths from BL, MS Egerton 1894, fo. 17. The scene, by an English artist of the 14th century (see p. 41), is set outside a shop or booth where knives, purses and girdles are being sold
Museum of London

Some shops were built of stone. The eight described *c.* 1220 were said to be of stone, and there was a ninth, probably also of stone, adjoining them to the east. This row appears to have been part of the same stone structure as the substantial house behind. The shops were used by ironmongers and spurriers, for whom a fireproof structure may have been appropriate, yet men in the same trades also occupied the wooden shops which adjoined these stone shops to the west.[30] The landlord's ability to invest in substantial building, and his desire to make an impression by doing so, were probably at least as important as more utilitarian considerations in determining whether shops were built of stone or of less durable materials. Some of the most imposing Cheapside shops were probably those within the substantial stone house erected in front of the church of St Mary le Bow during the 1270s for Canterbury Cathedral Priory, to a high architectural standard (the principal mason later built the Great Cross in Cheapside) and at great expense. This house, still a notable Cheapside landmark in the 16th century (see Plate IV), seems to have been built as much to express the priory's presence in the city, and for the use of its officers, as to provide a source of rental income.[31]

In Cheapside, and indeed throughout the city, most shops were built of timber, even if, as is recorded in several cases, they were partially supported by the stone wall of a house behind or by the stone party wall between two properties.[32] There are references to the boarded partitions between shops, and an agreement of 1314 concerning the maintenance of a ground-floor corner shop, which was in separate ownership from the room above, mentions the corner post, the joists, the plates and the planks, as well as the hooks for the shutters.[33] Late 14th-century repair accounts from a group of shops nearby contain many references to the doors with their locks and to the windows of what were evidently timber-framed structures with tiled roofs. Most frequently renewed were the cords and pulleys for the windows, by means of which stalls in front of the shops were presumably raised at night.[34] The stall itself was evidently used in much the same way as the modern shop counter, and in one late 15th-century case the shop stall of one year's repair account was described as the shop board in another.[35] This counter in front of the window seems often to have been protected from the weather by an overhanging shelter or pentice. Four new shops erected in Ironmonger Lane around 1420 were provided with pentices roofed, at least partly, with lead. They appear to have been cantilevered structures, suspended from 'pentice hooks'.[36] Such projections over shop windows were common in Cheapside in 1246, when an inquiry into encroachments revealed that practically every house there had a pentice.[37] The projecting stalls beneath the pentices, being moveable, seem not to have been regarded as encroachments, although in the 17th century some Cheapside property-holders erected in front of their shops more permanent structures known as stalls or 'bulks' which the city authorities attempted to remove or for which they exacted rents.[38]

Contemporary illustrations show many of these external features of medieval and later shops with varying degrees of realism.[39] One of the most vivid representations is by a mid-13th-century artist, perhaps a Parisian or working under Parisian influence, but possibly an Englishman (Plate VB).[40] So far as we can tell, Parisian shops of the time were similar to their counterparts in London,[41] and this depiction very clearly shows the wooden fabric of the shop, its narrow doorway, its window closed with a shutter, and the overhanging pentice. The artist's juxtaposition of this building with a stone one of higher status evokes a scene which would have been familiar to Cheapside shoppers.

Shops in Cheapside and the streets nearby invariably had rooms or 'solars' above them. They were sometimes used by the occupant of the shop below, but were often in separate tenure or ownership. At a shop near the corner of Ironmonger Lane in 1288 a staircase was inserted so as to provide a way up for the occupants of the recently-contrived lodgings above, while in a part of the cellar beneath, a latrine pit was made to accommodate the needs of the new arrivals.[42] The sources, which use such phrases as 'shops with solars above', do not enable us readily to determine how many floors above the ground floor these shop structures contained. Some probably had no more than two storeys above ground, but a reference in 1288 to a small shop which had two solars above[43] suggests that at that time shops with two storeys above them may have been common in the Cheapside area, as they certainly were in the 15th and 16th centuries.[44] As well as being used as lodgings, the rooms over the shops could also be put to commercial use, for storage or as places in which to trade. This is indicated by the occurrence in the early 14th century of chests and cupboards as fixtures in some of these upper rooms, and by the use in the 15th century of the term 'shop' to denote rooms on the first and second floors of houses on the Cheapside frontage.[45]

The terrace-like row made up of units with a shop on the ground floor and rooms above was a standard feature of the London street scene. Frequently, though perhaps less in Cheapside than elsewhere, the structural units corresponded to domestic ones, so that the family dwellings of the 'retaylers' and 'artificers', the largest of all classes in London society according to John Stow,[46] were often known as shops. A London building contract of 1369 for a row of twenty dwellings stated that they should be made 'in the manner of shops'.[47] Four small three-storey houses erected in Ironmonger Lane in about 1420, each measuring about 10 ft next to the street and 22 ft in depth, were described initially as shops. Later they were described as tenements (the standard term for a house of any size), and the term shop was used to denote only the ground-floor room.[48] The length of such rows of shops or dwellings depended upon the width of the property next to the street. In Cheapside, where during the 13th and 14th centuries the small frontage widths reflected the high demand for access to the market-place, shops were generally erected or managed in groups of three or four (cf. Fig. 1), although the names which were applied to them — Goldsmiths' Row,

Mercers' Row, and the like — were analogous to street-names and denoted longer lengths of the frontage which extended across several properties and were in the control of many different owners and occupiers. Relatively lightly constructed, timber-framed buildings of this type could be easily altered. Thus we find shops being divided, thrown together, or removed so as to create an entry into the house behind, without apparent difficulty.[49]

It is tempting to suggest that structures such as these first came into existence as encroachments on to the street. If this was the case in Cheapside, the development must have taken place well before 1200, when the documentary sources begin to be comprehensive. It is more likely, however, that, as in Winchester, ordinary householders were prevented from extending their houses on to the principal market street (except for the fixed stalls in the middle of the street) from at least as early as the 11th century onwards, and that in the side streets where substantial encroachments were made in order to accommodate small houses or shops this process had come to an end by 1100.[50]

At the eastern end of Cheapside, where the streets now known as Poultry and Bucklersbury converge, there was an exception to this in the form of a row of shops, which came into existence as a result of encroachment during the 13th century. In 1246 the owner of the house facing west down Cheapside in the angle between the other two streets was said to have encroached by building a pentice above (ultra) his cellar. Within twenty years this structure had been rebuilt, following further encroachment, as a row of four shops with rooms above, which was said to stand 'in the gable' of the stone house to the east.[51]

Shops were often incorporated in or partially supported by other structures. Thus it is not uncommon to find shops as part of a timber-framed building erected on top of a masonry cellar or vault. This arrangement sometimes resulted in ground-floor shops being set a little above street level. At one property in 1216 there were two small shops over a cellar and on either side of a doorway leading off Cheapside. Beneath at least one of the shops was a window lighting the cellar: the owner of the shop was not to obstruct the window by making a pentice or by other means, and the owner of the cellar was not to interfere with the shop by enlarging the window. There was a similar arrangement at the much larger stone house belonging to Canterbury Cathedral Priory.[52]

Apart from being fitted out with chests, stalls and other fixtures for the display and storage of goods, shop interiors were probably sparsely furnished. In the later 16th and early 17th centuries, few shops appear to have included fireplaces,[53] and, in the Cheapside area, their walls were hardly ever panelled with timber, unlike many of the other rooms in the houses of which they formed part.[54] In this context, the Cornhill draper's shop which in 1475 was furnished with 'a piece of black buckram stained above round about the shop', seems exceptional. The other furnishings or fixtures in this shop included a 'cowcheborde boarded behind and covered above with boards and canvased from the backside to the ground', another 'cowcheborde' canvased behind, a 'shewyng borde' covered with canvas, and a stall with an iron bolt through the post holding the stall to the windows. In the warehouse behind the shop were a 'shewing table' and more 'cowchebords', which were boarded and canvased as in the shop, and had a painted cloth 'crested about' above them.[55] In the 16th century similar fittings, including 'warechestys' and 'shoppe shetys', are recorded in mercers' shops in Cheapside and elsewhere.[56] Elaborate and doubtless attractive display arrangements of this type, perhaps not unlike the franchise stall in the modern department store, were probably more characteristic of the later medieval period, when shops, and living conditions generally, were more spacious than in the 13th and early 14th centuries.

In the earlier period many shops were probably packed to their ceilings with goods, and there may have been little room for elaborate displays. An impression of these crowded conditions is conveyed by a rare inventory of 1332 concerning the goods which had belonged to the recently-deceased mercer, Richard de Elsyng, and which were accommodated in his shops in Soper Lane.[57] The goods were in the care of his three apprentices, and so may have been in three shops. One of Richard's shops, containing two chests and three stalls, and with a room above, measured about 5 ft by 10 ft,[58] so that the three may have had a total ground floor area of 150 square feet, possibly representing a total area of 300 square feet if the goods were kept on two storeys. Within this space were stored some 1,750 separate items, worth £284. They ranged from kerchiefs counted by the dozen to 102 yards in length of Wilton linen cloth. Other fabrics included woollens, worsteds, fustian, taffeta and silk. The goods came from London, Aylesham (in Richard's home county of Norfolk), Elmham, Winchester, Amesbury, Cornwall, Ireland, Flanders, Cologne, Cambrai, Valenciennes, Paris, Rennes (or Rheims; or Rayne in Essex), and Lucca. Some cloths were plain, others were coloured, and some had designs containing roses or popinjays. Particular items included bed covers, chasubles of cloth of gold, coverchiefs, gorgets, cushions, bankers, and a piece of arras. Other items in stock were gold thread, a silver brooch, a silver seal, and silk belts with silver and enamelled fittings. The riches of this collection demonstrate that it was not at all inappropriate to use the term 'shop' to denote the Biblical treasure house.

Shops were the most obvious private space in which retail trading was conducted. But in Cheapside c. 1300 there was, every eight yards or so, an entry leading off the street into one of the larger trading establishments, known as selds, which lay behind the shops. The Cheapside selds are best described as privately-controlled, off-street bazaars. In many respects they resembled the exchanges or bazaars which appeared in the western suburb during the 17th and 18th centuries, although they seem to have been much more numerous. The term 'seld', cognate with the word 'settle',[59] seems primarily to have denoted a building where groups of people sat in order to trade. The business of those who occupied the selds was not unlike that of the traders in the shops, but the selds were larger. In Winchester in 1148 the term 'seld' was used to denote a large establishment where the linen trade was conducted,[60] and in the 13th century, at St Giles's Fair just outside the same city, the selds were long structures accommodating up to about fifty traders in booths which were described as windows (*fenestre*).[61] In London, and especially in Cheapside, the term was in common use by the beginning of the 13th century.[62] Occasionally, as elsewhere, the term was synonymous with 'shop', but almost invariably the seld was an off-street bazaar. Around 1200 one Cheapside seld, set behind two shops, measured 74 ft 3 in. by 17 ft 3 in. This was probably a common size, although other selds were up to twice that width.[63]

The Cheapside selds were solid structures, with stone outer walls, minimising the spread of fire. They were roofed over, and at least one had a louvre.[64] Some of them seem to have been single-storey buildings, open to the roof, but in many instances, selds occupying the ground floor are known to have had rooms over them.[65] Since selds occupied the full width of adjacent properties their interiors must frequently have been dark and gloomy, fitfully lit by lamps or torches. Both selds and shops were sometimes constructed over cellars in which taverns might be accommodated.[66] The land extending 70 ft and more back from Cheapside was thus devoted entirely to commercial uses, at least at ground level and below. Only further to the rear of the longer properties were to be found the houses which served as residences for some of the wealthier inhabitants of the area. Such men were above the 'shopkeeper' class, but were not the major merchants whose homes were in more remote locations. Houses of this type might be separated from the seld by a small yard, but were sometimes an integral part of the seld structure.[67]

The space inside the selds was divided into plots or stations, on which, in most Cheapside selds before *c.* 1350, chests, boxes, benches, cupboards, and counters stood. These installations resembled those in the shops (although cupboards were a much more common feature of selds than of shops), and were used by traders who rented them from the landlord of the seld or, just as often, themselves had freehold possession of the small plots of land on which they had been erected. The market in these plots, and in the rents charged on them, was an active one, and from its records we can reconstruct the internal arrangement of the selds. At a small seld near Soper Lane in the 1220s seven separate freeholders, paying annual quit-rents ranging from 4*s.* to £1 3*s.*, possessed plots with chests, and there were almost certainly other traders there who held their plots as tenants at will. The occupants of this seld traded in gloves and other leather goods, although by the end of the 13th century their interests had shifted to a specialised trade in girdles and in mercers' wares. About 1250 (see Fig. 2) the fourteen plots containing nineteen chests which occupied the rear part of this seld are recorded in detail. They were ranged on either side of a central passage about 4 ft wide, and most of them were a little over 5 ft wide by between 7 ft and 8 ft in depth. Altogether this seld probably contained about 21 plots and 30 or more chests, manned by a corresponding number of traders.[68] Few selds are as intensively documented as this one, but arrangements of this type, often with plots or stations of even smaller dimensions, were typical of most Cheapside selds where the traders dealt in small goods. There was an exception at Tanners' Seld, run on a communal basis by the city's tanners, where the plots were said to be fitted out with stalls, tables and boards on which hides could be laid out. About 1300 at least eighteen tanners occupied this seld.[69]

From an early date the selds were distinguished by names. Indeed, they are the type of Cheapside property for which names appear first in the written record, suggesting that selds were notable for their size and appearance. They seem to have had a clear identity as landmarks and as places to meet,[70] rather like that of the modern department store. This identity would help to attract customers in off the street, past the shops which in most instances concealed the interior of the seld from passers-by. The early names denote the appearance of the seld, its ownership, or the goods traded there. The 'Painted Seld', so called by *c.* 1220, was later known as the 'Great Seld' or the 'Broad Seld' (it was about 30 ft wide). Next door was 'St. Martin's Seld' (it belonged to the collegiate church of St Martin le Grand), later known as the 'Girdlers' Seld' or as the 'Narrow Seld' (*la Streyteseld*: it was just over 12 ft wide near the street).[71] The 'Long Seld' in 1287 (it may have been 230 ft long) was known as 'Anketyn's Seld' in the 14th century, after its former owner Anketyn le Mercer.[72] There are indications that by the early 14th century, with the increase in the scale and density of trading, the owners or occupants of selds were making efforts to attract business by erecting signs on the Cheapside frontage.[73] Thus 'Brantefeld's Seld' of the late 13th century (named after William de Brantefeld who had died before 1260) was known in 1321–2 as the 'Seld of the Boot' or the 'Seld of the Hose' (*selda del Huse*), and by 1408 as 'The Leg'.[74] A sign showing a leg presumably both identified the house and indicated that hose were sold there. Two doors away in 1330 was a seld known as 'The Three Leggs'. It belonged to the Godchep family, one of whom, alive some seventy years earlier, had included on his seal a prominent representation of a leg or a piece of hose.[75] In this case the sign may have served to denote both a particular trade and, in the manner of a modern trademark, a family or business identity. The communal 'Tanners' Seld' of the 13th and 14th centuries was known by 1433 as the 'Cow Head', presumably because of a sign which the tanners had suspended there.[76] This change in the style of naming selds, from a system in which names were attributed by customers and passers-by to one in which landlords or stallholders themselves asserted an identity, may reflect a significant development in the practice and experience of trading and shopping in London.

The shops which occupied the street frontages did not have names, at least in the crowded period before the Black Death. Nevertheless, while shops were individually anonymous, rows or groups of them did acquire distinctive names, denoting the trading specialisms of shopkeepers who congregated there. In Cheapside the practice of naming parts of the street in this way was well established before the end of the 12th century, but reflects a widespread and much older practice of naming streets in medieval towns.[77]

Between them the shops and selds contained accommodation for a very large number of traders. In 1300 Cheapside probably contained some 4,000 stations for traders in selds, in addition to 400 or so shops. The actual number of traders was probably greater than the total of these two figures, because of multiple occupancy in the shops. Cheapside traders on their own were sufficiently numerous to populate a market town of considerable size.

These totals and these arrangements imply that well before 1300 London had a retail trading system of great density and great complexity. But we know little in detail about the operation of this system. Some men and women held several shops and trading stations in selds. Sometimes they probably regarded such holdings simply as a way of investing capital in return for income in the form of rent, but it was also possible, as the example of Richard de Elsyng seems to show, for such people to run several trading outlets at once, using apprentices, servants, or other agents to mind them. These shops or trading sites in selds might all be in one place or might be scattered in several locations. Richard de Elsyng, evidently a wealthy man, may have busied himself with the supply and wholesale side of the business, perhaps visiting producers in Norfolk and elsewhere, dealing with the Italian merchants from whom he would have obtained his silks, and contracting with the girdlers and other craftsmen in the streets around Cheapside whose products he also sold. At the other extreme, as we have seen, single individuals who were relatively poor, or at least in reduced circumstances, might occupy a part of a shop or a seld where they traded on their own account. Some retailers of this type probably purchased their stock in trade on a wholesale basis from 'mercantile shopkeepers' like Richard de Elsyng. Some were too poor even to do this, and undertook to trade in goods on behalf of the person who owned them, presumably handing over to that person the money received from sales less a certain amount as commission. This practice is well documented in the late 13th century and later,[78] but the records of the London rules concerning the taking of distress for arrears of rent suggest that it was also widespread in the early 13th century, particularly in selds, where the poorest indoor traders are likely to have been found. The rules stated that goods were not to be taken as distress in selds, where people left many things for selling (*v lum cumande multes choses pur vendre*). Such goods did not belong to the person who paid the rent for the place where they were being sold, just as the cloths at a dyehouse (another location where distress could not be taken) did not belong to the dyer who ran it.[79] Time devoted to the display and selling of goods thus added to their value in much the same way as the process of dyeing added to the value of cloth.

In considering the storage and distribution of goods in medieval London it is necessary also to take account of the warehousing facilities which the wealthier merchants presumably maintained at the houses where they lived. Such houses included substantial stone halls and cellars, ranges of chambers, outhouses and stabling and generally occupied secluded sites a little distance from the busiest commercial frontages. Clearly they had the space for storing large quantities of goods which could be distributed to retail outlets in Cheapside and elsewhere, but we know very little about the specialised uses of parts of these establishments and even less about their use for storage. At the end of the 13th century several very large properties close to Cheapside which belonged to alien merchants with wide interests, including the textile trade, came to be used by aristocratic families as wardrobes, an indication, perhaps, of the actual and potential use of this type of establishment for the storage of goods on a large scale.[80]

Retail trading in shops and selds offered a means of earning a livelihood to a very wide range of individuals. In particular, it provided an opportunity for women, who might organise the distributive side of the family economy while their husbands manufactured items in the workshop or travelled in search of goods. Women might also look after a shop or a stall at the same time as supervising a household or children. In some retail trades, concerning textiles for example, they might contribute processing skills traditionally associated with women. Above all, perhaps, as in later periods, retailing either in the shop or in a bazaar offered the 'industrious female' who lacked capital, perhaps as often the young unmarried one as the widow, a degree of independence which few other activities could provide.[81] That women regularly looked after shops is indicated by the provision made for widows to continue trading in part of their former husband's shop, as well as by the relative frequency with which they occur as owners or tenants of shops in their own right. Out of sixteen tenants known for a group of three shops in Soper Lane between 1369 and 1418, nine were women, a much higher proportion of the total than was the case with normal households headed by women.[82] At one of these shops a woman paid rent for the pentice on her own account, while her husband paid the rent for the rest of the shop. She presumably occupied a prominent position by the shop window. The independence of the silkwomen who kept shops in 14th- and 15th-century London is well known.[83] They had worthy predecessors in the 13th century, including Gunnilda Fierbras who around 1260 purchased a plot in a seld and, perhaps a little later, a shop nearby in Soper Lane. Her occupation or status was described simply as 'woman' (*mulier*).[84]

Gunnilda's byname suggests that her 'proud arms' may have been one of the features which attracted customers to do business with her. Women were often to be seen in shop windows or doorways, and this was presumably part of a strategy for drumming up trade. Dedicated shoppers like Samuel Pepys (to come no nearer to the present) clearly found shop women one of the attractions of the activity, and in Cheapside *c.* 1600 the shopkeeper's wife played an important role in attracting custom by her beauty and wit.[85]

Women probably also congregated at or near shops as customers, particularly for the personal accessories, clothing and textiles which were to be found in Cheapside. This is perhaps one reason why a 14th-century English illustrator of Genesis chose to set Dinah's encounter with the women of the locality, whom she had set out to see, in close proximity to a shop or booth. The powerful attractions associated with shopping had their disreputable side, and the rape of Dinah which followed this meeting is portrayed as taking place virtually at the shopkeeper's feet (Fig. 4).[86] A 13th-century artist who portrayed a shop seems to have had similar considerations in mind, for he shows it as occupying the ground floor of a house in the open upper window of which sits Bathsheba naked in her bath, being eyed by King David from across the street (Plate VB). In shops, perhaps, it was customary to agree, or to force, assignations which were consummated near by. Soper Lane, full of shops, was part of a particular concentration of lanes and alleys leading off Cheapside, and it is probably no coincidence that before the end of the 13th century the two lanes nearest to it had come to be known as Popkirtle Lane and Gropecunt Lane (Fig. 1).[87]

The monetary values of these trading sites were very high, testimony to the major contribution which shopping and the distributive trade made to the urban economy. In the mid-13th-century plots in Cheapside selds could be obtained for between 6*d.* and 2*s.* a year rent, and at one seld in 1256–7 chests were worth an average of 2*s.* a year each. This was about half the rent of a two-storey cottage in Winchester at about this date.[88] Shops commanded a higher price, having rental values which ranged between £1 and £2 c. 1260, rising to between £3 and £4 by the third decade of the 14th century. Land values near the street frontage were higher than those to the rear. Thus in one seld c. 1250 the annual rental value per square foot ranged from 0.055s. for a plot at the rear to 0.2s. for plots nearer the street.[89] In 1988 values,[90] the plots in the latter group were perhaps worth £40 a square foot. A shop on the street frontage near by had a site value of 0.37s. a square foot in 1270, rising to 1.429s. by 1325.[91] The shop had a room over it, so that the mean values per square foot of accommodation were half these figures. In the seld, however, the plots had no additional storey over them. In 1988 terms, the annual rental value per square foot of accommodation in the shop (both upstairs and downstairs) rose from £35.8 in 1270 to £107.1 in 1325. These sums are in the same range as the rental values of office space in the same central area of the city today, although the multi-storeyed structures of the modern city contain a much greater quantity and concentration of accommodation at this value than the two- to three-storeyed buildings of the 13th century. Valuable as this space was, it was probably often eclipsed in worth by the goods stored within it. If Richard de Elsyng's goods worth £284 in 1332 were stored in three Soper Lane shops, it is likely that the capital value of those shops was not much more than £120.

While many of the practices associated with the shops and selds of 13th- and 14th-century London can also be recognised in the shops and bazaars, and even in the department stores, of much later periods, it is clear that during the 14th and 15th centuries there were major changes in the physical environment in which retail trade was conducted. They arose in the first instance from the demographic and economic problems of the second decade of the 14th century, and were accelerated by the depopulation associated with the Black Death of 1348–9 and later pestilences. Well before the Black Death there was a sharp fall in the demand for sites in the Cheapside area, reflected both in the trend in land values and in the pattern of building. Some adjacent shops were amalgamated, creating more spacious structures. The trend is even more visible after the Black Death. Buildings were replaced by vacant plots, and on one side of Soper Lane in the 15th century a whole row of shops was taken down and its site added to the street. One of the shops in this row was, in real terms, worth in 1370 about half what it had been in 1325.[92] Selds in Cheapside which were to remain in use throughout the 15th century had site values of about 0.16s. per square foot at the beginning of that century, in real terms about half what selds had been worth two hundred years before.[93]

With the reduced pressure on space, but with a lively demand for goods among a population which was smaller and enjoying rising living standards, the selds were rearranged. While the seld names survived, the new structures differed from their predecessors in that they now consisted of shops or warehouses, often of two storeys, ranged along alleys open to the sky, in a much less dense pattern of occupancy than before. 'St. Martin's Seld', for example, which in 1250 contained about 21 plots with chests, in 1360 contained eleven plots, some of which were described as shops and had rooms above (Fig. 3). There seem to have been eleven shops on the site in 1516, when the property may have been worth less than half as much as in 1360.[94]

Towards the mid-16th century there was a marked revival in the demand for Cheapside properties and within fifty years land values again equalled their late-13th-century levels. Some of the larger shops which had been created were divided,[95] but the proliferation of minute shops and trading sites which had characterised the 13th century did not reappear. This contrast in structural arrangements between the two periods, reflecting changes in the pattern and legal framework of property tenure, probably parallels one in the organisation of retail trade. In earlier periods this trade was in the hands of a very large number of small-scale operators, who traded on their own account from establishments, however small, which they themselves controlled, even if they did not actually own the goods they sold. At the later date the typical retail trading unit was more substantial, occupying larger premises, and probably with a larger stock. By 1550 or 1600 there may have been as many individuals concerned in running this trade as there had been in 1300 (although this is by no means certain), but a higher proportion of them may have been the servants of others, enjoying, nominally at least, a smaller degree of freedom of action than their predecessors.

The property once known as the 'Broad Seld' provides a good example of this change. In the 13th century there were four small shops on the Cheapside frontage plus an entry to the seld behind. About 1530, following a period of decay, the property, now known as 'The Key', was rebuilt. It now contained only one 'great shop' measuring 60 ft 6 in. by 21 ft. There was a narrow entry beside it leading to a warehouse and domestic accommodation. In 1588 three young members of the Mercers' Company, all once servants of the recently-deceased householder, himself a tenant of the company, were running the shop at the Key, as they had presumably done when their master was alive. They controlled a space (1270.5 square feet) confined to the ground floor, which was perhaps more than four times the size of that controlled by Richard de Elsyng's three apprentices in 1332 (possibly 300 square feet on two storeys). This great shop itself had a name, 'The Key' or the 'Golden Key', which was presumably displayed as a sign.[96] This was one of the largest shops in Cheapside, but by this date many others seem to have approached it in size, and most of these shops had a name and a sign (now quite evidently serving as a trademark), as the selds had done before them.

The verbal distinction between the shop and the warehouse was one which seems to have arisen in the course of the 15th century.[97] The warehouse was generally larger than the shop and almost invariably occupied an off-frontage site, immediately behind the shop or still further back, often on land where a seld had once stood. It was perhaps used mainly for storage and as a setting for wholesale transactions, although the similarity between the fittings in warehouses and those in shops suggests that, in the textile business at any rate, some retail trading also took place in the warehouses. This recalls the propensity of 19th-century distributive traders to call their businesses warehouses when they considered that the size of their business 'merited a more impressive description than that of shop'.[98] The combination of shop and warehouse which was emerging by the early 16th century as typical of many 'artisan/shopkeeper' establishments, as well as of mercantile ones, again seems to illustrate the relative increase in the scale of retail trading businesses.

Despite these changes, many of the structural features of the 17th-century shop would have been familiar to the 13th-century citizen and many long-established customary trading practices still continued. Even at the Golden Key in 1652, 'Goodwife Smith' was allowed to sit 'at the door'. She was left five shillings by the prosperous mercer who occupied the shop, and presumably in her declining years earned a small income from the customers who, as they entered or left the shop, made purchases of her small wares, perhaps often with a charitable intent. A few years later the wealthy shoppers at the Key included Samuel Pepys 'with a company of fine ladies', who had come to see the Lord Mayor's show, and after his visit Pepys entertained the shopkeeper at the tavern next door.[99]

Shops and the practices associated with them have been a constant feature of English town life from the early Middle Ages to the present day. Throughout this period they have occupied a central position in the system by which urban wealth was created, and they have shown a clear response to economic, demographic, and social change.

D

ACKNOWLEDGEMENTS

The detailed research on which this paper is based was undertaken at the Institute of Historical Research as part of the Social and Economic Study of Medieval London, funded by the Economic and Social Research Council (grant number 000/23/004), an anonymous donor, the Bank of England, and other institutions. Thanks are due to Martha Carlin, David Crouch, Vanessa Harding, Joanna Mattingly, Olwen Myhill, and John Stedman for help with the research.

Figure 1 appears by permission of the Museum of London, Plate VI by permission of the Society of Antiquaries of London, and Plate VII by permission of the Pierpont Morgan Library, New York.

REFERENCES

1. The origin of this misconception seems to be Davis (1966). See also Clark (1981), esp. p. 7. The views of P. J. Corfield have undergone a modification: Corfield (1972), esp. p. 289; Corfield (1982), 19. Mui (1989) provides a welcome reassessment of the prevalence and importance of shops in 18th-century England.
2. See Wood (1965), 221–2 and Pl. 34 (for 15th-century examples); Stenning (1985), 35–8.
3. Corfield (1982), 19; Davis (1966), 192–3 (citing Defoe).
4. *Henry VIII: Letters*, XI, 333.
5. *Island of England*, 42–3. The editor's translation has been modified, and her interpretation of 'The Street' as The Strand, is clearly wrong.
6. Reddaway (1963), 181–206. The lists of 1558 and other years on which this article is partly based, cover goldsmiths trading in Cheapside and in other city streets and not, as Reddaway sometimes implies, those who were tenants of the Goldsmiths' Company.
7. Stow, I (1971), 295–6, 345–6.
8. *London Eyre* (1971), nos 370, 372.
9. Keene and Harding (1987), passim; Keene (1985b), 18.
10. Bosworth and Toller (1898), 839. See Luke 21.1: 'he looked up and saw the rich putting their gifts into the treasury'.
11. Barlow *et al.* (1976), 38 (no. 27).
12. Keene and Harding (1987), nos 105/22, 23.
13. *Magnum. Rot. Scacc.*, 147.
14. Cf. Ekwall (1947), 26, 110, 180; Ekwall (1951), passim. Ekwall cites several 12th- and early 13th-century instances of the name *le Sopere*, but interpreted it (with some hesitation) as meaning 'soaper', as he did also in the case of Soper Lane: Ekwall (1965), 117. The close association between the *sopparii* or *soperes* and the shops of the Cheapside area (Keene and Harding (1987), passim), however, leaves little doubt that in this context the term means 'shopkeeper' rather than 'soap-maker' or 'soap-seller'. Cf. Godefroy, III (1884), 395, s.n. *eschopier*.
15. Ekwall (1965), 182–3.
16. *Rot. Hund.* Vol. I 408, 416, 421; *De Ant. Leg. Lib.*, 168.
17. Plate IV. Anglo (1969), 198, 255, 284–90, 321.
18. *De. Ant. Leg. Lib.*, 7, 20, 116, 119, 161; *Chrons Edward I and Edward II*, Vol. I, 102, 315–6, 354.
19. *Memorials*, 435; *Letter-Book H*, 131–3.
20. CLRO, Repertories 21, ff. 543–4. For a summary of the later medieval pattern of street marketing in the city, see Archer *et al.* (1988), esp. pp. 1–15. Ibid., p. 65 shows how the Cheapside monuments might serve to define the spatial organisation of the street market.
21. *Memorials*, 532–3; *Letter-Book B*, 391.
22. *Lib. Cust.*, Vol. I, 96–7; Gray (1985), 16–9.
23. Keene and Harding (1987), no. 105/26.
24. Ibid., nos 145/31, 34.
25. Keene (1987), 11; Keene (1988).
26. Keene and Harding (1987), nos 105/16, 17.
27. Ibid., no. 145/5B.
28. Ibid., nos 145/5A, 7.
29. Ibid., passim, but especially nos 145/20, 37.
30. Ibid., no. 105/26.
31. Ibid., no. 104/20.
32. Ibid., nos 104/33, 105/17, 145/9.
33. Ibid., nos 105/17, 145/26, 34; *Assize of Nuisance*, no. 206.

34. Keene and Harding (1987), no. 145/5.
35. Ibid., no. 145/28–9.
36. Ibid., no. 95/5.
37. *London Eyre*, nos 370–95.
38. Keene and Harding (1987), no. 105/14; CLRO, Repertories 51, f. 114.
39. Evans (1966), 262–3. Hartley and Elliot (1925), Pls 32-3, and id. (1928), Pls 22, 36–7.
40. Cockerell and Plummer (1969); Branner, IX (1977).
41. Leguay (1984), 42, 127–30; Cleret (1941), 31–8.
42. Keene and Harding (1987), no. 105/14.
43. Ibid., no. 145/3.
44. Ibid., nos 95/5, 104/33.
45. Ibid., nos 104/33, 145/9E.
46. Stow, II (1971), 208.
47. Salzman (1968), 441.
48. Keene and Harding (1987), no. 95/5.
49. Ibid., nos 104/33, 105/16–7, 145/31.
50. Barlow *et al.* (1976), 37–8 (no. 23, n. 1); Keene (1985a), 48–50. There is some indication of a similar pattern of encroachment at the Cheapside end of Bow Lane: Keene and Harding (1987), nos 104/10, 104/17–9.
51. Keene and Harding, no. 105/25.
52. Ibid., nos 104/20, 104/37–41.
53. Schofield (1987), passim.
54. Keene and Harding (1987), passim: inventories attached to leases in this period regularly list panelling, doors, and other timber fixtures which tenants were to leave *in situ* at the end of the term of the lease.
55. PRO, C146/902.
56. E.g., Keene and Harding (1987), nos 145/9–10; PRO, C239/1/15B.
57. PRO, E154/1/18a.
58. Keene and Harding (1987), no. 145/5A.
59. *New English Dictionary*, s.n.
60. Keene (1985a), 517.
61. Ibid., 1092, 1098–9.
62. For early uses of the term in London sources, see *Westminster Charters*, nos 135, 295. See also Keene and Harding (1987), nos 11/8–9, 10, 104/29–30, 37–41. Selds are mentioned in a spurious royal charter dated 1081, the text of which may describe genuine arrangements of the early 13th century: *Regesta I*, no. 141; *EHR*, 43 (1928), 617.
63. Keene and Harding (1987), nos 11/10, 145/10.
64. Ibid., nos 105/11, 145/8.
65. Ibid., nos 104/14, 15, 27, 32, 33, 37–41.
66. Ibid., nos 104/20, 37–41, 105/11, 145/10.
67. Ibid., nos 11/6, 8–9, 104/32, 34, 37–41.
68. Ibid., no. 145/8.
69. Ibid., no. 104/42.
70. *Cal. Inquis. Misc.* iii, no. 155.
71. Keene and Harding (1987), nos 104/10, 145/8; see also Fig. 2.
72. Ibid., no. 104/29–30.
73. For an example, from 1391–2, of expenditure on painting a sign and hanging it from a pole on the Cheapside frontage, see ibid., no. 145/8.
74. Ibid., no. 104/34.
75. Ibid., no. 104/32.
76. Ibid., no. 104/42.
77. For early 'row-names', see ibid. nos 104/29–30, 105/26. See also Ekwall (1965), 41–2, 72–8; Brooke and Keir (1975), 277–8.
78. Keene (1985), 252; *Novae Narrat.* 17; Milsom in ibid. 'Legal introduction', clxxx. For the legal position of such agents, cf. Plucknett (1954), esp. pp. 23–4, 30; and Milsom (1981), 279–81. The law of agency, which by the 18th century had replaced the late medieval notion that the bailiff had title to the goods in his care, appears to have resembled the earlier medieval practice.
79. Bateson (1902), 494.
80. For properties in this category, see Keene and Harding (1987), 95/8–12, 13–5, 104/23, and Keene (1987), 9–11 and Appendix pp. 8–16.
81. Cf. Davis (1966), 122–5; Adburgham (1981), 19–20.
82. Keene and Harding (1987), nos 145/5, 25–6; Keene (1985a), 266.

83. Lacey (1985), 24–82; Dale (1932–4), 324–35. For shops in Cheapside acquired by silkwomen a few years before they married, see Keene and Harding (1987), nos 145/9B, 9C.
84. Keene and Harding (1987), nos 145/5B, 8C.
85. E.g. *Pepys*, VII, 156, 196–7; Davis (1966), 109.
86. British Library, MS Egerton 1894, f. 17. Reproduced in James (1921b); see Pächt (1943), 51–71. Part of the scene is redrawn in Cowgill *et al.* (1987), 61.
87. See Fig. 1; Ekwall (1965), 140, 164–5.
88. Keene and Harding (1987), no. 11/10; Keene (1985a), 237–8. In this discussion values are consistently expressed as annual rentals. Capital values have been converted to annual ones on the assumption (justified by many instances in the sources) that at this period annual rents were generally sold for sums equal to 10 years' income.
89. Keene and Harding (1987), no. 145/8.
90. Conversion to modern values is a process fraught with difficulty, and the values suggested here should be treated with a great deal of reserve. There is, however, no other readily comprehensible means of expressing the real value of medieval properties. For the purposes of the following discussion the building craftsman's daily wage rate has been used as an index, with the following values: 1250–1300, 3*d.* a day; 1320s, 4*d.* a day; 1370–1400, 5*d.* a day; 1988, £50 a day.
91. Keene and Harding (1987), no. 145/5B.
92. Ibid.
93. Ibid., nos 104/33 (0.056*s.* a square foot, *c.* 1200; 0.16*s.* a square foot in 1419), 104/34 (0.165*s.* a square foot in 1408), 104/42 (0.158*s.* a square foot in 1405).
94. Ibid., nos 104/32, 33, 34, 145/8.
95. Ibid., nos 105/18, 19.
96. Ibid., no. 145/10.
97. See ibid., no. 105/33 for warehouses in 1475, and passim for 16th- and 17th-century references. For a rare 14th-century reference to a warehouse, described as a 'house for merchandise', see Salzman (1968), 464.
98. Adburgham (1981), 14.
99. Keene and Harding (1987), no. 145/10.

The Romanesque Architecture of Old St Paul's Cathedral and its Late Eleventh-Century Context

By Richard Gem

The London region is the only place in England where we can be confident a fully-developed Romanesque style of architecture was established before the Norman Conquest: at Westminster Abbey, begun in the late 1040s or *c.* 1050.[1] However, a remarkable fact seems to be that Westminster, for all its progressive qualities, did not constitute the most influential model for post-Conquest Romanesque architecture in the region. Rather, the last two decades of the 11th century saw the formation of a new regional style, intimately linked with Canterbury. It is this late 11th-century phenomenon that will be examined in this paper, with special reference to Old St Paul's Cathedral, but considering also the probably contemporary church of St Mary le Bow and the somewhat earlier works of Bermondsey Priory and the Tower of London.[2]

THE TOWER OF LONDON

The most impressive late 11th-century monument to survive in London is undoubtedly the White Tower,[3] the construction of which seems to have been under the supervision of Gundulf, a protegé of Archbishop Lanfranc. Gundulf was certainly acting for William I in this supervisory capacity sometime during his tenure of the bishopric of Rochester, that is *c.* 1077–87;[4] but whether this dates the start of the building is uncertain.

The Tower is constructed of rubble work with ashlar dressings of Caen and Quarr stone cut in small, evenly-sized blocks. This ashlar technique indicates a change from Westminster Abbey (where large ashlar blocks were used in the early works) and a shift in the centre of technological influence towards Caen. This shift is no doubt related to the growth of the Caen stone industry, but it is also symptomatic of the stylistic emergence of Calvados with the creation of the Norman High Romanesque style at St-Etienne in Caen. Both developments, technological and stylistic, are ones that had already affected Canterbury before the works had opened at the Tower of London; but thereafter London and Canterbury may both have been in direct contact with Normandy in a parallel relationship.

The Tower is of great importance from the point of view of castellology: but, on account of the chapel of St John, it is also of fundamental significance to the study of ecclesiastical architecture — which is the subject here under consideration. The general form of the chapel is well known (Pl. VIA),[5] but its relationship to contemporary great church design has not so often been analysed — which is surprising since in conception it is closely similar to the eastern arm of a great church, bereft of transepts and nave. The ambulatory *parti* is adopted for the chapel, but not for any real functional reason since there are no radiating chapels to which the ambulatory could give access. In elevation the aisle is surmounted by a gallery, which is to some extent explicable in terms of the relationship of the chapel to the main domestic block of the construction, but which is also a feature of display, and part of the formula taken over from a great church. There is no clerestory — and in the context one could hardly have been included — but the omission of this in a building with a barrel vault is perhaps to be expected anyway.[6]

If a specific parallel to the conception of the chapel were sought in a great church, the most obvious and relevant example would be the presbytery of St Augustine's Abbey, Canterbury, which was begun by Abbot Scolland c. 1070–3 and completed in its eastern parts by 1087.[7] In the two buildings are to be seen a similar ambulatory plan, probably a similar use of uniform columnar supports in the main arcade, and probably a similar appearance of some arches of a continuous plain rectangular order with no impost. Apparently a similar system of measurement was also used for laying out the dimensions of the buildings: the length of the two central vessels is closely comparable, while in total width the chapel is half the comparable dimension of the presbytery.

That there should in fact be a direct connexion between the works at the Tower and at Canterbury is by no means improbable. Gundulf had been Lanfranc's domestic administrator at Canterbury before being made Bishop of Rochester and he must have known the works at the cathedral and St Augustine's. Vitalis, the *Exactor* for the procurement of building stone for the King's works at the Palace of Westminster (and possibly the Tower?) was a confrater of St Augustine's and procured stone for the works there also.[8] Furthermore, there was already a link in relation to building work established between Duke William, Lanfranc and Gundulf when the latter were in Caen and responsible for building the ducal abbey of St-Etienne.

The Canterbury works in the 1070s were the foyer of High Romanesque architecture in England. Thus if the royal works at the same period were linked intimately to the same organisational network as Canterbury, then St John's Chapel (and indeed the Tower itself) might be seen as an integral part of that same achievement. In short, London was participating in the forefront of High Romanesque architectural creativity, as it had already done under Edward the Confessor in relation to the Early Romanesque.

ST SAVIOUR'S PRIORY, BERMONDSEY

The major lost London monument of the latter years of William I's reign, contemporary with the Tower, is the priory of Bermondsey. According to the priory's own tradition recorded in the 15th-century *Bermondsey Annals* the origins of the house went back to the year 1082 when Alwin Child, a London citizen, gave various rents in the City to the monks of La-Charité-sur-Loire. However it was the manor of Bermondsey, which formed part of the royal demesne, that was to be the site of the new monastery; and this suggests that the king himself, if not the originator of the idea, was actually responsible for the foundation.[9] Domesday Book records under the royal manor of Bermondsey: *ibi noua et pulchra aecclesia* (there is there a new and beautiful church);[10] so construction must have been well advanced by c. 1086. Three years later in 1089 a group of four monks was sent from La-Charité to colonise the new house, which by then was presumably ready to receive the community. William II gave the manor of Bermondsey to the priory and Alwin elicited donations from various other people before his death in 1094.

Excavations by Corbett and Grimes on the site of the priory uncovered the foundations of part of the eastern arm of the church, and from these it is clear that the building was of the greatest interest. The building stretched some 20 m east of the crossing before coming to a *chevet* that superficially resembles in plan an eastern transept with apsidal chapels to either side and three apsidal chapels to the east. The main crossing itself was flanked by fully-developed transept arms, provided with twin apsidal chapels on the east side.[11]

The reconstruction of the superstructure from the foundation plan raises important issues (Fig. 1). The total internal width of the eastern arm must have been about 10 m, which would have been about the same as St John's Chapel in the Tower: however, the chapel is

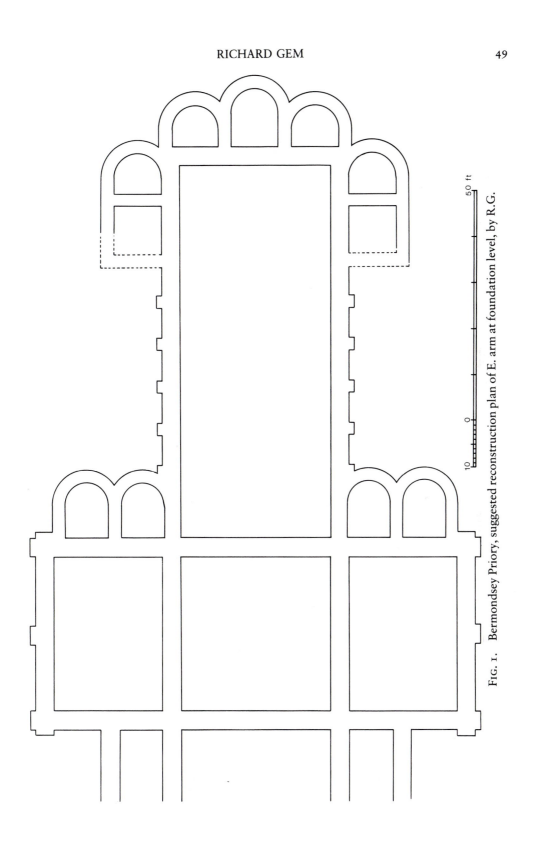

Fig. 1.   Bermondsey Priory, suggested reconstruction plan of E. arm at foundation level, by R.G.

some 6 m shorter along the east and west axis. It seems improbable that the aisled arrangement of the chapel was drawn out to fit the length of the Bermondsey presbytery, for this would have formed an extraordinarily long and narrow tunnel effect. On the other hand, the total width of Bermondsey is similar to that of the nave only, without the flanking aisles, of St Augustine's Abbey. It seems most plausible to suppose, therefore, that the Bermondsey presbytery was unaisled — a contention that would be supported by the fact that an aisle was added outside the 11th-century north wall in the 14th century. Such a design seems distinctly 'primitive' and makes it almost certain that the eastern arm was built c. 1082–7 — and was not an extension in the 12th century of an earlier and simpler eastern termination (Grimes had thought it likely that the excavated building was 12th century, although he had found no clear evidence of a preceding 11th-century church).[12]

The plan of the rest of the building as recorded by Martin[13] would suggest that west of the transept lay an aisled nave of perhaps nine or ten bays, and work on a building of such dimensions is likely to have continued into the early 12th century. On the other hand a photocopy has recently been discovered of a lost 19th-century copy of a drawing of 1550–1 by S. Robbus showing the still-standing church with only a four-bay nave:[14] this is probably the result of schematisation in the drawing, although the details otherwise suggest a degree of representational accuracy. The drawing confirms the survival of the Romanesque nave and transept until the Dissolution, but indicates that the eastern arm was a Gothic replacement (even if it is difficult to make the drawing tally with Grimes' plan).

A date for the start of the building at Bermondsey in the 1080s would be of considerable interest. The plan at first sight might be loosely interpreted as belonging to the Cluniac double transept group and as showing the influence of the great church of Cluny III. However, Cluny was begun only in 1088 (even though preparations began perhaps as early as 1085) and this makes any influence on Bermondsey unlikely or impossible. On the other hand, not only is Cluny itself to be seen in the context of other contemporary Continental buildings experimenting with more or less similar plans, but also it is doubtful whether the Bermondsey plan is really of double-transept type. The apsidal features flanking the eastern termination are comparatively small chapels in plan and it is most unlikely that they rose open the full height of the main vessel of the presbytery. Flanking chapels in a comparable position and not constituting true transepts may be seen in the eastern arm of the famous abbey of St-Benoît-sur-Loire begun by Abbot William, 1067–80, and early enough to show that this feature precedes the influence of Cluny III. At La-Charité itself the church that was dedicated in 1106–7, and which therefore may have been begun not later than the 1080s or 1090s,[15] probably had an *échelon* of five eastern apses terminating an aisled presbytery. Five apses disposed so as to terminate an unaisled presbytery would inevitably resemble Bermondsey quite closely. But some explanation seems called for to explain the reduction to an unaisled plan. Perhaps it was reasons of economy, and of speed so that the building could be ready to receive the monastic community as soon as possible. Whatever the exact circumstances, however, it may be noted that a comparable reductionist tendency was in operation at this time at Rochester Cathedral, reducing an orthodox Romanesque apse *échelon* scheme to a bizarre rectangular form with a single chapel projecting beyond its main east wall.[16] Moreover the contemporary rebuilding of York Minster was preceding on an unaisled plan — though one very different in scale from Bermondsey.[17] But whether Bermondsey had any close relationship in the details of its design with Bishop Gundulf's Rochester — and beyond Rochester with Canterbury — cannot be determined on the available evidence.

ST PAUL'S CATHEDRAL

History

Whatever the precise appearance and history of the fabric of St Paul's Cathedral as it stood in the middle of the 11th century (matters which, unfortunately, are deeply obscure), there is no evidence that Bishop Robert of London (1044–51) or Bishop William (1051–75), who were both Norman appointees of Edward the Confessor, took any steps towards a rebuilding of their church to parallel the new splendours of Westminster Abbey up the river. Nor does it appear that William the Conqueror's first bishop, Hugh de Orival (1075–85), changed the situation. This may, of course, reflect a lacuna in the documentary sources, or it may to some extent bear witness to the scale of the Anglo-Saxon cathedral church. Be that as it may, by the time of Bishop Maurice's appointment in 1085 the cathedral can hardly have seemed any longer commensurate with the dignity of the bishopric: at the Council of London in 1075 the Bishop of London was recognised as next in precedence after the two metropolitans, and he was also regarded as 'Dean' of the church of Canterbury.[18]

In the late summer of 1087 came Bishop Maurice's opportunity when, as the Anglo-Saxon Chronicle records, 'the holy minster of St Paul, the cathedral church of London, was burnt down, and many other churches, and the largest and noblest part of all the city'.[19] The *Life of St Erkenwald* (written *c.* 1148 by Arcoid the nephew of Bishop Gilbert I[20]) describes the fire, in which Erkenwald's relics were unharmed, and then goes on to say that Bishop Maurice:

aliam ecclesiam a fundamentis incepit, opus uidelicet, ut multis uidebatur, inconsummabile, uerum si consummari posset, honor et decus Londoniae. Peractis denique criptis, sanctissimi corpus Erkonwaldi ibidem collocari precepit

(began another church from the foundations — a work which, it seems to many, is incompleteable, or if it could be completed the honour and glory of London).[21]

Bishop Maurice died in 1107 and was succeeded in 1108 by Bishop Richard I de Beaumais who *incepte muros ecclesie mirabiliter auxit* (wonderfully extended the walls of the church that had been begun)[22] as well as creating a close around the cathedral.

The same works were described by William of Malmesbury, writing *c.* 1120–5 (and thus during Richard I's episcopate). He says of Bishop Maurice that:

Magnanimitatis certe ipsius est inditium basilica sancti Pauli quam incohauit Lundoniae. Tanta est decoris magnificentia, ut merito inter praeclara numeretur edifitia. Tanta criptae laxitas, tanta superioris aedis capacitas, ut quamlibet confertae multitudini uideatur posse sufficere. Quia igitur Mauritius erat mentis immodicus, laboriosi operis impensam transmisit ad posteros. Denique, cum Ricardus successor eius omnes redditus ad episcopatum pertinentes aedificationi basilicae transcripsisset, aliunde se suosque sustentans, propemodum nichil efficere uisus est. Totumque censum ad hoc prodigus exhauriebat, et parum in effectum prodibat. Quare, impetus boni quem in initio episcopatus habuit, procedentibus annis desperatione lassescens, paulatim elanguit.

(The mark of Bishop Maurice's great-mindedness is the basilica of St Paul which he began in London. Such is the magnificence of its beauty that it deservedly may be numbered among famous buildings. So great is the breadth of the crypt and so great the capacity of the upper building that it may seem able to suffice for a multitude however dense. Because Maurice was thus a man of unrestrained mind, he transmitted to his successors the expense of a burdensome work. At length, when his successor Richard assigned all the rents belonging to the bishopric to the building of the basilica, maintaining himself and his household from other sources, almost nothing seemed to be achieved. The unsparing man was well-meaningly pouring out all his wealth but advancing too little in result. For that reason the impetus for good which the bishops had in the beginning, grew weak with despair as the years went by, and gradually faded).[23]

Henry of Huntingdon, writing c. 1125–30, only says that Bishop Maurice *templum maximum quod necdum perfectum est incepit* (began the great church which is still not yet complete)[24] and does not refer to Bishop Richard's work. However, Orderic Vitalis, writing c. 1136–7, says of Bishop Richard that *in constuctione prefatae basilicae quam antecessor eius incohauerat summopere laborauit, et inceptum opus magna ex parte consummauit* (he laboured greatly in the construction of the basilica, which his predecessor had undertaken, and he completed a great part of the work which had been begun).[25]

For the history of the fabric following Bishop Richard I's death in 1127 we are very poorly informed by the surviving sources. The *Life of St Erkenwald* says rather unhelpfully of Bishop Gilbert I the Universal (1128–34) that this was not the place to relate what he did for his cathedral.[26] However, it was in his time that took place the great fire of 1133[27] in which *maxima pars Lundoniae ciuitatis, cum principali ecclesia beati Pauli Apostoli . . . igne combusta est* (the greater part of the city of London, with the principal church of Blessed Paul the Apostle, was burnt by a fire).[28] This might therefore mark a serious setback to the work of the cathedral still in progress, while the situation could have been compounded by the seven-year vacancy in the see between Gilbert I's death and the appointment of Robert de Sigillo (1141–50).

It was in these years shortly before the middle of the 12th century that took place various events connected with the shrine of St Erkenwald described by Arcoid. There was an attempt made to steal the relics from their *loculus ligneus* (wooden coffin) in the crypt and this led to the decision to enclose them *in tutiori loco* (in a securer place).[29] But pressure of opinion then decided that the relics should also be transferred *ad locum honorabiliorem* (to a more honourable place).[30] Accordingly a solemn translation was celebrated on 14th November 1140 and the relics in their leaden cist were carried *ad locum de nouo paratum* (to the place newly prepared) — but where this was is not specified — and there placed in a stone receptacle.[31] Two translations are recorded in the *Short Chronicle of St Paul's*: one in 1140, and a second on 14 November 1148.[32] Dugdale says that at the 1148 translation the relics were transferred to a place behind the high altar of the main church,[33] but since he only quotes the *Short Chronicle* (*sc.* 'Matthew of Westminster') as his source, and this does not mention the place of translation, this is probably an unfounded assumption.

The *miracula* described by Arcoid in the section of his text following the 1140 translation are not placed chronologically and it is not necessary to assume that all of them are later than 1140 in occurrence — though one is stated specifically to be so. One miracle took place *eo tempore quo ipsius sancti presulis prefati corpus adhuc in cripta in sarcophago seruabatur, testudo eiusdem cripte pingenda fuit* (at that time when the body of the aforementioned holy bishop was still laid up in the crypt and the vault of the same crypt was to be painted).[34] Two other miracles refer to the construction of a wooden feretory covered with silver and gold for the relics of the saint — work in which the silversmith Eustace was involved.[35] Subsequently Arcoid recounts some miracles which he places specifically in the reign of King Stephen (1135–54), and later still in the sequence of his text he tells of an incident which refers to *Erkenwaldus . . . habens sepulchrum in dextero latere altaris sancte Fidis* (Erkenwald who has his sepulchre on the right side of the altar of St Faith).[36] St Faith, at least at a later date, was the principal dedication in the crypt.

Bishop Robert was succeeded by Richard II de Beaumais (1152–62), of whom nothing is recorded in relation to the fabric. The next bishop was then Gilbert II Foliot (1163–87), who around May 1175 appealed for funds towards the work of the cathedral 'which was begun what is now a long time ago, and which is already in large part built' (*que a multo iam tempore fundata, et ... magna iam sui parte constructa*), so that 'you may see the too-long protracted work completed in your day' (*ut in diebus uestris diu protractum opus ... completum uideatis*).[37] However, it is not necessary to conclude from this late 12th-century campaign of work that the construction of the main Romanesque fabric had been protracted continuously since 1087. It is arguable that the substantial body of the cathedral had been erected under Maurice and Richard I, that there had then been an interruption(s) in the work, and that what was undertaken in the later 12th century was the completion of the more peripheral elements. But before assessing further the implications of the documentary sources, it is necessary to review the evidence for the Romanesque fabric itself.

The Fabric

Putting together a picture of the early phases of the Romanesque fabric of St Paul's (Fig. 2) is not an easy matter because of the sparse and sometimes contradictory evidence.[38] *A priori* it might be expected that Bishop Maurice's work between 1087 and 1107 included the determination of the dimensions of the building as a whole and the commencement of those parts of the structure that were needed first for the liturgy: that is, the sanctuary in the eastern arm and the canons' choir in the crossing and easternmost nave bays, together with the immediately adjoining parts.

Of the crypt beneath the sanctuary, which was certainly built by Maurice, there is little direct evidence, but its extent can probably be inferred from the plans of the 13th-century crypt and upper church given by Dugdale and from the Wren plan (Pl. IXB).[39] The crypt of St Faith beneath the New Work accounted for eight bays of the fabric above (counting from the east) and at its west terminated in a straight wall: any apse to the original 11th-century crypt further west, therefore, must have been demolished. On the not unnatural assumption that the 13th- and 11th-century work actually joined on the chord of the former apse, the original presbytery would have accounted for the first four straight bays east of the crossing in the 13th-century work, with the apse projecting beyond — and it is precisely the fifth bay of the 13th-century presbytery that the Dugdale plan shows as wider than its neighbours at both upper and crypt levels. Confirmation of this is provided by the Wren drawings for a crossing rotunda, which also indicate the fifth bay of the Gothic presbytery as wider than its neighbours (Pl. XVI). The existence of an ambulatory and radiating chapels about the main apse may be no more than inferred as a likelihood — in view of the contemporary references to the extravagant scale of the work — for no firm evidence is recorded. Finch's claim that the Dugdale plates of the choir and of the tomb of Bishop Roger Niger show cylindrical Romanesque piers surviving at the putative point of springing of the original main apse must be treated with caution (Pls XIIB, XVA).[40] However, if the Romanesque presbytery was actually divided into four bays between the crossing and the apse (that is, if the 13th-century Gothic piers of the later presbytery stood above Romanesque crypt piers), these were considerably narrower than the nave bays and a uniform system of columnar piers might seem one possibility. On the other hand, the contrast between the bay lengths of the presbytery (approximately 16 ft 6 in.) and nave (approximately 24 ft 6 in.) would find a good parallel at Winchester (approximately 15 ft 8 in. and 22 ft) where there was an alternating system in the presbytery, and this seems the preferable alternative for the design of the St Paul's piers — especially since uniformly spaced columnar piers would have resulted in a column on the axis of the main apse. The other possibility altogether is that the 13th-century presbytery was laid out without reference to the 11th-century crypt plan.

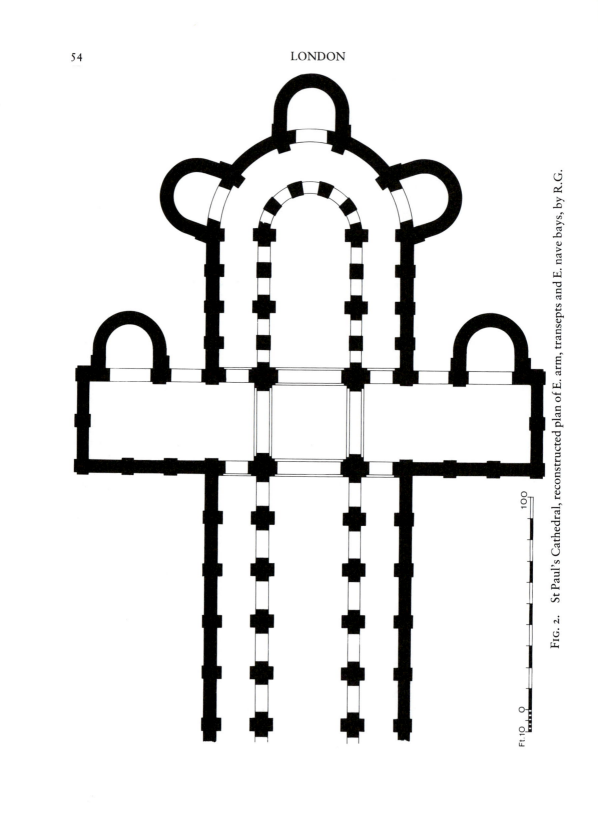

Fig. 2. St Paul's Cathedral, reconstructed plan of E. arm, transepts and E. nave bays, by R.G.

Ft.10   0   100

Access to the crypt beneath the presbytery seems to have been provided by steps leading down from the transepts through doorways in the east walls of the latter (shown by Hollar) (Pl. VII).

The original form of the transepts is probably the most controversial element in any reconstruction. It has frequently been assumed that the Romanesque transepts were of the same scale as those that in Gothic guise survived until the Great Fire: an assumption loaned credibility by the supposed extravagant scale of the work. However, there are objections to this assumption. In the first place, the total length of the transepts (as shown on Dugdale's plan) appears impossibly out of scale with the rest of the Romanesque cathedral. On any hypothesis that aisled transepts were laid out or built as part of Bishop Maurice's work, their dimensions (as at the contemporary Winchester and Ely) might be expected to have been integrated with the scale of the eastern arm to provide some form of symmetrical arrangement about the crossing: but this the aisled transepts at St Paul's did not do. The length of the latter was considerably greater than the eastern arm, and this can only be taken as evidence that they were planned as part of a different project (cf. Pl. IXB).

Perhaps even more conclusive is the 17th-century graphic material showing the transept elevations, for this indicates that the Gothic aisled transepts in fact incorporated elements from an earlier Romanesque unaisled arrangement. Hollar's interior section, depicting the east side of the crossing and part of the transepts (Pl. VII), shows the first bay of either transept projecting beyond the line of the presbytery aisles as containing Romanesque arched openings (above the doorways to the crypt), pierced through a solid wall on a line north and south of the eastern crossing piers. Above these larger openings are shown smaller ones, likewise round-headed but flanked by trefoiled blank arcading. Above these again is the clerestory (see further below). The two levels of round-headed openings are most plausibly interpreted as windows corresponding to the aisle and gallery levels in the Romanesque (presbytery and) nave, but here providing light directly into the main transept space. Thomas Wyck's drawing of c. 1667, showing the ruins of the south transept from the north-east following the Great Fire, confirms the Hollar evidence.[41] Again it shows the first transept bay projecting beyond the line of the presbytery aisles as having a solid east wall in the line of the crossing piers. This wall below clerestory level has a circular window, below which is a band of blank arcading and then, lower still, a large Romanesque window. Equally important, the Wyck drawing shows the next bay of the transept as having an apsidal projection eastwards from the line of the solid wall. The same apsidal projection is shown in plan in Wren's pre-Fire design for adding a domed rotunda to the crossing of the medieval church.[42]

The evidence for the Romanesque transepts thus seems to point to an east elevation, moving outward from the crossing piers, which was composed thus: Bay 1, gave access to the presbytery aisles and galleries — but no evidence survives for the Romanesque fabric here. Bay 2, projected beyond the line of the aisles and was a solid wall with four levels of openings — that is, a doorway to the crypt, a large arched window, a smaller window (possibly circular) and finally the clerestory window. Bay 3, was broader and opened into an apsidal chapel. If then the length of each transept arm was approximately comparable to the length of the presbytery including the apse (deduced from the Dugdale and Wren plans), the transept terminated with Bay 3. This means that Bays 4 and 5 as they stood in the 17th century formed part of a different campaign of work.

For the west side of the transepts there is little direct evidence for the Romanesque fabric, but it would seem likely that if there were no aisles on the east side originally then there were none on the west either. In this case the addition of west aisles could belong to the same

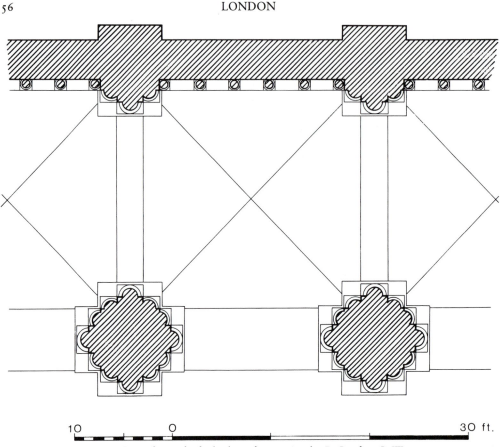

FIG. 3.   St Paul's Cathedral, plan of nave pier, by R.G. after C. Wren

phase of remodelling as the lengthening of either arm by two bays. A substantial rebuilding of the transepts in the 13th century seems a plausible hypothesis (while the Wren plan indicates the proposed classical remodelling).

In contrast to the transepts the nave design can be reconstructed in a fair degree of detail. West of the crossing the nave and aisles ran through for twelve bays up to the west front. The elevation was of the standard Anglo-Norman three-storeyed form, comprising aisles, galleries and clerestories, the general appearance of which is well conveyed by the Hollar engraving (Pl. VIB). At ground-storey level the main piers were of uniform composite type, with a major half-column and minor angle colonnettes in *each* of the four directions (Fig. 3). Towards east and west the piers carried an arcade of two moulded orders, the outer of which had a hood apparently decorated with a bead ornament. No fragments of these hoods seem to survive, although other moulded elements from the Romanesque fabric are now preserved in the south nave gallery of the present cathedral. The aisle walls had responds matching the outer faces of the main piers, and between these responds an arcaded dado ran along beneath the windows — to be seen beyond the Beauchamp tomb. The aisles in the 17th century, as seen above the Kempe chantry as well as in the longitudinal view of the nave by Hollar and in the Wyck drawing, were covered by rib vaults, which seem likely to have been part of the Romanesque fabric or a later remodelling of original vaults.

The aisles were surmounted by galleries which opened towards the nave through large arches of two orders without subdivision. Externally the galleries were lit in the 17th century by oculus windows (Pl. IXA) which, where they had not been remodelled by Inigo Jones, had a band of blank arcading running beneath them. The fact that a similar window design occurred on one of the transept bays that preceded the putative 13th-century remodelling suggests that this was the original Romanesque design. There is no clear evidence as to whether the galleries were vaulted or open-roofed, but the absence of any evidence for gallery vaulting in the Wyck drawing is suggestive.

The most problematic element in the elevation is the clerestory design. The Hollar view of the interior shows a window of uncertain form flanked by blank arches with Gothic tracery, while externally the clerestory windows were for the most part round-headed but belonging to the Inigo Jones remodelling. Hollar, however, shows on the south side of the nave adjacent to the crossing two bays that escaped Jones and these seem to have triangular heads. These heads may suggest Tudor arches — which could be interpreted as a localised repair in the vicinity of the crossing consequent upon the 1561 fire that destroyed the spire. The Wyck drawing is sadly unhelpful in relation to the nave clerestory, although it might have been looked to for evidence of any clerestory wall passages. It does not seem possible thus to draw any positive conclusions on the nave clerestory: whether the Romanesque clerestory had ever been built, or whether it had been built and substantially remodelled in later campaigns of work. At this point it is perhaps appropriate to return to the question of the transept clerestory (Pl. VII), the discussion of which was deferred above. The Hollar view of the transepts shows in Bay 1 a single triangular-headed window, then in Bay 2 a window flanked on either side by a lower arch. Despite the triangular arch heads (which could result from similar circumstances to those postulated above for the nave east bays) the stepped arrangement of openings suggests the perpetuation of a Romanesque clerestory with a central window flanked by openings to a wall passage. Unfortunately the Wyck drawing throws no further light on this, for the clerestory of the Romanesque section of the transept had obviously collapsed by 1667, while the standing sections of the west and south walls look fully Gothic.

The quadripartite rib vault that covered the nave in the 17th century would seem to have been Gothic in execution and perhaps 13th century (Pl. VIB). The construction of this might then have involved work also to the nave clerestory. However, it may be that there was an intention from the start to vault the Romanesque nave. If the main nave piers were uniformly of 11th- or 12th-century construction, then they always included towards the nave a main half-column with dosseret and flanking colonnettes. These members were carried up as wall shafts to the base of the clerestory level, from which point the Gothic vault sprang, and it is arguable that their purpose always was conceived in relation to a high vault over the nave, of groined or ribbed form.

Discussion

Enough is known of the Romanesque building to attempt at least a provisional assessment of its place in late 11th- and early-12th-century architecture. The presbytery of four straight bays and the underlying crypt place St Paul's alongside such major projects as Winchester and Bury St Edmund's: while in actual dimensions the length of the eastern arm and also its width (so far as these can be calculated) are closely comparable with Winchester. Alongside this may be placed the suggestion made above that St Paul's had a similar system of alternating piers in the presbytery to Winchester. The length of the eastern arm, on the other hand, was not the most ambitious among Anglo-Norman churches of the late 11th century, being exceeded, for example, at St Alban's (where, however, there was no crypt or ambulatory) and at Canterbury in the Glorious Choir.

Each of the transept arms was similar in length to the presbytery, and this length was again comparable to Winchester (including the transept aisles). But there was a marked difference from Winchester in the absence of aisles and galleries to the transepts, and in this respect the transepts were more akin to the open transept arms of St Augustine's, Canterbury, and St Alban's — though much larger in scale than these latter.

The nave was comparable in its twelve-bay arrangement to Westminster Abbey, St Augustine's and Winchester, but did not reach the fourteen bays of Norwich. In its actual dimensions the nave is difficult to calculate exactly, but was considerably greater than the first two buildings and appears to have been closely similar to Winchester — excluding the western massif of the latter.

In view of these comparisons it is difficult to avoid the conclusion that St Paul's was specifically intended to emulate in scale the new cathedral of Winchester, which was designed to be one of the largest churches in Europe since Antiquity.[43] But St Paul's was more restrained than Winchester and omitted the aisles and grouped towers to the transepts and the great massif at the west end. Despite its size, Winchester, begun in 1079, was certainly well on the way to completion within thirty years. Given adequate financing, therefore, there would seem little reason why the St Paul's project could not have been substantially finished by the 1120s — and this, in fact, is what Orderic Vitalis implies was actually the case when he says that Bishop Richard I 'completed the work in great part' before his death in 1127. None the less, the less optimistic statements of William of Malmesbury, Henry of Huntingdon and Arcoid must certainly indicate that some parts of the fabric were not completed until after his death. These latter parts, however, may have been such elements as the west façade, the crossing tower and the nave high vaults: these were necessary to the completion of the whole, but they did not hold up the bringing of the main functional parts of the building into use and they were relatively non-urgent. The solution that is put forward here, therefore, is that Bishop Maurice between 1087 and 1107 completed the main fabric of the crypt, the presbytery, the transepts and the easternmost nave bays. Bishop Richard I between 1108 and 1127 then went on to complete the greater part of the nave. After this the original impetus lagged and when the work was damaged by the 1133 fire the repairs and completion of the fabric dragged on into the second half of the century — or even, as perhaps with the nave vault, remained unexecuted and were overtaken by the great 13th-century programme of works.

Apart from the strong evidence for thinking that the scale of the new building was an emulation of Winchester, and that the system of presbytery piers may have been copied from there (or, equally, from Westminster), it is difficult to be precise about the other influences that may have contributed to the design, because the evidence is sparse for the finer decorative and technological details of the building. In general, however, it may be seen that the plan combining an ambulatory and crypt in the eastern arm with unaisled transepts looks to the tradition of St Augustine's, Canterbury,[44] which was the fountainhead of much English Romanesque architecture. The elevation as seen in the nave was also related to Canterbury and, beyond there, to St-Etienne in Caen — especially in its pier forms and in its use of undivided gallery arcades. Also of Canterbury origin is the use of cushion capitals,[45] which Hollar shows throughout the nave. A simultaneous relationship with Canterbury and Winchester would be in no way surprising, since Winchester itself was deeply indebted to the Canterbury tradition.

St Paul's may probably be seen as a rather conservative essay, but one ambitious in scale, in interpreting the architectural traditions that had been established in the Canterbury,

Winchester and probably London ambit in the 1070s and 1080s under the patronage of the crown and its leading ecclesiastical magnates. It may have been a metropolitan and court workshop but despite this, or perhaps because of it, its work exhibited none of the eclectic features that characterised other major projects of the 1080s and 1090s elsewhere in England, where Canterbury traditions were being increasingly transformed in the interests of regional variation.[46]

THE CHURCH OF ST MARY LE BOW

The most complete ecclesiastical building to survive in London from the last two decades of the 11th century is the crypt of St Mary le Bow; and, having examined the better dated but less well preserved monuments, it is opportune to try to relate this building to them. The documentary evidence[47] appears to indicate that the church was of pre-Conquest origin and that by the time of William I if not before it belonged to Christ Church, Canterbury. The church became the centre of the Christ Church fee in London and from at least the 12th century was adjoined on the north by a substantial stone-built lodging house fronting onto Cheapside. The importance of the church in the 12th century is indicated by its provision of a school — a status shared with St Paul's and St Martin le Grand alone.[48]

Whether the church was one of those burnt in the city fires of 1077 and 1087 is not known, but a structure was certainly here in 1091 when its roof was blown off in a gale. William of Malmesbury records this last disaster, which *tectum ecclesiae sanctae Mariae quae 'ad Arcus' dicitur pariter subleuauit* (at the same time lifted off the roof of the church of St Mary which is called 'le Bow'),[49] providing evidence that by the second quarter of the 12th century the church had acquired its present cognomen. In a second disaster in 1270 the tower of the church collapsed, falling towards Cheapside and damaging the adjacent stone house.[50]

The medieval church apart from its crypt was destroyed in the Great Fire of London, but the building as existing up to that time is shown in the maps of Ralph Agas (*c.* 1560) and others. The church was a four-bay aisled building with clerestory, and there was a tower prolonging the south aisle westward a further bay. Beneath the whole church extended a crypt which still survives (Fig 4).[51] This crypt comprises a four-bay central vessel, flanked by aisles opening from it through arches carried by rectangular piers. The central vessel is vaulted in three spans of groin-vaulting (rebuilt in the 17th and 20th centuries) carried on two rows of monolithic columns with mitred-cushion capitals (Pl. VIIIA). The main piers and outer aisle walls have responds of three rectangular orders to carry the vaulting (Pl. VIIIB); indicating that the original vaults were of groined form with wall arches and transverse arches. The aisle and west wall windows are of narrow, internally splayed, form, while the east wall has a series of arched niches which probably had further windows pierced through their backs. At the north-west corner of the north aisle is a small vice which must have led to the main upper floor, but this may be of slightly later construction. The outer walls of the crypt are built of rubble, while the piers and associated detail are of coursed ashlar with broad joints between the stones.

The crypt of St Mary le Bow, besides its high architectural quality, is a monument of twofold interest: as to its function, and as to the evidence it provides for the architectural relationships of this London workshop. The existence of a crypt at all in this church is not to be explained by the lie of the land, for the upper church did not need made ground for its construction, while the crypt was sunk only partly below the 11th century ground level. The crypt, therefore, is present for one or both of two reasons: as a mark of prestige; or because it forms part of an architectural formula to which a two-storeyed arrangement was integral.

E

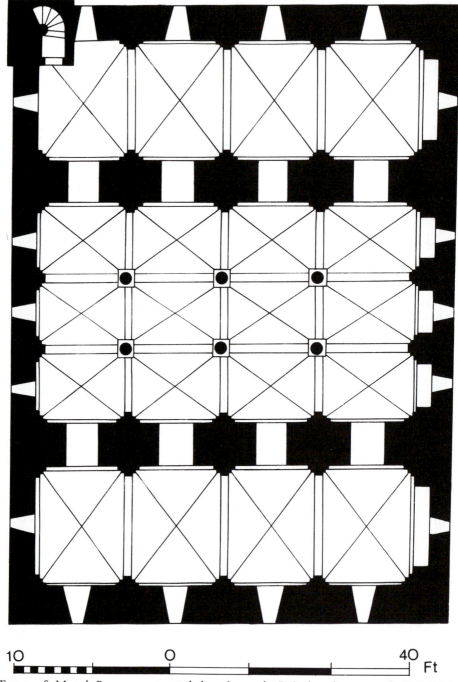

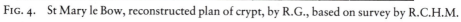

FIG. 4.   St Mary le Bow, reconstructed plan of crypt, by R.G., based on survey by R.C.H.M.

In its actual form and scale the crypt is closely similar to a crypt beneath the eastern arm of a major church (such as the crypts of Christ Church and St Augustine's, Canterbury, and of Rochester Cathedral), but there is no evidence that it was ever in fact intended to form part of a project for a larger church — and the west windows seem to exclude this positively. On the other hand, it has been observed above that the chapel of St John in the Tower reproduces on a reduced scale the format of the eastern arm of a larger church. St John's does not have a crypt, properly speaking: but elsewhere it can be seen that the two-storeyed formula was fairly standard for royal and also episcopal palace chapels. The two-storeyed chapel tradition in western Europe was established as early as 800 with Charlemagne's palace chapel at Aachen. Subsequent to this the two-storeyed arrangement was favoured sometimes in association with the octagonal form of Aachen and sometimes dissociated from it. It is a tradition that can be seen still alive at the end of the 13th century at St Stephen's Chapel in the Palace of Westminster. For the 11th century in England there are the examples of the episcopal chapels of Hereford (attaching to a German tradition)[52] and Durham (to be paralleled in Maine),[53] the latter being the closer in conception to St Mary le Bow. This raises the question of whether St Mary's could be seen as an episcopal chapel for the Archbishops of Canterbury in London: but in reply it would have to be stated that there is no evidence for any episcopal lodging or residence attached to the church (unless such were the origin of the stone lodging house on the north side?). Be this as it may, the architectural form of St Mary le Bow proclaims it as standing apart from ordinary parish churches, and the contention that it was of extraordinary status might well find support in the parallel drawn above to St Paul's and St Martin le Grand in the matter of the attached school.

Returning to the question of the architectural relationships of the workshop, it may be observed that the plan of the crypt is most closely comparable to the crypt of Lanfranc's cathedral at Canterbury begun c. 1070, and to Gundulf's cathedral at Rochester begun c. 1077, which was a building closely related to the Canterbury workshop of the later years of Lanfranc's archiepiscopate.[55] The main piers of the Bow crypt are comparable in Canterbury to the Christ Church dormitory (1080s) and the Glorious Choir crypt (c. 1095 ff), and to the St Augustine's crypt (c. 1075); and in Rochester to the cathedral crypt. The construction with a sparing use of ashlar and with wide jointing is characteristic of the 1070s and 1080s in the Canterbury workshop, but was superseded by more extensive use of ashlar and thinner jointing as the Glorious Choir proceeded. Mitred cushion capitals first appeared in the Canterbury workshop in the 1070s and spread thence throughout England.[56] Finally, if, as seems likely from the surviving fragmentary evidence, the vaults at Bow were originally constructed with rubble transverse arches, this would compare with the crypt of St Augustine's and with the first phase of the Glorious Choir.

The relationships of the work, therefore, are very much with the Canterbury workshops of the period from the 1070s to the 1090s. This perception helps not only to reinforce the concept of a London and Canterbury axis, but also helps to date Bow church itself: between the late 1070s and the early 1090s seems the most probable stylistic range. An important question then remains as to whether the church predates or postdates the fire of 1087. If it postdates this fire, then it is a distinct possibility that the design and construction are directly related to the workshop of St Paul's. This would both reinforce the evidence for St Paul's itself being related to the Canterbury workshop, and also would provide some insight into the quality of the early fabric of the Romanesque cathedral finally consumed by the Great Fire of London. However, the earlier date is a distinct possibility on stylistic grounds, because the design and construction of St Mary's could have derived directly from Canterbury without the necessity of St Paul's acting as an intermediary. In the case of the earlier date being correct, it would seem almost inevitable to conclude that the work was commissioned by Lanfranc himself — possibly following the 1077 fire. But a final resolution of the problem cannot be provided by the architectural historian and, therefore, the documentary historian and archaeologist must be looked to for providing, by some happy fortune, new evidence.

REFERENCES

1. Gem (1980), 33–60.
2. Too little unfortunately is known about the 11th-century buildings of St Martin le Grand to include them in this analysis.
3. RCHM *London*, v, 86–92; Colvin and Brown (1963), 29–31, 96 ff.; Brown (1979), 99–108.
4. *Text. Roff.*, 212.
5. See n. 3.
6. Compare the transepts of Le-Mont-St-Michel; also the evidence for barrel vaults at Gloucester, Tewkesbury and Pershore — see papers by P. Kidson, R. Halsey, M. Thurlby and C. Wilson in BAA CT, vii, *Gloucester and Tewkesbury* (1985).
7. Gem (1982), 1–45.
8. Gem (1987), 85–92.
9. Ann. Bermund., 425–6. See also Graham (1926), 157–84; Brooke and Keir (1975), 210–17. In fact Bermondsey had first been founded at a much earlier date, for the monastery of St Peter there had received a privilege from Pope Constantine, 708–15 (*Councils and Eccles. Docs*, 276–8). If this early church had continued into the Late Anglo-Saxon period as a minster, it may have shared the lot of many of its class which were given to Continental monasteries in the years immediately following the Conquest. If the church of Bermondsey (as distinct from the manor) had been given to La Charité already in or by 1082 it might explain why the rents given in that year came to be regarded as the start of the endowment of the later monastery.
10. DB, 30.
11. Grimes (1968), 210–17. More recently further excavation by David Beard has taken place on the site of the monastic offices and touching the south-east corner of the church (vid. *Lond. Arch.*, v, 1986, 186–91). He has also re-examined the site records from the earlier excavations, which indicated that the interpretation of the evidence is less straightforward than Grimes' published account suggests. I am most grateful to Mr Beard for discussing with me his work in progress, the final results of which may modify some of the suggestions put forward here.
12. That is to say, he did not interpret the structures which he and Corbett certainly did encounter as belonging to a discernible 11th-century Romanesque church plan. It is difficult now to interpret the walls and other features discovered, some of which could perhaps have been of Anglo-Saxon date. It is worth noting that the north chapel of the great Romanesque church cuts an earlier grave, which suggests the proximity of an earlier church.
13. Martin (1926), 192–228.
14. *The Times*, 19 January 1985.
15. Philippe (1905), 469–500. See also Renimel (1976), 167–229 (though Renimel's interpretation may be disputed).
16. See plan in Gem (1982), 12.
17. Phillips (1985).
18. Barlow (1979), 47.
19. *A–S Chron.*, *sub anno*.
20. Brooke and Keir (1975), 356.
21. The *Life* is only published in the version of it by Capgrave (1901), i, 396 (also *Acta Sanct.*, *Aprilis*, iii).
22. Ibid.
23. *De Gestis Pontificum*, 145–6.
24. Huntingdon, x, 208.
25. Orderic, vi, 144.
26. Capgrave (1901), 396.
27. Brooke and Keir (1975), 33, 212.
28. Florence ii, 93. Following probably this fire the bishops had assigned certain revenues to the fabric, see *St Paul's Charters*, 45–6.
29. Capgrave (1901), 397.
30. Ibid.

31. Ibid. *Acta Sanctorum* (as noted in Horstman's footnote to Capgrave (1901)) emends to 1148.
32. *St Paul's Chron.*, 41. Whether there really were two translations is perhaps open to doubt.
33. Dugdale (1716), 22.
34. Capgrave (1901), 398.
35. Ibid., 398–9.
36. Ibid., 404.
37. *Foliot Letters*, 306–8; also *PL*, CXC, 928. See also Graham (1945–7), 73–6.
38. The principal source is obviously Dugdale (1658 and 1716). The main modern studies of the Romanesque cathedral are: Lethaby (1930), 671–3, 862–4, 1091–3; Finch (1935), 728–30; Cook (1955).
39. It is important to note that the plans given by Dugdale do not appear to be strictly accurate, but are more in the way of schematisations.
40. Finch (1935), 730.
41. Most recently published by T. Cocke in Zarnecki *et al.* (1984), cat. no. 503 (though the view is from the north-east and not the north-west as there stated).
42. Wren Soc. *St Paul's*, pl. vi (All Soul's College, Oxford, vol. II, no. 4).
43. Gem (1983), 1–12.
44. Gem (1982).
45. Gem (1987).
46. Gem (1984), 233–72.
47. I am most grateful to Dr Derek Keene and his colleagues working on the Social and Economic Study of Medieval London and at the Museum of London for discussing with me the documentary evidence relating to the early history of St Mary's.
48. Barlow (1979), 235.
49. *De Gestis Regum*, 375.
50. Ann. Lond., 81.
51. The principal published account of the crypt is RCHM *London*, IV, 79–80.
52. Gem (1986), 87–96.
53. See Pré (1961), 353–72. The Durham chapel, being a secondary feature of the castle founded in 1072, is not dated by documentary evidence: it could therefore be as late as the episcopate of William of St-Calais, *c.* 1080–8, since he came from Maine.
54. Strik (1982), 20–5; Gem (1982), 3–4.
55. Ibid., 11–12.
56. Gem (1987).

The First Façade of Old St Paul's Cathedral: Did it have Flanking Towers?

By J. Philip McAleer

Although the rebuilding of the Cathedral of London was undertaken by Bishop Maurice (*c.* 1085/7–1107), perhaps as early as 1087, construction of the large building dragged on for well over a hundred years.[1] As a result, and judging from the engravings of the interior by Wenceslaus Hollar, the first façade was probably partly Romanesque and partly Early English, or at least Transitional, in style.[2] It is essentially still 'visible' in the engravings and drawings of Hollar, *c.* 1658, showing the west front after the alterations and additions of Inigo Jones during the years 1634–43 (Pl. IXA). The façade finally completed for this building appears to have been of a modest character: it was basically a 'sectional' façade, that is, it was simply a west wall shaped as if following the result of a section cut across the nave and aisles. This was a type that had been very common among Romanesque churches in England, as façades with two towers were not the exclusive norm and other types were rare.[3] Sectional façades and twin-tower ones also continued to be characteristic façade types in Gothic England as well.[4]

One can see from the views by Hollar,[5] and others, how the basic sectional form of the Medieval façade was adopted and adapted by Jones.[6] His famous Corinthian portico covered the entire width of the lower part of the façade, and rose to the height of the aisles. Above this level, the wall was covered by drafted masonry. There are three tall, narrow, round-headed windows which may be either a direct reflection of Romanesque ones, or a slight alteration of the pointed arches of Gothic lancets. The prominent buttresses between nave and aisles, in the line of the nave arcades, containing newel-stairs and inherited from the Romanesque/Gothic structure, terminated in tall pedestals supporting obelisks. In addition, large volutes hid the slope of the aisle roofs, whereas the gable corresponded to the original steep pitch of the nave roof.

This composition is flanked by two towers. On the south side, there is also a small structure next to the tower. This was the church of St Gregory, its portal-less west face in the same plane as the west wall of tower and church. The towers themselves are shown as being of two equal stages, and rising to a height corresponding to the sill of the clerestory, a level about halfway between the aisle and nave eaves. Each tower terminates in a third, octagonal, stage, with an oval window in each face and volute buttresses between them, and is capped by a conical roof with concave sides. The question may be asked: were these flanking towers, in their essential structure, part of the original façade design as finally completed in the early 13th century?

When Edmund B. Ferrey made his plan, view from the south-west, and aerial view of Old St Paul's in 1868,[7] perhaps the first reconstruction of the post-Conquest building, he showed a sectional façade in plan, with three portals and four buttresses, and with newel-stairs behind the middle pair of buttresses. No towers were included, apparently because, as he stated, 'no drawings or plates are known to exist which would settle the question'. The view from the south-west showed a simple sectional façade with flat buttresses and, in the nave-end, a central portal, a triple window and an oculus. The aerial view did not directly show the west face of the façade, but no pinnacles were included as terminations to the buttresses. The small three-aisled parish church of St Gregory was shown as being built snugly up against the cathedral's aisle wall, its five bays corresponding to the three west ones of the south aisle of St Paul's. A model of Old St Paul's, following Ferrey's reconstruction drawings, was made by John B. Thorp in 1912.[8]

In the 1890s, H. W. Brewer made a series of restoration drawings which appeared sporadically in *The Builder*, and from which, eventually, a model was made.[9] His restoration of the façade was much grander than Ferrey's, as, despite Ferrey's caveat, it not only included two low flanking towers (with short spires), but a double-storeyed, five-aisled narthex that projected five bays from the west wall. In spite of its two floors, the narthex was rather low, so the slope of the aisle roofs was visible above it, and the west wall had a composition of three lancets, with an oculus above flanked by lancets, and, finally, three small lancets in the apex of the gable.

Much later, in the 1930s, several other authorities also accepted the towers as part of the original façade design, a decision based primarily on evidence for them in Christopher Wren's plan of the cathedral, now preserved at Oxford. W. R. Lethaby wrote: 'These towers are shown much more clearly on the Oxford Plan than by Hollar. It has been doubted whether these were ancient ... It is evident, however, from the way that the old Bishop's hall abutted against that on the north, and the one on the south projected into St Gregory's Church, that they must have been ancient. Such extensions of west fronts were common in late Norman and early Gothic works (compare St Albans, Ely, Wells, etc.)'.[10] R. H. C. Finch followed Lethaby's restoration of a façade design with flanking towers in his restoration drawings.[11] Later in the 1950s, G. H. Cook accepted the 'Lethaby-Finch' restoration, although he also reproduced a plan that did not include flanking towers.[12]

Another set of restoration drawings was made about the same period as Finch's. They were by A. E. Henderson,[13] who proposed a far more grandiose façade which included flanking towers in a design clearly based upon the façade of Wells Cathedral. The towers were integrated into a screen-type façade, and were capped by spires and tall corner pinnacles; three strongly projecting, gabled porches sheltered the three west portals.

Both the plan by Hollar, of 1657,[14] and the Oxford Plan of Wren, c. 1661/3–6,[15] were made after the renovations of Jones. However they do not show an identical structure. Hollar's plan shows towers rectangular — the long axis north-south — on the interior, with the east walls of the towers partially overlapping the buttresses on the aisle walls. The walls of the towers are rather thin, and the towers lack angle buttresses, as indeed is accurate in one sense, as whether or not they existed in the medieval construction, the towers were not buttressed in Inigo Jones' design.

Unlike Hollar's plan, Wren's plan of a few years later does not show the work of Jones at the west end (Pl. IXB). Wren's plan also shows towers rectangular on the interior but with the long axis east-west, with heavy walls, and with exterior angle buttresses, all features in contrast to Hollar's rendering. Wren also places the newel-stairs at the exterior angles (as in the transept) in contrast to their apparent position in Jones' façade. It is, probably, an attempt at a restoration of the original façade. In plan this was easily accomplished: he had only to eliminate the portico and, in order to make the towers appear more authentic, add angle buttresses to them. These simple details, like the exterior splay of the three west portals, Wren could have 'invented' from his knowledge of Gothic architecture. Born in 1632, it is unlikely that Wren himself would have consciously seen the façade of St Paul's before Jones' remodelling.

It is interesting to observe that Wren rendered the plan of St Gregory's as only a thin exterior wall, without any specifics: not even a nave arcade is represented. The way in which the south tower is shown by Hollar as intruding into the parish church of St Gregory's suggests that it was, indeed, an intrusion. The rhythm and dimensions of the nave arcade are clearly unrelated to the size of the tower. This is all the more surprising as it seems the parish church of St Gregory's was pulled down by Jones who was forced to rebuild it as a result of the outrage of the parishioners. On the other hand, if the plan is to be taken as representing a medieval tower, and not a building or rebuilding of Jones, then it seems difficult to interpret it as a construction either earlier than the church of St Gregory or contemporary with it, as one might expect, in either case, that the bay system of the church would have been co-ordinated with the dimensions of the tower (or vice versa). Unfortunately, there appears to be no evidence to indicate a date for the original construction of St Gregory's, or of its pre-Jones form, and the extent to which he may or may not have altered the original *parti*.[16]

Based on the visual evidence, it would be tempting to propose that the towers were built by Jones. Indeed, J. Summerson implied that the north tower was produced by Jones in order to balance the southern one of St Gregory's: '. . . [he] was obliged, also, to incorporate and classicize the Gothic tower of St Gregory-by-St Paul's on the south and, moreover, to repeat it for symmetry on the north'.[17] Cook, in his book on St Paul's, also suggested Jones may have rebuilt the towers: 'Both towers are depicted in Hollar's drawing of the west front of S. Paul's, as they appeared after Inigo Jones had modernised if not rebuilt them'; and, again, 'The small towers flanking the west front evidently rebuilt by Jones . . .'[18]

There is, however, other evidence for the existence of towers than the plan of Wren, or of Hollar. In 1598 John Stow wrote: 'At either corner of the west ende, is also of auncient building, a strong tower of stone, made for bell towers, the one of them, to wit, next to the Pallace, is at this present to the use of the same Pallace, the other towards the south, is called the Lowlardes Tower, and hath beene used as the Bishoppes Prison, for such as were detected for opinions in Religion, contrary to the faith of the church . . . Adjoyning to this Lowlardes Tower, is the Parish Church of Saint Gregorie . . .'[19] Nevertheless, early views of the church, dating before Inigo Jones' renovation, suggest that the towers mentioned by Stow may not have been part of the façade design, and could have been constructed at later dates.

Possibly one of the earliest views is an anonymous woodcut panorama of London, simply titled *Civitas Londinum*.[20] The point of view is to the south and slightly to the west of Old St Paul's and consequently the façade is portrayed obliquely and is rather heavily shadowed. What is shown is the nave-end, with indications of small windows, flanked by apparently round turrets with conical terminations. The chapter-house and what might be the west end of the south aisle and its sloping roof are also shown, but there is no sign of flanking towers or St Gregory's church.

Another of the earliest views is an engraving depicting the cathedral from the south, looking from across the Thames (the foreground is reversed), and inscribed, 'A prospect of parte of ye citye of London Southward to ye Thames whern you may beholde ye very forme of ye most famous church of St Paule' (Pl. XA).[21] It must date after 1561, as it records the fact that the steeple of St Paul's was destroyed by lightning in that year. As Bulmer's water tower at Broken Wharf is not shown, a *terminus ante quem* of c. 1594 is likely. The upper part of the west front of St Paul's is shown prominently: the nave end is depicted with three lancet windows, the central one tallest; a quatrefoil-shaped window appears above each side lancet; three small pointed-arched windows fill the gable and echo its shape in their positions; the gable is flanked by tall pinnacles, presumably terminating buttresses which are not shown. The nave clerestory, sloping, lean-to aisle roofs, and south aisle wall (without windows) are also shown, though not with any stylistic detail. No flanking towers are visible. There are only two somewhat ambiguous vertical, flat-topped masses of unequal height that do not rise higher than the aisle roof. They are located towards the west end of the south nave aisle. These forms could represent the Lollard's Tower.

From about the same period there are several other panoramas of London which include St Paul's, although less prominently than in the engraving just discussed. One is a woodcut map-view probably executed sometime between 1561/2 and 1570. The others are two drawings attributed to Anton van den Wyngaerde, most likely dating to 1558–62.[22] The latter both show St Paul's from the south-east, so once again the west front proper is not shown. Both do, however, clearly show the pinnacled turret between nave-end and south aisle, and the slope of the south aisle roof. Both also depict, near the west end of the nave, a large, low, flat-topped tower that appears to have had a small flat-topped turret on the south-west corner; thus, van den Wyngaerde's renderings perhaps allow a more accurate interpretation of the forms ambiguously shown in the early engraving, as representing a tower with a turret on one corner. Other details are not very distinct. The larger drawing, which is a bird's-eye view, appears to show a largish window in the south face of the tower — round arched, but van den Wyngaerde does not carefully distinguish between round and pointed arches elsewhere in his drawings of St Paul; only the merest indication of a tiny window is shown in the smaller drawing. Neither drawing, then, provides any specific information about the date of the tower, or its exact relationship with the west wall. Indeed, both drawings suggest that the Lollard's Tower stood a little apart from the west front and the south aisle.

The view of St Paul's in the woodcut map-view of London, *Civitas Londinum*, formerly attributed to Ralph Agas, shows the church directly from the south (Pl. XB).[23] A low crenellated wall, with three windows and a door, parallel to the south aisle of St Paul's, can be identified as the church of St Gregory. At its west end is a tower of three stages, flat topped with a crenellated parapet. One large window is indicated on the middle stage, and two on the upper. The tower does not rise higher than the nave aisles, and an east face indicated by shading creates the impression that the tower stood to the south of the wall of St Gregory's. This view is similar to that in the small scale map-view, *Londinum Feracissimi Angliae Regni Metropolis*, that appeared in G. Braun and F. Hogenberg's atlas, *Civitates Orbis Terrarum*, published in Cologne in 1572.[24] Both were probably based on the earliest known map-view of London, the Copperplate Map of *c.* 1553–9, of which the sheet with St Paul's has not survived.[25]

St Paul's appears again, without its spire, in the *Bird's-Eye View of London* of John Norden, from the year 1600.[26] Although represented very distantly and, therefore, small in scale (relative to the scope of the total engraving), a tower on the south side of the nave can be distinguished. As in other representations, it is rather low, and allows the turrets, or more accurately, the southern of the turrets, flanking the nave end to be clearly visible. Whether or not the indistinct form should be identified with the south or Lollard's Tower, is almost unimportant, as the view is not specific enough to determine the exact shape. A few years later, William Kip's engraving of the arches of triumph erected for the entry of James I (15 March 1603 [1604]), by Stephen Harrison, shows a low, flat-topped tower with a crenellated parapet, which seems to stand to the south of St Gregory's, at the west end of St Paul's, as it appeared in the model of the City that formed the arch ('*Londinium*') erected in Fenchurch Street.[27] Here again, it can be seen that the façade of the cathedral was sectional in outline. As shown in the engraving, the tower did not rise higher than the eaves of the aisle roof; the slope of the roof and the turret at the end of the clerestory are clearly depicted. Two small windows are shown in the south face of the tower at the highest level, with a larger feature in the middle of the stage below.

Another view, from a position a little further to the east, is found in the second sheet of Claes Jansz Visscher's *Long View of London From the South* of 1616 (Pl. XD).[28] The west wall is not included; however, the buttress-turret between the nave and south aisle is clearly shown, as well as the edge of the slope of the aisle roof. A tower with a corbelled parapet is visible,[29] overlapping the west end of the aisle: its basic form is similar to that shown in the woodcut map-view of 1561/2–70. Flat-topped and built on a square plan, it rises scarcely higher than the aisle eaves, and the way the tower is depicted makes it appear to stand a short distance away from the aisle. Nothing that can be securely identified as the parish church of St Gregory is visible.

Yet another view is a painting by John Gipkyn, also of 1616 (Pl. XC).[30] Although it is a close-up of the cathedral, which is the only building portrayed, it appears much less accurate in terms of stylistic details. The nave is only two or three bays long — the same length as the north transept — which may be the result of pictorial 'necessity': the long building would not 'fit' into the vertical format of the picture area. The east, rather than the west façade is included, as the view is from the north-east. Nevertheless, tall buttress-turrets ending in pinnacles are shown flanking the nave-end and there is no sign of any flanking towers, nor, especially, of the north tower adjacent to the Bishop's Palace.

In all of these views of St Paul's dating from the later 16th to early 17th centuries, the precise form and shape of the south tower remains vague and elusive; and there is no visual record of the north tower at all. The available evidence suggests that the Lollard's Tower was no taller than the south aisle, was perhaps not immediately adjacent to the aisle and was flat-topped, either with a turret at the south-west corner or with a crenellated or a corbelled parapet. As any tower that might be identified in the views as the Lollard's Tower also lacks any buttresses, a date early in the Gothic period does not seem likely. Indeed, construction during the late 14th or early 15th century, if not at an even later period, may be deemed more probable.[31] The lack of buttresses also gives it the air of being military rather than ecclesiastical, a quality that it, however, shares with a number of church towers in the vicinity of St Paul's.

Additional arguments against the thesis that the 'ancient' towers, recorded as being in existence at the end of the 16th century, belong to the period *c.* 1200, may be advanced on the basis of other representations, all earlier than those so far discussed.[32] The earliest of these, a 'view' of London attributed to Matthew Paris, includes a very simplified, but prominent, rendering of St Paul's which can be easily interpreted in its broad outlines as representing a building composed of a choir with a flat east end, transept and crossing tower with a tall spire, and nave. No towers of any kind are shown at the west end. The drawing comes from one of Matthew Paris's itineraries from London to Apulia, associated with his *Historia Anglorum*, specifically British Library, MS Royal 14. C. VII, f. 2a. Similar depictions occur in others of the itineraries, notably Corpus Christi College, Cambridge, MS 26, f. 1a. The British Library manuscript is dated 1250–9, and the Cambridge one to *c.* 1240–53, about the time of the dedication of the Cathedral.[33]

Drawings of cities in three manuscripts of the 14th century are also said to reflect Old St Paul's. A second manuscript in the British Library, MS Royal 13. A. III, a copy of the *Historia regum Britanniae* of Geoffrey of Monmouth, dating to the late 13th century, includes drawings of towns inserted in some bottom margins early in the next century.[34] The drawing of London on f. 14 is very faint, but is said to include Westminster Abbey, St Paul's with its spire, and the Tower as the major defining landmarks.

The second manuscript is the Luttrell Psalter, British Library, MS Add. 42130, of before 1340.[35] On f. 164b a view of Constantinople is shown as a walled city containing a church with a central tower and a tall spire surmounted by a weathercock which has led to the supposition that a 'standard' view of London was used to represent the otherwise unimaginable and distant city. The west façade is represented as a pair of enormous doors between flanking pinnacles. Presumably, if towers had formed a significant part of the façade, they would have been shown in some form.

A third manuscript, also in the British Library, MS Cotton Nero D ii,[36] of which the first 198 folios comprise a *World Chronicle* down to the death of Edward I (1307), dating to *c.* 1377, includes a small depiction on f. 18, as if a section through the transept, with the tower, tall spire and a weathercock.

A drawing of a large church, possibly seen from the west, has been identified as St Paul's because of the tall tower and spire. It is found in Lambeth Palace, MS 1106, f. 96b, in that section of the composite manuscript forming an anonymous chronicle down to 1341.[37] Once again no other towers are shown, whether the front we see is the west one or the transept.

Yet another representation from this period is the drawing scratched on the north wall of the interior of the west tower of Ashwell Church (St Mary's), Hertfordshire, probably sometime between *c.* 1360 and 1462.[38] Depicting a very large building with a transept, it is generally thought to represent Old St Paul's from the north-east, including the freestanding bell tower at the east end. A north-west tower is not shown: the profile suggests a sectional façade, as the slope of an aisle roof appears.

Rather later in date, *c.* 1500, is a full-page illumination in the Flemish style, although probably executed in England, in the British Library, MS Royal 16. F. II, f. 73.[39] Yet again it is only a tall central tower that characterises St Paul's and thereby helps to identify London.

The last view is a woodcut of 1510, from Richard Pynson's printing of the *Cronycle of England*.[40] It, too, shows the cathedral as a building composed of a flat-ended choir, transept, crossing tower with a tall steeple, and nave — a nave without any towers at its west end.

Although it is obvious that the accurate depiction of architectural forms and details is not to be expected in manuscripts of the 13th and 14th centuries, especially at such a small scale and in minor illustrations, it would seem that large memorable elements such as the central tower, spire and weathercock of St Paul's could be recognisably indicated. This suggests that west towers did not form a similar prominent feature: yet if they had existed, they should have been unusual enough to be another distinctive characteristic — aiding recognition and identification. And one might imagine that if they had been completed in the early 13th century, they might have received some sort of terminating spires which would have emphasised their presence.

Hollar's engravings do not tell us about the towers *before* the work of Inigo Jones, nor, I think, does Wren's plan. Engravings before 1634 only tell us that the towers were not very conspicuous or prominent. Stow informs us that towers existed to north and south but provides no evidence for their size, date of construction or, indeed, if they were symmetrical or contemporary. The available evidence suggests that it is most probable that the towers were *not* part of the original façade design, and could well have been built separately at independent dates, and that they were never very tall.[41] Both towers could have been regularised by Jones, and raised in height in order to produce the classically desirable symmetrical design. Of course, a façade with towers flanking the west bay, instead of being placed at the ends of the aisles, as at Durham Cathedral, or Southwell Minster and Worksop Priory, would not have been an impossibility early in the 13th century, or even late in the 12th. This, as Lethaby pointed out, was the arrangement soon to be constructed at Wells Cathedral, *c.* 1215, and which had been contemplated, *c.* 1195, at St Albans Abbey.

At Wells Cathedral,[42] the flanking towers do not stand free, but serve to create a screen façade, as there is a wall rising up to fill the space over the end of the aisles between the towers and nave. The result is a large rectangular wall covered with tiers of arcading. The Wells façade stands in notable contrast to the reconstruction proposed for Old St Paul's by Lethaby and Finch, not only in the relative bareness of the wall at St Paul's, but most especially in the independent nature of the towers at the latter. For the period before Wells, the evidence, although rather slight, points to the probability that flanking towers were so located in order to create a wide screen façade. Enough does survive at St Botolph's, Colchester, to establish the certainty that flanking towers and an arcaded screen wall, very likely the first example, were constructed there c. 1160–70.[43] Foundations of flanking towers remain from the priory churches at Earls Colne, Essex (late 12th) and West Acre, Norfolk (early 13th); both are near Colchester and were very likely influenced by it.[44] As mentioned, a façade with flanking towers was started at St Albans but was soon abandoned.[45] One was actually built in the early 13th century at Coventry Cathedral, of which the entire lower courses survive above ground.[46]

The 'Lethaby-Finch' restoration generally observes a sectional profile for the west wall, but the line of the slope of the aisle end is much higher than the actual level of the roofs: so what is shown is a quasi-screen façade, in spite of the fact that all the engravings indicate that the south aisle's west wall did not rise higher than the slope of the aisle roof. Even the nature of Inigo Jones' design makes it evident that there was not a screen wall rising in the line of the aisles: his volutes above the portico serve to hide the sloping aisle roofs and, to an extent, to link the towers to the centre. In his restoration drawings, the few details of the façade are based by Finch on the 1561–94 engraving: the central composition of three lancets, two quatrefoils and three gable windows. The pinnacles are elaborated plausibly, even though none of the engravings are of a scale to permit the inclusion of such details. Small plain, blind oculi are shown on the aisle screen wall and the three west portals, with carved tympana, are shown as Romanesque in style: for all of these details there is no evidence. Of course, the towers are purely hypothetical: as shown, they rise barely to the height of the nave eaves, and are capped by low pyramidal roofs.

If flanking towers were part of the late 12th- or early 13th-century design, they would have been unique, and would seem to have been contrary to the tendency towards, not only wide façade structures, but screening façades during the late 12th and early 13th centuries. The development of the type with flanking towers can be paralleled by that with flanking stair-turrets — the type of Salisbury Cathedral, as preceded by Lindisfarne, Croyland and Malmesbury abbeys[47] — and also by the more complicated structures of Ely Cathedral (west transept), Bury St Edmunds (west transept expanded by octagonal towers) and Peterborough (west transept plus porch flanked by towers) abbeys, and, eventually, Lincoln Cathedral (screen surrounding the Romanesque façade-block). The subsequent Gothic period abandoned the screen façades of these varied types, or even those of Wells and Salisbury, in favour of the sectional or twin-tower types. Freestanding, flanking campanili also had no successors; if they had appeared at St Paul's, it would have been a unique instance. However, I believe the available evidence does not support the uniqueness of St Paul's, and instead suggests that it was one of the many sectional façades constructed during the Romanesque and Gothic periods.[48]

REFERENCES

1. For a discussion of the documentary sources see *supra* pp. 51–3.
2. Hollar's engraving of the nave, made prior to its destruction in the Great Fire of 1666, records details of the clerestory and ribbed vaulting which strongly suggest the early 13th century as the period of the last phase of

construction: see Dugdale (1658), 167, or (1716), between pp. 144 and 145 (by J. Harris); reproduced in Cook (1955), pl. I.

3. A tabulation done by me some years ago found evidence of thirty certain examples of twin-tower façades and twenty-seven major sectional ones, in the hundred years or so following the Conquest: see McAleer (1984), 330, Appendix I, Table IA, and 358–9, Appendix IV, Tables IAi and IIA, respectively.

4. Later examples of twin-tower façades include Lichfield, York and Canterbury Cathedrals, Westminster Abbey and Beverley Minster; of sectional façades, Worcester and Gloucester Cathedrals, Romsey, Binham and Bath abbeys.

5. Dugdale (1658), 164; reused in Dugdale (1673), between pp. 296 and 297; a similar engraving by J. Harris appeared in the second edition of Dugdale (1716), between pp. 150 and 151.

6. Gotch (1928), 168–76, pl. XVIII; Lees-Milne (1953), 90–4; Lang (1956), frontispiece, pls I, IX, XII; Summerson (1966), 93–103 and pls 44–5.

7. They appeared in Longman (1873), 3 (view from SW), facing 15 (aerial view), and were compiled by F. Watkins from drawings by E. B. Ferrey; also reproduced in Bond (1913), I, 3 (plan), 4 (aerial view); Cook (1955), pls 5 (view from SW), 18 (aerial view).

8. Thorp's model is now in the London Museum, where it is displayed in a wall case so it is impossible to see the west front at all.

9. Brewer's drawings appeared in *The Builder*, LI (6 November 1886), 662 and after 686 ('The "New Work", Old St Paul's'); LVII (6 July 1889), 10 and after 18 ('"Paul's Walk": The Nave of Old St Paul's; A Reconstruction'); LXII (2 January 1892), 11 and after 20 ('Old St Paul's Cathedral from the North-east'); and LXX (4 January 1896), 10–11 and after 26 ('Ludgate in the time of Henry VIII'). Brewer's reasons for including a galilee are given on p. 11. The latter view was reproduced in Brewer (1962), pl. 11. I am grateful to Ms Judith Nelson for bringing this item to my attention as it helped me locate the original date of publication in *The Builder*. The model, made for *The Builder* by Partridge's Models, is now in the crypt of St Paul's.

10. Lethaby (1930), 1091–3, 24–6.

11. Finch (1935), 728–30, 772–3 and 778–9; plan between pp. 778 and 779; reconstruction of west front, p. 779.

12. Cook (1955), cf. 30 and 31–2; Pevsner in B/E *London I: The Cities of London and Westminster* (1973), 124 and B/E *Wiltshire*, 2nd ed., rev. (1975), 398; B/E *North Somerset and Bristol* (1958), 284 also accepted two west towers outside the aisles.

13. They appeared in Henderson (1937) and included, 'The Norman Cathedral: View from the South', 'The South Side of the Cathedral about the Year 1537', and 'The Norman Cathedral, the West Front'.

14. Dugdale (1658), 161; Hind (1922), no. 36, 56–7, pl. XXXIV; Cook (1955), 83, fig. VIIIb. Cook (1955), 24–5, reproduced a restored plan of St Paul's based on Hollar's: the portico is eliminated; there is a thick west wall with stairvices in the middle pair of buttresses; St Gregory's is altered to five bays plus an apse; cf. p. 30, fig. III (plan in 12th century).

15. Oxford, All Soul's College, Wren Drawings, vol. II, no. 1: see *Wren Soc.: St Paul's*, 9; Lethaby (1930), 1092, fig. 3.

16. On the pulling down of St Gregory's see Dimock (1900), 48; Cook (1955), 83. The date of the construction of St Gregory's has not been determined, and there does not seem to be any clear evidence for it. According to Harben(1918), 277, a church of St Gregory was first mentioned *c*. 1070 (MS Cotton Titus B. II. 1); £2,000 was spent on repairs and its beautification in 1631–2 (Strype (1720), I, iii, 227); and the church was partly pulled down in 1641. Equally little appears to be known about the building history and form of the Bishop's Palace on the north of the nave: see Simpson (1905), 13–47; Kingsford (1917), 28–81, esp. 35–8. My thanks to Dr Caroline Barron for the above references.

17. Summerson (1953), 82.

18. Cook (1955), 73 and 83 respectively.

19. Stow (1598), 302 or (1603), 372. Dimock (1900), 38, noted that the north tower was also used as a prison, and that the south was also both bell and clock tower. From Stow (1598), 302 or (1603), 372 comes the additional information that there were three west portals. Various accounts indicate that in the 16th century the towers were linked by passageways in the thickness of the west wall: John Philpot, *Examinations and Writings*, quoted in *Foxe Acts*, VII (1838), 647–8; other references: Dimock (1900), 38; Lethaby (1930), 24; Cook (1955), 72–3. The thickness of the west wall in Finch's restoration is based upon the Oxford Plan — according to Lethaby (1930), 24, 'some 10 or 12 feet'; a theoretical position for the passageway was not indicated. The locations of the six or seven doors the prisoner passed through before gaining his cell on the top level of the north tower are also not clear, see Simpson (1881), 113–20; id., in *St Paul's Docs*, 214–18 (Appendix K); they could have been in the north tower itself, rather than in the west front.

20. Pepys Library, Magdalene College, Cambridge: Schofield (1984), 133, fig. 107. I am indebted to John Schofield, of the Museum of London, for bringing this woodcut to my attention.

21. A copy is preserved in the Society of Antiquaries of London: Harley Collection, IV. *London Plans*, etc., p. 3*; 33.2 cm by 22.9 cm. A portion is reproduced in Barker and Jackson (1974, 1983), 45. This engraving is apparently one of the least documented of the early panoramic views of London. Although it includes the spire of the central tower, it dates from after 1561, as above the spire it states: 'This/spere whc/was of ti/ber coverd/with lead/was in hei/ght 260/feet, &/in [an]no/D 1561/wass bur/nte/dow/ne'. Mr John Fisher of the Guildhall Library, London, brought to my attention the fact that there is no sign of Bulmer's water tower, constructed in 1594, at Broken Wharf.

22. The drawings are in the Sutherland Collection, Ashmolean Museum, Oxford; facsimilies have been published by the London Topographical Society: *View of London (ab. A.D. 1550) by Antony van den Wyngaerde*, Publication No. 1 (1881–2), and *View of the City of London between the Fleet River and London Bridge from a drawing by Antony van den Wyngaerde, c. 1550*, Publication No. 77 (1944). They are reproduced in Barker and Jackson (1974, 1983), 50, 55.

23. Overall (1873–6), 81–99 and Overall (1874). Another facsimile was published by the Lond.TS.: *Plan of London (circa 1560–1570) by Ralph Agas*, Publication No. 17 (1905). Two copies are preserved: in the collections of the Guildhall Library, London, and the Pepys Library, Magdalene College, Cambridge. See also: Fisher (1981), Introduction and sheets 4–10, esp. sheet 8.

24. Fisher (1981), Introduction, and sheet 3. Also Lond.TS: *Hoefnagel's Plan of London from Braun and Hogenburg's 'Civitates Orbis Terarum'*, Publication No. 2 (1882–3).

25. Fisher (1981), Introduction.

26. Hind (1952), 30, 199–202, pl. 112. Facsimile: Lond.TS: *A View of London in 1600 by John Norden (from the engraving in the de la Gardie Collection in the Royal Library, Stockholm)*, Publication No. 94 (1961). Another contemporary view, *The View of the Cittye of London from the North towards the South*, Utrecht, University Library, MS No. 1198, Hist. 147, does not reveal any towers at or near the west end: see Barker and Jackson (1974, 1983), 98–9.

27. Hind (1955), 17–29, pl. 2; Adams (1983), 3–6, fig. 1.

28. Hind (1955), 96–111, pl. 50. Facsimile: Lond.TS, *View of London A.D. 1616 by Nicholas John Visscher*, Publication No. 4 (1883–5). Views of St Paul's similar to that in Visscher's Panorama are also found in other works of the period; for example, oil paintings attributed to Claude de Jonghe (Stepney Public Library) and Thomas Wijck, and engravings by de Jonghe, Matthew Merian the Elder, and others such as Rombout van den Hoeye and Dancker Danckerts. See Scouloudi (1953), 42–5, 50–2. As Scouloudi observes, it is impossible to state the exact relationship between the various views and artists — especially Visscher, de Jonghe, and Merian — and to determine who borrowed from whom: or, as she asks, was there a common source? Facsimile: Lond.TS, *View of London engraved by Matthew Merian, from 'Neuwe Archontologia Cosmica . . . durch Johann Ludwig Gottfried, Franckfurt am Mayn, 1638'*, Publication No. 49 (1922).

29. This tower is overlapped by another similar but shorter; two more are in the same line nearer to the river: it is difficult to identify any of these with the two prominent ones shown in the *c.* 1561–94 engraving.

30. Now in the Society of Antiquaries of London. It is the right-hand panel of a diptych painted for Henry Farley: Scharf (1865), No. XLIII, 32–8. An engraving after the painting is in Wilkinson (1816), pls. 155–8. A similar view is depicted on the map of Middlesex in Speed (1611–2): Hind (1955), II, 78–9, pl. 42.

31. The vast majority of post-Anglo-Saxon church towers, from the Romanesque to the Perpendicular styles, had buttresses of some form at the angles. The central tower of Old St Paul's would seem to have been somewhat unusual for its period, if it did not have angle-buttresses, as Harvey (1978), 228, 230, claims. However, the pictorial evidence is somewhat equivocal. The view of 1561–94 includes angle buttresses as does Gipkyn's painting of 1616; Visscher's view does not; Hollar's view from the west suggests that the prominent stepped buttresses may have been added when the stabilising flying buttresses were constructed (1462?). Later, the central tower of Wells Cathedral, of *c.* 1315–22, attributed to Thomas Witney, was unbuttressed, perhaps influenced by the parish church at Witney (Oxfordshire). At the end of the century, the unbuttressed tower had a certain 'popularity': examples are the Westminster Clock Tower of Henry Yeveley, begun 1365, his tower for St Mary Overy in Southwark (1380/90–1424), as well as the flanking towers of the façade of Westminster Hall, 1397–9; William Wynford's tower for New College, Oxford (1396–1400); the central tower of Arundel Collegiate church in Sussex, *c.* 1380 onwards, a building associated both with Yeveley and Wynford and in type similar to the central tower of Edington Priory church in Wiltshire (1352–60) with a polygonal turret at one angle; the west tower of All Saints Pavement, York, from 1395; the clock tower at St Albans, by Thomas Wolvey, *c.* 1405–10. See Harvey (1978), especially pp. 135, 228, 230 and pls 18, 60, 61, 81, 82, 86, 96, 100.

32. Two of the 'views' to be discussed were reproduced by Lethaby (1930), 25, figs 3 and 4. In spite of his use of these views for information — in addition to the post–1561 engraving in the Society of Antiquaries (his fig. 5) — about the spire of the central tower, Lethaby apparently did not consult them about the towers at the west. Fifty years before Lethaby, Simpson had also looked at manuscript representations of Old St Paul's: Simpson (1881b), 123–34.

33. For the itineraries, see Vaughan (1958), 242, 247–50, pls XII, XIII. For BL, MS Royal 14. C. VII (*Historia Anglorum*; *Chronica Minora*, and *Chronica Maiora*, pt. III), see Morgan (1982), 142–4; reproduced in Barker and Jackson (1974, 1983), 25, fig. 1. For CCCC MS 26 (*Chronica Maiora*, pts. I, II), Morgan (1982), 136–9. Lethaby (1930), 25, fig. 3: he did not identify the source of the Matthew Paris 'view'.

34. Warner and Gilson (1921), II. *Royal MSS. 12.A.i to 20.E.x. and App. 1–89*, 74–5. Simpson (1881b), 131–2, no. 3; also reproduced in Barker and Jackson (1974, 1983), 25, fig. 2.

35. BM *Cat. Mss Addit.*, 195–202; Millar (1932), 42, pl. 81. Reproduced in Barker and Jackson (1974, 1983), 25, fig. 4.

36. BM *Cat. Mss Cott.*, 237. Simpson (1881), 128–9, no. 2; also reproduced in Barker and Jackson (1974, 1983), 25, fig. 3.

37. Todd (1812), 255; Simpson (1881), 125–6, no. 1.

38. Sherlock (1978), 3–5, pl. III. Also Dickins (1967), 181–3 (Appendix III); Coulton (1914–5), 54, 56, 57, 58 (who wrongly stated it was a 'drawing of Westminster Abbey in the fourteenth century [miscalled Old St Paul's] . . .'). I owe these references to the kindness of John Clark, Senior Assistant Keeper, The Museum of London. In B/E *Hertfordshire*, 2nd ed., rev. (1977), 74–5, it is incorrectly identified as the south rather than the north side of Old St Paul's. A cast of it is found in the Museum of London.

39. Warner and Gilson (1921), 203–4 (especially p. 204, no. 2); colour reproduction, Warner (1901), pl. 54; Simpson (1881b), 132.

40. Cockerell (1900), 51, pl. facing p. 51; Lethaby (1930), 25, fig. 4; also reproduced in Barker and Jackson (1974, 1983), 35. A late 16th-century drawing was reproduced by Simpson (1881b), 133–4, no. 4. It was a crude drawing from the Diary of Alessandro Magno, dated 1562, and portrayed St Paul's as if it were an Early Christian basilica with side apses and a sectional façade. A tower over the east end of the nave was drawn so as to suggest to Simpson that it represented the stump of the tower of St Paul's after the fire, wrapped in scaffolding and with a 'rude capping to keep out the rain'. It might be mentioned here that the view of St Paul's that was included in the mural of the Coronation Procession of Edward VI from the Tower to Westminster in 1547, formerly in the dining parlour at Cowdray (destroyed in a fire in November 1793, but known from engravings published by the Society of Antiquaries in 1778 and 1787, and from a water-colour copy made in 1785 by S. H. Grimm, now at the Society of Antiquaries) is rather a poor show as it is unclear if the aisleless structure depicted is meant to be the choir, transept or nave, and the central tower certainly does not rise over a crossing. See St John Hope (1919), 56–7, pl. XVI; Barker and Jackson (1974, 1983), 66, fig. 1.

41. Dimock (1900), 37–8, worried over the existence or non existence of the west towers: he concluded that they had existed; the real question for him was when were they built? As he noted, p. 36, the excavations of 1878 by Francis C. Penrose (1883), 381–92, esp. 391–2, pl. XIV did not solve this problem.

42. The west façade at Wells may have been designed as early as 1175–80: see Harvey (1982), 55–6, 59.

43. Peers (1917); B/E *Essex*, 2nd ed. (1965), 136–7.

44. Fairweather (1937), 279–86; B/E *Essex*, 2nd ed. (1965), 163–4; Fairweather (1926–8), 375–6; B/E *North-West and South Norfolk* (1962), 371–2.

45. Page (1898), 21–6; B/E *Hertfordshire*, 2nd ed., rev. (1977), 293–306; especially pp. 295, 301–2.

46. Woodhouse (1909), 16–8; Tickner (1919), 34–6; B/E *Warwickshire* (1966), 248, 262–3; Hobley and Lambert (1971), especially pp. 84–6, 90–1, pls 22–5.

47. Thompson (1949); B/E *Northumberland* (1957), 185–7; Clapham (1932), 349–51; B/E *Lincolnshire* (1964), 503–6. 'Plan, Elevations, and Sections of Malmesbury Abbey Church', *Vet. Mon.*, v, pl. III; Brakspear (1913), 419–20; B/E *Wiltshire* (1975), 321–6.

48. Well after completing the research for this study, I quite accidentally, and in a very different context, came across a reference to: 'Front of Old St Paul's', *Gentleman's Magazine*, LI (April, 1781), 217. Rather disappointingly, this item did not prove to offer any definitive evidence for the appearance of the façade. Instead, it turned out to be an enquiry by one 'Architectus' of 'Mr Urban' as 'to whether there is such a thing in being as a drawing or print of the West front of Old St Paul's before the alteration by Inigo Jones . . .'. The belated reply to this question would seem to be 'Alas, no'.

The New Work at Old St Paul's Cathedral and its Place in English Thirteenth-Century Architecture

By Richard K. Morris

By Tuesday morning churchyard and Cathedral had become part of the vast conflagration; for two days and nights Old Paul's was wrapped in flames ... The climax came when, with a rending crash followed by a roar as of thunder, the main roof of the choir caved in and vanished ...[1]

The loss of Old St Paul's in the Great Fire of 1666 has relegated it to a place of relative obscurity in the study of our medieval cathedrals. Not that its importance nationally or in the context of London could be in doubt. The cathedral literally towered over the medieval city: its steeple was taller than Salisbury, its length exceeded Winchester by over fifty feet, and its eastern arm was as large as that of York.[2] Yet architectural historians have generally focused their attentions on buildings which survive, and most accounts of the development of English medieval architecture afford St Paul's little more than a token mention.[3]

In mitigation it could be said that the study of medieval buildings relies heavily on the assessment of extant fabric for historical documentation, given the relative paucity of other forms of evidence. None the less, St Paul's is not lost to us in the sense that it has left no visual record, like most of the great churches destroyed at the Reformation. We have the unique set of engraved views by Wenceslaus Hollar in Dugdale's *History of St Paul's*,[4] and several other 17th-century drawings from just before or after the Great Fire,[5] which taken together provide a vivid picture especially of the Gothic eastern arm and its fittings (Pls VII, XI–XVI). The accuracy of Hollar's engravings is not above suspicion, but his illustrations of the architectural details of St Paul's will be shown to be generally convincing in relation to the surviving fabric of other Gothic churches, particularly in close-up views.[6]

The concern of this paper is with the eastern arm of the cathedral, as extended and remodelled in the second half of the 13th century. This work has not escaped the attentions of previous writers on the cathedral, of whom the most discerning from an architectural point of view was Lethaby,[7] and therefore a word of justification is necessary for a further treatment of this subject. The approach adopted here is to examine the evidence for the style of the building in greater detail than has been attempted hitherto, and particularly to set its features in the wider context of English ecclesiastical architecture during the experimental period when Early English and French Rayonnant ideas intermingled at the beginning of the Decorated style. The parallels which will be drawn between St Paul's and great churches contemporary with it will be used to help validate most of Hollar's observations. My main purpose, however, is to demonstrate that the execution of the work was a slow process, so that it is unlikely that it was all designed at its inception. Rather, the creation of its various elements was spread over several decades at least, as the work progressed.

In this comparative method lies the danger that the pre-eminence of the new work at St Paul's may be disguised: that the reader may gain the impression that it is no more than a reflection of the works with which it is compared. Inevitably exchanges of ideas must have taken place as masons moved from the provinces to London and vice versa, but the new work was literally the largest ecclesiastical undertaking of the later 13th century and its location in London in a period of increasingly centralised government guaranteed that it would be regarded as a showcase for architectural fashion. No other English church of the 1270s and 1280s has a better claim to be the trend-setter of its generation.

To commence with the documentary evidence for dating, it is necessary first of all to dispose of a misconception which still appears in some of the literature. The eastern arm as rebuilt in the 13th century consisted of twelve bays (Fig. 1), and it is well known that it was divided for the purposes of funding into eight eastern bays — the 'New Work'[8] — and four west bays which housed the choir. Lethaby demonstrated convincingly more than fifty years ago that Dugdale's dates of c. 1221–40 for the choir bays were too early for the style of the fabric as shown in Hollar's engraving (Pl. XIIb), and yet these dates have still been followed by some writers.[9] Undoubtedly the choir bays incorporated reminiscences of the Romanesque east end in their narrow spacing and in parts of their fabric. Hollar's engravings clearly indicate responds with Romanesque bases in the choir aisles, but Gothic bases and responds in the aisles of the New Work (cf. Pl. XIVa, XVc).[10] It is also possible that differences of detail in the choir arcades may have stemmed from a superficial updating of the Romanesque fabric in the second quarter of the 13th century,[11] and it can be argued that Lethaby, in denying this, places too much faith in the Wren section drawing, in which the uniformity shown between the east and west bays may actually have been contrived by Wren as part of his intended tidying-up of the medieval fabric (Pl. XVI).[12] None the less Lethaby's conclusions remain fundamentally correct. All the features of the choir bays which are depicted in sufficient detail for evaluation to be possible — especially the tracery and the main vault — belong indubitably with the New Work and to the style of the second half of the 13th century (Fig. 6, Pls XIII, XVc). Thus for the purposes of this paper, all twelve bays of the eastern arm will be regarded as parts of one process put in hand in the 1250s.

Exactly when work started in that decade will probably never be known for certain. Three different dates for the commencement have come down to us — 1251 (Stow), 1256 (Dugdale) and 1258 (*Chronicle of the Mayor and Sheriffs*).[13] There is little to choose between them, though 1258 is the most precisely expressed entry and finds the widest acceptance nowadays.[14] With regard to completion, Dugdale's frequently quoted judgement that 'the main brunt was over' by c. 1283[15] has been challenged by Lethaby, who sees the work on the whole eastern arm as continuing until about 1314,[16] an interpretation which is followed in this paper. If one examines comparable and well-dated works, such as the Angel Choir at Lincoln or the nave of York Minster, one finds that the average rate of progress is roughly one complete bay for every five years. Comparisons of this kind are obviously fraught with hazards, because no two buildings are ever alike in their circumstances.[17] However the fact remains that the application of this rule-of-thumb to the twelve-bay eastern arm of St Paul's produces a hypothetical completion date in the second decade of the 14th century: which is more or less when the bulk of the documentary evidence suggests that it should be finished.

The main dates relating to the completion are these.[18] Around 1315 the whole cathedral was officially measured,[19] including its total length and the height of the eastern arm, which suggests that the New Work was complete in all its main essentials. In 1314 the altars of the Lady Chapel were dedicated,[20] and the years around these dates were taken up with fitting out the eastern arm. An altarpiece for the high altar was commissioned in 1309.[21] A contract for paving four bays at the east end of the New Work was signed in 1312–13.[22] The foundation stone for the shrine of St Erkenwald, which stood in bay 5 of the New Work, was laid in 1313; work on the shrine itself was recorded in 1319, and the saint's relics were apparently transferred to it in 1326 (Pl. XVb).[23] Finally in 1327 the canons entered their new choir in the remodelled older bays of the eastern arm, and the high altar between bays 5 and 6 of the New Work was consecrated (Pl. XIIb).[24] The delay between 1314, when the

F

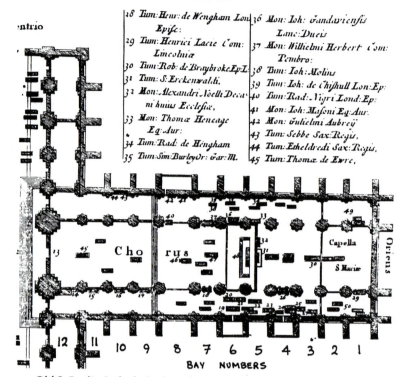

28 *Tum: Henr: de Wengham Lon:* 36 *Mon: Ioh: Gandavensis*
    Episc: *Lanc: Ducis*
29 *Tum: Henrici Lacie Com:*   37 *Mon: Willielmi Herbert Com:*
    Lincolnia   *Pembro:*
30 *Tum: Rob: de Braybroke Ep: L.* 38 *Tum: Ioh: Molins*
31 *Tum: S: Erckenwaldi.*   39 *Tum: Ioh: de Chishull Lon: Ep:*
32 *Mon: Alexandri Noell Deca-*   40 *Tum: Rad: Nigri Lond: Ep:*
    ni huius Ecclesia,   41 *Mon: Ioh: Mssoni Eq: Aur:*
33 *Mon: Thoma Heneage*   42 *Mon: Gulielmi Aubrey*
    Eq: Aur: 43 *Tum: Sebbe Sax: Regis,*
34 *Tum: Rad: de Hengham*   44 *Tum: Etheldredi Sax: Regis,*
35 *Tum: Sim: Burley Or: Gar: M.* 45 *Tum: Thoma de Ewre,*

FIG. 1.   Old St Paul's Cathedral, plan of eastern arm: based on Dugdale (1716), detail

New Work was apparently complete, and 1327 may indicate that work had continued on updating the four west bays of the old fabric during these years.[25] Some substantiation for this hypothesis may be derived from the fittings shown in Hollar's engravings. The stylistic features of the shrine and especially the screens accord well with a process of fitting out the New Work from *c.* 1310 onwards (Pls. XIII, XVB); but the screen in the link bay with the old work (Pl. XVA), and especially the pulpitum at the entry to the choir (Pl. VII), look more likely to have been made nearer *c.* 1330.[26]

Indications from documentary sources about the progress of construction are sparse, though burials and chantries provide a few clues. Hollar's engravings of the tomb of Bishop Wengham (d. 1262) shows that the dado arcade of the aisle is complete in front of his recess in bay 3 of the south aisle (Pl. XIVB; and Fig. 1, No. 28). One explanation for this could be that the aisle wall was built after his death and, as the new crypt would precede work on the aisles, this would tend to reinforce Lethaby's view that a date in the later 1250s is the most likely starting date for the crypt.[27] In contrast, the illustration of the tomb of Bishop Chishull (d. 1280) in bay 7 of the north aisle may be interpreted as indicating that a pre-existing dado has been modified to accept his monument (Pl. XIVA; and Fig. 1, No. 39).[28] If so, the aisle wall at this more westerly point must have been constructed before 1280 at the latest. On this basis, *post quem* and *ante quem* dates can be established for the lower parts of the aisle walls of the New Work: some time after 1262 and before 1280. It also appears significant as an indicator of slow progress on the building that no further burials are known in the New Work until the first decade of the 14th century.[29] The most important were those of Henry de Lacy, Earl of Lincoln (d. 1310) and Bishop Baldock

(d. 1313), both of whom are singled out in Dugdale as major benefactors of the New Work.[30] Both were buried in the area of the Lady Chapel, which suggests that the east façade and the easternmost bays were completed no later than the early years of the 14th century. Corroboration that construction continued as late as this is found in the reference to 'new vaults' in four east bays of the New Work in the paving contract of 1312/3.[31]

We may now turn to the main focus of this paper, namely to examine the building in as far as it can be recovered from old views and the few surviving fragments. In overall form, the eastern arm was characterised by its monumental simplicity — a huge rectangle uncluttered by any eastern transepts or projecting chapels, and with its main vessel continued at full height to form the centrepiece of the great east front (Pl. XIA, B). It has not escaped the notice of some modern commentators[32] that this scheme is strikingly different to the French chevet adopted at Westminster Abbey, and that the contrast may have been intended. Certainly there must have been rivalry between the two great churches, as existed in the 12th century when Edward the Confessor was canonised,[33] and it is likely that the royal rebuilding of the Abbey from 1245 was a vital factor in spurring the cathedral chapter to undertake the New Work on the grandest scale to provide a modern setting for the relics of St Erkenwald. However, Westminster is exceptional in the English context because it is obviously inspired by the French royal coronation church of Reims Cathedral,[34] whereas it is more relevant to stress the strong connections of St Paul's with the latest design for great churches in the east and north-east of England. This was the 'flush' east end with its terminal wall filled with glazing, which must have seemed more attractive in an age of developing window size than the stepped elevation with lower eastern chapels, epitomised by Salisbury (1220 sqq.). Flush east ends are numerous in the later 13th and 14th centuries,[35] but at the inception of the New Work at St Paul's they were rarer and the outstanding exemplar to be followed would have been Bishop Northwold's splendid east arm at Ely Cathedral, newly completed in 1252. At Ely, as at St Paul's, the new work was intended to create a more spacious setting for the shrine of the patron saint, and the general arrangement of eastern chapels, feretory and sanctuary is strikingly similar in both churches.[36]

The examination of the fabric will commence with the crypt, and then consider the interior elevation and the tracery; and finally the exterior of the superstructure, parts of which would be amongst the last works to be executed. It is highly probably that the New Work was constructed from east to west, with the old east end left in use as long as possible before it was modernised and linked up with the new;[37] the link is represented by the wider eighth bay.[38] Preceding any of this work would have been the crypt, which is an unusual feature for a 13th-century cathedral, but is at least partly explained here by the need to house the parish of St Faith's, whose existing church had to be demolished to accommodate the eastward extension of the New Work.

Remarkably, the south-east corner respond of the crypt survives relatively intact in a deep hole beneath a metal cover in St Paul's churchyard, east-south-east of Wren's cathedral (Pl. XVIIA, B).[39] The existence of this important fragment ought to be much better known, and urgent consideration should be given to its better conservation.[40] The respond was excavated by Penrose in 1878,[41] as also were the footings of three of the buttresses of the east front, one of which can still be inspected from a manhole in the churchyard (Pl. XIA, 'x'; and Fig. 2e). The survival of the respond testifies to the general accuracy of Hollar's view of the crypt (Pl. XIIA), though two minor differences may be observed.[42] First, the plinth of the respond forms part of a dodecagon in plan (Fig. 2d), unlike the plinths of the piers, which Hollar shows as irregular octagons (Pl. XIIA).[43] Second, the minor shafts of the respond interrupt the mouldings of the capitals and bases of the main shafts (Pls XVIIA, B; Fig. 2d.i), and one would assume that this treatment would also have been applied to the piers.[44] The

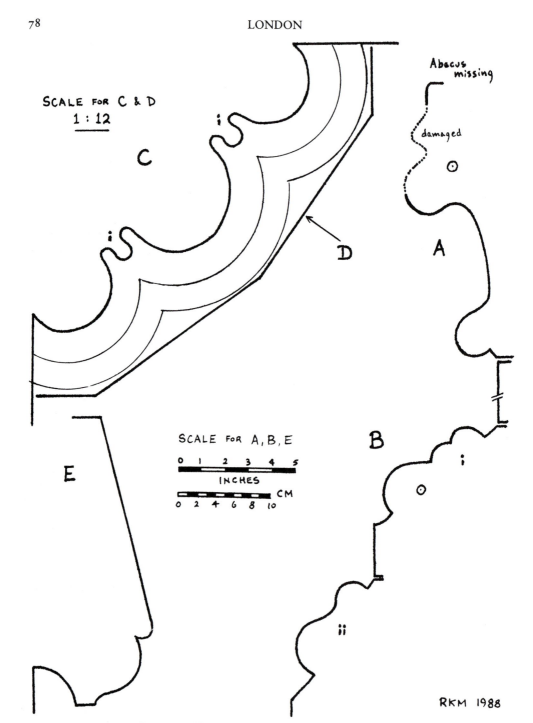

FIG. 2.   Old St Paul's Cathedral, crypt of St Faith's.
A,B: south-east vault respond, capital and base (Purbeck marble). C,D: south-east vault respond,
section of respond (free-stone) and plan of sub-base (Purbeck marble). E: exterior stringcourse on
buttress of east wall (free-stone)

latter feature was developing in advanced northern French architecture from the mid-13th century,[45] and an early example in England can be seen at Netley Abbey (Hampshire), in the processional door from the cloister, which probably dates from the 1250s,[46] the same decade in which the crypt of the New Work was begun. The door compares closely with the crypt respond in the way in which the bands of capitals and bases which incorporate the termination of the minor shafts are fashioned in Purbeck marble, whereas the minor shafts are carved in free-stone (Pl. XVIIA, c).[47]

The best preserved moulding profile of the respond is the base (Pl. XVIIB and Fig. 2b),[48] and its features are recognisable also in Hollar's view (Pl. XIIA). The base proper consists of the triple roll form (Fig. 2b.i), which had been growing in popularity since c. 1220, and was the standard design for Purbeck marble bases by the 1250s.[49] It was in use in the City by the 1230s, for example, in the main arcades of the chancel of the Temple Church; though its appearance at Westminster Abbey (1245 sqq.) was more reticent.[50] There it was finally adopted in the transept arms, c. 1250, and in a maturer form in the east bays of the nave, mainly after 1259. More distinctive is the bell profile of the sub-base of the respond (Fig. 2b.ii), probably ultimately of French Rayonnant derivation but rare in England in the 13th century.[51] There are two instances earlier than St Paul's which are particularly relevant — in the work at Westminster Abbey, including most of the main sub-bases in the chevet (1245 sqq.),[52] and in the sub-bases of the nave arcade at Lincoln (c. 1230).[53] Either could be the source for this feature at St Paul's,[54] but the case for a Lincoln provenance is furthered by the fact that it is used in conjunction with a plinth of dodecagonal form. During the first half of the 13th century, plinths of polygonal plan were becoming more common, usually based on an octagon or an irregular octagon. This is the form shown in Hollar's interior of the crypt (Pl. XIIA) and is also found, for example, at Westminster Abbey and in certain bases at Lincoln.[55] However, it is specifically at Lincoln that a rare usage of the dodecagon for plinths is found in the bases of the nave arcades,[56] and this is one of a number of links to be encountered between that cathedral and the New Work.

In sum, this analysis has demonstrated that a starting date in the 1250s is credible for the crypt, and it should be added that the style of the ground-course mouldings of the buttress from the east wall is also compatible with a date in the mid-century (Fig. 2e).[57] In addition, the examination of the surviving respond has been important in demonstrating the relative accuracy of Hollar's interior view of the crypt, and this corroborates what has already been noted about his perceptive observation of details in the choir aisles.[58]

The completion of the crypt — or at least of its east bays — would have cleared the way for construction to commence on the main elevation of the New Work. This stage would have been reached at some time after 1262, as we have seen; probably in the later 1260s. The elevation is very typical of an English great church of the years c. 1245–80, and it has often been remarked how conservative it is in form, even though certain details, notably the tracery, are right up-to-date with developments in France. The relationship of the triforium, clerestory and vault is particularly typical of the period (Pl. XIII). In each bay the triforium consists of two units, each filled with two lights of openwork tracery, which creates an impressive display around the middle level of the church; albeit of a rather traditional kind. The twin-unit design was probably the most popular form of triforium in great churches for three-quarters of the 13th century,[59] and the incorporation of bar tracery into the design at Westminster Abbey after 1245 gave it a new lease of life which inspired a number of followers,[60] of which St Paul's appears to have been one. In this matter, however, one should not entirely preclude the possibility of more recent French influence, stemming from works such as the remodelled east arm of Meaux Cathedral (1254–c. 1275/8) near Paris, which has a prominent traceried triforium incorporating delicate pointed trefoils,[61] as in the

New Work. This sort of triforium would be attractive to an English architect, and further possible links with Meaux and Paris will be cited below.[62]

The twin-unit triforium also had the advantage, in comparison with triforia which employed a super-arch,[63] of allowing more height for the clerestory.[64] This potential was realised to a certain extent at St Paul's, where the proportions of the elevation were similar to those of the Angel Choir at Lincoln, but with slightly more space being given to the arcades and clerestory at the expense of the triforium.[65] However the impact of the clerestory tracery would probably have been lessened on the interior because it appears to have been set back behind deep window splays (Pl. XIII), a shortcoming remedied at Lincoln by duplicating the window pattern in openwork tracery on the internal wall-plane.[66]

Another characteristic which St Paul's shares with the Lincoln Angel Choir and virtually all other English churches of this generation, except Westminster Abbey, is that the vault sprang from triforium level,[67] thus partly burying the clerestory in the vault. This relationship began to change towards the end of the century with the adoption of the narrow banded triforium as at St Albans and Chester (c. 1278);[68] or with the omission of the triforium altogether as in the original elevation of the presbytery at Exeter (c. 1290); or with the linkage of triforium to clerestory as at York Minster (after 1291). All these solutions put the springing of the vault somewhere in the clerestory, in contrast to the lower springing point of the New Work. Overall the thinking behind the design of the elevation of the New Work is of the third quarter of the 13th century. In reality, however, its upper parts could belong to any time before c. 1290, because only York, of the group of churches mentioned above, presents a fair comparison with St Paul's, for its great size makes it hard to do without a triforium. Thus, one can say that it was not until the 1290s and York nave that an alternative elevation to that used in the New Work appeared in a really great church in England.

The vault itself was a tierceron star vault, apparently springing from the spandrels of the triforium (Pl. XVI), as was the fashion at Lincoln.[69] It almost certainly had a main ridge rib and probably transverse ridge ribs, as well as carved bosses at almost all intersections, despite the fact that these features are omitted in Hollar's engravings (Fig. 6, Pl. XIII).[70] Not only does the Wren section drawing indicate bosses, and almost certainly ridge ribs too (Pl. XVI),[71] but also a large foliage boss has survived and is kept with other fragments in the south triforium of the present cathedral.[72] The boss appears to derive from the intersection of a continuous ridge rib and two tierceron ribs and, considering its size, it must belong to one of the main vaults, which could only mean the high vault of the eastern arm.[73] The general pattern of the vault follows the three early examples of tierceron vaults executed between c. 1240–70: Lincoln nave, Ely presbytery and Westminster nave. Had the vault been designed much later than c. 1290, one might have expected it to reflect the enhanced decorative quality of the next generation of vaults, such as additional tierceron ribs as at Exeter,[74] or just possibly the early appearance of some lierne ribs as in the undercroft of St Stephen's Chapel, Westminster Palace.[75] In this case, however, it is most probable that the direct inspiration for the design came from its near neighbour, Westminster Abbey, the latest of the first generation of tierceron vaults (c. 1260–72).[76] The pattern was introduced there in the nave either by Master Robert of Beverley (after 1260), whose name implies that he came from the pioneer area of tierceron vaulting,[77] or by his predecessor at the Abbey, Master John of Gloucester (shortly before 1259), as has recently been argued.[78] The east bays of the vault were certainly complete by King Henry III's death in 1272.[79] With regard to the design date of the St Paul's vault, little more can be said except that it belongs between the 1270s and the 1290s: and that, with regard to execution, four bays of it were sufficiently recent to be described as 'new' in 1312/3. More precise clues for dating are provided by the window tracery and other details.

From an English point of view, an unusual feature of the elevation is the emphasis placed on the vertical lines of the shafts between each bay (Pls XIII, XVI). The impression of each vault shaft rising from the floor to the vault springer, which is captured best in Wren's drawing (Pl. XVI), exudes a certain Frenchness and is reminiscent in a general way of the French-inspired elevation of Westminster Abbey. It contrasts strongly with the English practice during much of the 13th century of springing the vault shaft from a corbel usually placed in the spandrel of the arcade,[80] thus negating any vertical linkage to the shafts of the pier below. Only very rarely is this sort of vertical linkage encountered in England outside Westminster after the early 13th century,[81] as in the interesting nave design at Lichfield (1260s sqq.), which shows an awareness of French ideas, and in the nave of York Minster (1291 sqq.), where French inspiration is not in doubt.[82]

At Lichfield and York, the shafts rise to the springing point of the vaults without interruption from capitals or stringcourses. This effect is partially reproduced in the New Work, in the way in which the vault shafts continue in front of the triforium stringcourse (Pls XIII, XVI).[83] The dominance of the vault shaft over the stringcourse would appear to be an idea gaining popularity in England only from the 1260s and 1270s,[84] which is helpful in giving an indication of date for the design of the elevation of the New Work.

Another relevant detail which has escaped comment by all writers about the New Work is that the vault shafts appear to spring from their own bases directly above the capital level of the piers. Hollar clearly depicts these bases in his interior view of the eastern bays (Pl. XIII), and the veracity of his perception is made more credible by the fact that he omits them in the four western bays next to the crossing (Pl. XIIB). In other words, he is representing actual differences of detail which existed between the New Work and the remodelled older fabric: or, at least, between the eastern bays and the western bays.[85] On the other hand, Wren's drawing, which is always taken to be more accurate, fails to show this feature (Pl. XVI), perhaps because it was not actually present in the three bays illustrated — bays 7, 8 and 9, the link area between the New Work and the old.[86] Alternatively, he may have omitted it deliberately, because it could be argued that his drawing shows modifications he intended to make to the eastern bays to impart more uniformity to the medieval fabric.[87] His drawing was not intended to be used as an archaeological record.

If Hollar's view of the interior is therefore preferred to Wren's, the overall effect of the elevation of the eastern arm was fussy in the way in which the vertical articulation was broken at the arcade capitals, rather more reminiscent of Westminster Abbey than of York nave; and we should not be surprised if the design was influenced by Westminster.[88] However, the specific details of bases on the vault shaft, occurring directly above the pier capitals, is not found at Westminster and indeed had not been in regular use in an English great church since the early 13th century.[89] It had been employed at Lincoln in St Hugh's east end,[90] and had continued in use there as far as the east elevations of the main transept arms (c. 1220). Given other connections of the New Work with Lincoln,[91] it is therefore possible that this feature is a conscious reference back to the Lincoln design, and in this respect it is interesting that the idea was revived again at Lincoln at some date after 1256 for the westernmost piers of the Angel Choir. As these piers are part of the eastern crossing which links to St Hugh's work, the most obvious reason for the revival would appear to be the negative one of desired uniformity with the earlier fabric. None the less, it is important to note that all the components of the piers in question are in the style of the Angel Choir, and therefore that a master at Lincoln had direct experience of handling this somewhat anachronistic feature at about the same time that parts of the New Work at St Paul's were being designed.

An alternative source of inspiration, not necessarily incompatible with a Lincoln source, is France. The combination of a vault respond with bases above a shafted pier remained in use longer there, having been popularised by its adoption at Chartres Cathedral. In Picardy and the Ile-de-France, it was included in major works begun in the 1230s, such as the east end of Amiens Cathedral, and more than two decades later it is still found in the east end of Meaux Cathedral.[92] Bases on vault responds were also popular in eastern France, and remained in use there at least as late as the nave of Metz Cathedral (begun 1257).[93] There were strong links through the English court with Savoy[94] and other parts of France, and the francophile leanings of King Henry III are well-known, so that French influence in the elevation of the New Work cannot be ruled out.[95] In particular, a connection with major work in the Paris area, such as Meaux Cathedral, would be worth further consideration.

Hollar shows that the arcades of the New Work contained a number of features of interest, particularly the piers and their bases (Pl. XIII). The latter appear to be similar in general form to those of the crypt (Pl. XIIA), except that each of the main shafts is given its own polygonal plinth projecting from the main core of the pier (Pl. XIII); an idea also utilised in the aisle responds (Pl. XIVA). This treatment is virtually certainly of French Rayonnant derivation and can be found in important Parisian and Picard buildings from the 1230s onwards, such as Amiens Cathedral and the Sainte-Chapelle in Paris.[96] In England it is rare in the 13th century, the only major examples outside St Paul's being isolated bases in the early work around the feretory at Westminster Abbey (1245 sqq.) but not continued in the rest of the work there;[97] and in bases of the chapter house (c. 1280) and nave (1291 sqq.) at York Minster.[98] In the 14th century examples became more common, as in the new presbytery at Winchester Cathedral (c. 1310 sqq.). These dates demonstrate potentially how late in the 13th century a start on the main part of the New Work could be, though in the context of the building as a whole, it is unlikely in fact that the first bases were laid later than c. 1270. Rather the form of the plinths should be viewed as an indication of fairly direct French Rayonnant influence, as at Westminster and York. In fact, this was probably true of the style of the bases as a whole, for the evidence from Hollar (Pls XIII, XIVA) suggests that the sub-bases made more prominent use of the French-derived bell moulding than those in the crypt (Pl. XIIA and Fig. 2b.ii).[99] Details like these emphasise the importance of the New Work as a repository of up-to-date Rayonnant ideas in the period between Westminster and the emergence of the Decorated style towards the end of the century.

With regard to the profile of the base proper, it is not possible to tell whether it consisted of a triple-roll moulding, as in the crypt examples, or whether it was the typical Decorated design which appears in England from the 1280s.[100] On chronological grounds the former is more likely, but given the use of advanced Rayonnant features in the sub-base and plinth, the Decorated design cannot be ruled out and would be a pioneer example of this French-derived type in England.

The piers of the main arcade are important for introducing into the London area the richly shafted forms found mainly in the great churches of north-east England before this time. The sixteen-shafted pier[101] is particularly a feature of Lincoln Cathedral (main transept, nave, Angel Choir) and of the main transept at York Minster, and it was probably the sheer size of these churches and of St Paul's which led to its employment in all three works. In the New Work, Hollar indicates that within each pier there was an alternation of major and minor shafts, as in the piers of the north-eastern churches (Pl. XIII), but unlike them, there is no evidence that any detached shafts were included. Had they been present, Hollar — and possibly Wren also — would almost certainly have not omitted to show annulets on the shafts (Pls XIII, XVI), as annulets are visually very prominent in surviving mid-13th-century examples.[102] The extensive use of detached shafts was beginning to lose favour in the last forty years of the century,[103] and it is with the appearance of sixteen-shafted piers built entirely of coursed masonry that those of the New Work have their closest affinity, as in the feretory of St Albans Abbey (?c. 1270s) and the presbytery at Exeter Cathedral (c. 1290). Indeed St Paul's is probably the prototype for this feature at both churches.

If these conclusions about the pier type are correct, then the plan drawings of the piers in Lethaby[104] and Cook[105] cannot be correct, in that both indicate that the minor shafts are detached. Lethaby gives his source of information as a plan of 1894 made after Penrose's excavations in 1878, saying that here the plans of the piers of the ground arcade were given with detail that suggested that there must have been good evidence for the form.[106] In fact, Penrose's excavations were below floor level of the New Work, so that it is very unlikely that any evidence for the design would have been located, except for the remote chance that a large piece of a pier, capital or base had fallen intact into the crypt and been recovered.[107] So, it is suggested here that the reconstruction illustrated by Lethaby should be put aside, unless tangible evidence appears to disprove Hollar's depiction of this feature.[108] The same strong reservations should be applied to Lethaby's indication in the same drawing that the main shafts were filleted. The inclusion of fillets would accord nicely with other stylistic affinities which the New Work has with the north-east and Lincoln, where filleted shafts were a regular feature, but the archaeological evidence for the reconstruction is lacking. Even the affirmation by both Lethaby and Cook that the piers of the New Work were made entirely of Purbeck marble appears to be no more than an assumption:[109] but in this case a credible one. Given the extensive use of coursed English marble for the piers at Westminster Abbey and in Lincoln Angel Choir, it is very likely that a prestigious undertaking like the New Work would have aspired to the same; and in this respect, it may well have been the direct prototype for the coursed Purbeck piers of Exeter Cathedral. At the very least, the moulded capitals and bases must have been of Purbeck, given that marble was used for these features in the crypt (Pl. XVIIA, B).

The visual sources cannot help us further with the details of the elevation, but at least three stones from arches have survived which allow us to gain some idea of the style of the arch mouldings (Pl. XVIIIA).[110] Each of the stones seems too small to have belonged to the main arcade arches, and in fact their exact provenance is unknown. The moulding formation is asymmetrical in two of them, perhaps implying the rere-arch of a window (Fig. 3a, b and Pl. XVIIIA), whereas the third, illustrated by Lethaby,[111] is virtually symmetrical and might come from a rib or a small arch from a window or door (Fig. 3c). Two stylistic features deserved comment. First, the axial moulding of two stones (and probably of the mutilated third stone originally) consists of a roll-and-fillet moulding with lateral canted fillets ('roll and triple fillets', Fig. 3a.i, c.i). This is combined in two instances with deep hollows which continue as an S-curve into an adjacent roll moulding (especially Fig. 3a.ii). The first important use of this idea appears to be in the ribs and arcade arches of Westminster Abbey (1245 sqq.).[112] It is not usually found until the last three decades or so of the 13th century, when it began to be taken up at other works especially in the south-east,[113] amongst which the closest parallel is to be found in St Etheldreda's, Holborn, the former chapel of the bishops of Ely. In the south door in the west bay of the chapel, each order of the arch is very close in design to OSP1003 (Fig. 3a), though smaller in scale and fully symmetrical (Fig. 3d). The chapel is now generally accepted as belonging to the years 1284–90,[114] and as it lies only half a mile from St Paul's, it must certainly reflect the latest style of work at the cathedral, as other similarities will prove.[115]

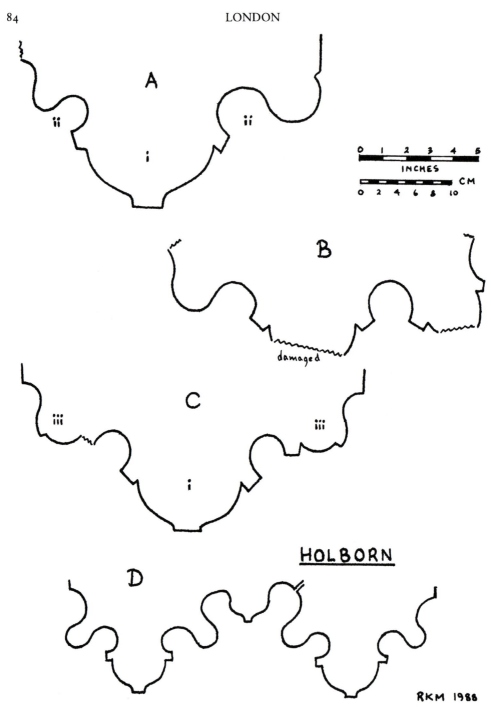

FIG. 3.   A,B,C: Old St Paul's Cathedral, loose stones from arches — Warwick Mouldings Archive OSP1003, OSP1024, and Lethaby (1930) 235 Fig. 8 (redrawn to ¼-scale). D: St Etheldreda, Holborn, south door arch (detail) — *Architectural Association Sketchbooks*, 8 (1874–5), Pl. 23

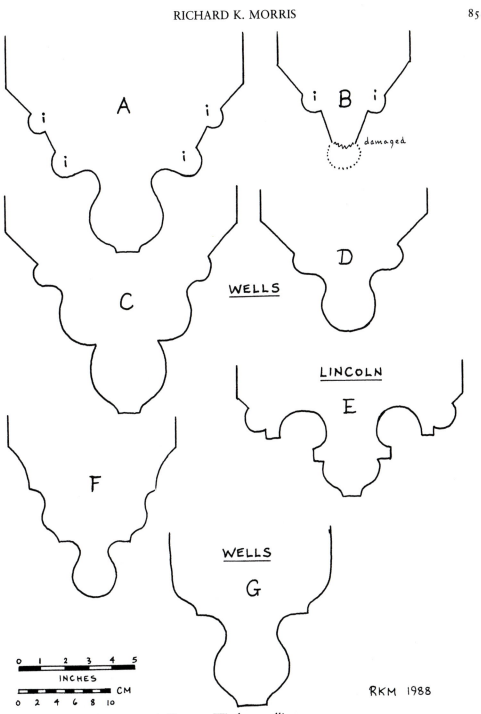

FIG. 4.   Window mullions.
A,B: Old St Paul's Cathedral, loose stones, major and minor profiles — Warwick Mouldings
Archive OSP1007 and OSP1006. C,D: Wells Cathedral, chapter house, major and minor
profiles. E: Lincoln Cathedral, Angel Choir, south aisle, east window, interior profile. F: Old St
Paul's Cathedral, loose stone — Warwick Mouldings Archive OSP1002. G: Wells, Bishop's

The second feature, the employment of the scroll moulding (Fig. 3c.iii), is potentially significant for the purposes of attribution, because it suggests a connection with the north-east, especially Lincoln. The scroll moulding is indigenous to England, and rare in occurrence before the later 13th century. The first usage of it as a component in arch mouldings is in St Hugh's Choir at Lincoln (c. 1200), and it continues to characterise the Lincoln workshop during the first half of the 13th century, as in the chapter house and some of the nave ribs.[116] During this period, it begins to appear in other works in the north-east,[117] and almost certainly Lincoln is also the source for its appearance in the nave arcades and rib profiles at Lichfield Cathedral (1260s sqq.), an undertaking contemporary with the New Work at St Paul's. The next major example known to the author is Exeter Cathedral, also in the main arcades and ribs (c. 1290),[118] but by this stage it is possible that the influence is by way of St Paul's. In other words, if this one surviving stone gives a representative indication of the usage of the scroll moulding in the New Work, it appears that a northern feature was adopted at St Paul's and thus given a wider currency.

The only other elaborate mouldings presumed to be from the New Work, and about which we have any knowledge, derive from window tracery (Pl. XVIIIB, C). Lethaby illustrated them and they have been redrawn to scale here from the surviving stones (Fig. 4a, b, f).[119] The profile which can be associated most convincingly with the New Work belongs to a general type of mullion common in the 13th and 14th centuries, the 'roll and chamfer family'.[120] Here, however, it is distinguished by two extra roll mouldings applied to the chamfer plane of the major profile (Fig. 4a.i); or one extra in the case of the minor profile (Fig. 4b.i).[121] In the third quarter of the 13th century, elaborate mullions in this family tend to have the chamfer plane between the roll mouldings cut away by a deep hollow, as in the Angel Choir windows at Lincoln (Fig. 4e). The 'flatter' treatment afforded to these St Paul's mullions is rare, and the timing of its appearance can be pinpointed closely from surviving examples in other buildings. A design fairly comparable to the minor mullion profile is found in the interior profiles of the mullions of St Etheldreda's, Holborn (1284 sqq.).[122] Only slightly later, the mullions of the chapter house at Wells Cathedral (c. 1290–1306, Fig. 4c, d) also relate to those at St Paul's, and the chapter house is another work influenced by the style current in London.[123] In this respect it is interesting to note that a different mullion design found amongst the fragments from St Paul's[124] bears a resemblance to the mullions of the important chamber over the services in Bishop Burnell's great hall at Wells (c. 1290, Fig. 4f, g). The design is unusual and cannot be ascribed with certainty to the New Work, but this connection with Wells makes it more likely that it belongs with late 13th- or early 14th-century works in the eastern arm or just possibly in the transept aisles.[125]

The exact location of one of the tracery pieces in the eastern arm has been discussed by Lethaby. He considered that the largest piece (Pl. XVIIIB) belonged in the clerestory, above the centre light of one of the three-light window designs shown in the Wren drawing in bays 7 and 9 (Pl. XVI).[126] This identification is convincing both in design and scale. The other tracery piece which employs a similar profile, but which was not discussed by Lethaby (Pl. XVIIIC), is difficult to place in the clerestory or the aisles. A possible location would be in the subsidiary tracery of one of the radiating lights of the eastern rose window. This accords reasonably well with the asymmetry of the cusping of this piece, with its scale, and also with the fact that it is from a minor profile (Fig. 5 and Pl. XIA).[127] If this reconstruction is valid, it means that the clerestory and the rose employed a mullion type coming into vogue in the 1280s. Moreover, it seems a reasonable assumption that the profile was also used in the aisle windows, because their tracery relates especially closely to St Etheldreda's, Holborn.[128]

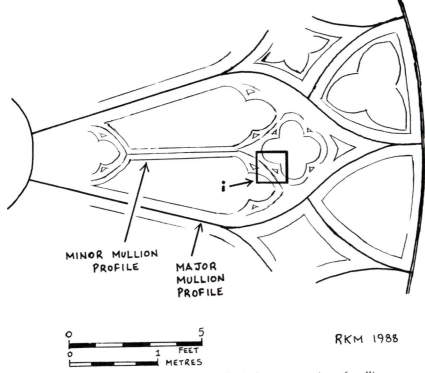

MINOR MULLION
PROFILE

MAJOR
MULLION
PROFILE

RKM 1988

FEET
METRES

FIG. 5. Old St Paul's Cathedral. Hypothetical reconstruction of mullion stone (Warwick Mouldings Archive OSP1006) in eastern rose window

The New Work is second in significance only to Westminster Abbey for the introduction of French Rayonnant tracery. After the initial impetus given to bar tracery in England by its adoption at the Abbey, St Paul's was the first major display of a second generation of French tracery motifs, such as the impaled trefoil. It was also an important pioneer of the great traceried east window,[129] the forerunner of the spectacular examples at Gloucester and York in the next century. However, the repetitive uniformity of the tracery patterns in the aisle and clerestory windows[130] denotes that the architectural thinking behind the New Work is of the 1270s and early 1280s, in contrast with the insistent variety which is a feature of such early Decorated works as Exeter Cathedral, and the chapels of Merton College, Oxford, and the bishop's palace at Wells.

Certain features of the tracery provide an invaluable guide as to the chronological progress of the New Work. The standard aisle windows[131] each consist of a triplet of lights surmounted by three oculi (Pls XIB, XIII), a tracery pattern familiar in England in works begun in the later 1250s and 1260s, e.g. Lincoln Angel Choir, Hereford north transept, Lichfield nave.[132] However, the significant development at St Paul's is that an impaled figure is introduced into the head of the light. In the lateral windows, it is an impaled trefoil, probably in all three lights (Pl. XIII), but in the east windows Hollar shows a less distinct form over the centre light only (Pl. XIA): these might have been the first windows executed. This motif had begun to appear in France around 1260,[133] and in one of the earliest examples, the clerestory of the apse at St-Urbain at Troyes (1262–6), the unobtrusive way in which it appears only in the centre light of a triplet design recalls the aisle east windows of the New Work (Pl. XIA). In surviving works in England, the motif is extremely rare before the 1280s,[134] after which it grows rapidly in popularity.[135] At St Etheldreda's, Holborn (1284 sqq.), it is employed with a consistency and maturity which suggests that it was not a new feature in London by that date,[136] and it is reasonable to assume that the source for St Etheldreda's, as for other examples outside the capital, was the experimentation with this feature at St Paul's. Indeed, one can argue that the fondness for sex-foiled and octo-foiled oculi at St Etheldreda's also derives from the aisle windows at St Paul's, and particularly the grouping of three large oculi in the west window of the chapel. Thus all the signs point to the aisle windows of the New Work being designed in the 1270s, and acting as an intermediary between the latest French architectural thinking and the acceptance of features like the impaled trefoil in the rest of England a decade later.

By the time the triforium and clerestory had been reached, the pointed trefoil had come to dominate the tracery patterns, especially inscribed in a curved triangle (Pl. XVI).[137] The invention of this combination can be traced back to the south transept at Notre-Dame, Paris (1258–67); and around Paris, delicate trefoils, though not actually set in curved triangles, appear in works like Meaux Cathedral (1254–c. 1275/8).[138] Another idea found in the transepts of Notre-Dame is the subdivision of a unit of tracery into six foiled figures,[139] and this was taken up in the New Work. Wren's drawing indicates that each oculus in the clerestory windows was subdivided into six triangular figures, which were alternately trefoiled or left void (Pl. XVI). Over the rest of England, examples of this sexpartite design involving either trefoils or curved triangles began to appear towards 1290,[140] generally five to ten years later than the spread of the impaled trefoil. One cannot be categorical in asserting that the same remove of time separated the design of the aisle and clerestory patterns in the New Work, but this evidence suggests that the clerestory was not created until the later 1270s or early 1280s.[141]

The great rose window shares certain features in common with the clerestory and was probably the last of the tracery designs to be executed, given its size and position (Pl. XIA). Its twelve-light design was almost certainly derived from the south transept rose of Notre-Dame, Paris, and therefore one can be fairly sure that the foiled figures depicted around its circumference are trefoils in curved triangles (Pl. XIA, XIII and Fig. 5). The most enigmatic feature of the window is the treatment of the heads of the twelve radiating lights. Were the heads given explicit ogee arches, as suggested in Hollar's exterior view (Pl. XIA) and as reconstructed by Lethaby;[142] or were ogee arches merely implied, as in the south rose at Notre-Dame?[143] The question will probably never be answered convincingly, but the rate of progress argued here for the New Work means that the rose window stage was probably not reached until the 1280s, and the execution of the tracery could be even later. The detailing of its design is thus very close to the time in the early 1290s when the ogee arch made its better known appearance in a series of works by court masons,[144] and it is therefore by no means inconceivable that the motif was a conscious feature of the rose, and not merely one implied by the juxtaposition of other patterns in the tracery. This would make it the first prominent usage in a window of the ogee arch,[145] and a credible source for this key feature of Decorated tracery.

As for the rose itself, it is generally accepted that this distinctively French Gothic form of window never gained popularity in England, but one can point to a number of subsequent examples set above a row of lights and probably inspired ultimately by 'Paul's window'.[146] Occasionally they follow the arrangement of radial lights, as in the south transept window at Minchinhampton church, Gloucestershire (c. 1330–40), which looks like a reduced copy of that at St Paul's, as Lethaby remarked.[147] The more common type, however, employs a more fluid composition of foiled figures, taking the arrangement of foiled figures around the circumference of the St Paul's rose to its natural conclusion. Major examples are the window of St Anselm's Chapel, Canterbury Cathedral, the west window of Exeter Cathedral, and almost certainly the lost east window of St Stephen's Chapel in Westminster Palace: all works of the 1330s.[148]

The rose window was set into an east front bristling with pinnacles (Pl. XIA), and bearing a general resemblance to the house shrine of St Erkenwald, which is probably more than coincidental (Pl. XVB). Particularly unusual is the suggestion[149] that in the east front, an additional upright was placed over the apex of each of the aisle east windows, giving the impression of a double range of flying buttresses. This must have been restricted to the façade for obvious structural reasons (Pl. XIA).[150] A single row of flying buttress was employed in the side elevation, as one would expect in a church without double aisles (Pl. XIB). Thus, the decorative multiplicity of pinnacles in the east front suggests at the very least a general intention to impress, and perhaps specifically to communicate to the outside world the image of St Erkenwald's shrine, with its triple tiers of uprights and pinnacles (Pl. XVB).[151]

The other distinctive features of the exterior included the decorative parapets above the eaves (Pl. XIB), and the paired angle buttresses which add a sense of spatial depth to the corners of the east front (Pl. XIA, B). The form and delicacy of the parapets is probably another conscious allusion to precious metalwork. Hollar shows that they were pierced with a band of quatrefoils, and Lethaby is probably correct in attributing one large surviving piece amongst the fragments to this part of the building (Pl. XVIIID).[152] Small-scale cornices decorated with foiled figures were coming into fashion in the 1290s, in court commissions associated with the Kentish school of craftsmen, such as the Eleanor Crosses and the tomb of Edmund, Earl of Lancaster, in Westminster Abbey.[153] On a larger scale, the closest parallel to the combination of foiled parapets and flying buttresses at St Paul's is to be seen over the nave aisles at York Minster, officially begun in 1291, but where the relevant work was probably not executed until around 1310 and later.[154] Parallels for the paired angle buttresses also belong to the 14th century. They were employed on the crossing tower of Hereford Cathedral (before 1319), but a more comparable usage to that at St Paul's is found in the Lady Chapel at Ely (after 1321) and the presbytery clerestory at Wells Cathedral, clasping the main gable of the superstructure (after 1325).[155]

This discussion provides further indications that the construction of the eastern arm dragged on well beyond the date of c. 1280 implied by Dugdale. Allowing for the huge scale of the whole undertaking, and assuming that the New Work proceeded mainly in horizontal layers, rather than each bay being built to full height sequentially, the chronology appears to be as follows. The completion of most of the new crypt would have delayed a start on the choir aisles substantially, and the detailing of most of their components appears to belong to around 1270 and the years following. Above arcade level, the same stage of development would probably not have been reached before c. 1280, and the form of some elements in the superstructure may not have been finalised until a decade or so later. Moreover, the completion of certain elements, such as the high vaults and the remodelling of the older fabric, seems to have carried over into the early years of the next century.

Thus, in about 1270, St Paul's took over from the abbey church at Westminster as the greatest architectural undertaking in the London area, and it was to retain this position until at least the 1290s, when King Edward I commissioned the new chapel of St Stephen at Westminster Palace. In its heyday, the importance of the St Paul's workshop must have been a major attraction for established and aspiring masons in the London area and beyond. It is therefore appropriate that this article should conclude with a brief consideration of the possible identities of some of these craftsmen. For one of the most remarkable things about the New Work is the anonymity surrounding its creation and design. Only towards the end of its construction do we learn of the names of two masons engaged there — Master John de Weldon, appointed late in 1308 (?1308/9) to have charge of works and repairs, including the New Work; and Master Adam le Marbrer, who contracted in 1312/13 to pave four bays of the New Work.[156] For the 13th-century work, however, we are left to speculate.

Dr John Harvey has implied the involvement in the New Work of Master Michael of Canterbury, the royal master mason, on the basis of shared details with St Etheldreda's, Holborn.[157] Given the recurrence of certain features from St Paul's in the court works of the 1290s, it is highly probable that the cathedral workshop provided valuable experience for masons who went on to work for the crown in the 1290s, such as Michael of Canterbury. In this case, his only documented presence in London before c. 1290 was working for Christ Church Priory, Canterbury, on the prior's house next to St Mary le Bow;[158] suggestively close in proximity to the east end of St Paul's, but we have no evidence beyond this inference. So the matter must be left open.

There are several other important masons of the royal works in this period, however, for whom stronger claims may be advanced for involvement on the New Work around the 1280s. Chief amongst these are Masters Richard Crundale and Simon Pabenham.[159] Crundale has the advantages for our purpose of being an established master mason in the City by 1281, and of being the principal mason under Master Robert of Beverley at the Tower of London. Pabenham was also working at the Tower in Beverley's time, and went on to become a master of considerable status and property in the City by the early 14th century. However, our real interest in him lies in the implication that he was a relative of the Simon de Pabenham who was warden of the work on the Angel Choir at Lincoln around 1270, perhaps later to become the master mason of York nave.[160] Links between the New Work and York Minster have been described above and, as Harvey mentions,[161] the presence of members of the Pabenham family in London and the north-east could help explain elements of the court style at the Minster. More significant, however, are the connections with Lincoln and with Robert of Beverley.

It has been shown that the great churches in England which had the most influence on the architectural style of the New Work were Lincoln and Westminster Abbey. Certain details of the New Work seem to relate particularly to Lincoln, such as the scroll moulding and the treatment of the shafts of the high vault. In Robert of Beverley we have a mason whose career combines a probable acquaintance with Lincoln and a close knowledge of Westminster. His name implies that he had been trained in the north-east, and from 1253 he is documented as working at Westminster Abbey under John of Gloucester.[162] The circumstances suggest that it was his idea to introduce the Lincoln tierceron vault to London, in the nave of the Abbey,[163] whence the vaults of St Paul's derived their inspiration. In 1260 he succeeded John of Gloucester as chief mason at the Abbey and as King's Master Mason, and in the latter capacity he was engaged in the City on various works at the Tower between 1271 and his death in 1284.[164] As we have seen, these were the years when the main part of the New Work began to take shape, and it is therefore highly probable that his ideas were influential on its design. Moreover, with regard to a source for the French influences observed at St Paul's, the works at the Tower could provide a possible foyer for the interchange of ideas between Master Robert and leading foreign craftsmen engaged on Edward I's castle-building programme.[165]

Whether Master Robert ever held the post of master mason at the New Work is more problematic, for he appears to have been extremely busy in this period, especially on royal works, as Harvey's biography demonstrates.[166] However, as the outstanding mason in

FIG. 6.   Old St Paul's Cathedral, upper parts of choir
(Dugdale, 1716), detail

London in the 1260s and 1270s, he would have attracted a following, a school of masons, amongst whom must be numbered Richard Crundale and perhaps also Simon Pabenham. It was quite conceivable that the New Work was in the hands of masons from this background in its formative years, under the tutelage of Master Robert until his death. Indeed it is tempting to speculate that Richard Crundale made his name at St Paul's in the 1270s, initially in a junior capacity, and that Pabenham worked there in the 1280s and 1290s. This can be no more than conjecture, however.

The irony of St Paul's is that the importance of its workshop in these years was not matched by speed of completion of the work. By the time that the eastern arm was finished and ready to view, its decorative vocabulary had been largely superseded by further developments, especially in vault patterns and window tracery, in workshops in the west and in East Anglia. Moreover, the sheer size of the work deterred potential patrons from emulating the whole scheme: the notable exception being the subsequent rebuilding of the nave and eastern arm of York Minster, the work which best evokes the lofty spaces of the New Work.

ACKNOWLEDGEMENTS

This paper is substantially the same as the one given at the British Archaeological Association Conference in London in April, 1984, to which has been added further discussion of surviving fragments of the fabric, and of the masons involved. I am grateful to the following for assistance with various points in this paper, especially since the conference: Dr Richard Fawcett, Dr John Harvey, Philip Lankester, Georgina Russell, Christian Schueler, David Stocker, Jane Waddington and Dr Christopher Wilson. For facilitating my research at St Paul's Cathedral, I am grateful to Robert Potter (former Surveyor to the Fabric), Frank Atkinson (the librarian), the late A. R. B. Fuller (former librarian), Commander Charles Shears (Registrar and Receiver), and the Clerk of Works (R. L. Harvey) and his staff.

REFERENCES

1. Lang (1956), 22–3, based on accounts by Evelyn, Pepys and others.
2. For the dimensions, see Lethaby (1930), 235–6.
3. For example, see Bond (1906), Index of Places — compare the number of references to Old St Paul's (p. 736) with those for, e.g. Lichfield or Lincoln (pp. 754–5); and note that in his Chronology of English Churches (pp. 638–57), St Paul's is omitted altogether. Also Webb (1956) and Kidson (1979), in both of which the coverage is restricted mainly to the east window and the chapter house. Brieger (1957), 231–2, understood the significance of the 13th-century work — '... the most important piece of building, both for its own sake and because of its influence in shaping a new style, was the "new work" at Old St Paul's'; but the short account of the building which follows this statement is disappointing. Bock (1962), 25–6 and 86–7, partly inspired by Brieger, gives the Gothic parts of Old St Paul's a more balanced coverage. For other works which deal in more specific detail with the 13th-century eastern arm, see below, n. 7.
4. Dugdale (1716). Unless stated otherwise, all references in this paper are to the 1716 edition, but their content has been checked against the 1658 edition.
5. Notably Wren Drawings; Pl. XVI in this article is a detail from his section drawing.
6. Ideally one would wish to study Hollar's preparatory drawings for these engravings, but only one is known to have survived, unsigned but attributed to Hollar. This is in the Ashmolean Museum, Oxford, and shows the cathedral from the north; see Brown (1982), 84–5 and pl. VI. I am grateful to Christian Schuler of the University of Berlin for drawing this to my attention and also to Philip Lankester for informing me about a *Collection of Monuments in Various Countries*, by Sir William Dugdale (1640–1), which includes drawings of monuments and other fittings in Old St Paul's; this volume is on loan from the Trustees of the Winchilsea Settled Estates to the British Library (Loan MS 38). The drawings in the latter do not appear to include any architectural views, nor apparently are they by Hollar, though the Dugdale connection is suggestive and Hollar may have had access to them (Philip Lankester, communication to the author); see also Cook (1955), 54–5. I have not had an opportunity to check MS 38.
7. Lethaby (1930). For the main literature on Old St Paul's, see the bibliography in Cook (1955), 107, of which the best is Lethaby (1930). To Cook's list should be added Hastings (1955), ch. 1; B/E *London I: The Cities of London and Westminster* (1962), 115–18; and Bony (1979), 5 and 10–11. The text of Cook (1955) is the most convenient modern summary of material relating to Old St Paul's, but lacks a scholarly apparatus; it is weak as an analysis of the architecture. The reconstruction drawings by E. B. Ferrey in Longman's book (Cook (1955), 107) should be regarded with great caution as an archaeological record, and they have been reprinted in other books, e.g. Cook (1955). Less widely known but much to be preferred are the drawings submitted for the Pugin Studentship by Finch (1935), 729 and 778–9, which take account of the archaeological discoveries of Penrose and the research of Lethaby; I am grateful to John Harvey for first drawing them to my attention some years ago.
8. For the distinction in administration and funding of the 'New Work' and the 'old fabric', see VCH *London*, I, 420–3, passim; and Cook (1955), 33–4.
9. E.g. Brieger (1957), 231–7; B/E *London I* (1962), 115–6, though noting that the upper parts of the choir bays are later; and Schofield (1984), 65.
10. Also Hollar shows the piers between bays 8 and 9 apparently as having a plain cylindrical surface, which could be a survival of Romanesque fabric at the junction between the new and old work (Finch (1935), 728, interpreted it in this way); or just possibly the circular core of a shafted pier of the kind used at Salisbury Cathedral (1220 sqq.) and Westminster Abbey. Both piers are visible in the distance in Pl. XIIb, but the clearest view is in Pl. XVa (right).
11. The main difference is that Hollar shows the choir bay piers with eight shafts, and the piers of the New Work with sixteen (Pls XIIb, XIII); B/E *London I* (1962), 116, treats the former as belonging to c. 1221–40.

Another detail shown by Hollar in the choir bays is an annulet on each of the vault shafts at the level of the base of the triforium, perhaps an extension of the presumed stringcourse at this level (Pl. XIIB); this idea was probably more common in England in the first half of the 13th century than in the second half, but it is hardly a safe indicator of date.

12. Lethaby (1930), 193–4, where he accepts the drawing of Wren the architect as more accurate than the engravings of Hollar the artist, but without questioning Wren's purpose; also Finch (1935), 772, describes Wren's drawing as 'much better evidence than Hollar'. As the plan for the pre-Fire Design (Wren Drawings, No. 4) indicates proposals for major changes in the floor levels in bays 8 and 9, compared with those shown in Dugdale's plan (Fig. 1), one could argue that the uniformity of the pier bases in this area represents modifications intended by Wren rather than being an accurate record of the medieval fabric. Likewise the prevalence of the eight-shafted pier on the plan, shown both for the choir bays (where most authorities would accept its existence) but also for the New Work (where Hollar shows piers with sixteen shafts); and also Wren's omission in the wide bay, no. 8, of the inserted pier and arches, which are shown by Hollar (Pls XIIB, XVA).

13. For a summary of these references, see Lethaby (1930), 193, and Hastings (1955), 5. Note that Stow applies Dugdale's date of 1256 to the start of work on remodelling the transepts ('cross aisles'), a work beyond the scope of this paper; Stow (1955), 292.

14. Accepted by, e.g. Lethaby (1930), 193; Finch (1935), 730; Hastings (1955), 5; and Bony (1979), 5. Note also, however, Harvey (1974), 232, in which 1251 is preferred.

15. Dugdale (1716), 15.

16. Lethaby (1930), 193.

17. For example, at St Paul's, a crypt had to be constructed under eight bays of the New Work, which would have slowed progress, but the additional time needed for this would be at least partly compensated for by the fact that the four west bays of the eastern arm were not entirely a new build; both these factors are absent from the works at Lincoln and York.

18. For some of these dates there are slight discrepancies between the various sources (e.g. see n. 19), and another source of potential confusion arises from contracts and other documents which would have fallen in the old year by medieval reckoning, but in the new year by modern convention: see e.g. n. 22, and Harvey (1984), xxii. I have not attempted to update or make compatible any of the dates from the sources.

19. 1313 according to VCH London, I, 414, n. 123, citing the Chrons Edward I and Edward II, I, 277: St Paul's Chron., 44–6 gives 1314: Dugdale (1716), 17, implies 1315. The measurement must have taken place after the completion of work on the spire in 1314; see n. 25.

20. St Paul's Chron., 45. The three altars were those of the Virgin Mary, of St Dunstan (which definitely stood at the east end of the south aisle) and of St Thomas (which Lethaby places at the east end of the north aisle). Lethaby (1930), 193, takes this event to be the dedication of the whole New Work, and in this he has been followed by other authorities, such as Hastings (1955), 7.

21. Dugdale (1716), 16.

22. For the contract for the paving, see Salzman (1952), 419–20. The date of the contract is 25 January 1312/3, which puts it in 1313 by modern convention; see Harvey (1984), xxii and 327.

23. For a summary of the dates relating to the shrine, see Coldstream (1976), 24–5; St Paul's Chron., 51, gives 1326 for the translation of the relics.

24. See VCH London, I, 414 and 125, citing the Chrons Edward I and Edward II, I, 338 and 368; St Paul's Chron., 56, puts the consecration of the high altar in 1339.

25. The delay may also be related to work on the spire recorded in about 1314, the completion of which appears to be related to the official measurement of the cathedral; see further n. 19.

26. See Hastings (1955), 12, 112–15, 129–30, for a comparative account of their features with the style of the Kentish masons and with the work of Master William Ramsey. As he remarks, in the pulpitum, the design of the doorways into the choir aisles (Pl. VII) is remarkably similar to the work of William Ramsey in the vestibule of St Stephen's Chapel, Westminster Palace, which is dated by Harvey to after 1337 — Harvey (1961), 149–50 and Harvey (1984), 243. Ramsey was certainly working at St Paul's from 1332. To this it should be added that the only section of the choir screen illustrated by Hollar (Pl. XVA) is generally reminiscent in design to Archbishop's Meopham's tomb at Canterbury (1334–6), with quatrefoil tracery similar to that in the windows of the hall at Penshurst Place (c. 1341); Ramsey's name has been associated with the latter — Harvey (1984), 244. For the most recent account of Ramsey's work, see Wilson, (1980).

27. The earliest reference to the crypt is in 1271, when a guild chapel of St Anne is recorded — VCH London, I, 424, n. 354, citing Historical MSS. Commission Report; though Dugdale (1716), 120, gives 1371 as the date, and Cook (1955), 52, follows this. The context of Dugdale's reference implies that this chapel was in the crypt of the New Work, rather than in the older crypt which is assumed to have existed under the original four west bays of the eastern arm.

28. Similar differences are also illustrated between the tombs of the Saxon kings, which would have been a planned reburial in the north aisle, bay 10 (Pl. XVc), and the tomb of Canon Ralph Hengham (d. 1311), which appears as an insertion into the dado arcade of the north aisle, bay 5. See Dugdale (1716), 102.

29. Information about the burials and chantry foundations is found mainly in Dugdale (1716), 16 and 30–3; and in Stow (1955), 297–300. In chronological order, the earliest ones in the 14th century are — first mention of a chantry in the New Work, Reginald Brandon, 1305 (Stow, who places it in the Lady Chapel) or 1307/8 (Dugdale); Henry Lacy, Earl of Lincoln (1310), between the Lady Chapel and the altar of St Dunstan (Fig. 1, No. 29); Canon Ralph Hengham (1311), in the north aisle, bay 5 (Fig. 1, No. 34); Bishop Baldock (1313), in the centre of the Lady Chapel (Fig. 1, east of No. 30); Canon William Chateslehunt/ Chaldeshunt (1321 or 1322); Sir Nicholas Wokenden (1322 or 1323); Canon Roger Waltham (1325 or 1326).

30. Dugdale (1716), 16.

31. See n. 22.

32. E.g. Brieger (1957), 232–7; Bock (1962), 25.

33. See Scholz (1961), 38 sqq.

34. For the most recent treatment of this connexion, see Wilson (1987), 75 sqq.

35. Most notably Lincoln (1256 sqq.) and York (1361 sqq.), but also, e.g. Carlisle, Ripon, Bridlington, Guisborough and Selby. Major examples earlier than St Paul's, other than Ely, are Beverley Minster (c. 1220 sqq.) and Worcester (1224 sqq.), both with pronounced eastern transepts, unlike St Paul's; and notably Rievaulx (c. 1225 sqq.) amongst the Cistercian houses. Examples of the staggered east end remain mainly southern and south-western: apart from Salisbury, major examples include Winchester Cathedral, St Albans, Wells, Hereford and Exeter. Gloucester (1337 sqq.) is an interesting hybrid, achieving the 'flush' effect of a great east window extending almost to the floor, yet also including a lower Lady Chapel to the east.

36. See further Draper (1979), 10 sqq. The only difference is that the longer eastern arm of St Paul's allowed the choir to be accommodated in it as well, whereas at Ely it extended into the crossing.

37. This would accord with the procedure followed when extending the eastern arm of other cathedrals, e.g. Worcester in the 13th century, and Wells and Lichfield in the 14th. It is hard to concur with Harvey (1984), 327, that the Lady Chapel was not built until 1307–12; though I agree that the major features of this part of the church, the tracery of the east window and the high vaults, were amongst the last items of work to have been completed.

38. Lethaby (1930), 194, suggested that it was much wider to mask the difference between the narrow bays of the old fabric and the wider bays of the New Work. It is also usually assumed that the apse and ambulatory of the Romanesque cathedral lay on this site: see Clapman (1934), 31–2.

39. I am very grateful to Christopher Wilson for pointing out its existence to me during the conference; and also for supplying me with copies of drawings relating to this area, on which my Fig. 2c and e is based. His copies were made from drawings in the Surveyor's Chest at St Paul's.

40. Especially of the Purbeck marble capitals and bases (Pls XVIIa, b).

41. Penrose (1883), especially 390–1 and pl. XIV.

42. Hollar's view of the crypt (Pl. XIIa) is taken from the west and does not illustrate the area of the surviving respond nor any corner respond, so the differences noted here need not be construed as mistakes by the artist.

43. The plinths of the piers may well have taken the octagonal form because all their main shafts were equal in diameter, as Hollar's view suggests, whereas in the corner respond the centre shaft is larger than the two lateral ones, so the plinth is given an extra angular projection to accommodate it. The observation about the piers applies particularly to the two outer rows of piers which, being larger than the middle row, each had eight main shafts, and thus three main shafts on each diagonal face (Pl. XIIa).

44. The profile of a crypt pier published in Cook (1955), 35, fig. IV/4, is almost certainly wrong, in that it omits the continuous curves linking the minor and major shafts, as exist on the respond (Fig. 2c); and in that there is no evidence that the corner shafts of the pier were larger in diameter than the intermediate ones.

45. See Morris (1979), 24: the example at St-Germer-de-Fly (Lady Chapel vestibule) is illustrated in Branner (1965), pl. 105.

46. For Netley, see Thompson (1973); and Colvin and Brown (1963), I, 158. Earlier examples can be found in England in which minor shafts are treated with smaller capitals and bases (e.g. Worcester Cathedral, choir piers, c. 1230; Lincoln Cathedral, entrance to nave south aisle from south transept, c. 1230), but the mouldings of the bases and capitals in these remain uninterrupted.

47. The only difference is that at Netley the main shafts were detached, presumably of Purbeck marble (they are lost), whereas at St Paul's all the shafts of the respond are built of coursed free-stone. Unfortunately the moulding detail of the Purbeck capitals and bases at Netley has been lost through weathering and decay.

48. Only the necking and part of the bell mouldings of the capital are preserved (Fig. 2a), and correspond to the two lower projecting profiles shown on the capitals in Hollar's view (Pl. XIIa); the abacus block is lost. The

surviving mouldings are not particularly distinctive, being of a general type found in Purbeck marble capitals from *c.* 1220 onward (e.g. Salisbury Cathedral, main aircade of presbytery/choir).

49. See Morris (1979), 26. Major early examples of the triple roll base are — Salisbury Cathedral, 1220 sqq. (used throughout); Winchester Castle Hall, 1222–36 (main arcades); Temple Church, London, *c.* 1230–40 (main arcades only); Lambeth Palace Chapel, *c.* 1230; Worcester Cathedral, *c.* 1230 (western two bays of choir); Ely Cathedral, 1234–52 (Northwold's east end). All these examples are executed in Purbeck marble except Worcester.

50. The persistence of the water-holding type of base in the earliest work in the chevet may be due to the predilection for French forms on the part of the first master of the work, Henry of Reyns: for the most recent account of him, see Wilson *et al.* (1986), 26 sqq. Alternatively, the water-holding bases may have been prepared in the period 1220–45, before King Henry III took over responsibility for the rebuilding of the whole church.

51. Morris (1979), 28.

52. Illustrated in RCHM *London*, I, 95, bottom row.

53. An exceptionally early example occurs in the retrochoir of Winchester Cathedral (*c.* 1200–20), in the Purbeck marble sub-bases of the main arcade; this might be an indigenous derivation from the torus base type.

54. The Westminster sub-bases are in Purbeck, as at St Paul's; the Lincoln nave sub-bases are in free-stone.

55. Employed at Lincoln, for example, for the main crossing piers and some of the bases in the north transept. Early examples elsewhere include — Wells Cathedral, e.g. nave (*c.* 1200–30); Salisbury Cathedral, corner piers of retrochoir (1220 sqq.); Ely Cathedral, Northwold's east end (1234–52).

56. The dodecagonal plinth was also used in the east bay of the Angel Choir at Lincoln (1256 sqq.), but the plinths in the rest of this work reverted to a form which is more or less an irregular octagon.

57. The undercut roll-and-fillet moulding, with a bead moulding attached and turned downwards, is typical of this date, though I have been unable at a quick check to find an exact parallel in a ground-course moulding.

58. See further p. 76 and n. 28.

59. E.g. Lincoln, where it is a consistent feature of all parts of the work from St Hugh's Choir onwards; St Albans, nave; Worcester, east end; Rievaulx. The seminal work for Early English Gothic is Willam of Sens' choir at Canterbury Cathedral (1175 sqq.). For a fuller account of the design of English church elevations in the 13th century, see Jansen (1979).

60. Lincoln, Angel Choir (1256 sqq.); Hereford, north transept (1260s); Lichfield nave (1260s sqq.).

61. Kurmann (1971), ch. III and pls 1, 37. The triforium is twin-unit over the lateral bays, but reduced to a single unit in the narrower chevet bays. It has openwork tracery in the spandrels, a feature not found in the triforium at St Paul's.

62. See pp. 82, 88. The judgement in Branner (1965), 75, that Meaux represents a trend that 'was sorely out of date' seems rather harsh, especially as the work at Meaux is linked (as he acknowledges) to one of the most inventive Rayonnant churches of the period, St Sulpice-de-Favières, in which impaled trefoils are used in the tracery at an early date; a motif also found, incidentally, in the aisle windows at St Paul's.

63. E.g. Salisbury Cathedral; York Minster, transepts.

64. This potential advantage was not always exploited: note the small clerestories of Hereford, north transept, and Lichfield nave.

65. Observations based on the right-hand bay in Wren Drawings, 7 (Pl. XVI).

66. See further Peter Kidson's important account of the early development of bar tracery in England, in P. Kidson *et al.* (1965), ch. 4. It is usually assumed that the New Work had no wall-passage at clerestory level (like Westminster Abbey, Lichfield nave and Hereford north transept), on the basis that Hollar does not show this feature in his views (Fig. 6, Pl. XIII). However, a clerestory passage is not shown in his views of the Romanesque fabric either, where one would almost certainly have existed, so this issue has to be left unresolved.

67. The top of the triforium/gallery level is the most common position, examples of which include Salisbury, Worcester, Rievaulx, Much Wenlock, Ely, Lichfield, Hereford, Tintern. Occasionally the springing point is in the spandrels of the triforium, as in the transepts at York, and it is a particular characteristic of Lincoln (transepts, nave, Angel Choir). This was the springing level used in the eastern arm of St Paul's, if we accept the evidence of Wren's section drawing (Pl. XVI) over that of Hollar's views (Pls XIIB, XIII), as I think we must in this matter. A rare example, before Westminster, of a vault springing from the clerestory zone in a three-stage elevation is the eastern arm of Beverley Minster (*c.* 1220 sqq.).

68. Jansen (1979), 228.

69. See further n. 67.

70. Except that he includes one boss in the main intersection of each bay.

71. A transverse ridge rib is actually drawn in only in the wide centre bay, bay 8, so it cannot be certain whether the other bays had them. A longitudinal ridge rib is presumably represented by the continuous horizontal

line slightly below the stippling of the cross-section of the vault cell. It would be unprecedented at this date for a tierceron star vault to omit a longitudinal ridge rib and some form of transverse ridge ribs. For the latter, the type favoured amongst the early examples is what Bond calls 'abbreviated', running from the centre boss only as far as the intersections of the tiercerons, e.g. Lincoln nave, Ely presbytery, Lichfield nave: Bond (1906), 323–37. The other major early example, Westminster nave, has transverse ridge ribs the full width of the vault, and this is the type indicated for the wide bay at St Paul's in the Wren drawing (Pl. XVI).

72. The boss is about 15–20in. (40–50cm) in diameter, very worn in condition, and in 1984 it was on the bottom shelf of the racking in the triforium. It is too heavy to move single-handed for closer examination, but its importance is clearly such that it should be properly recorded in due course. No catalogue of the fragments appears to exist, though various architectural historians have studied them and recorded items of interest for their research — e.g. John Harvey, Christopher Wilson and presumably W. R. Lethaby: Lethaby (1930), 1098, urges the 'adequate publication of the ancient fragments stored in the church'. Profile drawings of many of the Gothic fragments are available in the Warwick Mouldings Archive, ℅ Dr R. K. Morris, History of Art, University of Warwick, Coventry CV4 7AL.

73. Hollar's views of the other high vaults in the cathedral (as well as the vaults of the aisles and crypt of the New Work) show simple quadripartite rib vaults only.

74. I.e. the Lady Chapel at Exeter Cathedral, the earliest example of a star vault with additional tiercerons. The vaults of the Lady Chapel, with the conventional star vaults of the flanking chapels and of the Bishop's Palace chapel at Wells, are the first examples of the appearance of the tierceron star vault in the West (c. 1290): see Morris (1984), 200–2. Exeter appears to have been influenced in a number of its features, not just the vaults, by the style of the New Work: see Lethaby (1930), 1090, and Morris (1972), i, 48.

75. Designers were obviously contemplating the application of lierne ribs to vaults in the closing years of the 13th century — see most recently Wilson et al. (1986), 82–3, passim; but whether any examples were actually executed before the second decade of the 14th century remains open to question. On the basis of the style of the bosses, the undercroft vault of St Stephen's Chapel, Westminster Palace, may not have been executed until c. 1320, and the choir vault of Pershore Abbey, Worcestershire, not until c. 1310; whilst the more developed example in the main vault of St Augustine's, Bristol (now the Cathedral) is unlikely on stylistic grounds to pre-date c. 1320.

76. In contrast to the Westminster nave vault, the other major tierceron vault of the period, in the Angle Choir at Lincoln, moves away from the symmetrical star vault pattern by omitting the lateral tiercerons in each bay, and is thus less likely to be directly influential on the St Paul's design.

77. The stylistic connections between the Early English works at Lincoln and Beverley Minster are well known, e.g. B/E Yorkshire: York and the East Riding (1972), 172–3; even though the tierceron vault pioneered at Lincoln was not actually followed at Beverley.

78. Wilson et al. (1986), 66.

79. Ibid., 29.

80. Examples earlier than, or contemporary with, the New Work include Worcester (east arm), Beverley Minster (east arm), Much Wenlock, York Minster (transepts), Netley, Lincoln (nave and Angel Choir), Hereford (north transept), Tintern: later 13th-century examples include Chester (east arm), Ripon (east arm), Guisborough and Exeter. Less common variations are to spring the shaft from a corbel at the top of the arcade spandrel, just below the base-line of the triforium, e.g. Ely (Northwold's work), Rievaulx, St Albans (presbytery); or from the triforium spandrel, e.g. Salisbury.

81. Examples occur in earlier Gothic elevations of the late 12th and early 13th century, e.g. Worcester, nave west bays (c. 1175 sqq.); Southwark, chancel, c. 1212 sqq.

82. For French influence at York, see Harvey (1977), ch. IV; and Coldstream (1980), 92–4.

83. In the west bays of the old work, Hollar shows an annulet on each shaft at triforium level (Pl. XIIB), a feature omitted by Wren. I would not accept that Wren is necessarily more accurate than Hollar in this matter, and it may be that this feature relates to an earlier remodelling of this part of the fabric; see also n. 11.

84. Early examples in this period are Hereford (north transept), Lichfield (nave), St Albans (presbytery, upper levels); then Chester St Werburgh (presbytery), York Minster (nave), Guisborough and Ripon (east arm). Interestingly, at Westminster Abbey, the stringcourse at the base of the triforium interrupts the vault shafts in the presbytery and transept; and in the east bays of the nave, both triforium and clerestory stringcourses run across the shafts.

85. It cannot be certain that the bases were used in all the bays of the New Work, because Hollar has left no close-up view of bays 5–8, with which to compare Wren's drawing of bays 7 and 8. Another detail which Hollar shows as differing between the eastern and western bays is the form of the vault respond, which consists of three shafts in the New Work (Pl. XIII) — the norm for England in the 13th century; but only a single shaft in the old work (Fig. 6, Pl. XIIB), which is closer in visual effect to the nave elevation of York Minster, though in fact the latter is triple-shafted, with the main shaft much larger than the lateral ones.

86. See n. 85.

87. Wren Drawings, 7, implies this intention; whereas the exterior elevation, 6, suggests an alternative scheme in which all the Gothic features of the eastern arm would be suppressed.

88. Westminster uses the four-shafted *cantonné* pier form (changed to eight shafts in the nave), and the vault shaft springs from above the capital of the appropriate pier shaft. The vault shaft is thus set slightly forward of the vertical plane of the pier shaft, an awkward detail which may also have been present in the New Work at St Paul's.

89. Whereas bases on vault shafts springing from corbels are common, e.g. Ely (Northwold's work), Lincoln (nave, and Angel Choir except east crossing), York (transept), St Albans (nave west bays, and east end).

90. For example, the south-west pier of the east crossing, which still provides some indication of what the crossing piers of St Hugh's period were like. I am grateful to David Stocker for advice about this point, and about the date of the fabric in the piers of the east crossing in general.

91. This elevation at Lincoln also employs piers with sixteen shafts, a feature also taken up in the New Work at St Paul's: see further p. 82.

92. Other major French examples are St Denis (chevet only, *c.* 1230) and, further west, Tours Cathedral (east end, after 1233); in all these examples, bases are applied to the lateral shafts of the vault respond, but not to the main shaft. Examples in the lesser churches include Brie-Comte-Robert (1230s) and Cambronne (ded. 1239), the latter considered by Bony (1979), 5, to be a type of Parisian elevation influential on the north transept at Hereford Cathedral, its main feature being a prominent triforium — as at Meaux and St Paul's.

93. See Bony (1983), pl. 371. Earlier examples in eastern France include Auxerre Cathedral (east end, 1215–33), the stylish church of Notre-Dame at Dijon (nave, 1228–40), and Semur-en-Auxois (choir, *c.* 1225–35): all in Burgundy. Also, the nave of St Bénigne, Dijon (*c.* 1290), is unusual for its date in having the vault shafts springing directly above the pier capital, though there are no bases on the shafts. This shows how late these ideas were still in play in eastern France. With regard to St Paul's, it is just possible that the inclusion of this feature (with bases) in the New Work might be connected with the presence in England in the 1270s of Savoyard craftsmen, engaged primarily on the Edwardian castles in Wales (1277 sqq.), and whom Jansen (1979), 228, has argued were influential on the design of St Werburgh's, Chester (*c.* 1278). A date in the 1270s is perfectly possible for the arcade stage in the development of the New Work. Moreover, John Harvey has hinted that a potential contact between the foreign craftsmen engaged on the Welsh castles, and masons working in the London area, would be the royal works undertaken at the Tower of London immediately after Edward I returned from crusade in 1274: Harvey (1984), 267–8 ('Master James of St George'). The master in control of works at the Tower in this period was Master Robert of Beverley, who may also have played a major role in the design of the New Work, as will be discussed later in this paper.

94. E.g. the Savoyard, Pierre d'Aigueblanche (Aquablanca), Bishop of Hereford and the initiator of the smart Rayonnant-style work in the north transept of the cathedral.

95. Attention to French precedents for the New Work has focused mainly on the tracery, whereas it has generally been assumed that the form of the elevation is entirely of English derivation.

96. See further Morris (1979), 26 and n. 251. For illustrations of relevant details in these buildings, see e.g. Branner (1965), pls 65, 66.

97. Mainly restricted to piers between the feretory and the ambulatory, especially in the east, south-east and north-east bays of the ambulatory. These are used on *cantonné* piers (rather than the compound piers of St Paul's), and therefore the effect is closest to the nave at Amiens (1220 sqq.), where polygonal plinths were first used in combination with Chartrain arcades.

98. Chapter House examples illustrated in, e.g. Bony (1979), pl. 90.

99. The general accuracy of Hollar's observation of bases is suggested by the way he differentiates between the pier bases of the New Work and the bases of the subsidiary pier in the wide bay (no. 8), inserted either when the eastern arm was being fitted out or perhaps as a structural precaution: in either case, presumably later than the New Work. The bases of the latter are shown with polygonal plinths between the base and sub-base (Pl. XVA bottom left), a treatment appearing only from the late 13th century in England. In contrast, the plinth in this position in the main bases of the New Work is shown as circular in plan (e.g. Pl. XIVA).

100. See Morris (1979), 26.

101. The Wren drawing (Pl. XVI) has only eight large shafts in the piers of bay 8, the only piers shown in their entirety. This may be because only the main shafts have been included in the drawing, or it may have been the actual situation in the link bay 8: certainly Hollar shows some eight-shafted piers in the bays west of bay 8 (Pl. XIIB).

102. E.g. Lincoln, York transept, Westminster Abbey.

103. An early example of this tendency may be seen in the east bays of the nave of Westminster Abbey (late 1250s–69), where the pier design changes to eight-shafted, of which the four axial shafts are attached; whereas the *cantonné* pier employed in the eastern parts of the Abbey uses detached shafts only. Also, at

Lincoln, the piers of the Angel Choir (1256 sqq.) make more prominent use of attached shafts than had the piers of the nave.

104. Lethaby (1930), 194, fig. 3.

105. Cook (1955), 35, fig. IV/3: in this drawing, his plan of the plinth is also completely at variance with that shown by Hollar. In addition, Cook's figure IV/2 shows eight detached shafts for the piers in the four western bays (9–12), which is also unlikely unless these piers were fashioned in the period 1221–40, the date assigned by Dugdale to these bays: see further p. 75.

106. Lethaby (1930), 194, col. 3.

107. Even in such a fortunate eventuality, the very nature of a detached shaft would mean that it would be hard to prove its provenance unless the socle for such a shaft was found on a surviving capital or base from a pier.

108. The most likely place where such evidence might appear is amongst the fragments on the shelving in the south triforium of the present cathedral. Several cursory inspections have failed to reveal any relevant pieces, but obviously a thorough survey is need of this collection.

109. Lethaby (1930), 194, col. 3; and Cook (1955), 35–6. Lethaby gives his reason for Purbeck as follows: 'judged from the amount of Purbeck marble in the existing part of the old Chapter House [1332 sqq.], it must have been liberally used in the church . . .'.

110. All three stones are on the shelving in the south triforium of the present cathedral (April 1984). Profile drawings of two of the stones, OSP1003 and OSP1024, are in the University of Warwick Mouldings Archive, and I have checked Lethaby's drawing of the third against the surviving stone: Lethaby (1930), 235, fig. 8. According to a note on one of the stones (Pl. XVIIIA, Warwick Archive drawing OSP1003), it was found reused in a pier of the crypt of Wren's cathedral during maintenance work in either 1931 or 1937 (the last digit is abraded); though this gives no clue as to its location in the medieval cathedral.

111. Lethaby (1930), 235, fig. 8.

112. Illustrated in RCHM *London*, I, 95, 'Eastern Arm and Transepts' — arch-mould and transverse ribs; 'Nave 1st to 5th Bays' — arch-mould and vaulting ribs. Note that in these examples the lateral 'fillets' of the roll-and-triple-fillet mouldings are bead mouldings or small-scale beak mouldings instead.

113. Apart from St Etheldreda, other examples of this idea are found at Rochester Cathedral, in the north transept dado arches of the west wall; at Chichester Cathedral, in some of the chapels off the nave north aisle, especially the diagonal ribs (beads used instead of lateral fillets, as at Westminster Abbey, see n. 112 above); at St Stephen's Chapel, Westminster Palace (1292 sqq.), in the main rib profile of the undercroft vault (with some differences of minor detail).

114. For the date, see Bony (1979), 12 and 74, n. 10.

115. For example, the grouped bases of the window rere-arches employ prominent octagonal plinths; and the window mullions and tracery relate to the New Work (see further below, pp. 86, 88).

116. Examples in the chapter house and its vestibule are illustrated in the *AASB* 1st ser. 9 (1875–6), drawing by Stevenson, February 1876. As these drawings show, the scroll is frequently inverted at Lincoln, in comparison to the better known use of the moulding in the Decorated period. The scroll does not continue as a feature of Lincoln in the Angel Choir.

117. E.g. Rievaulx Abbey, choir, illustrated in Sharpe (1848), pls 7, 16, 17, 28; and at York Minster, south transept, triforium arch (personal communication from Jane Waddington).

118. The profile of the main rib from Exeter is illustrated in Morris (1979), fig. 15, D; see also ibid., 20, for a brief account of the appearance of the scroll moulding used in capitals, which seems to have taken place at a slightly later date than its early use in arches.

119. Lethaby (1930), 234, fig. 6: my drawings differ slightly from his in the relative proportions of the features.

120. Morris (1979), 1–4.

121. One stone of each profile survives, in the triforium of the present cathedral, with the other stones (Pl. XVIIIB, C). The drawing reference numbers in the Warwick Mouldings Archive are OSP1006 (minor profile) and OSP1007 (major profile).

122. For the mullion profile, see *AASB*, 1st ser. 8 (1874–5) pl. 25, drawing of the west window by Lohr, May 1875; I am grateful to Christopher Wilson for a copy of this drawing.

123. For the dating of the chapter house, see most recently Morris (1984), 197–203. Other features which relate to St Paul's are the use of grouped polygonal plinths on the bases (e.g. the centre pier of the chapter house) and the window tracery; see further Morris (1972), I, 46–8.

124. At least two pieces of this type of mullion survive amongst the fragments in the south triforium of the present cathedral: their drawing reference in the Warwick Mouldings Archive is OSP1002, and the profile was also illustrated, not quite accurately, in Lethaby (1930), 234, fig. 6 (left).

125. See also Morris (1978), 25, where I tentatively ascribed it to the later chapter house/cloister works, an association which is now made less likely by the discovery of this link with earlier work at Wells.

126. For the reconstruction drawing, see Lethaby (1930), 234, fig. 5.

127. In Fig. 5, I have accepted Lethaby's reconstruction of the rose window; Lethaby (1930), 234, fig. 7.

128. There is no clue as to the original location of the other mullion profile (Fig. 4f), because the two surviving pieces are simply straight lengths of mullion. We have no direct evidence for the form of the mullion in the aisle windows, but I would doubt if these would be the source because this mullion profile looks slightly later in design than the one which has been shown to have been employed in the clerestory. It is conceivable that it comes from an isolated window in the eastern arm, of a different design to the others and perhaps executed later; for example, Hollar shows two variant tracery designs in the north aisle, bays 1 and 8 (Pl. XIB). There was also work under way in the east aisles of the transept about this time, judging from the style of the tracery (Pl. XIB), but this is beyond the scope of this paper.

129. It has been estimated that the east window of the New Work was about 35ft wide and over 60ft high (10.7 by 18.3m): Lethaby (1930), 234.

130. I.e. in the bays of standard width in the eastern arm, one design was employed for all the aisle windows and another probably throughout the clerestory.

131. By this I mean the windows in every bay except the wider bays 1 and 8, judging from the north elevation (Pl. XIB).

132. For the French development of the triplet pattern, see Branner (1965), chs IV, V.

133. E.g. St Sulpice-de-Favières (aisle, east window), St Urbain at Troyes (apse), Clermont-Ferrand Cathedral (chevet): all illustrated in Branner (1965), pls 90, 117 and 110 respectively.

134. Examples which may belong to the 1270s are found at St Albans, retrochoir (south aisle, east window) and at Hereford Cathedral, north transept (window in north gable, lighting the roof-space), but neither is well dated. The design of the latter closely recalls the hesitant introduction of the impaled figure in the aisle east windows at St Paul's.

135. E.g. works in the 1280s and the 1290s — St Etheldreda, Holborn; the Eleanor Crosses; Dover, Maison Dieu; Oxford, Merton College Chapel; York Minster, chapter house and vestibule; Ripon Minster, east window; Bridlington Priory, nave, south side; Howden, west window; Wells, chapter house and Bishop Burnell's hall; Exeter Cathedral, Lady Chapel.

136. For illustrations of all the windows at St Etheldreda, see Bony (1979), pls 63, 64, 66, 67.

137. Hollar's rather distant view from the north (Pl. XIB) implies that the pattern of the clerestory tracery is the same as that for the standard windows of the aisles, but here Wren's closer view must be preferred (Pl. XVI), which shows that in bays 7 and 9 the three oculi were filled with trefoils in curved triangles (shown most clearly in the single larger oculus in bay 8). The assumption is that this pattern was also used in bays 1–6 of the clerestory of the New Work.

138. For the development of the trefoil motif in France and England in the 13th century, see Morris (1974), 30–1; and Bony (1979), 10–11.

139. Inside the north transept, the 'propeller' pattern executed in blind tracery over the door, and in the south transept, at the top of the blind tracery added internally to the east and west walls of the south bay: see Branner (1965), pls 95, 114.

140. E.g. York Minster, vestibule to chapter house, c. 1290 (but not the chapter house); Ripon Minster, east window, after 1286; Lincoln, cloister, c. 1296; Exeter Cathedral, Lady Chapel, c. 1290; Oxford, Merton College Chapel, 1289–94; Howden, west front, aisles. The design used in the clerestory of the nave at Lichfield must certainly be earlier (?1270s), but its use of one large curved triangle reflects the influence of Westminster Abbey. Also, the disposition of its oculi seems more related to the earlier 'triplet' design, and the tracery details lack the metallic sharpness of the trefoils and triangles at St Paul's.

141. An analysis of the context of the larger pointed trefoil design used in the openwork tracery of the triforium (Pl. XIII) suggests the same conclusion: see further Morris (1974), 30 sqq.

142. Lethaby (1930), 234, fig. 7.

143. See Bony (1979), 23 and pl. 56.

144. Described in Bony (1979), 22 sqq., to which one should add the tomb of Archbishop Peckham (d. 1292) in Canterbury Cathedral: Bony avoids mention of the rose window at St Paul's.

145. Other early but more subtle examples are the windows of the undercroft of St Stephen's Chapel, Westminster Palace (after 1292), and of the chapter house at Wells (1290s–1306).

146. Chaucer's term for shoe patterns based on the window, and cited in Lethaby (1930), 234.

147. Lethaby (1930), 234. The Minchinhampton window is illustrated in Bond (1906), 286–7; an identical rose, but not used over a row of lights, is found in the east windows of the north transept at Cheltenham parish church, Gloucestershire — see Morris (1972), I, 163–6.

148. Other surviving roses in the Decorated period include the curvilinear 'Bishop's Eye' in the south transept at Lincoln, and gable windows in the great halls of the Bishop's Palace at St David's and of the Bishop of Winchester's Palace at Southwark, the latter a rectilinear reworking of the curved-triangle motif of St Paul's — illustrated in Schofield (1984), fig. 74. Christopher Wilson has suggested that the composition with foiled figures derives from the centrepiece in the head of the west window at St Etheldreda's, Holborn, a work which we have seen is closely connected with the New Work at St Paul's.

149. The additional uprights are shown only in Hollar's east view (Pl. XIA), but are not clearly visible in his north view (Pl. XIB), so some doubt must remain about the reliability of this observation. However, the feature is so prominent in the east view that its authenticity is accepted here; see also n. 150.

150. Any scepticism about Hollar's accuracy in depicting the potentially dangerous combination of a buttress support over a window arch is confounded by the fact that both the east wall and its buttresses were very substantial. Penrose's excavation revealed that the north buttress of the east wall was 9 ft (2.9 m) thick (excluding foundations), and he commented on 'its great thickness and that it corresponded with the large angle buttress shown by Hollar' (Pl. XIA): Penrose (1883), 389. Also Hollar's interior view shows that there was a deep relieving arch around and over the great east window (Pl. XIII), which would imply the same treatment for the east windows of the aisles.

151. As evidence has been cited above to suggest that work on the upper parts of the eastern arm continued into the early 14th century, it is conceivable that the design of the shrine was known when the details of the architectural superstructure were being finalised. Another complication in the evidence is that Hollar's depiction of the shrine (Pl. XVB) was based on an old drawing, as the shrine itself had gone at the Reformation: see Dugdale (1716), 24. For dates relating to the shrine, see n. 23.

152. Lethaby (1930), 235, fig. 9. The surviving fragment in the triforium of the present cathedral indicates that each quatrefoil would have been about 2 ft (61 cm) across. Admittedly, the detail of a vertical division between the quatrefoils is not indicated in Hollar's views (Pls XIA, B), though it is paralleled in such contemporary work as the Coronation chair in Westminster Abbey (1299–1300): Hastings (1955), pl. 51.

153. See Bony (1979), 20–2; Harvey (1961), 161–2.

154. For the chronology of the nave, see Harvey (1977), ch. IV. The elaborate display of flying buttresses at York Minster was also followed at Beverley Minster, nave aisles (c. 1311–34): Coldstream (1980), 102 sqq. An early example of the pierced quatrefoil parapet on a large scale is the west front of Newstead Abbey, Nottinghamshire, probably dating from c. 1290–5; the aisle parapets at St Paul's would probably have been erected by this date.

155. For Hereford, see Morris (1985), 100: the four prominent pinnacles are a modern addition to the original pairs of angle buttresses. For Ely Lady Chapel, see Coldstream (1979), 28 sqq.; and Coldstream (1985), 5 sqq. For a review of the dating of Wells, see Morris (1984), 194, 196, 203 sqq.; old views suggest that the pinnacles were never completed. The execution dates for the relevant features at Wells and Ely are probably c. 1330 and c. 1340 respectively.

156. See Harvey (1984), 259 ('Rothinge, Richard') and 327; and Lethaby (1930), 235. Unfortunately nothing else is known about the career of John of Weldon, except that presumably he came from the quarry area of Weldon (Northamptonshire).

157. Harvey (1984), 45–6. I agree with Harvey about the stylistic similarities between the two works, but not that the east bays of the New Work (the Lady Chapel) belong entirely to the years 1307–12; they were begun about 1270, as argued in this paper.

158. Ibid., 45.

159. For their biographies, see ibid., 77 ('Crundale, Richard') and 225 ('Pabenham, Simon II').

160. For this Master Simon, see ibid., 224–5 ('Pabenham, Simon de I') and 274 ('Simon the Mason I').

161. Ibid., 225.

162. Ibid., 23–5.

163. Even if the first springer stones for the vault were laid in the time when John of Gloucester was still officially in charge, as Christopher Wilson has argued — Wilson et al. (1986), 66.

164. Harvey (1984), 23–4.

165. See further n. 93.

166. Harvey (1984), 23–4.

Restorations of the Temple Church, London

By C. M. L. Gardam

On the night of 10 May 1941, incendiary bombs hit the roofs of the Temple Church. The water mains had already been hit so it was impossible to control the ensuing fire. The roof and wooden vault of the nave collapsed in flames. Burning timbers and molten lead fell into the interior, and the whole church was gutted.[1]

All the piers and decorative details of Purbeck marble were severely 'fractured and scaled'. The rest of the stonework was badly calcined, particularly in the lower half of the church. However, the vault of the circular nave aisle and choir vaults remained intact. The porch, west doorway and wheel window above were relatively untouched. So were the pentitential cell and north stair turret placed at the junction of the choir and the nave.[2]

The church was shored up and made waterproof and in 1947 the architect, Walter Godfrey, was appointed to superintend its reconstruction.[3] He welcomed the opportunity to restore the church, as far as it was possible, to its original 12th- and 13th-century appearance; for prior to the air raid of 1941 the whole church had undergone many repairs, alterations and restorations over the centuries. 'Nothing', he wrote, 'could have been more thorough than the way in which every ancient surface was repaired away or renewed so that in the end the result was a complete modern simulacrum of this superb monument.' However, he believed that 'behind the restorer's veneer there is sufficient of the old fabric remaining to make one feel there is still a life to be prolonged and much that is significant to be preserved'.[4]

Godfrey based his restoration on a series of drawings made by Frederick Nash in 1818 (Pls XIX, XXA, B),[5] before the three principal restorations of the 19th century, in 1826–7,[6] 1840–2[7] and 1861–2.[8] However the evidence of these drawings is limited. First, with the exception of the west doorway, Nash did not illustrate the exterior, probably because much of it was 'shut out from view by houses for occupations most mean and despicable'.[9] Secondly, much of the interior, particularly of the choir, was clad in timber wainscoting[10] and elaborate monuments,[11] and thus his depiction of plinths, pier bases, etc. is suspect. And thirdly, the church had already undergone fourteen recorded repairs and alterations before 1818, and probably many more of which there is no record.[12]

This paper uses the evidence of engravings, watercolours, and written accounts from the 17th century onwards, to establish as precisely as possible which features at the Temple Church owe their appearance to 12th- and 13th-century architects, and which must be considered the products of later architectural fashions and re-interpretations.

THE CHURCH EXTERIOR

The basic problem here is that for centuries the church was surrounded by shops, houses and tenements built up against it, which prevented artists from recording much of its exterior (Pls XXD, XXIB).[13]

After a great deal of discussion the accretions were removed from the south side of the nave in 1826;[14] from the south and north sides of the choir in 1810, c. 1819 and 1840–1;[15] and finally, the Middle Temple Benchers ordered their removal from the north side of the nave, from around the belltower and the porch in 1861–2.[16]

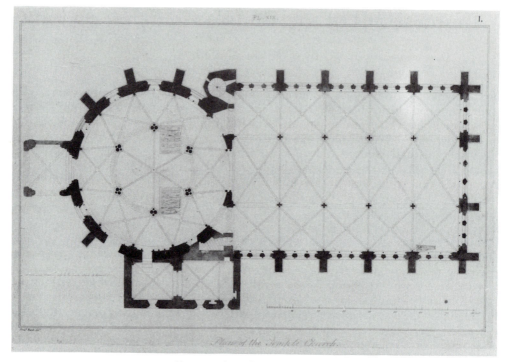

FIG. 1   Plan of Temple Church

The West Porch

The west porch has suffered severely over the centuries. In the second half of the 17th century it was crowned by a dome (Pl. XXc),[17] its responds encased in ashlar[18] and its vault heavily plastered.[19] The north opening was blocked,[20] and early in the 18th century a three-storey set of chambers was built on top of it (Pl. XXIb). A shop was situated inside the porch in 1695[21] and, despite several orders from the Inner and Middle Temples to remove it,[22] it was not finally demolished until 1840.[23]

In 1841, the Benchers decided that 'the porch should be restored as nearly as possible to its original state'.[24] By 1842 *The Gentleman's Magazine* was able to announce that 'the entrance porch is for the most part new'.[25] However, it was not until 1862 that St Aubyn removed the three-storey chambers from on top of it, unblocked the north opening and restored the north archway (Pls XXIA, c).[26] But in 1912, Caroe described the porch as having 'been covered with paint and putty and dirt so as to present to the eye little more than a black mass of decayed stone'.[27] As a result the porch was, once again, heavily restored. Thus the porch as it stands today (with the exception of two capitals) is the product of the 19th and 20th centuries, despite its relative escape from the effects of the Blitz. How accurately did the architects concerned replace the 12th-century stone?

Two surviving 12th-century capitals were uncovered by St Aubyn when he unblocked the north archway in 1862. They are the northernmost capitals of, respectively, the north-east (Pl. XXIVA), and north-west (Pl. XXIVB) responds. They were painted in their unrestored condition by Archer (Pl. XXIVc), but both have received a certain amount of 19th-century patching. St Aubyn retained both capitals and repeated their design when reconstructing the inner capitals supporting the soffit arch. But there is no evidence that any other porch capitals survived beneath the 17th-century casing, which was removed by Smirke and Burton in 1841–2. Thus, although the basic design of the responds, with clustered shafts, moulded bases and ornate capitals can be presumed to be in character with the original 12th-century design,[28] the exuberant detail cannot, and has to be accepted as 19th century.

In 1841–2 the abaci of the respond capitals were each designed with a flat, rectangular band immediately above the capital with a broad cavetto moulding above, a quirk, and a narrow, flat rectangular band above that. However, in 1862, St Aubyn uncovered two fragmentary 12th-century abaci above the surviving capitals of the north archway. The abacus of the north-western respond capital survived in a damaged condition and was illustrated by Archer when it was first revealed (Pl. XXIVc). It can still be seen today, with a quirk immediately above the waterleaf capital; a flat, rectangular band above that, with a delicate roll above and a deep cavetto moulding rising to the upper, flat rectangular band. St Aubyn restored all three of the other newly exposed respond abaci of the north archway to this design. However, Archer's watercolour of the newly exposed capital and abacus of the outer north-east respond, shows that the design of the 12th-century abacus in this position was much more ornate, with ribbed leaf and beaded flowerhead, similar to those of the richly foliated abaci on the west door as illustrated by Nash in 1818, before it was restored. However, St Aubyn did not attempt to reconstruct such an abacus and replaced it with one based on the design of the other more complete 12th-century abacus on the north-west respond.

The richly moulded north, west and south archways have also been heavily restored. According to St Aubyn in 1862: 'The north arch of the porch, the only one of the three not tampered with, was in a very shattered and almost falling condition, but with great care we were able to preserve it.'[29] Archer's watercolour reveals the careful shoring up with wood (Pl. XXIc). However, despite the various restorations and St Aubyn's claim of 'past tampering', the archways retain their original design according to pre-restoration drawings.

The most noticeable feature of the soffit mouldings of these archways is the use of the notched roll, and this relatively unusual feature helps to establish the chronological relationship between porch and nave. When St Aubyn lowered the ground level of the porch during his restoration work of 1862, he took the opportunity to excavate beneath it.[30] There he discovered the foundations of two western buttresses of the nave and concluded that the porch was not an integral part of the round nave, but was added some years later. George Gilbert Scott also witnessed these excavations but came to a slightly different conclusion: 'By the manner in which the walls are bonded to the church,' he wrote in June 1862, 'and by the exact similarity of its details to those of the church itself . . . it was an improvement effected by the original Architect while the erection was actually in hand.'[31] Archer's watercolour of the restoration of the porch reveals a clear masonry break between the porch and nave (Pl. XXIa). This tallies with St Aubyn's interpretation. However, the notched rolls used in the porch can also be found in some of the aisle vaults of the nave. Although such rolls are found in other buildings well into the 13th century, it seems reasonable to accept that the porch was built soon after the completion of the nave.

Before the restoration of 1840–2, the rib vault of the porch 'was covered in a thick coat of plaster, so that the bold effect of the ribs was lost'.[32] Records of that restoration do not make it clear whether the vault and ribs were completely rebuilt, partly so, or only cleaned. They certainly had to be cleaned in 1912.[33] Examination of the ribs suggests that they were partly replaced at some time. However, the degree of deterioration of the stone has been so great during this century that such a suggestion can only be tentative. The present design is closely comparable to the plaster-covered rib vaults depicted before c. 1840, and thus probably close to the original 12th-century design.

The massive buttresses to the west of the porch were built by St Aubyn in 1862 and further extended in 1875.[34] St Aubyn discovered the fragmentary plinths of two 12th-century buttresses and erected his buttresses in the same positions. However, the height and positioning of the set-offs is entirely 19th century.

With the removal of the chambers in 1862, part of the gabled parapet running above the north arch was revealed in a fragmentary condition (Pl. XXIA). St Aubyn rebuilt such gables on all three sides of the porch, but his justification for doing so is questionable, since the porch seems in the 12th century to have been one bay of a cloister that ran to the south of the church.[35]

The West Doorway

The degree of restoration undergone by the west doorway is a problematical and controversial issue.[36] The doorway is in an appalling state of deterioration and the various contemporary reports concerning the restoration works of the 19th and early 20th centuries are ambiguous, and it is unknown if all their recommendations were carried out.

For several hundred years before November 1840 the west doorway had been repaired piecemeal with patchings of plaster covered over with paint.[37] However, at that date, the Benchers of the Inner Temple decreed that 'the ancient doorway and porch be repaired and restored to its original state'.[38] A report to the Benchers of both the Inner and Middle Temples by Sydney Smirke and Decimus Burton, in August 1842, made it clear that they considered that the doorway should be completely restored with new stone: 'We find with regret that the defective state of the carved work was but imperfectly known to us, and on removing the plaster and colouring that filled up the enriched archivolts which are surprisingly perforated and sunk, we find that these carved stones are so perished as to be for the most part incapable of recurring reparations and that they ought to be entirely new — we find also that on close examination of the six shafts of the door jambs (originally of polished Purbeck marble) stone has since been substituted in some cases, whilst in others new Purbeck marble shafts have been supplied having a Roman entasis altogether unsuited to the style of the original work'. On reading this report, the Benchers allocated £400 to carry out these recommendations.[39] However, there are no detailed written accounts of the actual work done.

Only fourteen years later, Smirke was called on to advise on its continuing deterioration.[40] And by 1912 it was crumbling away so fast that the Surveyors of the Inner and Middle Temples wrote: 'we fear that it will be requisite to re-instate the whole of the grouped, moulded and carved columns and arches'. They estimated such work would cost £600.[41] The exact character of the work they carried out is not recorded; however photographs of the doorway taken by the Royal Commission in 1929 reveal it in almost pristine condition[42] which suggests that the restoration of 1912 was considerable.

The design of the capitals of the plain shafts in the 1929 photographs is very different from that depicted by Nash in 1818. This difference was noted by T. H. Baylis in 1893,[43] and thus the present designs must date from the 1842 restoration rather than that in 1912. After examining the doorway closely in 1975, Professor Zarnecki noticed that 'the capitals and busts on either side of the doorway are made of only two blocks of stone'.[44] As a result the capitals and busts must almost certainly date from the same period and be products of Smirke and Burton's restoration. There is the possibility that the capitals were just re-cut rather than completely replaced in 1842. Smirke described that restoration in 1856 as 'restoring to its original sharpness the old masonry of the doorway'.[45] However, despite Smirke's claim that he re-cut the old masonry, Paul Williamson has shown that considerable sections of stone in the voussoirs over the doorway were completely replaced at that date;[46] thus the doubt about whether the busts and capitals were re-cut or replaced must remain. All that can be asserted with any confidence is that the general design of foliate capitals alternating with the unusual small busts, is 12th century.

Some of the original voussoirs are in the Victoria and Albert Museum.[47] They are entirely compatible with the voussoirs shown in Nash's drawings. By comparing the V. & A. fragments with Nash's drawings, and with the present doorway, Paul Williamson has recently shown that the innermost order of portal voussoirs have been completely replaced.[48]

When one compares the foliate voussoir from the V. & A. with the present outer order of the archway, it is clear that this order was also entirely replaced in 1842. Nash's drawing of the voussoirs concerned is compatible with the V. & A. fragment (Pl. XXA). However, the present voussoirs in that order, more clearly seen with the recent cleaning, are not. The four petalled leaves that curl back and meet point to point are spread much further apart on the doorway today, with a very large beaded fruit in between. Likewise the second and third orders, today, differ in detail from those depicted by Nash. Thus all the voussoirs of the archway are replacements.

Thus, taking into consideration the restorations of both 1842 and 1912, the precise detail of the west doorway must be treated carefully, although the remarkably rich general design can be accepted as 12th century.

The Wheel Window

While restoring the nave interior in 1840, James Savage discovered a fine 12th-century wheel window set over the porch.[49] St Aubyn exposed it on the exterior when he removed the chambers from above the porch in 1862 (Pl. XXIA). As Archer's watercolour of 1862 reveals, the wheel was remarkably intact (Pl. XXVA). A few of the sculptural details of the heart-shaped openings between the spokes were broken off, and these were replaced by St Aubyn. It is this combination of 12th- and 19th-century work which exists today.

Archer's watercolour also revealed that the window was flanked by single vertical bands of stone. These suggest that the window is an insertion, a later embellishment to the original fabric.[50] St Aubyn retained the flanking bands of stone and they can still be seen despite the heavy pointing of the rubble wall.

The Round Nave

Where the south side of the round nave was not masked by other buildings, it was embellished in the Baroque style in c. 1682 and 1695.[51] The rubble walls of the lower parts of the south side and the whole upper drum were encased in ashlar.[52] The second window to the south-west of the porch was reduced to half its size and a 17th-century doorway, complete with open pediment, eared architrave and Doric entablature, inserted underneath (Pl. XXC). The window mouldings at both levels were either encased or replaced by plain, deeply moulded architraves. The lower buttresses were built out with re-entrant curved set-offs and topped with heavy scrolls.

However, part of the south side escaped such embellishment. A three-storey tenement of c. 1700, visible in Malton's watercolour (Pl. XXIB), encased the earliest of the additions to the round nave: a two-storey, early 13th-century building that included a chapel, possibly dedicated to St Anne.[53] It was blown up in 1678 to prevent a fire in the Temple from spreading to the church;[54] and in time its ruins were incorporated into the tenement.

When Robert Smirke supervised the restoration of the nave in 1826, he noticed, on removing the tenement, that beneath the ruined chapel's north wall 'the original carved and moulded work' of the 12th-century fabric had 'retained all the freshness of recent execution'.[55] This can also be seen in Buckler's watercolour of 1826 (Pl. XXIIA). As a result of this survival, Smirke claimed he was able to restore the south side of the nave's circular aisle to its original design.[56] However, instead of retaining, or copying the coursed rubble walling of the 12th-century design, he continued the work of the 17th-century architects and either replaced, or encased it with fine quality Bath free-stone ashlar.[57] When St Aubyn restored the north side of the aisle in 1862 he left the rubble wall exposed (Pl. XXIA). Today, despite the thick 20th-century pointing, the north side of the aisle walling is basically 12th century, whilst the south side is 19th century.

The string course running eleven feet above the ground round the north and south sides of the circular aisle cannot be seen in either Buckler's or Malton's watercolours of the south side of the nave (Pl. XXIA). However, it is visible in a fragmentary condition in several of Archer's watercolours of the north side (Pl. XXIc). Therefore, it may be presumed that the presence of a string course in this position does date from the 12th century, and that it was removed from the south side during the 17th-century embellishments.

The buttresses of the circular aisle have been altered over the years. After restoring the south side in 1826–7, Robert Smirke insisted that 'the buttresses were in every part discovered to have had the form and projection which I have given them'.[58] He removed the 17th-century embellishments and rebuilt the buttresses in two stages, 5 ft 5 in. deep at the base. However, Billings, in 1838, dismissed them as being totally 'of modern construction'.[59] The original buttresses were probably of slighter proportions. John Carter described them in 1808 (probably basing his view on those on the north side). He wrote: 'Between the windows, plain pilasters, which pilasters have had worked against them in later times (for support) buttresses'.[60] Suggestions of a more pilaster-like buttress, with two stages of a larger buttress built up against it, can be seen in one of Archer's watercolours of a damaged buttress, made during St Aubyn's restoration of 1862 (Pl. XXIc). St Aubyn claimed that he restored the buttresses on the north side back to their 12th-century profiles after carefully examining them stone by stone.[61] However, he retained the irregular design of the north-westernmost buttress, as illustrated by Archer (Pl. XXIA). Thus it appears that he preserved the buttresses on the north side as he found them, rather than returning them to their original 12th-century more uniform pilaster design.

Likewise the slender clerestory buttresses appear to have been given greater emphasis at some period before the late 17th century. Today they have the two slight set-offs that can be seen in the earliest known, detailed engraving, depicting the exterior in c. 1682 (Pl. XXc), and all subsequent illustrations. However, Carter described them in 1808: 'some alterations have been made, yet with caution, but at what period it is difficult to determine; such as adding a small buttress to the pilasters'.[62] Although Carter's architectural judgement must be viewed with caution,[63] he did have the advantage of having much more of the original fabric in front of him than we have today, for his analysis pre-dates the re-casing of the upper drum with ashlar in 1842.[64] It seems possible that the severely simple pilaster buttresses of the circular aisle were echoed by similar, slimmer buttresses in the clerestory.

When Robert Smirke wrote to the Benchers in 1827, he claimed that by using the fragmentary remains preserved under the chapel of St Anne, he had been able to restore the windows of the south side of the circular aisle to their original 12th-century design. He wrote: 'the original jambs and mullions were such as they now appear. Many of the small remains of this ancient stone work which have served to authorize these restored parts, have been left in their original places where they were not too much destroyed and mutilated.'[65] The general design, with the tall, round-headed lancet flanked by single nook shafts with simple scalloped or foliate capitals, is certainly based on 12th-century evidence. Buckler's watercolour shows clearly the simple voussoired head of such a window and the capital and upper part of the right-hand nook shaft, beneath the rubble of the dilapidated chapel (Pl. XXIIA), while Archer shows three such windows on the north side of the circular aisle, just before their restoration in 1862 (Pl. XXIA). They have lost their nook shafts, but several of the capitals are intact, and are still in position today (Pl. XXVB). St Aubyn appears to have retained much more of the original fabric than Robert Smirke, despite the claims of the latter.

The clerestory windows were originally much longer,[66] and probably flanked by nookshafts. They retain their essentially 17th-century appearance with plain, deeply moulded architraves, for none of the restorers of the 19th or 20th centuries attempted to return to the original 12th-century detail.

When he removed the chapel of St Anne in 1826–7, Smirke exposed fragments of the original nave aisle corbel table.[67] This can be seen in Buckler's watercolour (Pl. XXIIA). There was a corbel table of some kind above the rest of the south aisle. Malton's watercolour of 1792 shows it as a classical modillioned cornice; while Emmett's engraving of c. 1682, before the parapet above was built, shows a dentillated band. However, Smirke restored the corbel table on the whole of the south side according to the fragments under the chapel of St Anne.[68] St Aubyn revealed the corbel table on the north side of the circular aisle in 1862. Archer's watercolour shows that it was in a fragmentary condition in the westernmost bay, but almost intact in the two bays to the east (Pl. XXIA). St Aubyn appears to have retained the 12th-century corbelling and it is this combination of 12th- and 19th-century work which exists today (Pl. XXVB).

The broad coped parapet running round the circular aisle seems to be largely due to Robert Smirke. He wrote: 'The height of the parapets with the coping . . . have been the only subject upon which I was obliged to exercise any invention, and in doing so, careful reference has been made to the analagous parts of this building and others of corresponding era in several parts of the country.'[69] Smirke may have been guided by the parapet above the north nave aisle, but this was not 12th century. There was no parapet when Emmett drew the church in 1682. It was probably built shortly thereafter — Archer's 1861–2 watercolour shows that the parapet was of ashlar-encased brick (Pl. XXIA) — when the roof over the triforium was removed so that people could walk round above the circular aisle in the open air, without fear of falling off. Billings makes this fact clear in 1838 when he wrote that the top of the circular aisle had been 'flatted and plastered' outside so that it could be covered in lead; and that the steps leading up from the staircase were very worn, which suggested some other use for the triforium than a mere roof space.[70]

After much discussion St Aubyn was able to remove the parapet from both the north and south sides of the nave in 1862, and substitute it with moulded eaves (Pl. XXVC).[71] The steeply pitched triforium roof which he built was completely destroyed in the Blitz, and Godfrey decided to reinstate the broad parapet and change the angle of the roof to a shallower pitch to obtain greater height in the otherwise cramped triforium.[72] Thus the parapet is totally 20th century, and is based on a 17th-century safety measure. The 12th-century design was probably very similar to that at the late 12th-century Temple Church in Paris,[73] with a corbel table, and steeply pitched triforium roof rising to just below the clerestory windows, as, indeed, they appear in Emmett's 1682 engraving. In short,

H

St Aubyn's solution to this particular problem would have been more satisfactory than the present arrangement.

The battlements running round the top of the upper drum also disappeared in the 19th century, only to reappear under Godfrey's supervision. In Malton's watercolour of 1792 they appear to have been of rendered ashlar with moulded eaves running below and coped above (Pl. XXIB). They are known to have been restored in 1706[74] and can be clearly seen in Emmett's engraving of c. 1682 (Pl. XXc). They could well be based on 12th-century rubble battlements. Since the church was the headquarters of the Knights Templar in England, the battlements would have reflected the military function of the Order. The 12th-century round-naved chapel of St Mary Magdalene in Ludlow Castle has rubble battlements, but of much broader proportions, and clearly, the crenellation of a chapel was thought appropriate in military surroundings in the 12th century.

In the restoration of 1827, the battlements were replaced on the south side by a corbel table (similar to that round the circular aisle); and a low-pitched roof was hidden behind a plain parapet.[75] In 1862, when St Aubyn changed the pitch of the roof, the parapet (and battlements on the north side), were removed leaving only the corbel table (Pl. XXVc).[76]

The pitch of the roof over the central vessel of the nave has undergone several alterations and its original 12th-century appearance is unknown. The Emmett engraving of c. 1682 shows the nave with a dome crowned by a cupola (Pl. XXc), while a rather crude engraving of 1770 of a drawing of 1671 reveals it with a pointed, almost tent-like roof with gabled dormer windows (Pl. XXD). By Malton's watercolour of 1792 (Pl. XXIB), the roof is of such a low pitch that it is no longer visible above the battlements. Robert Smirke retained this low pitch when he replaced the battlements with the parapet, but in 1862 St Aubyn had very different ideas, erecting a very heavy, steep cone covered in lead with four tiny, cusped, gabled and finialled ventilator openings near the apex (Pl. XXVc). He claimed that such a pitch was more in character with 12th-century architecture and believed that the church of the Holy Sepulchre in Jerusalem had originally had such a profile.[77] Godfrey restored the roof to the low pitch of the late 17th century, defending his decision on three points. First, he wrote 'In western countries the "round" seems to have been covered by a roof of shallow pitch hidden behind a parapet (compare Paris, London and others).'[78] Secondly, he wrote that it was impracticable to go to the expense of rebuilding such a cone because the nave had already been provided with a flat, reinforced concrete roof immediately after the air-raid, which was perfectly watertight. Thirdly, he considered that it would 'dwarf the proportions of the building and have the effect of isolating it from the magnificent Quire to the east'.[79]

The Chancel

Like the nave, the chancel also suffered from accretions both inside and out, and from a series of confident alterations, piecemeal repairs and major restorations.[80] Today, not a single visible stone can be dated back to the original 13th-century fabric; every surface and every detail has been replaced. However the chancel is a much less complex and controversial structure than the round nave.

The original rubble of the chancel was gradually encased over the years: the plinth and gables of the east end in 1736;[81] the south side in 1827;[82] and the remainder of the east end and what was left of the north side after the construction of an organ chamber, in 1840–2.[83] The lower sections of the octagonal north-west turret were not re-cased until 1861[84] when the small buildings were removed from around it, although the upper sections were completely rebuilt in 1842.[85]

The three-stage buttresses with ashlar-dressed plinths and angled set-offs were almost entirely rebuilt, on the south side in 1826–7[86] and on the east and north sides in 1840–2.[87] However, a comparison with those in engravings of the south side of 1671 and c.1682 (Pl. XXc, D), and with those depicted by Billings on the east and south sides in 1838,[88] suggests they have retained their original 13th-century proportions and design.

When an organ chamber was added to the north side in the early 1840s, its advantages as a buttress to the structurally suspect north wall were stressed by the architects concerned.[89] The vestry was built in the same style as the chancel, with three stage buttresses, triple lancets, corbel table and parapet. After the Blitz Godfrey replaced it with a much more massive structure with the air of a modern fortification.

Today the chancel has five doorways. One is in the south side and set in a rectangular, ashlar-dressed porch built by Godfrey in 1953.[90] There was no precedent for either a porch or doorway in that position. However, Emmett's pre-restoration engraving of the south side depicts a doorway set beneath the central group of lancets. Its outer shafts are suspiciously Doric, and it is possible that this doorway is imaginary, since it is not mentioned by any of the restorers, or in any of the records of the Inner or Middle Temples.[91]

Two small plain doorways flank the altar in the east end of the chancel and give the Benchers of the Inner and Middle Temples private access to the church. They are not depicted by Nash in 1818 or Billings in 1838, but they do appear in photographs post-dating the 1840–2 restoration,[92] and were probably inserted during it.

Nor do the fourth and fifth doorways have medieval antecedents. Before 1840, a vestry, furnace room and catacombs were situated against the north-east side of the church.[93] However, there is no evidence for a doorway giving access from them to the chancel. When the new organ chamber and vestry were built against the north wall in the early 1840s, a doorway was inserted underneath the organ loft. After the destruction of the 19th-century organ in the Blitz, Godfrey built the new organ chamber and vestry, and in so doing inserted a vestry doorway to the east.

Thus none of the five doorways to the chancel are of medieval origin. It appears that in the 13th century, the only access to the chancel was gained through the round nave.

The five windows on the south side of the chancel are largely the product of Robert Smirke's restoration of 1826–7.[94] He had a major task in reinstating them, for a description of the church in 1808 reveals that the windows had been 'most shamefully despoiled a short time back of their columns and architraves'.[95] William Emmett's pre-restoration engraving of c.1682 reveals that the original windows were basically very similar to Smirke's replacements except that they did not have hood moulds and label stops (Pls XXc, XXIIIb).

The five windows on the north side and the three windows of the east side have, and always did have, the same basic design as those on the south side, the only difference being that the triple lights of the central east window are a little taller and a little broader than the others. They were completely reinstated by Savage, Sydney Smirke and Burton in the 1840–2 restoration,[96] while the details of the east window had to be replaced once again in 1935.[97]

The three west gables were cased in ashlar by Robert Smirke in 1826;[98] while the three east gables, encased in ashlar in 1736, were completely taken down by James Savage, and re-erected by Sydney Smirke and Burton in the early 1840s.[99] The lights into the roofspaces in each gable were first made as small pointed openings in either 1726 or 1736[100] and in the 19th century they were opened up and dressed with nook shafts with moulded capitals and heads, hood moulds and head label stops.[101] In 1736 the gables were all crowned with flaming urns.[102] These were replaced by cross finials, on the west gables in 1826–7, and on the east gables in 1840–2.[103]

A coped parapet runs along the north and south sides of the chancel, and beneath it, a corbel table. Emmett's engraving of c.1682 does not show this corbel table (Pl. XXc). However Robert Smirke insisted that he discovered just such a corbel table in a fragmentary condition on the south-west side of the chancel when he removed the two-storey chapel of St Anne (Pl. XXIIA),[104] and he built a corbel table based on it along the full length of the south side. In the early 1840s a similar corbel table was built on the north side when the parapet on that side was rebuilt.

The parapet on the north side was discovered in 1840 to be built of 'modern' brick encased in ashlar,[105] like the parapet running round the circular aisle of the nave. The parapet that Robert Smirke replaced on the south side dated from 1737 when the Benchers of the Inner Temple paid for a hundred feet of new coping.[106] However the 13th-century building probably had some sort of corbel table and parapet.

Today an octagonal ashlar bell turret crowns the pentitential cell in the north-west corner of the chancel. Its exterior is entirely 19th century (Pl. XXVc), and it survived the Blitz intact. An engraving of 1770 of a drawing of 1671 (Pl. XXD) shows an octagonal wooden structure in this position, towering over the church and crowned with battlements. A very steep flight of steps leads down from the top of the tower to the roof of the round nave. A slightly different turret is depicted by Emmett in c.1682 (Pl. XXc). The lower sections appear to be tile-hung, while above, a slender octagonal wooden turret rises with numerous rectangular slit lights illuminating the staircase inside. A small bridge, supported by a curved brace, gives access from the top of the turret to the domical roof of the round nave. Billings, in 1838, does not show the bell turret although he gives a detailed account of the penitential cell. From this one can presume that the upper wooden structure had been dismantled. However the lower sections were almost certainly always of stone, which had been patched with brick over the years.[107] The upper stages of the present bell turret therefore entirely date from the early 1840s,[108] whilst the lower stage is an 1861 casing of medieval fabric.[109]

THE CHURCH INTERIOR

The interior of the Temple Church has suffered from the changing fashions in both church fittings and restoration over the centuries. In 1682 an organ and wainscot screen, complete with Corinthian pilasters and cherubs, were set up between the choir and nave (Pl. XXIIB), and the upper parts of the north and south arches were blocked and plastered over.[110] At the same date the floors were covered in black and white marble, and the chancel was encased up to the window sills in wainscoting. A large reredos blocked the lower sections of the east window. In 1706 the piers of the round nave were clad in six feet of wainscoting;[111] and by the early 19th century, the walls, piers and sculptural details of both halves of the church were covered in monuments and layers of plaster and paint.[112]

By 1840, the screen and organ were so dilapidated that they had to be taken down. The resulting 'vista' was considered so attractive that it was retained, and the new organ placed in the central bay of the north wall of the choir with a chamber built behind to accommodate it.[113] The black and white marble was also removed and the ground level lowered and covered in encaustic tiles based on those in Westminster Abbey's Chapter House.[114] In the 1950s Godfrey moved those that survived the Blitz into the triforium, and replaced them with plain ashlar.

The architects and Benchers of the 1840s decided to stop patching with plaster and hiding the repairs under paint. Instead they had the original stone and marble cleaned of all such excrescences, which exposed the true dilapidation of their condition.[115] The architects involved in the resulting major restoration, James Savage, Sydney Smirke and Decimus Burton, insisted that their work was based entirely on the original 12th- and 13th-century structure. Godfrey, in turn, based his restoration of the interior on the fabric that they had left behind and on Nash's engravings of 1818.

The Nave

In 1826 Robert Smirke cleaned and restored the lower sections of the nave aisle wall with its blind arcade and marble responds, and blocked the doorway leading from it to the recently demolished two-storey chapel of St Anne. He reported his progress to the Benchers, in detail. On removing the thick coats of plaster from the billeted arches, ornate capitals and grotesque heads set in the spandrels of the wall arcade, he discovered that they were in a very shattered condition.[116] He renewed all the grotesque heads with almost no reference to their original designs.[117] Some of the cast-off heads were used to prevent the workmen's carts from rolling away.[118] According to Nash's pre-restoration drawings, the billeted arches were restored accurately, but the two soffit decorations in each arch, and the ornate spurs on the arcade shaft bases were too small to appear in the pre-1826 drawings and engravings, so it is not known if they are based on 12th-century evidence.

Nash illustrated one bay of the wall arcade before Robert Smirke's restoration (Pl. XXB), and Billings illustrated all the wall arcade capitals after the restoration.[119] None of those by Billings tally with those by Nash. Clearly most of the present arcade capitals owe their appearance to Smirke rather than to the masons of the 12th century. However, in 1838, both Billings and Godwin claimed that a few of the capitals were reused.[120] Certainly, the similarity between one of the capitals depicted by Billings (in the south aisle) and one on the pre-restoration doorway of St Mary's Church, Hemel Hempstead, is too striking to be ignored.[121] Both have hooked and beaded spearheads on the points of beaded chevron. A very similar capital, but on a much smaller scale, can be seen on one of the exterior nook shafts of the north-eastern window of the round nave (Pl. XXVB), and this too may be a 12th-century survival.[122]

The present marble aisle vault responds are post-War replacements, based on marble responds dating from the 1840s. However, Robert Smirke had already discarded the original 12th-century Purbeck marble responds in 1827, replacing them with stone. There is no way of assessing his accuracy.[123] Savage's replacement of these stone responds in 1840 differed from Robert Smirke's in detail. Billings depicted four of Robert Smirke's capitals in the north aisle:[124] one with richly veined leaves, one waterleaf and two crocket. In 1840, the veined and crocket capitals were replaced by simple waterleaf designs, while the single waterleaf capital was replaced by one with veined leaves folding back upon themselves. The base mouldings were also altered.[125] Smirke gave them a simple roll on a chamfered plinth, whilst Savage gave them doubled rolls. Thus, although the basic idea of slender marble responds with moulded bases, shaft rings and ornate capitals can be considered as 12th century, the precise details must be attributed to the masons employed by James Savage.

For many years the ribbed vault of the circular aisle was patched with plaster and covered with paint. It escaped Robert Smirke's 1827 restoration, and so Billings was able to illustrate the richly complex rib profiles in 1838.[126] But by November 1840, when James Savage removed the years of cosmetic patching, it was discovered to be in 'a very loose and shattered state'.[127] Savage only managed a small portion of the 'careful reparation' recommended before his disgrace and replacement by Sydney Smirke and Burton. However, in 1845 the latter confidently boasted that: 'The vaulting of the aisles and the whole inner surface of the walls were restored, and in great part rebuilt'.[128] The basic rib design and the rich variety of rib profiles, however, seem to tally on the whole with those depicted by Billings before the restoration of the 1840s.

In the 1840s, Savage, Smirke and Burton make clear, again and again, that the lavish use of Purbeck marble, both structurally and decoratively, was based on the original 12th-century fabric. The six arcade piers of the nave were so decayed by damp and shattered by the attachment of wainscoting and monuments that they had to be completely replaced.[129] The same difficult operation had to be carried out again after the Blitz.[130] The unusual pier design of four detached shafts with single shaft rings is certainly 12th century,[131] and can be seen in several pre-restoration engravings (Pls XIX, XXIIB) and was described in similarly early texts. The design of the à bec abaci are also 12th century, as a pre-restoration description of them makes clear: 'The capitals in their abacuses are remarkable taking angular directions front and rear, and square ditto sideways from division to division'.[132]

When the wainscoting was removed from the arcade piers in 1811, the design of the base mouldings was lost. John Carter condemned the new bases inserted at that date as being 'not with an eye to the architecture of the church . . . but to some Batty Langley's or Gibbs' Five Orders of Roman and Grecian architecture',[133] so that Nash's illustrations of the bases in 1818 (Pl. XIX) are unreliable. However, the unusual plinth design, with large corners cut off so that the straight sides of the rectangle are shorter than the diagonals could be 12th century. An undated engraving in the British Museum shows the 18th-century wainscoting arranged round the piers in the same, uneven octagonal shape.[134] It seems unlikely that this awkward arrangement was due solely to 18th-century caprice.

When Savage replaced the capitals of the arcade piers he insisted that the workmen cleaned up the original capitals and took casts of them to ensure the replacements were accurate.[135] Comparison with pre-restoration engravings shows that the capitals have retained their basic designs, though they are flatter and less exuberant than the originals.[136] Unfortunately, the capital of the first pier from the west on the north side was swapped with the capital from the corresponding pier on the south side. When Godfrey rebuilt the arcade piers after the war, he retained the 19th-century alterations.[137]

The marble shafts and capitals of the triforium arcade were described by Carter in 1808, as being 'sparingly enriched';[138] while in 1838, also before their restoration, Billings claimed that their design was 'scarcely discernible from the effects of repeated coats of whitewash'.[139] In 1842, when Smirke and Burton took over the restoration of the church from the disgraced James Savage, they deplored the fact that the forty-two triforium shafts had already been removed and destroyed before new ones could be made.[140] They duly renewed them and gave them simple waterleaf capitals.

The vault over the main vessel of the nave had already undergone several major changes before Godfrey rebuilt it in its present form after the war. The earliest description of the vault is in Strype's edition of Stow, in which he describes it as 'something like a dome'.[141] But by c. 1682 Emmett's engraving reveals that most of the vault had either fallen or been dismantled, and six stone springers supported a flat ceiling.[142] It is unknown whether originally the stone springers supported a stone vault or a wooden one. Sydney Smirke and Burton believed in the latter, claiming that the clerestory buttresses did not rest on any solid foundation and thus could not have supported a stone vault.[143] As a result they replaced the flat ceiling with a wooden domical, six part rib vault. However the cylindrical form of the nave walls would probably help to carry the load of a stone vault, as at the round nave of the Temple Church in Paris, built only a few years later than that in London.[144]

The Chancel

Over the centuries before 1840, the interior rubble walling and the Purbeck marble and ashlar dressings of the chancel were covered in many layers of plaster and paint, masking the variety of textures and colours.[145] However, Savage, Sydney Smirke and Burton presided over the complete removal of the paint and plaster in 1840–2, and much of the original fabric as well. The rubble walls were cut back and encased in ashlar,[146] whilst a new ashlar casing, in turn, replaced the Victorian stonework after the Blitz.[147]

On the removal of the plaster and paint from the rubble walls, a number of aumbries and a piscina were discovered and opened up.[148] Single trefoil-headed aumbries in the north and south aisles near the east end were completely restored with hood moulds and label stops. Likewise a double piscina in the south wall, with Purbeck marble details, was also completely restored in the 19th century and can be seen today, in its Blitz-scarred condition.[149] On the removal of the 17th-century altar in 1840–4, three niches were discovered.[150] That in the centre was larger than those flanking it, and had a semicircular head. The others were trefoil-headed. They remain today, concealed beneath the 17th-century reredos which was reinstated after the Blitz.[151]

The marble string course beneath the windows also underwent complete replacement in both the 19th and 20th centuries. So did both the slender ashlar and marble shafts of the responds between the windows, and the delicate freestanding nook shafts that articulate the windows themselves.[152] Today the details agree with those depicted by Nash and Billings before the two major restorations and thus their basic appearance can be accepted as 13th century.

The Purbeck marble piers and responds of the north and south arcades were not wholly replaced until the 20th century.[153] In the 1840s, sections of the marble were cut out and replaced, mostly in the lower half of the arcade where they had been encased in wainscoting and pews.[154] The plinths had to be lengthened out to the original floor level which was also excavated at that date. Today the base mouldings agree with those depicted by Nash before the major restorations. Godfrey must have turned to the Nash drawings in the reconstruction of the bases, for Sydney Smirke and Burton did not consistently keep to the original 13th-century design. They write in a report to the Benchers of the Inner Temple that some of 'the bases and footings' have been cut away and 'commenced according to a new design'.[155]

When the ornate 17th-century screen and organ were taken down in the early 1840s, much of the Purbeck marble and ashlar of the three, newly unblocked, arches between nave and choir had to be replaced.[156] However, Billings was able to describe it in some detail before its restoration,[157] and on the whole the restoration appears to have been faithful. Four ornate foliate bands are remarkable. They decorate the lower sections of the responds of the north and south openings, running down to floor level from single corbel heads. The latter are replacements, but the foliate bands themselves appear to have survived the various restorations and the Blitz.

The west wall of the south choir aisle originally contained a doorway to the staircase to the upper storey of the Chapel of St Anne, situated to the south of the round nave.[158] With the partial demolition of the chapel in 1678, and its later incorporation within a tenement, the doorway was no longer needed. Billings drew it in 1838,[159] but, during the 1840–1 restoration, this section of wall was completely encased in new ashlar, removing all sign of the opening.[160] Godfrey did not attempt to reinstate it after the Blitz.

The rib vaults of the chancel, like much of the fabric, also underwent two heavy restorations in the 19th and 20th centuries. The restorers of the 1840s insisted that when they removed the paint and plaster from the vaults, not only did they discover cracks and shrinkage of the cells and ribs,[161] but also 'considerable remains were discovered on the ribs and vaultings of the Temple Church to prove that these had originally been painted in powerful colours but not in sufficient extent to warrant a restoration of any particular pattern'.[162] For £311, Mr Willemont repainted the vault and spandrels with richly coloured and detailed iconographic designs.[163] After the Blitz, Godfrey preferred the new stonework to remain uncluttered by such ornament.

Conclusion

Very little of the visible fabric of the Temple Church dates from the 12th and 13th centuries. Only the north side of the exterior of the round nave with some of the nook-shaft capitals and corbel table; two capitals of the porch; the underground Treasury;[164] and perhaps some sections of the porch and chancel vaults, escaped encasement or replacement by 17th-, 19th- and 20th-century stone and marble. However, the general design and aesthetic aimed at by the original architects is basically intact. Some details have been lost, especially in the nave, but their replacements are not incongruous. The impact of the single access through the west doorway has been destroyed by the insertion of other doorways in the chancel. However, the Temple Church remains one of the great historical monuments of London — the nave, because of the historic importance of its design for the introduction of the Gothic style into England, and both nave and chancel, for their very great beauty.

REFERENCES

1. Oswald (1958), 1104; Lewer (1968–9), 29.
2. Herd (1956), 2; Oswald (1958), 1104; Lewer (1968–9), 29.
3. ITBTO, 14 January 1947.
4. Godfrey (1953), 123. He worked in association with Messrs Carden and Godfrey. Oswald (1958), 1104.
5. *Vet. Mon.*, v, XX–XXV; Godfrey (1953), 123.
6. These were carried out under the auspices of Robert Smirke. ITL Misc., 4, 8 February 1825; ITBTO, 5 November 1827.
7. These were carried out, at first, under James Savage, but in April 1841 he was replaced by Decimus Burton and Sydney Smirke: ITBTO, continuous references during period 1839–42. For the circumstances concerning the dismissal of Savage: Mordaunt Crook (1965), 39–51.
8. These were carried out under the auspices of J. P. St Aubyn. MTMP (1861–6), numerous references covering years 1861–2; St Aubyn (1864), 153–5.
9. Carter (1808), 999.
10. Billings (1838), 46; Godwin (1838), I, pl. opp. 26; Burge (1843), 25; Baylis (1893), 64, 66; Crowle Pennant Collection, British Museum, VI, 186.
11. ITBTO, 2 November 1840, 8; Carter (1808) 999.
12. 1664, vestry to south; Baylis (1893), 64. 1682, interior 'beautified and adorned' by Wren; Hatton (1708), II, 563; Colvin (1978), 926. 1691, south-west exterior; Hatton (1708), II, 563. 1695, west doorway restored, ibid., 563; 'Clerk of the Temple Church, His Book', Inner Temple Library, no pagination. 1706, interior plastered and gilt, new fittings; Hatton (1708), II, 563. 1707, east end exterior restored; Baylis (1893), 65. 1717, north and east exterior repaired; ibid. 1734, south side repaired; ITBTO, 10 January 1734. 1736, whitewashing, buttress set-offs, coping and battlements repaired, urns placed on choir gable ends; ITBTO, 16, 18 May and 10 August 1736; 13 June 1839. 1737, south-east of choir repaired and 'beautified'; ITBTO, 13 June 1737. 1750, unspecified general repairs; ITBTO, 5 August 1750. 1793, nave and roofs repaired and restored; BOPMT, 1776–1797, 364. 1802, repairs to north side; BOPMT, 1798–1813, 149–51. 1807, north side repaired; ibid., 26 January 1807. 1809, repairs to north side, ibid., 412. 1810–11, repairs and restoration, ibid., 27 June and 13 November 1810; 21 May 1811. The Inner Temple was responsible for the south side of the church, and the Middle Temple for the north side.
13. A few drawings pretend these accretions did not exist, eg. British Museum, Crowle-Pennant Collection, VI, no. 191, but their value is limited.
14. ITL Misc. XX, 5 November 1827; ITBTO, 18 May 1821, 11 May 1824, 10 February 1826.

15. See respectively: ITBTO, 16 November 1810; Baylis (1893), 65; ITBTO, 2 November 1840; 4 October 1841.
16. MTMP S. (1861–6), 22 November, 130–1.
17. The evidence for this is based purely on Emmett's engraving and may be suspect.
18. ITBTO, 2 November 1842.
19. ITBTO, 4 November 1842; Baylis (1893), 66.
20. St Aubyn (1864), 155.
21. 'Clerk to the Temple Church, His Book', no pagination.
22. Carter (1808), 999; ITBTO, 10 November 1820, 12 November 1824, 18 May 1827.
23. ITBTO, 2 November 1840 (Cottingham's Report).
24. BOPMT, 5 November 1841, 273; ITBTO, 17 July 1841 (Smirke and Burton's Report).
25. *The Gentleman's Magazine* (November 1842), 521.
26. J. W. Archer, Drawings, IX (1862), British Museum, 4, 8. MTMP S. (1861–6), 130, 223, 311.
27. *Report on the Temple Church* 17 December 1912, 3. For earlier reports of deterioration; *Reports and Opinions*; A. W. Blomfield, 29 October 1895, 5–6; T. G. Jackson, 18 February 1903, 7, 14.
28. ITBTO, 4 November 1842. Report by Sydney Smirke 'We found clear indications of the form of the original piers which rendered it very evident that the original work consisted of a cluster of detached pillars standing within square rebates.' The Benchers agreed to remove the splayed jambs 'and to substitute Pillars as described above'. Billings (1838), pl. XIII.
29. St Aubyn (1864), 153.
30. Ibid., 154–5.
31. *Reports and Opinions*, G. G. Scott, 24 June 1862, 3.
32. Baylis (1893), 66.
33. *Report on the Temple Church*, 17 December 1912.
34. MTMP S. (1861–6), 131; *Report on the Temple Church*, 6.
35. Godfrey (1953), 134; Billings (1838), 36.
36. Zarnecki (1975), 246–53; Williamson (1983), 96–9; Zarnecki (1984), 238; Williamson (1985), 716.
37. ITBTO, 4 November 1842.
38. BOPMT P. (1840–6), 20 November 1840, 77; 5 November 1841, 273.
39. ITBTO, 4 November 1842.
40. MTMP R. (1855–60), 21 November 1856, 16 January 1857.
41. *Report on the Temple Church*, 17 December 1912.
42. RCHM *London*, IV, 137. Photographs in NMR and CL.
43. Baylis (1893), 9.
44. Zarnecki (1975), 248.
45. MTMP R. (1855–60), 16 January 1857.
46. Williamson (1985), 716.
47. Williamson (1983), 96. They were originally given to the Architectural Association by Decimus Burton in 1855.
48. Williamson (1985), 716.
49. ITBTO, 2 November 1840; Report of Joint Committee, 3; Report of Mr Cottingham, 18.
50. I would like to thank Christopher Wilson for pointing this out to me.
51. Hatton (1708), II, 563.
52. The upper drum was encased again in 1840. ITBTO, 2 November 1840.
53. Thenceforth, this building will be referred to as the chapel of St Anne. Baylis (1893), 53–4; *The Gentleman's Magazine*, II (1824), 127–8; ITL Misc. XX, 5 November, 1827; ITBTO, 8 November, 1825; Godfrey (1953), 28–9.
54. Dove (1967), 165.
55. ITBTO, 5 November 1827; Allen (1827), 392.
56. ITBTO, 5 November 1827.
57. Ibid.
58. Ibid.
59. Billings (1838), 47.
60. *The Gentleman's Magazine*, May 1827, 386.
61. St Aubyn (1864), 154. He also replaced the weathered Reigate ashlar dressings with Bath stone.
62. Carter (1808), 999.
63. For example he considers the porch to have been added 'in Tudor times'. Carter (1808), 999.
64. ITBTO, 2 November 1840; 9 August 1841.
65. ITL Misc. XX, 5th November 1827.

66. Various illustrations in the Crowle Pennant Collection, VI, show the insertion of fabric blocking the lower half of the windows (No. 192) or the windows at their full length (No. 188).
67. ITL Misc. XX, 5 November 1827.
68. Ibid.
69. Ibid.
70. Billings (1838), 38.
71. MTMP S. (1861–6), 241, 251, 265. Includes letters from Sydney Smirke, St Aubyn and G. G. Scott.
72. Godfrey (1955).
73. Christ (1947), 84. The Paris Temple can be dated stylistically *c*. 1185–90 and must have been influenced, at least in its use of the rounded nave, by its London equivalent, see Gardam (1983), 60–7, pls 38–46.
74. Hatton (1708), II, 563; Billings (1838), 47.
75. Billings (1838), 47 describes how these battlements had been replaced on the south side in 1827. NMR engraving by J. Carter, 1828.
76. MTMP S. (1861–6), 26 June 1862; 5 December 1862.
77. Ibid., 5 December 1862; 13 November 1863.
78. Comparison with the round nave of the Temple Church in Paris does not give credence to his case, for it had a plain dome, see Christ (1947), pl. 84.
79. Godfrey (1955).
80. For example: BOPMT, 22 June 1792; 14 June 1793; July 1802; 16 May 1806; 6 June 1806.
81. ITBTO, copy of a letter, 13 June 1839.
82. BOPMT, 2 February 1827.
83. ITBTO, 12 November 1841; 16 March 1842.
84. St Aubyn (1864), 153. MTMP S. (1861–6), 22 November 1861, 131.
85. ITBTO, 14, 22 June, 17 July and 11 August 1841; Essex and Smirke (1845), 3.
86. Billings (1838), 35, 47.
87. ITBTO, 2 November 1840, Cottingham's Report, 9.
88. Billings (1838), pls IV, XX.
89. For example, ITBTO, 2 November 1840, Cottingham's Report, 10; Report of Joint Committees, 6.
90. Lewer (1971), 1.
91. The doorway can also be seen in this position in Stow, 1 (1720), 131. However, a more detailed view in 1, 271 reveals the buildings hemming in the south side and not showing the doorway. It is altogether more accurate in detail than the former.
92. NMR; CL.
93. ITBTO, 6 October and 2 November 1942; Report of Joint Committee, 7.
94. ITBTO, 10 February 1826.
95. Carter (1808), 1000.
96. ITBTO, 6 October 1842.
97. *Reports and Opinions*, report of C. G. Swanson, 15 October 1935.
98. ITBTO, 10 February 1826.
99. ITBTO, 6 October 1842.
100. Carter (1808), 1000.
101. ITBTO, 6 October 1842; Billings (1838), 45.
102. Billings (1838), 47.
103. Ibid., 47, and pls III, IV.
104. ITBTO, 23 November 1826; 5 November 1827.
105. ITBTO, 2 November 1840, Cottingham's Report, 10.
106. ITBTO, 18 May 1737.
107. BOPMT, 14 June 1793, 364; ITBTO, 14 November 1816.
108. Essex and Smirke (1845), 3.
109. When the upper stages of the bell turret were dismantled, the bell was moved to a bellcote on the west end of the south gable of the chancel. In 1826–7, Robert Smirke removed the bellcote, considering it to be both incongruous and dilapidated. By 1838 Billings was able to draw it set under the roof of the round nave. The bell returned to the bell turret in 1842.
110. Burge (1843), 23, 24.
111. Britton (1811), 5.
112. *The Gentleman's Magazine* (February 1811), 100–1; ITBTO, 2 November 1840.
113. Burge (1843), 31–8, 41; ITBTO, 2 November 1840, report of Mr Burge, 2–3.
114. ITBTO, 13 January 1841.
115. ITBTO, 2 November 1840, report of James Savage, 8.
116. ITBTO, 5 November 1826.

117. *The Gentleman's Magazine* (October 1838), 292.
118. Mordaunt-Crook (1965), 40.
119. Billings (1838), Pls XXII–XIV.
120. Ibid., 55; Godwin (1838), I, 21.
121. Clutterbuck (1815), I, 421.
122. Although Archer's watercolours do not depict this particular window during St Aubyn's restoration of 1862, according to his illustrations the other windows of the north aisle did retain their capitals (Pl. XXIA, c).
123. ITBTO, 5 November 1827.
124. Billings (1838), pl. XVI.
125. ITBTO, 2 November 1840.
126. Billings (1838), pl. VIII.
127. ITBTO, 2 November 1840, report of James Savage, 11; Ibid., 17 July 1841.
128. Essex and Smirke (1845), 5.
129. Ibid., 5; Addison (1843), 55.
130. Oswald (1958), 1105. NMR, photographs of work in progress.
131. ITBTO, 2 November 1840; Cottingham's Report, 11; Ibid., 16 March 1842.
132. *The Gentleman's Magazine* (December 1808), 1086.
133. Ibid. (February 1811), 100.
134. Crowle Pennant Collection, no. 186.
135. ITBTO, 2 November 1840.
136. Billings (1838), pls XV, XVI.
137. Oswald (1958), 1104.
138. *The Gentleman's Magazine*, II (1808), 1086.
139. Billings (1838), 37.
140. ITBTO, 17 July, 1841. The interior of the upper drum was encased in ashlar. ITBTO, 15 April 1842; Essex and Smirke (1845), 5. Godfrey in turn cased it in Farmington stone; Oswald (1958), 1104. Paired rectangular openings were opened up in the triforium in the 1840s. The oldest engravings show four single openings (Pl. XXIIB).
141. Stow (1754), I, 751.
142. Crowle Pennant Collection, no. 192.
143. Essex and Smirke (1845), 3.
144. See above p. 116 n. 73.
145. Baylis (1893), 67; *The Gentleman's Magazine* (February 1811), 100. Early engravings do not emphasise the difference in colour and texture of the stone and marble, reflecting the fact that they were covered in plaster and whitewash.
146. ITBTO, 15 January, 17 July, 11 August, 6 October and 12 November 1841; 16 May 1842.
147. NMR.
148. ITBTO, 2 November 1841; *Reports and Opinions*, 8 December 1933, report of Charles Peers, 4.
149. ITBTO, 2 November 1841, report of James Savage, 6.
150. NMR; ITBTO, 13 June 1839, report of James Savage, 18; 2 November 1840.
151. Lewer (1971), 10. It is the original oak reredos installed by Wren and which was removed in 1840–2. It found its way to the Bowes Museum, and in 1953 was reinstated in the place for which it was designed.
152. ITBTO, 6 October 1841.
153. Oswald (1958), 1105.
154. ITBTO, 22 June and 13 July 1841.
155. ITBTO, 17 July 1842.
156. ITBTO, 5 November 1827; 6 October 1842.
157. Billings (1838), 41.
158. Addison (1843), 80; Carter (1808), 999.
159. Billings (1838), pl. XVI.
160. NMR.
161. The vault was in such an insecure state that the easternmost rib was held up by iron bars in the roof. ITBTO, 2 November 1841.
162. ITBTO, 6 October 1841; Essex and Smirke (1845), 6.
163. ITBTO, 6 October 1841.
164. MTMP S. (1861–6), 223; Godfrey (1953), 127–31.

'Liber Horn', 'Liber Custumarum' and Other Manuscripts of the Queen Mary Psalter Workshops*

By Lynda Dennison

INTRODUCTION

A classification has yet to be fully determined for the corpus of at least thirty manuscripts which bear some relationship to the 'parent' book, London, British Library Royal MS 2.B.VII, Queen Mary's Psalter. Elsewhere I have isolated the work of two of the illuminators of this group who constitute the 'central' Queen Mary Workshop.[1] I arrived at this grouping in part by following a method propounded by Delaissé (and termed by him 'the archaeology of the book')[2] in which a rigorous analysis of every aspect of a book's decoration, codicological structure and history is undertaken.[3] An analytical method of this kind highlights the need to identify individual illuminators, to ascertain where possible their methods of working and trace their development in a given group of manuscripts.[4] This type of analysis is of particular value when there has been more than one campaign in a book. As Delaissé has aptly noted 'many mediaeval books had a complicated and even sometimes a disturbed life: their execution shared by different craftsmen, or was even interrupted, and their content altered'.[5] I hope to demonstrate in this paper that by the archaeological method[6] it is possible to cast fresh light on two main areas of difficulty which constantly confront the historian of the medieval book: the localisation of artistic activity and the dating of the works produced. It is the exception, rather than the rule, at this period to find illuminated manuscripts which can be dated with precision. Moreover, liturgical evidence (if it exists at all) can be misleading and point in the general direction of the recipient, rather than to a centre of production.[7]

This lack of internal evidence, whether documentary or liturgical, means that certain manuscripts of major importance, such as Queen Mary's Psalter, remain undated and unlocalised.[8] However, it is often the lesser known and less elaborately decorated books, related to these *de luxe* volumes, which offer valuable insights into dating and provenance. Hence the importance of 'Liber Horn' and 'Liber Custumarum', the two manuscripts central to this paper, since they provide the much sought-after evidence for discovering the main centre of activity for the Queen Mary Group, and serve to affirm the chronology formulated for the central workshop.

From a colophon which occurs on folio 206 in 'Liber Horn', now in the Corporation of London Records Office, we learn that Andrew Horn was a fishmonger of Bridge Street in the City of London.[9] However, it is evident that he was no ordinary fishmonger because he held the office of city chamberlain from 1320 until his death in 1328.[10] During his term of office (and apparently earlier) he was responsible for compiling an impressive collection of documents containing, amongst other material, the laws of the early English kings and statutes and customs of the City of London.[11] According to his wish, on his death these books were to become the property of the City: 'I leave unto the chamber of the Guildhall of London one great book of the History of the English, in which are contained many things of utility; also, one other book on the ancient [laws] of England; with a book called "Bretoun", and with a book called "Mirror of Justices"; also another book composed by Henry of

Huntyngdone; as also another book on the Statutes of England, with many liberties and other matters touching the City'.[12]

THE IDENTITY OF THE BOOKS

Is it possible to establish the identity of the books listed in Horn's will? Riley, Ker and more recently Catto have hypothesised the following. Riley interpreted the wording of the will to imply six separate books; he concluded that the Britton, Mirror and the Henry of Huntingdon were no longer in the Corporation's possession (but he made no suggestion as to their present location) and that the second and sixth on the list: 'the book on the ancient [laws] of England' and the 'book on the Statutes of England, with many liberties and other matters touching on the City' comprised 'Liber Horn', now in the Corporation of London Records Office.[13] Ker on the other hand suggested that the six books were only four in terms of their medieval structure and identified a 'book on the ancient [laws] of England, with a book called "Bretoun" and with a book called "Mirror of Justices"', the second, third and fourth items, as MSS 70 and 258 in Corpus Christi College, Cambridge.[14] This then puts in question Riley's proposal that the second book on the list might be identified as part of the existing 'Liber Horn'.[15] It is clear from a close examination of 'Liber Horn' that initially it consisted of two books;[16] although Riley's suggestion that 'Liber Horn' comprises two distinctly separate volumes is to be endorsed, Ker and Catto's conclusion that 'Liber Horn' can be identified as the sixth item (i.e. the fourth book) mentioned in Horn's will seems to be the correct interpretation.[17] The description of this book as 'the Statutes of England, with many liberties and other matters touching the City' accords with its contents.[18] The book composed by Henry of Huntingdon remains unidentified and may no longer be extant. This then leaves the first on the list: 'one great book of the History of the English, in which are contained many things of utility', and about whose identity Riley and Catto are agreed. They share the view that it can be identified as the earlier part of the present-day 'Liber Custumarum' which, like 'Liber Horn', is still in the Corporation of London Records Office, a manuscript which no longer exists in its medieval form.[19] 'Liber Custumarum' is an amalgam of two separate works: folios ii, 1–102 and folios 173–86, the earlier of the two, Ker has named MS D, and the remaining folios, 103–72 and 187–284, MS C.[20] Other portions of C and D now exist in two further volumes: Oxford, Oriel College MS 46,[21] and London, British Library, Cotton MS Claudius D.II.[22] In effect, the two libraries and the City Corporation possess portions of what were two manuscripts before mutilation, at a time when MS C was called 'Liber Custumarum' and MS D 'Liber Regum (or Legum Regum) Antiquorum'.[23] Owing to the fortunate survival of 15th-century tables of contents for both manuscripts, Ker skilfully reconstructed the original order of the folios and gave a detailed account of their contents.[24] When in a single volume, MS D (the portion relevant to this paper) contained approximately 372 leaves and, despite the mutilation to which they were later subjected, almost all of them still exist: 117 leaves form part of 'Liber Custumarum' in the Corporation of London Records Office, 133 are in Cotton Claudius D.II and 103 leaves are in Oriel College 46.[25]

There is a good case for suggesting, therefore, that five out of the six books mentioned in Horn's will can be accounted for today. This is probably a unique instance in which a set of English manuscripts of this period and importance, listed in a will, can be successfully identified in extant copies.

As chamberlain it was Horn's responsibility to defend the City's privileges; not only are many of the texts in both 'Liber Horn' and 'Liber Custumarum' specifically related to the City of London,[26] but there is evidence of Horn's involvement as compiler and annotator.[27]

His hand can be recognised in the margins, interlinearly, and in the main text. The folio containing the colophon (Pl. XXVIA) in 'Liber Horn' offers further evidence of Horn's ownership of the volume; a shield of arms, depicting a fish and the saltire cross of St Andrew, is attached to a stem of foliage in the right-hand border.[28] This shield also occurs on folio 218 of 'Liber Horn', where it is held by a standing knight in a small historiated initial. A fish is occasionally found in the border decoration of 'Liber Custumarum', as on folio 66, where it accompanies the regulations concerning the unloading and selling of fish in the London fish market.

Horn's office as City chamberlain, his bequest of books and the specifically London nature of the texts secure without question a City of London origin. Of the books Horn bequeathed to the city the two in question are of additional interest on account of their illumination, but neither manuscript has as yet benefited from a detailed art-historical assessment. This paper therefore aims to define the styles of illumination, suggest possible sources, put forward a date and location for the artistic activity and determine what light, if any, might be shed on contemporary manuscript painting.

'LIBER CUSTUMARUM': DEFINITION AND SOURCES OF STYLE

In the words of Ker, 'Liber Custumarum' 'is and probably always was the finest of the city books, admirably written and illuminated'.[29] Both the border decoration and the figure types will be examined in order to arrive at possible sources for this style.

The borders consist of slender rectilinear shafts. Some are of interlace, and these terminate in flexible foliage extensions bearing paired leaves or simple flower forms (Pls XXVIB, XXVIIA, XXVIIIA). The grotesques are especially characteristic; they occur as an integral part of the border, the tail sometimes forming into a marginal flourish (Pl. XXVIB upper border), as a detached element at the end of a stem of foliage (Pl. XXVIB), or as completely isolated forms in the empty margins (Pl. XXVIIA). A precise precedent for these forms is not immediately obvious. However, they could be seen as deriving out of a group of manuscripts associated with the 'Queen Mary' group.[30] A psalter fragment from a Breviary, Oxford, Bodleian Library, Gough Liturg. MS 8, may lie at the root of this border style.[31] The method of placing grotesques at the extremity of the borders and in isolation in the margins, as in 'Liber Custumarum', also occurs in the Gough manuscript (Pl. XXVIIB), and is found as well in Cambridge, University Library, MS Dd.4.17, the Hours of Alice de Reydon.[32] The border decoration in the Reydon Hours further relates to that in London, British Library, Arundel MS 83, part I, the Howard Psalter (Pls XXVIIIB, XXIXA).[33] Although it is clear that a different artist was at work in the two manuscripts the borders can be seen to correspond in their structure and in the manner of incorporating decorative elements of tracery at focal points, which further has a parallel in 'Liber Custumarum'(Pl. XXVIIIA). The principal borders in the Reydon Hours in turn recall those in London, British Library, Additional MS 49622, the Gorleston Psalter (Pl. XXIXB).[34] This analogy is not surprising since an illuminator who can probably be identified as the Howard Psalter artist executed some of the initials in the Gorleston Psalter (much of the minor decoration may also be attributable to his hand),[35] and the style of one of the two historiated initials in the Reydon Hours (that to the Penitential Psalms on f. 79), is similar to that of the Gorleston and Howard artists.[36] The presence of three distinctly separate, yet closely related, artists at work here highlights the complexity and stylistic interdependence of these manuscripts. Grotesques of the 'Liber Custumarum' type (Pl. XXVIIA), which it has been indicated appear in the Gough Psalter and the Reydon Hours, also occur in the borders of the Gorleston Psalter.[37] The Gough Psalter (Pl. XXVIIB), moreover, can be seen to relate in aspects of its border decoration to the Bestiary portion of Cambridge, Corpus Christi College, MS 53, the so-called Peterborough Psalter and Bestiary.[38] The Gough artist used cusped border forms and grotesques with distinctive wing or peak-capped head-dresses (as on f. 17) which can be precisely paralleled in the Bestiary, as well as in the Gorleston Psalter.[39] The borders in the psalter section of MS 53,[40] however, denote a departure from the more organic forms of the Bestiary; they are composed of slender marginal bars adorned with simple leaf forms and there is an abundant use of distinctive bright green and orange pigments, enlivened with a textured application of white, borders which again have a parallel in 'Liber Custumarum'.

Despite a number of enigmatic parallels, the border artists of 'Liber Custumarum' cannot be identified in any of the manuscripts touched on above; the origin of the border style however does seem to lie in their direction.

Turning now to the figure style, the Peterborough Psalter and Bestiary is well-known for the cycle of full-page miniatures, illustrating the Life of the Virgin and Passion of Christ, placed before the psalter text.[41] They are by the artist who executed the closely related cycle prefacing the Reydon Hours,[42] as comparison of the scene of the Annunciation in each manuscript illustrates (Pl. XXXA, B). The figures are statuesque in quality, the faces delicately drawn, and the draperies are expansive and fairly fully painted. This miniaturist, to whom can also be attributed the illumination in the Sherbrooke Missal[43] and the Bangor Pontifical,[44] will be named the 'Subsidiary' Queen Mary Artist.

Corpus Christi MS 53 is a complex work for in addition to the artist of the Bestiary, and that of the prefatory cycle, a further illuminator can be assigned the miniatures of the prophets and apostles which are interspersed in diptych form on each paired recto and verso of the New Testament cycle.[45] This artist's facial types are similar to those of the historiated initials in the main text of the Psalter,[46] and affinities have been noted with the figure style in the Croyland Apocalypse, a manuscript in Magdalene College, Cambridge, MS F.4.5.[47] This Apocalypse and its companion volume, Oxford, Bodleian Library, Canon. Bibl. Lat. 62,[48] have been shown to relate to the group of manuscripts associated with the Peterborough Psalter in Brussels. The full relevance of the stylistic connection of Corpus Christi 53 with the manuscripts of this workshop is apparent on closer examination of the Gough Psalter: firstly, the border structures (Pl. XXVIIB) seem to have an origin in the Canticle section onwards of the Brussels Psalter;[49] and secondly, the Gough Psalter contains a cycle of miniatures, interspersed in diptych form throughout the text, which can be assigned to an artist (or artists) of the Peterborough Psalter in Brussels workshop.[50] The complex interrelationship of these manuscripts is further highlighted when it can be shown that the historiated initials in the Gough Psalter[51] (Pl. XXVIIB) are in a style which relates to the Subsidiary Queen Mary Artist (Pl. XXXA, B), that the full-page miniatures of the Prophets and Apostles in Corpus Christi 53 bear a marked resemblance to the work of the Howard and Gorleston artists and that the Croyland Apocalypse shows some influence of the 'Queen Mary' style.[52]

Further evidence in support of a correspondence between the works of the Subsidiary Queen Mary Artist and those of the Howard/Gorleston group is illustrated by the Downside Psalter-Hours, a manuscript partly illuminated in the style of the Virgin and Christ cycle in the Alice de Reydon Hours (and related works) and partly in the style of the Howard Psalter.[53] The border decoration by the 'Queen Mary' hand (possibly identifiable as the Subsidiary Artist) in the Downside manuscript (Pl. XXXIIA) has a precise parallel in that of the Psalter text of Corpus Christi 53,[54] and relates especially closely to that which occurs in the Oriel College portion of 'Liber Custumarum' (Pls XXXIB, XXXIIA).

The stylistic dichotomy, as exemplified by the Downside Psalter-Hours, is further manifested in British Library, Additional MS 24686, the Alfonso Psalter,[55] a final manuscript which will be considered as a source for 'Liber Custumarum'. Whereas the border decoration (Pl. XXXIIB) relates to that in the Howard Psalter (Pl. XXIXA), the Reydon Hours (Pl. XXVIIIB) and 'Liber Custumarum' (Pl. XXVIIIA), the prefatory cycle of miniatures (these occur in a separate gathering of four leaves at the opening of the volume and depict standing male and female saints) (Pl. XXXC) is in the style of the Subsidiary Queen Mary Artist (Pl. XXXA, B). Any differences discernible in the style might be accounted for here by the technique:[56] in the Alfonso miniatures the pigment is far more thickly applied to the faces and the draperies, with the result that it has flaked from the surface in certain areas. Although it could be argued that this illuminator is a close imitator of the Subsidiary Queen Mary Artist it is equally possible that it is a work of his hand at a different (possibly later) stage in his career. Since it is precisely this figure style and technique (Pl. XXXC) which characterise one of the artists of the British Library portion of 'Liber Custumarum'[57] (Pl. XXXD) (the miniatures in which this hand can be identified are detached from the accompanying borders)[58] this supports the conclusion drawn regarding the sources of the border style.

'LIBER CUSTUMARUM': DATING AND PROVENANCE

'Liber Custumarum' can be dated with certainty to 1321 or after on account of a list of City of London officials recorded there to that year.[59] There are no grounds for suggesting that there was more than one campaign of writing since the script of the dated portion is uniform with the remaining text (Pl. XXXIA, B). It is likely that the illumination was undertaken soon after the preparation of the text and certainly before 1324, the probable date of commencement of MS C,[60] with which each portion of MS D is now bound. Apart from the presence of the Subsidiary Queen Mary Artist and the border hands already outlined, at least two other figural illuminators can be identified in MS D.[61]

In the first part of this paper it was shown that the text of 'Liber Custumarum' originated in London,[62] and there is no reason to suppose that it was illuminated elsewhere. However, the origin of the style suggests quite a different location — the Fenlands and East Anglia. There are strong Fenlands associations for the Peterborough Psalter in Brussels and its group, to which the miniatures in the Gough Psalter relate,[63] and with the dioceses of Norwich and Ely for the majority of works containing material in the style of the Subsidiary Queen Mary Artist.[64] The Peterborough Psalter in Brussels group is broadly datable to the first two decades of the 14th century, extending into the third;[65] and where evidence exists it suggests that the Subsidiary Queen Mary Artist's activity was concentrated in the years 1310–20.[66] A date towards the end of the second decade of the 14th century for the standing saints in the Alfonso Psalter is suggested by their stylistic affinity to 'Liber Custumarum' of 1321.[67] The precise dates of the Howard and Gorleston Psalters remain unsolved but in the light of the proposed dating of between 1316 and 1322 for a Breviary, MS 10, in the Library of the Marquess of Bath, Longleat,[68] it is likely that they too were products of the second decade of the 14th century. A date of c. 1310 at the earliest for the Gorleston Psalter would be more realistic in relation to London, British Library, Stowe MS 12, the Stowe Breviary of 1322–5, which appears to be a late work by the Gorleston artist.[69]

Whether or not the Subsidiary Queen Mary Artist can be assigned some of the miniatures in 'Liber Custumarum', it is this version of the Queen Mary Artist's style which it exemplifies. Futhermore, the source of the border decoration in 'Liber Custumarum' clearly lies in the complex group of manuscripts with which this illuminator can be associated at an earlier stage in his development. Around 1320, after his activity in East Anglia and/or the Fenlands this artist may then have gravitated to the capital (from where he possibly originated and maintained contact) and undertaken work in the City of London for Andrew Horn, a patron of a different kind and one who adds a further dimension to the career of this illuminator.[70]

RELATIONSHIP TO THE CENTRAL QUEEN MARY WORKSHOP

The manuscripts in which the Subsidiary Queen Mary Artist participated have long been associated with the illuminator who produced Queen Mary's Psalter, British Library, Royal MS 2.B.VII.[71] But what is the precise nature of this relationship? As indicated in the introduction to this paper past studies have not clearly distinguished the manuscripts of the 'central' Queen Mary workshop from the large body of works illuminated in this general style. Michael was aware that some distinction should be made by using the label 'Queen Mary group "proper"' to denote the central workshop, but no classification for the manuscripts which constitute this workshop (as opposed to the Subsidiary one) emerged.[72] As stated earlier, I have isolated the manuscripts of the central group and proposed a sequence of production by tracing the development of the illuminator with whom the Queen Mary Artist collaborated.[73] Although it is not possible to discuss in any detail the conclusions of that study it is necessary to show how the manuscripts of the central workshop can be broadly distinguished from those in which the Subsidiary Queen Mary Artist participated. There are three basic distinctions; these occur in the areas of border decoration, technique and figure style.

Firstly, a page from a small psalter, MS Ancient 6 in Dr Williams's Library, London, a late example by the Queen Mary Artist's collaborator (the Ancient 6 Master) illustrates a border which is typical of the central workshop (Pl. XXXIIIA).[74] Almost twenty years may separate the production of this manuscript from what is probably this illuminator's earliest extant work, a Psalter in the collection of the Marquess of Bath, Longleat, MS 11 (Pl. XXXIIIB).[75] A transitional example of his work is provided by some of the decoration in Cambridge, St John's College, MS S.30.[76] The Ancient 6 Master was responsible for introducing a distinctive border design (Pl. XXXIIIA, B) in which a rich variety of leaf and flower motifs (the columbine is a particularly characteristic form) are arranged on a rectilinear structure of foliage stems, woven at intervals into lozenges and other shapes. Although these borders do not occur in Queen Mary's Psalter they are taken up and to a degree modified by the Queen Mary Artist in the Psalter of Richard of Canterbury, New York, Pierpont Morgan Library, Glazier MS 53.[77] In contrast, the Subsidiary Queen Mary Artist employs simpler structures and a more limited repertoire of forms, comprising wavy trefoils, clovers, heart-shaped leaves, and the occasional use of paired daisy buds, as in the Downside Psalter-Hours (Pl. XXXIIA), forms and structures which accord more closely than do those of the central workshop with 'Liber Custumarum', as illustrated by the Oriel College portion (Pl. XXXIB).

Secondly, the palette used by the central Queen Mary illuminators differs from that of the Subsidiary Artist which is characterised by an abundant use of bright orange and viridian pigments, to which a textured line of white is applied for the border decoration. The central workshop's palette is wider and is further distinguished by overlaying a dull green pigment with mosaic gold, a technique not employed by the Subsidiary Artist.

Thirdly, although the Subsidiary Artist's figure style and iconography are closely allied to those of the Queen Mary Artist, as comparison between the Nativity scene in the Reydon Hours and Queen Mary's Psalter illustrates (Pl. XXXIVA, B), the figures possess greater substantiality and the draperies are more expansive. The firmly circumscribed edges of the garments and well-defined facial features contrast with the sketchy, more spontaneous drawing style of the Queen Mary Artist, whose treatment shows extreme subtlety of line. Although the Queen Mary Artist uses full colour, close observation reveals that it is basically a wash technique, in contrast to that of the Subsidiary illuminator who employs more opaque pigmentation.

Furthermore, a division of hands has shown that in extant works the Subsidiary Queen Mary Artist cannot be identified working alongside either the Queen Mary Artist or Ancient 6 Master;[78] there is no sign of material in an 'alien' style. Indeed, the two artists work in such close harmony, consistently collaborating over a period of about fifteen years, that at one point in their development it is difficult to distinguish one hand from the other.[79] The pattern of development of the Subsidiary Queen Mary Artist, who does not appear to have had a lasting collaborator, is not as homogeneous. Although he was in contact with other illuminators, especially the artist of the Howard Psalter, he seems to have worked largely independently, sometimes entirely so, as in the Bangor Pontifical and Sherbrooke Missal, while at other times he provided portions of manuscripts in association (though not necessarily in collaboration) with other artists, as in the Alice de Reydon Hours, the Peterborough Psalter and Bestiary and the Downside Psalter-Hours (as well as in the Alfonso Psalter and 'Liber Custumarum', if these attributions can be accepted). The term 'workshop' has been avoided in the context of the 'Subsidiary' activity, since the working methods of those artists are by no means clear. Stylistic and codicological evidence suggests that they were an itinerant group of illuminators who had contact for short periods.[80] Whereas it would appear that the central Queen Mary artists enjoyed a stable working relationship over a fairly long period, this illuminator seems to have worked largely peripatetically and there is no evidence, as stated, of actual contact with the central artists.

'LIBER HORN': SOURCE OF STYLE

'Liber Horn' is the only surviving manuscript of the Horn bequest to have remained throughout its life in the safe-keeping of the City Corporation. In structure it is a far more complex volume than 'Liber Custumarum' and it has warranted a detailed codicological and palaeographical examination. The illumination is not homogeneous and the style of the two artists who participated is apparently unrelated. One hand (Artist A) illuminated the portion of text from folios 206 to 226, a section containing London documents (Pl. XXVIA), and he can also be assigned the portion comprising the Statutes of the Realm, from Magna Carta on folio 21, to the first Westminster Statute on folio 35v (Pl. XXXVIA). The latter is found in two gatherings of eight leaves. He participated, therefore, in a relatively small portion of the 376 folio volume and at widely spaced intervals. It is a linear style, and although by a competent artist the work is not of the highest quality. There may be some affinity with one of the border artists in 'Liber Custumarum' (Pls XXVIA and B, XXVIIA, XXVIIIA, XXXVIA) and a figural illuminator in a manuscript which will be discussed below, but it has not been possible, as yet, to identify this artist in any known work. It can be stated without reservation, however, that Artist A's style is totally unrelated to that of the central workshop.

The forms of Artist B are easier to locate. He was responsible for the decoration at the beginning of each statute, following on from those of Artist A at folio 49, the Second Statute of Westminster, to that of the Seneschal on folio 168. He also illuminated the Kenilworth Statute, now placed before Magna Carta, in a gathering of five leaves at the beginning of the book from folios 16 to 20. This style is quite different in that it has no figural illumination, except in the form of grotesques and bas-de-page vignettes (Pls XXXVB, XXXVIB). There are decorative initials with organic leafy extensions, or single rectilinear shafts which give support to a fairly wide range of leaf and flower forms (Pls XXXVIB, XXXVIIIB). These can be paralleled for the most part in the manuscripts of the central Queen Mary workshop; this artist derives his border types directly from those of the Ancient 6 Master, as demonstrated in the Longleat Psalter (Pls XXXIIIB, XXXVIB, XXXVIIIB).[81] Furthermore, most of the drolleries and vignettes in 'Liber Horn' have an exact parallel in Queen Mary's Psalter. Certain closely related examples (Pl. XXXVA, B) suggest that Artist B either had contact with those illuminators or access to a pattern book of that workshop.[82] The latter is probably the case, since 'Liber Horn' is not a product of that atelier; the artist is never found working with those illuminators, nor has it been possible as yet to identify his hand in any other manuscript. Close examination has revealed that despite these correspondences certain aspects of border decoration are alien to those artists. There is, for instance, an extensive use of bright orange and viridian pigments, and the structures are more diluted than those in central works, with an emphasis on paired clovers and trefoil leaves (Pl. XXXVIIIB). In these respects there is a closer affinity with those manuscripts in which the Subsidiary Artist participates, as comparison with the Downside Psalter-Hours demonstrates (the clover leaves, though absent from the Psalter-Hours, are used by the border artists of 'Liber Custumarum') (Pls XXXIIA, XXXVIIIB). Furthermore, certain grotesques (Pl. XXXVIB) are clearly of a different kind from those of the central workshop and relate more closely to types in the Hours of Alice de Reydon.[83] But Artist B, like Artist A, cannot be identified amongst the hands of the 'Subsidiary' group.

There are subtle yet important differences which suggest that this illuminator's work is derivative stylistically.[84] However, it is a highly competent imitation of the style current at the time and it was probably executed in the vicinity of the central workshop, hence the heavy reliance on those forms. It is therefore unlikely that 'Liber Horn' can be credited as a source of inspiration for the central Queen Mary workshop.

'LIBER HORN': DATING

Part of the volume, at least, can be dated fairly securely to 1311 by the colophon on folio 206.[85] It is rare in an illuminated manuscript to have such an informative colophon, giving not only the date of execution but also for whom the book was made, Andrew Horn, of Bridge Street in the City of London (Pl. XXVIA). This colophon occurs half-way through the volume on a page decorated in the style of Hand A. It is questionable, however, that this date can be applied to the book as a whole without first making a closer investigation, since 'Liber Horn' appears to consist of two completely separate volumes bound as one. The page containing the colophon would seem to represent what was the initial opening of the book. Consequently, whereas the illumination by Artist A can be dated with some assurance to 1311, that by Artist B, which occurs only in Part I of 'Liber Horn', cannot.

This then poses two questions: can 'Liber Horn', Part I (that is ff. 16–176 and 176^v–204^v which are in effect additions) be dated; and how can the anomaly of the two gatherings in this section, containing Artist A's style, be explained? Close examination of folios 21 to 49 suggests that there was an interruption to the campaign which affected both the scribe and illuminator. These folios were mostly written by a scribe (Scribe One) who relates closely to that in Part II, an affinity which is supported by the presence of the same illuminator in these portions (Pls XXVIA, XXXVIA). A change in scribe, however, occurs between folio 41 recto and 41 verso (Pl. XXXVIIA, B), the third leaf of the sixth gathering of eight,[86] in the middle of the First Westminster Statute.

The characteristics of the first campaign are well illustrated by the text on folio 41 recto where the minims are provided with feet (Pl. XXXVIIA). In this, there is agreement with the script on folios 206 to 225 verso,[87] also of the first campaign, and where further work by Artist A can be found (Pl. XXVIA). The text (Pl. XXXVIIA) is interspersed with distinctive capital letters of the same colour as the script; there are red and blue capitulum marks in the left margin; and forty-one lines of justified text set within three vertical lines of black ruling.

Although there appears to have been some attempt by the scribe of folio 41 verso (Scribe Two) to imitate the script of the first campaign for the first five or six lines (this he does by imitating the upright nature of the text) (Pl. XXXVIIB), the script soon assumes the character of the remaining text decorated by Artist B. The script of the second campaign (ff. 41^v–176) lacks the feet given to the minims (Pl. XXXVIIIA); there are no capital letters within the text, nor are there any opening coloured initials or capitulum marks. There are small letters, placed by the scribe in the left-hand margin indicating the opening letter required but these were never filled in by the rubricator. Furthermore, the textual area does not compare exactly with that of the first campaign; there are thirty-seven to thirty-eight lines of unjustified text and not forty-one justified lines, as on folio 41 recto. Although ruling of a similar type is just visible on folio 41 verso, by 42 recto it is lighter and clearly very different. Codicological, palaeographical and stylistic evidence demonstrate beyond question that a break in campaign occurred at this point, but as only to be expected from an interruption to the work the script and general appearance of the text up to the end of this gathering on folio 47 verso remain uneven in quality. Further evidence of this break is shown by the last folio of this, the seventh quire, and the first of quire eight (f. 48) where a few lines were omitted by the scribe. Horn, realising this, has added the required lines and his own catchword to correspond with the opening line of text on folio 48. On this folio, throughout gathering eight and beyond, a consistent writing style is achieved by the second scribe. Moreover, there is the return of the coloured initials and capitulum marks, although they are of azure and carmine, and not the ultramarine of the first campaign. Whereas there are no catchwords evident in the first campaign, they occur regularly in the second; ruling is barely visible and the parchment is white and smoother in quality. With a change in scribe for the text of the Statutes comes a change in scribe for the headings (probably the scribe of the main text in each case). The first of these by Scribe Two occurs on folio 46, where further evidence of the transition to the second campaign is apparent in the empty space left for an illuminated initial which was never filled in (Pl. XXXVIIIA). The following Statute, that on folio 49, is illuminated, and the decoration from here to folio 176 is in the style of Artist B.

Since the illumination by Artist A and the accompanying scribe (Scribe One) accord with the dated portion, it suggests that the first campaign in Part I (ff. 21–41) also dates to 1311, and that Hand B is later; but how much later? Some indication of a possible date for the style of Artist B is offered by the annotations and additions in the volume. On folios 109 to 110 verso three writs on the statute have been added in the margins, giving the dates of 1306 and 1315. It is clear that they were all written at the same time and in Horn's own hand, the hand it would appear which also wrote the colophon. Although these annotations cannot establish a definite date, since it is not certain when they were added, they could well have been prompted by the writ of 1315 and would therefore date the illumination by Artist B to some time before 1315. This hypothesis is strengthened by further additions in an unilluminated portion which immediately follows: folios 177 to 189 contain an ordinance of 1312 and writs of 1312 and 1315. Again, this cannot give a certain date of before 1312 for the illuminated material which precedes it, but the likelihood of this increases when the volume is considered as a whole. Although clearly consisting of two separate books, each part (the unilluminated material which follows folio 226 in Part II comprises mostly

London documents dating from 1313 to 1318) represents a gradual (and thus chronological) accumulation of material by Horn and as such illustrates the essentially working nature of the volume.[88]

Although there was obviously a break in campaign, which interrupted both the writing of the text and its decoration, there is a strong case for suggesting that the illumination in the style of Artist B followed on closely from that of Artist A, and that both campaigns date to 1311, thus pre-dating the earliest additions of 1312. Catto has noted that by 1319 the volume had been reorganised and given a new table of contents.[89] This suggests that the two parts which now comprise 'Liber Horn' were bound together around 1320, possibly in time for Horn's installation as Chamberlain. In any event, by 1328 it certainly existed in its present form (the original binding survives) (Pl. XXXIVc) since it is referred to as a single volume in Horn's will. Clearly, 'Liber Horn' was Andrew Horn's working volume of the second decade of the 14th century. After his installation in 1320 he seems to have set in motion his plans for 'Liber Custumarum', datable to 1321 or soon after.

DATING AND PROVENANCE OF THE CENTRAL QUEEN MARY WORKSHOP

The study of these two dated works, largely illuminated in a version of the 'Queen Mary' style, sheds important light on the dating and localisation of the central workshop, comprising the Queen Mary Artist and the Ancient 6 Master.[90] This is demonstrated by three factors.

Firstly, 'Liber Horn' is without question a London product; Horn is likely, therefore, to have called on local illuminators. It would appear that the forms Hand B appropriated from the two central artists are in themselves sufficient evidence to localise the central workshop to the capital.

Secondly, forcible support for this is given by twenty-four leaves, apparently removed from 'Liber Custumarum' before the medieval foliation was made, which now form folios 16–39 of 'Liber Albus' in the Corporation of London Records Office.[91] These folios, not previously noted in an art-historical context, are of considerable interest since the miniature on folio 16 (Pl. XXXIVd) closely resembles the hand of the Queen Mary Artist, as comparison with historiated initials from La Somme le Roi illustrates.[92] Closer examination, however, reveals subtle differences in the palette and drawing technique (this is only observable from the originals), which suggest that the 'Albus' illuminator, like Artist B of 'Liber Horn', was a very skilful imitator of the Queen Mary Artist's style.[93] This is supported by the border decoration which here forms an integral part of the miniature and is of the 'Liber Custumarum' type, alien therefore to the central workshop. It is the 'Albus' artist who probably also illuminated the vignette of the 'Wreck of the White Ship' in the British Library portion of 'Liber Custumarum'.[94] Although it is not possible to assign these two miniatures to the hand of Queen Mary's Psalter they are an effective witness to the presence of the central artists in the city.

Thirdly, although the central Queen Mary manuscripts do not abound in internal evidence for localisation, what does exist clearly supports London for their origin. A Breviary, in which the two artists of the central shop collaborated, was owned by the monks of Chertsey Abbey and its liturgy is of special significance for London.[95] MS Ancient 6 in Dr Williams's Library has clear associations with Queen Philippa: her arms occur alongside those of England and France on the Beatus page (Pl. XXXIIIa); the calendar is Franciscan and there is evidence that she patronised the church of the Grey Friars in London.[96]

It has been stated that the manuscripts of the 'Queen Mary group "proper"', including Queen Mary's Psalter itself, can all be dated to after 1320'.[97] However, as has been demonstrated, 'Liber Custumarum' of 1321, on which this claim is based, is not a member of the central workshop; and it is clear that the central workshop was functioning probably as early as *c.*1310. A detailed account of my method for dating these manuscripts appears elsewhere, only a brief synopsis of which can be given.[98] Broadly, by identifying and tracing the development of a single illuminator (the Ancient 6 Master) with whom the Queen Mary Artist collaborated, a chronology was formulated. Added to this there is reliable dating evidence for two of the manuscripts assignable to the Ancient 6 Master: there is a *terminus post quem* of 1327/8 for Ancient 6 itself; and a date of 1318–20 for Oxford, Bodleian Library, MS Rawlinson C.292, a book of statutes.[99] By virtue of this illuminator's collaboration with the Queen Mary Artist it was further possible to form some impression of the latter's stylistic development and thus place in sequence all the manuscripts of the central group, including Queen Mary's Psalter. It emerged that amongst those manuscripts apparently post-dating 1318–20 was Cambridge, St John's College, MS S.30 and pre-dating 1318–20, the Longleat Psalter and Queen Mary's Psalter. Moreover, since the clearly derivative 'Liber Horn' dates to between 1311 and 1312, it presupposes the existence of the central workshop some time before then. Queen Mary's Psalter could therefore date to as early as 1310.

There appears to be no stylistic or documentary evidence in support of the view which has been expressed that the East Anglian version of the Queen Mary style, namely the works with which the Subsidiary Artist can be associated, were the source of inspiration for the central workshop.[100] On the contrary, it is the artists of 'Liber Custumarum' who appear to represent a later offshoot of what might be termed the Subsidiary Queen Mary group, evolving out of the Harnhulle Psalter-Hours and related manuscripts. It has been demonstrated in this paper that the stylistic correspondences between 'Liber Custumarum' and Michael's Artist B are greater than those which exist between the latter and the products of the central shop. There is support for Michael's dating of the manuscripts I have now termed 'Subsidiary' to *c.*1310–20,[101] but rather than the central Queen Mary workshop evolving out of the Subsidiary material, as Michael has suggested, its foundation (there are strong indications that it came into existence around 1310) and a substantial part of its production might also be placed in that decade. It would appear that the two workshops were approximately parallel chronologically, hence the fundamental connections existing between them in style and iconography, but possibly located in different areas from *c.*1310 to 1320 — London and East Anglia respectively.

It can be stated with some assurance that the Subsidiary Queen Mary Artist was active in East Anglia from at least *c.*1315 to 1320. It may be possible to demonstrate that he began his career in London or had contacts with the capital while in East Anglia by reference to Paris, Bibliothèque Nationale, MS latin 1332, an English Franciscan Missal (Pl. XXXIXA, B). In this manuscript he worked alongside another illuminator whose style is difficult to place but which is not dissimilar to Artist A of 'Liber Horn' (Pls XXXVIA, XXXIXB).[102] The iconography of the Subsidiary Artist's initials exactly parallels that in the Sherbrooke Missal. However, unlike all the other liturgical books illuminated wholly or in part by this artist containing any internal evidence for localisation, London rather than East Anglia is suggested for the Missal. Of the few non-Roman saints celebrated in the calendar there are only two which may have any local significance, the Deposition of St Erkenwald on 30 April, venerated at St Paul's, and St Louis, King of France, on 25 August. There was a chapel dedicated to St Louis in the London Greyfriars, probably at the east end of the south aisle of the nave, which was erected in 1305.[103]

Unfortunately, nothing has as yet been uncovered which relates specifically to the presence of illuminators in the City of London at this time (i.e. *c.*1310–1320/25), an area which requires further investigation. By 1328 there was a fraternity of painters dedicated to St Luke in St Giles, Cripplegate, where apparently many of them lived, but the distinction between illuminators and painters, if indeed there was one at that date, is difficult to establish from surviving documents.[104] The manuscripts themselves, however, are the most powerful testimony to the presence of illuminators in the capital, even though they may have been small in number. The central Queen Mary workshop comprised only two artists, 'Liber Horn' also two, and 'Liber Custumarum' a further three or four.[105] It would appear that from c. 1310 to 1325 much of the illumination was being produced in East Anglia and possibly also the Fenlands.[106]

CONCLUSION

It can be stated with confidence that the style practised in the capital was that of the central Queen Mary workshop. Moreover, Artist B of 'Liber Horn' and the artists of 'Liber Custumarum' were most likely imitating the style current in the city at that time, of which the Queen Mary Artist and Ancient 6 Master were the innovators. It is indeed rare to be able to date illuminated manuscripts with precision. As a result the two books which have been the subject of this paper are of considerable importance; they can be used to support the dating of the central Queen Mary workshop and its localisation to London, problems which once looked insoluble owing to the paucity of internal evidence.

ACKNOWLEDGEMENTS

I wish to thank all the Librarians and their staff who have facilitated my work on the manuscripts discussed in this paper but especially Miss Betty Masters, and more recently Mr James Sewell, of the Corporation of London Records Office, and Dom Philip Jebb and Dom Daniel Rees of Downside Abbey for their generous co-operation. This paper was prepared for publication during my tenure of the Joanna Randall MacIver Junior Research Fellowship, offered to me by the Principal and Fellows of Lady Margaret Hall, Oxford, to whom I should also like to express my gratitude for their support.

REFERENCES

* This paper was submitted for publication before the appearance of Sandler (1986). My analysis and conclusions remain unchanged from those presented in 1984, but in March 1988 I made the appropriate bibliographical updatings so as to include references to it and to other relevant publications.

1. See Dennison (1986a), 287–314, pls XL–LV.
2. See Delaissé (1967), 423–35.
3. I have employed this method in my unpublished Ph.D dissertation, Dennison (1988).
4. I use the term 'group' to describe manuscripts which share certain family characteristics (features of style, iconography and sometimes those of liturgy and ownership) and the term 'workshop' as a subdivision of this larger group; a workshop, in turn, may comprise one or more illuminators ('hands'). I offer these definitions in the context of my own work in response to Michael Camille's statement (see Camille (1988a), 104) that terms such as 'hand', 'workshop' and 'group' have not been used with sufficient care in the past. However, for my attempts at a narrower definition of these terms, as demonstrated by a detailed stylistic and codicological analysis, see Dennison (1986a). Further research on the Queen Mary manuscripts resulted in the present paper (delivered in 1984) which indicated that there were probably two subsidiary workshops, practising the style of the central one. It is my intention to place certain other manuscripts (see n. 105 below), as yet uncategorised (they are not central works), into their correct context.
5. Delaissé (1967), 428.
6. And not mere 'connoisseurship' which is an implied criticism sometimes levelled against any art historical method which involves making stylistic assessments as a necessary component of that analysis. See Michael Camille's concluding comments in Camille (1988b), 144.
7. For a discussion of this question and its implications see Dennison (1986b), 49 ff.
8. For the suggested chronology of Queen Mary's Psalter in the context of other closely related material see Dennison (1986a). The question of a provenance for these workshops is addressed in the present paper and a closer dating is proposed for Queen Mary's Psalter itself.

9. 'Iste liber restat Andree Horn piscenario London de Breggestrete in quo continentur Carta et alie consuetudines predicte Civitatis.' The remaining part of this colophon will be discussed in a later context.

10. For further details on Horn see Catto (1981), 367–91, especially 367–71.

11. Ibid., 369.

12. Translation taken from H. T. Riley's edition of *Lib. Cust.*, x. See also *Husting, Wills*, 344–5. For the Latin transcription (CLRO, Hustings Roll 57, no. 16) see Catto (1981), 370–1. The wish accompanying his will was that these books should always remain in the Chamber of the Guildhall.

13. *Lib. Cust.*, x.

14. Ker (1954), 37–8.

15. *Lib. Cust.*, x, n. 4, where Riley notes that 'Liber Horn' consists 'of two separate works, bound up together'. In this paper I am only concerned with isolating 'Liber Horn' and 'Liber Custumarum'.

16. An explanation for this is given in later discussion.

17. Ker (1969), 34; Catto (1981), 371.

18. For these see Catto (1981), 371–2.

19. *Lib. Cust.*, xi; and Catto (1981), 376–8 where the contents of the volume are discussed.

20. Ker (1954), 37–45. See also Ker (1969), 20–2.

21. Oriel College MS 46, ff. 1–108 are Ker's MS C and ff. 109–211, MS D. For MS D see also Alexander and Temple (1985), no. 280, pl. xvii.

22. Cotton Claudius D.II, ff. 116–23 (119–26) are Ker's MS C (the numbers given in brackets represent the new foliation since Ker's reconstruction) and ff. 1–24 (4–27ᵛ), 30–40 (33–43ᵛ), 42–115 (45–118ᵛ), 124–35 (127–38) and 266–77 (269–80ᵛ), MS D. For MS D see also Millar (1928), 16, 56, 81, pl. 40(c), and Sandler (1986), no. 68.

23. Details of their dismemberment and later history are given in full by Riley (see *Lib. Cust.*, xii–xiii, xvii–xxiv). The portion which was in Cotton's hands bears ample evidence of his ownership (as does the portion returned to the Guildhall by Tate), since a number of the decorative initials have been disfigured by the quarterings of the Cotton and Bruce arms. For a useful summary (and a slightly different interpretation of later events) see Ker (1954), 41–2. Ker notes that it was not until the detached portions were returned to the Guildhall by Tate, that they were bound together in one volume and given the collective title 'Liber Custumarum'. See also Catto (1981), 376.

24. Ker (1954), 37–41.

25. Ibid., 42–5 for a table of the contents of MS D, with medieval foliation, and the present location of the leaves. See Sandler (1986), no. 68 for a summary of Ker's reconstruction. For ease of reference MS D will be referred to by its modern appellation, 'Liber Custumarum', rather than its medieval title, and will encompass all three portions, unless otherwise stated.

26. For the contents of 'Liber Custumarum' see *Lib. Cust.* See also Ker (1969), 20–1; Catto (1981), 376–7. For the contents of 'Liber Horn' see Ker (1969), 27–34; Catto (1981), 371–2.

27. See Catto (1981), 369–70 and 383–4 for further details.

28. For a description of the arms see *Husting, Wills*, 344, n. 4. Sharpe wrongly states that the arms were added later.

29. Ker (1954), 39.

30. The style associated with London, British Library, Royal 2.B.VII. See Warner (1912). For further discussion and bibliography see L. Dennison (1986a), passim.

31. For the Gough Psalter see Pächt and Alexander (1973), no. 545, where further bibliography is given, and pl. LIV. See also Lasko and Morgan (1973), no. 4; Sandler (1974), 10, 12, 38, 98–9 (no. 7), 119–21, 132, 133, 137 n. 10, 150, fig. 332, where reference is made to the material in question. The full-page miniatures which form part of this manuscript (see Pächt and Alexander (1973), no. 546, pl. LV) will be discussed in a later context. Oxford, Bodleian Library, MS Rawl. liturg. e.1*, a Breviary (ibid., no. 544, pl. LIV), containing one historiated initial and border, is in the same style as the historiated initials and borders in the Gough Psalter. See also Sandler (1974), 137 n. 10, 150, and Sandler (1986). no. 42.

32. Examples occur on ff. 23ᵛ, 33, 34, 35, 37ᵛ, 41ᵛ, 42ᵛ, 49, 50ᵛ, 62ᵛ, 63, 63ᵛ, 66, 70ᵛ, 71ᵛ, 97, 100ᵛ and 134ᵛ. For the Reydon Hours see *Cat. Mss Univ. Camb.*, I, 192–3, where it is erroneously dated to c. 1400; Millar (1928), 12–13, 51–2, 81 (no. 221), pls 27–9; Rickert (1965), 240 n. 19; Verdier *et al* (1972), no. 29; Lasko and Morgan (1973), no. 8; Sandler (1974), 132, 135, 143 n. 8; Michael (1981), 83, 84, 86, 87, 88, 89, 90, 93 n. 56; Marks and Morgan (1981), 19. See also Sandler (1986), no. 67 and *Age of Chivalry*, no. 570.

33. For the Howard Psalter see Millar (1928), 4, 45–6, 79 (no. 210), pl. 7; Rickert (1965), 132; Lasko and Morgan (1973) (mentioned under no. 20); Sandler (1974), 98–9 (no. 14), 128, 137 n. 13, fig. 340; Sandler (1976), 11, 12, 13, 14, 15, pl. 3b, c, d, f; Michael (1981), 81, 82, 83, 84, 85, 86, 87, 88, 89, 95 n. 69, pl. XIIIB; Marks and Morgan (1981), 76, where it is referred to under the discussion of the Gorleston Psalter; and Sandler (1986), no. 51.

34. For the Gorleston Psalter see principally Cockerell (1907). See also Lasko and Morgan (1973), no. 20 where further bibliography is given; Sandler (1974), 9, 12, 13, 88, 96, 98–9 (no. 13), 128, 130, 131, 134, 135, 136 nn. I.6, II.2, 6, 137 n. 24, 140 n. 15, 143 n. 5, 161, figs 298, 342–3; Sandler (1976), 10, 11, 14; Michael (1981), 82, 85 n. 15, 86, 90, pl. XVID, and also 83, 86, 87 n. 24, 88, 90 where reference is made to the 'Gorleston group' of manuscripts; Marks and Morgan (1981), 76 (pl. 19 is not typical of the decoration in question); Sandler (1986), no. 50; *Age of Chivalry*, no. 574.

35. These initials occur on f. 8 (Ps. 1), f. 35 (Ps. 26), f. 52ᵛ (Ps. 38), f. 86 (Ps. 68), f. 107ᵛ (Ps. 80), f. 167 ('Ad dominum cum tribularer'). An analogy with the Howard Psalter was first made in Lasko and Morgan (1973), no. 20. See also Michael (1981), 82–3. A possibly different but closely related hand (the Gorleston artist) appears to have been responsible for the remaining minor initials on ff. 68ᵛ, 69, 128, 146ᵛ, 190ᵛ. However, there is much overlapping of styles and the hands are not always easily distinguishable.

36. This was first noted by Michael (1981), 86 n. 22.

37. Examples, too numerous to enumerate, of the grotesque as a detached element with the tail extending into a stem of foliage, or as a completely isolated form in the upper or lower margin, occur throughout the Gorleston Psalter. A particularly close comparison can be made between one of the latter type on f. 64, almost identical examples of which can be found on f. 97 in the Reydon Hours, f. 27 in Gough Psalter and f. 3 in 'Liber Custumarum'.

38. For a complete facsimile see James (1921a), plates covering ff. 189–210. For discussion of this manuscript see James (1921a); Millar (1928), 11–12, 51, 81 (no. 220), pls 24–6; Rickert (1965), 125–6, 240 nn. 17–21, pl. 126; Lasko and Morgan (1973), no. 7; Sandler (1974), 95, 98–9 (no. 9), 108, 123–6, 132, 136 n. II.1, 137 n. 10, 140 nn. 14, 16, 154, figs 334–9; Michael (1981), 83, 84, 86, 87, 88, 89, 90; Marks and Morgan (1981), 19; and Sandler (1986), no. 23.

39. For examples from the Bestiary see James (1921a), plates covering f. 193ᵛ (winged head-dress) and f. 198 (peak-capped head-dress), and from the Gorleston Psalter, ff. 25, 35, 41ᵛ, 42ᵛ, 49, 63, 105, 106ᵛ, 132, 138ᵛ. Grotesques of this type can be found in the Reydon Hours (see ff. 20, 34, 36, 40ᵛ, 45ᵛ, 52ᵛ, 58ᵛ, 62ᵛ, 68, 100ᵛ).

40. The psalter extends from ff. 19–180; see James (1921a), Pictures in the Psalter 1–10.

41. This cycle is disposed in diptych form on ff. 7ᵛ–8, 9ᵛ–10, 11ᵛ–12, 13ᵛ–14, 15ᵛ–16, 17ᵛ–18. For a complete facsimile and subjects depicted see James (1921a), Pictures preceding the Psalter 2, 3, 6, 7, 10, 11, 14, 15, 18, 19, 22, 23. On this portion of the manuscript see also Sandler (1986), no. 66.

42. This is also disposed in diptych form from ff. 1ᵛ to 12. For the subjects depicted see Lasko and Morgan (1973), no. 8. See Millar (1928), pls 27–9 for reproductions of ff. 5ᵛ, 6, 7ᵛ, 8, 9ᵛ, 10; and Sandler (1986), no. 67, which illustrates ff. 1ᵛ, 2, 3ᵛ and 9ᵛ.

43. For the Sherbrooke Missal see Lasko and Morgan (1973), no. 18 where earlier bibliography is given; Michael (1981), 83, 88; and Sandler (1986), no. 65.

44. For the Bangor Pontifical see Ker (1977), 48–53. The attribution of the miniature on f. 8ᵛ to the artist of the prefatory miniatures in the Alice de Reydon Hours was initially made by Michael (1981), 88. See also Sandler (1986), no. 69, and *Age of Chivalry*, no. 109.

45. These occur on ff. 7, 8ᵛ–9, 10ᵛ–11, 12ᵛ–13, 14ᵛ–15, 16ᵛ–17, 18ᵛ. For a complete facsimile and subjects depicted see James (1921a), Pictures preceding the Psalter 1, 4, 5, 8, 9, 12, 13, 16, 17, 20, 21, 24.

46. These occur on f. 19 (Ps. 1), f. 38ᵛ (Ps. 26), f. 52 (Ps. 38), f. 64 (Ps. 52), f. 76ᵛ (Ps. 68), f. 92ᵛ (Ps. 80), f. 106ᵛ (Ps. 97), f. 122ᵛ (Ps. 109), f. 136 (Ad dominum), f. 153 (Confitebor). For illustrations see James (1921a), Pictures in the Psalter 1–10.

47. Sandler (1974), 132 and figs 136, 139–293 (odd numbers), 327. For further discussion of this manuscript see principally Sandler (1974), 9, 10, 12, 62–87, 104, 106–7, 122–3, 133, 134, 139 nn. 38, 39, 153–4. See also Lasko and Morgan (1973), no. 10 where earlier bibliography is given, and Sandler (1986), no. 93.

48. Sandler (1974), 9, 10, 12, 62–87, 100, 102, 104, 106–7, 122–3, 132, 139 nn. 38, 39, 151–2, figs 137, 138–292 (even numbers), 294–5, 326. See also Pächt and Alexander (1973), no. 573, pl. LVIII where earlier bibliography is given; Lasko and Morgan (1973), no. 11, and Sandler (1986), no. 92.

49. E.g. ff. 94–140ᵛ. This material is by two hands, ff. 94–101ᵛ and 102–40ᵛ respectively. For illustrations of some of the folios in question see Sandler (1974), figs 61–5. For further discussion of this manuscript see Sandler (1974), passim; Lasko and Morgan (1973), no. 2, and Sandler (1986), no. 40, where extensive bibliography is given. See also *Age of Chivalry*, no. 567.

50. For illustrations and discussion of these see Sandler (1974), 9, 10, 12, 38, 47–55, 88, 92, 94, 95, 119–21, 128, 150, figs 90–115, 333; and Sandler (1986), no. 42. See also n. 63 below.

51. These occur on f. 17 (Ps. 26), f. 27 (Ps. 52), f. 31 (Ps. 68), f. 38 (Ps. 80), f. 47 (Ps. 109).

52. For the Croyland Apocalypse see Lasko and Morgan (1973), no. 10; Sandler (1974), 132, 134, where this analogy has been previously noted..

53. For a division of hands, further bibliography and detailed discussion of this manuscript see Michael (1981), 81–4 and passim.

54. This correspondence has previously been noted by Michael (1981), 83, 86. Despite the analogy of the head types in the historiated initials in Corpus Christi 53 (see n. 46 above) with the style of the Howard illuminator, the figure types, drapery forms and border decoration are strongly reminiscent of those of the Subsidiary Queen Mary Artist and could well be by his hand, while under influence from the Howard miniaturist. For a good colour reproduction of the *Dixit insipiens* page (f. 93ᵛ) from the Downside Psalter-Hours, see Fitzgerald-Lombard (1981), 12.

55. Also called the Tenison Psalter. For reference to the manuscript as a whole see Bond (1863), 77–96; Watson (1979), 67, no. 296; Sandler (1986), no. 1; and *Age of Chivalry*, no. 357. It is the later campaign of 14th-century decoration which is under discussion, for which see Sandler (1974), 132, 135, 143 n. 7; Michael (1981), 87; and Sandler (1986), no. 1.

56. Michael (1981), 87, sees in these technical anomalies the work of a different hand, but Sandler (1974), 135, and (1986), no. 1, is of the opinion that they are possibly by the Reydon artist.

57. The palette and method of paint application, which renders the surface shiny, is identical, and in each the thick pigment has flaked from the surface of the vellum.

58. This figure style is particularly evident in the miniatures on ff. 73 and 76 and this technique in the miniature on f. 76.

59. This list is to be found on ff. 184ᵛ–186ᵛ in the CLRO portion of 'Liber Custumarum'. See *Lib. Cust.*, 239–46. For a discussion of the dating see Catto (1981), 378, who also refers to Riley's conclusions.

60. See Catto(1981), 378–9.

61. The hand closely analogous to the Subsidiary Queen Mary Artist may well have been responsible for all the miniatures (i.e. on ff. 33, 45ᵛ, possibly including the Wreck of the White Ship, ff. 72, 73, 76, 116) in the British Library portion. A further miniaturist painted the historiated initials on ff. 4, 5, 8, 11, 13, 15 and 20, the same hand it would appear who executed all the historiated initials (ff. 111ᵛ, 156, 163ᵛ, 169, 180, 183, 187, 189ᵛ, 196ᵛ), except for one (f. 109), in Oriel College 46; the illuminator of the initial on f. 109 does not appear elsewhere in MS D. The CLRO portion contains no figural illumination.

62. The London provenance is further attested by Cambridge, University Library, MS Gg.4.32 (see *Cat. Mss Univ. Camb.*, III, 177–82), a manuscript datable to *c.* 1315, with an undisputed London location, the main scribe of which is that of 'Liber Custumarum'. I am grateful to Dr A. I. Doyle for making this observation. This manuscript contains diagrams which recall those in parts I and II of London, British Library, Arundel 83, mentioned in an earlier context.

63. For details, see Sandler (1974), 106–26. See also Lasko and Morgan (1973), nos 2, 3, 4. In the light of the stylistic connections existing between the 'Queen Mary' and Fenland styles it is worth considering that the Gough miniatures did not appear in the Psalter as a result of a 'post-medieval forced marriage of two parts that never were intended to be wedded', as suggested by Sandler (1974), 121, although admittedly they are now incorrectly bound, as she notes. Sandler's overall conclusion (1974), 135, that these manuscripts may have been produced in a London atelier is doubtful in view of their strong Fenland affiliations, an opinion also expressed by Bennett (1982), 504–5, 508. Sandler (1986), i, 29, 30, seems now to favour a possible Norwich, but certainly East Anglian, place of manufacture.

64. Nicholas Rogers has pointed out to me that Cambridge, University Library Dd.4.17 (the Reydon Hours) has a calendar and litany which suggest an origin in the region of Huntingdonshire. Sir Robert de Reydon, Alice's husband, owned land in Ramsey (Raimes (1938), corrigenda slip opp. 107). The litany is probably based on a Fenlands monastic model, and although a complex one, has a number of features indicative of the Ely diocese and Huntingdonshire (i.e. Sts Neot, Botulph, Ivo, Etheldreda, Withburga, Sexburga and Radegund). For Downside Abbey MS 26533 see Michael (1981), 91–3, where he concludes 'that the book was probably designed for use somewhere in the region of East Anglia'. There is no indication of provenance for either the Sherbrooke Missal or Bangor Pontifical. Cambridge, Corpus Christi College MS 53 (the Peterborough Psalter and Bestiary) has a calendar which was originally intended for Norwich Cathedral Priory but was adapted in a closely contemporary hand for the Abbey of Peterborough; at the time of writing the litany a Peterborough destination was intended. For a discussion of this see Lasko and Morgan (1973), no. 7; Sandler (1974), 123–6; and Sandler (1986), no. 66. A Suffolk location (see Michael (1981), 87 n. 27) seems likely for the calendar of the Alfonso Psalter, decorated in an 'East Anglian' style; but it is not at all certain where the added miniatures, assigned to the Subsidiary Queen Mary Artist, were produced. Their close stylistic similarity to the miniatures in the British Library portion of 'Liber Custumarum', however, may point to a London provenance.

65. This question is fully discussed by Sandler (1974), 108–23. She concludes that 'the two earlier phases of development of the Fenland style belong to the first decade of the fourteenth century' while the 'third phase is probably of the twenties'. See also Sandler (1986), nos 40–2, 91–4. It is possible, however, that the Barlow Psalter (considered by Sandler as belonging to the third phase) was produced in the 1310s, for which see Bennett (1982), 505 where she concludes that the 'first campaign may have preceded 1321'. See also Lasko and Morgan (1973), no. 12.

66. For Cambridge, Corpus Christi College 53 see Lasko and Morgan (1973), no. 7; Sandler (1974), 125; and Sandler (1986), no. 66. For the Bangor Pontifical see Michael (1981), 88, and Sandler (1986), no. 69. There is no firm documentary evidence by which the Reydon Hours, Sherbrooke Missal and Downside Psalter-Hours can be dated more precisely. Sandler's suggested dating for the Reydon Hours of between 1320 and 1324 (see Sandler (1986), no. 67) is open to question. Alice de Reydon may have been dead by 1314 when John, her son and heir, was using the Reymes arms impaled with those of Reydon (Raimes (1938), corrigenda slip opp. 107). I am grateful to Nicholas Rogers for this information.

67. Sandler (1986), no. 1 forwards a date of before 1316 for the 14th-century material in the Alfonso Psalter, suggesting that the various additions were probably gathered together for Elizabeth de Bohun, daughter of Edward I and Eleanor of Castile, and wife of Humphrey de Bohun, fourth Earl of Hereford and Essex. Elizabeth, who died in 1316, presumably inherited the unfinished manuscript after the death of her brother, Prince Alfonso, in 1284. However, it cannot be established with certainty that the additions were made in her lifetime. If the book came into Elizabeth's hands soon after the death of her brother it had therefore remained incomplete for some twenty to twenty-five years of her usage (it is unlikely on stylistic grounds that the added material dates to before c. 1310 and it could well be later still), and may have remained in this state until it was owned by Humphrey de Bohun (for details concerning the Earl of Hereford see *Compl. Peerage*, VI, 467–70). It is possibly significant that it was not until after 1316 that this earl, who died in 1322, commissioned Longleat Library, MS 10 (see n. 68), the border decoration of which is not dissimilar to that in the later campaign in the Alfonso Psalter. The various obits inserted in the calendar cannot provide precise dating evidence; some of them were undoubtedly added, however, during Elizabeth's lifetime.

68. For the dating and illustration of the Longleat Breviary see Sandler (1976), 2–3, 14, pls 1 a–e, 2a, b, c; 3a, e, g; and Sandler (1986), no. 52. See also Sandler (1976), 12–5 where she advances the possible terminus of execution for the Howard Psalter from 1309 to 1326, but in Sandler (1986), no. 51, she prefers a date c. 1310 to c. 1320. Cockerell's identification of Roger le Bigod as the original patron of the Gorleston Psalter (Cockerell (1907), 8), who died in 1306, now looks doubtful; see Sandler (1986), no. 50. See also Lasko and Morgan (1973), no. 20.

69. For the dating of the Stowe Breviary see Lasko and Morgan (1973), no. 26 where earlier bibliography is given. See also Sandler (1974), 98–9 (no. 17), fig. 344; Sandler (1976), 4, 5, 9, 14–5; and Sandler (1986), no. 79 where further bibliography is cited.

70. Further securing a London provenance for this style is Edinburgh, National Library of Scotland, Advocates' MS 19.2.1, shown to have London origins (see Loomis (1942), 595–627). It is illuminated in a late (c. 1330) version of the 'Liber Custumarum' style; this is particularly evident from the foliage decoration.

71. See n. 30 above.

72. Michael (1981), 88 n. 30, uses this term 'to distinguish those books which have work by the artists of the Queen Mary Psalter or others who worked with them, from those books related to Downside *Artist B*', but this does not sufficiently account for the complex interrelationships which exist between the manuscripts illuminated in the 'Queen Mary' style. For an assessment of the group as a whole see Sandler (1986), i, 30–2 (illustrations 137–76), ii, nos 56–76.

73. See Dennison (1986a), passim. There is a book of hours in a private collection in Paris which Dr Patricia Stirnemann is to publish. She has kindly shown me slides of this manuscript and from what I have seen the work is by the Queen Mary Artist's collaborator, the Ancient 6 Master, for which see Dennison (1986a).

74. Ibid., 287–8 ff., where this manuscript is discussed in detail and bibliography given. Sandler (1986), no. 74.

75. Dennison (1986a), 291–3 ff., for discussion and bibliography. Sandler (1986), no. 73.

76. Dennison (1986a), 289–90 ff., for discussion and bibliography (see also pl. XLIIIa). Sandler (1986), no. 60.

77. Dennison (1986a), 295–6 ff., for discussion and bibliography. Sandler (1986), no. 57.

78. See Dennison (1986a), passim for a division of labour for the Queen Mary Artist and Ancient 6 Master and an analysis of this workshop.

79. Ibid.

80. It has been suggested (see Lasko and Morgan (1973), 7, no. 8) that the illuminator of the prefatory cycle of miniatures in the Hours of Alice de Reydon (now labelled the Subsidiary Queen Mary Artist) may have been itinerant. There is sufficient evidence to suggest that this miniaturist's collaboration with the artist of the Howard Psalter was well established (see Michael (1981), 88–9) but their working methods must be clearly distinguished from those of the central illuminators.

81. For discussion of the border decoration in the Longleat Psalter see Dennison (1986a), 291–3 and passim for the appearance of these structures in the other works of the central workshop.

82. Other examples in 'Liber Horn' which have a parallel in Queen Mary's Psalter include those on ff. 16, 160ᵛ, 161, 163, 173ᵛ, 174 and 174ᵛ. For comparison see Warner (1912), pls 143, 154, 166, 177, 180, 193, 194, 199, 205, 208, 213.

83. These are to be found on ff. 24ᵛ, 26ᵛ, 33, 34ᵛ, 35ᵛ, 36ᵛ, 49, 49ᵛ, 54ᵛ (a particularly good example), 66ᵛ, 68 and 116 in Cambridge, University Library, Dd.4.17, the Hours of Alice de Reydon, and can be compared

with those on f. 120ᵛ in 'Liber Horn'. Grotesques of this specific type (see for example ff. 65ᵛ, 89, 162ᵛ, 188ᵛ, 205, 207ᵛ, 215ᵛ, 216ᵛ, 220ᵛ, 222) also occur in the Gorleston Psalter.

84. See also n. 105 below.

85. The colophon (see n. 9 above) continues: 'Et carta libertatis Anglie et Statuta per Henricum Regem et per Edwardum Regem filium predicti Regis Henrici edita. Quem fieri fecit Anno domini mcccxi Et Anno Regni Regis Edwardi filii Reg' Edwardi vᵗᵒ.'

86. A ninth leaf (f. 40) has been inserted by Horn.

87. This correspondence has been observed by Ker (1969), 34; he notes that the writing is current, except for that on ff. 21–41 and 206–25ᵛ where the minims are provided with feet.

88. See Ker (1969), 34, and Catto (1981), 369, 371–2, 381, 382, 383–4.

89. Catto (1981), 372.

90. For an account of the activity of these two artists and a chronology of their works see Dennison (1986a), passim.

91. See *Lib. Alb.*, xxi–xxii; Ker (1954), 39 n. 11; Catto (1981), 377.

92. For illustrations of initials by the Queen Mary Artist from *La Somme le Roi* see Millar (1928), pl. 40(a), (b); and Sandler (1986), illustration 149.

93. The historiated initial on f. 109 in the Oriel College portion of MS D, which is by a close imitator of the Queen Mary Artist's collaborator, the Ancient 6 Master, and not as suggested (see Alexander and Temple (1985), no. 280, pl. XVII) by an artist of Cambridge, St John's College, MS S.30, should be similarly dissociated from the 'central' Queen Mary workshop. See also n. 105 below.

94. For an illustration see Millar (1928), pl. 40(c).

95. For discussion and bibliography see Dennison (1986a), 288–9 ff. For details of the liturgy see Alexander (1974), 73. See also Sandler (1986), no. 62 a and b.

96. For further details see Dennison (1986a), 298.

97. See Michael (1981), 89.

98. For a full discussion see Dennison (1986a), passim, and 305 for a suggested dating for the manuscripts associated with this workshop.

99. Ibid., 299, for discussion and bibliography.

100. Michael (1981), 89, 90.

101. Ibid., 88–90.

102. Michael (1981), 89, n. 37, has tentatively linked this manuscript with 'Liber Horn' and the artist of Queen Mary's Psalter, but he does not isolate the hands in question. Artist A of 'Liber Horn' bears some affinity to the illuminator of ff. 10, 25ᵛ, 231ᵛ, 235, 334ᵛ, 371ᵛ, 376 and 378, while that on ff. 241ᵛ, 264ᵛ, 271 and 422 is the work of the Subsidiary Queen Mary Artist, and not the Queen Mary Artist.

103. See Kingsford (1915), 202–3. Margaret of France, who died on 14 February 1317/18, the second foundress of the Greyfriars, was a granddaughter of St Louis. I am grateful to Nicholas Rogers for this reference.

104. For the Guild of St Luke see Unwin (1925), 96. I am grateful to Dr E. Veale for advice on this enigmatic question. She informs me that it is unlikely that lists exist of members of fraternities in the early 14th century.

105. There were certainly others. I have as yet to classify and postulate a date for further manuscripts which derive elements of figure style, iconography and ornament from the parent workshop. These include Baltimore, Walters Art Gallery, W.144; Cambridge, University Library, Dd.1.14; New Haven, Yale University Beinecke Library, G.B72, no. 2; Oxford, Bodleian Library, Canonici Misc. 248; Oxford, Bodleian, Rawlinson C.246; Oxford, Lincoln College 16; Paris, Bibliothèque Nationale, lat. 17155. The derivative nature of much of this material suggests, as in the case of 'Liber Horn' and 'Liber Custumarum' (and related manuscripts discussed in this paper), that central Queen Mary workshop pattern books were in circulation, principally in London but also in East Anglia.

The first sixteen folios of the Apocalypse, London, British Library, Royal MS 19.B.XV (see Lasko and Morgan (1973), no. 15 and Sandler (1986), no. 61) bear out this theory; they are not the work of the Queen Mary Artist, as hitherto believed. I shall substantiate this statement in a subsequent paper.

106. For evidence of London as a centre of illumination in the last decade of the 13th century see Bennett (1985), 15–30. The work of the Madonna Master in London, British Library, Arundel MS 83, part II, has been associated with Westminster and suggested to date *c.*1308, for which see Sandler (1986), no. 38 (with bibliography) and *Age of Chivalry*, no. 569. Michael (1988), 107–15, seems to confirm my conclusion that apart from those two artists working in the Queen Mary style (both the central workshop and derivative workshop(s), with the proviso that the Subsidiary Queen Mary Artist was probably itinerant, working in East Anglia and possibly also in London) between 1310 and 1320/25 the production of illuminated books was being done elsewhere, principally in East Anglia and the Fenlands. In addition, Michael produces evidence for Oxford as a centre, but where dates of specific manuscripts are given (see the captions to his illustrations 40–2) the inference is that this phase of production was of *c.*1320–30.

London, Londoners and Opus Anglicanum

By Penelope Wallis

The term Opus Anglicanum has often been used in a rather literal way to refer to any embroidery produced in England in the Middle Ages in its widest sense, and this is the definition adopted here. However, Opus Anglicanum is often taken to mean embroidery of the period *c.* 1250s–*c.* 1340s when this fine work produced in England reached its apogee of perfection. This is here referred to as the Great Period. Outside England, the term Opus Anglicanum was used in a literal sense in the inventories of churches to distinguish between English embroidery and that produced elsewhere.[1]

During the Great Period it seems that most of the embroidery was carried out in workshops in the City of London, by professional embroiderers — both men and women.[2] These workers served an apprenticeship of seven years as is shown in a Bill of Complaint brought by John Catour of Reading on 8 February 1369, against a brouderer of London, Ellis Mympe, for beating and ill-treating his daughter, Alice, who had been apprenticed for five years.[3]

The history of this fine English embroidery goes back to Anglo-Saxon times, the best known surviving examples from this early period being the so-called Stole and Maniple of St Cuthbert, now preserved at Durham.[4]

Surviving embroideries — both complete or near complete vestments and fragments — consist almost wholly of ecclesiastical vestments. Many vestments were destroyed at the Reformation in England and at other times of stress, often to reclaim the gold,[5] or just wore out. Sometimes the vestments were recut to form others, to have their life extended[6] or to bring them up to date.[7]

Various inventories of churches of both England and abroad reveal how popular vestments with English embroidered decoration were. The inventory of the Holy See in Rome of 1295 mentions more vestments with English embroidery than from any other country.[8]

The chronicler and historian of St Alban's, Matthew Paris, relates in his 'Historia Majora' this anecdote concerning Pope Innocent IV which took place in 1246:[9]

At about the same time the Pope seeing ecclesiastical vestments upon certain English priests such as choral copes and chasubles, desirably embroidered in gold, asked where they had been made. The reply was 'In England'. At this he exclaimed 'Truely England is for us a garden of delights; truely it is an inexhaustible well; from where so many things abound, many may be extorted'. Thus the Pope allured by the desire of the eye, sent letters, blessed and sealed, to almost all the abbots of the Cistercian order established in England, in order that they should send to him without delay, these embroideries of gold which he preferred above all others, and with which he wished to decorate his chasubles and copes, as if these acquistions would cost him nothing. The Pope's command did not displease the London merchants who traded in these embroideries and sold them at their own prices.

Thus Matthew Paris mentions the London merchants. There are also records of London embroiderers. Marc Fitch has drawn together evidence that a number of such workshops were operating in the area to the south of the church of St Mary le Bow.[10] He suggests that the occupational surnames of le Seur, le Asseur and le Setter applied to these embroiderers — certainly in the late 13th and early 14th centuries when Opus Anglicanum was at its height. Alexander le Settere, in 1307, received £10, in payment of £40, from Sir Poncius Roandi who was Chaplain to Master William Testa, Archdeacon of Lichfield and Coventry.[11] John le Setter (who is also referred to as le Asseur, le Asseyer and le Seur) had property in the Parish of All Hallows, Bread Street in 1281; Clement le Seur (also le Setter), in 1313, had a tenement in the Parish of St Andrew, Cornhill.[12]

The 'Golden Legend' tells of a noblewoman of the City of London 'which was right conning in silk work, which was desired to embroider certain garments to the Countess of Gloucester...' who discussed with 'a young demoiselle who was fellow with her and wrought the same work' whether to work on the Feast day of St Edward the Confessor and displease him, or not to do so and thus displease the Countess.[13]

In Royal accounts there are records of the Royal family as patrons of the London embroiderers: on 17 May 1317 fifty marks were given to Rose, wife of John de Bureford, citizen and merchant of London, for an embroidered cope purchased by Queen Isabella as a present to the Pope.[14] This is possibly the cope recorded by a watercolour drawing in the Walker Art Gallery, Liverpool and which was said to have been in Rome in the 17th century. This cope is dated by Donald King to 1315–35[15] and shows scenes from the Life of the Virgin and the Infancy and Passion of Christ framed by concentric registers of arcades which have scenes from the Book of Genesis and angels in the spandrels.

Not all the London embroiderers were above reproach, as can be seen in the Bill of Complaint brought against Ellis Mympe in 1369.[16] In 1382 it was awarded that William Soys, brouderer of the Parish of All Hallows, London, should be put in the pillory for cheating several times with a false chequer-board and that he should repay the complainants what he had won from them.[17]

SOME SURVIVING EMBROIDERIES WITH LINKS WITH LONDON

It is impossible to link any of the surviving vestments with individual workers or work-shops. It cannot even be said for certain that all the survivals were made in London. However, a number of surviving English embroideries are associated with Londoners and London Institutions. Although some come from outside the Great Period, nevertheless, they show a high quality of work. Perhaps one of the most famous of Londoners was St Thomas à Becket, born in Cheapside, the son of a merchant, Gilbert Becket. Several vestments from the late 12th century which traditionally are said to have been worn by St Thomas, whilst in exile in Sens, have been preserved in the cathedral there.[18] They include an alb with apparels, chasuble, stole and maniple and amice apparel, all worked with a design of crosses, circles and foliage in silver-gilt thread on silk. A further vestment from this group, an amice apparel, is now at Erdington Abbey.[19] A mitre which is also linked by tradition with St Thomas was, in 1842, presented to Cardinal Wiseman, Archbishop of Westminster, by the Archbishop of Sens and is now on loan to the Victoria and Albert Museum. The design consists of foliate scrolls and roundels in silver-gilt thread on white silk.

The inventory of St Paul's Cathedral, in London, of 1245 mentions a red samite (or rich silk fabric) cope with the Tree of Jesse embroidered on it.[20] It might have resembled the later so-called 'Jesse' cope in the Victoria and Albert Museum,[21] which shows, on a red silk background, the tree and figures worked in silver-gilt and silver threads and coloured silks. The figures include David and Solomon, and several other Old Testament figures, among them Moses, Abraham and Isaac and, at the top of the Tree, the Virgin and Child. The cope dates from the end of the 13th to the beginning of the 14th centuries.[22]

From somewhat later in the Middle Ages comes the chasuble which is connected with Sir Thomas Erpingham. Henry IV repaid Sir Thomas for his services with, amongst other things, a house near St Paul's in London.[23] Sir Thomas was a patron of the arts and is known to have given chasubles to Erpingham and other places. The chasuble of c. 1400–15, which is now in the Victoria and Albert Museum, is of Italian brocaded silk with an orphrey on the

FIG. 1   Brewers' Pall: detail of the
Assumption of the Virgin

FIG. 2   Brewers' Pall: detail of coat of arms

back and front which are of English work and which, according to Donald King, are of a group of orphreys produced between 1400 and 1430. Indeed, the actual iconographical design of the cross-orphrey on the back of the chasuble is close to that of a number of surviving orphreys of this later period, but here in the angles of the cross-arms are two shields which link this particular vestment with Sir Thomas Erpingham. On the left a shield displays the arms of Erpingham and, on the right, a shield contains several devices associated with Erpingham.

From the end of the 15th century come a number of palls, or hearse cloths, which still belong to some of the London companies. Apparently they were used to cover the coffins of members as they lay in state in the guild halls.

The Merchant Taylors Company owns two fine palls, the earliest being dated by Donald King to between 1490 and 1512.[24] Attached to the central panel, which is of cloth of gold, are four panels with embroidery in silver-gilt thread and coloured silks on purple velvet. Most of the iconography of these panels is associated with the Patron saint of the Merchant Taylors, St John the Baptist. In the centre of the long sides is the Baptism of Christ with, on either side, two representations of the Agnus Dei, alternating with St John himself and an angel with St John's head on a platter; at each end is a pair of shears. On the short sides, between representations of the Agnus Dei, are: the Presentation of St John's head to Salome and St John's Entombment. The scrolls behind the head of St John on the long sides are inscribed 'ECCE AGNUS DEI', and those of the angels 'CAPAT IOHANNIS BAPTET IN DISCO'.

The Brewers' Pall of c. 1490–1538[25] also has a cloth of gold central panel with four sides — here of red velvet. The Assumption of the Virgin is embroidered as the central scene on each long side (Fig. 1), separated from the coat of arms of the Brewers' Company (Fig. 2) by ears of barley. An inscription on the scrolls on either side of the shields is part of the antiphon to the Nunc Dimittis used at Compline during part of Lent in the Sarum Breviary ('Sancte Deus Que Cognoveris Occulta cordis Parce Peccatis Nostris. Sancte Fortis Et misericors Salvator Amare morti Ne tradis nos'). The Patron Saint of the Brewers' Company, St Thomas of Canterbury, is shown on each short side, vested and with mitre and cross-staff.

The Saddlers' Pall of 1490–1538[26] also has four side panels which are embroidered in silver-gilt thread and coloured silks on red velvet with the Assumption of the Virgin. An interesting feature of this pall is that after the Reformation the Virgin was hidden behind panels with the monogram 'IHS' inscribed on them. Either side of the Virgin are the arms of the Saddlers' Company and on the long sides is the inscription which is the concluding phrase of the Te Deum ('In te Dñe Speravi nõ Cõfundar In eternũ').

From the Great Period of Opus Anglicanum come two rare survivals in the form of seal bags protecting the Great Seal on two charters which are dated 8 June 1319.[27] The first is attached to a Confirmation, by Edward II, of articles for the better government of the City of London. On one side is the coat of arms posthumously attributed to Edward the Confessor, and on the other side a shield with St Paul — the coat of arms of the City of London.[28]

The second seal bag protects the seal on a Grant of the full use of liberties to the citizens of London. On one side is a shield with leopards, the arms of England and, on the other side, St Paul — again the arms of the City of London.[29] Both seal bags are embroidered in coloured silks and silver-gilt and silver thread.

Although much of the evidence is tentative there are a number of connections between London, Londoners and the high quality embroidery which was produced in England in the Middle Ages. It has been suggested that the bulk of this work was produced in London where the names of some of the workers are known and there are records that amongst their patrons were members of the Royal Family. Many examples of English embroidery survive from the Middle Ages but unfortunately, however, it is not possible to link surviving vestments with particular workers or workshops, although it is possible to see in these fine works the kinds of items which were produced in the London workshops.

ACKNOWLEDGEMENTS

I am particularly grateful to Mr Donald King who has always been ready with help and advice and to Miss S. Levey, Keeper, and her Staff of the Textile Department, Victoria and Albert Museum who have been extremely helpful in allowing me access to the many English embroideries in the Museum collection. I also wish to thank the Worshipful Companies of Saddlers, Merchant Taylors and Brewers who kindly allowed me to see their Companies' Palls. Also, thanks are due to the Administrator, Westminster Cathedral; Mme M. Flury-Lemberg, Abegg-Stiftung Bern, Riggisberg; the Director, Pinacoteca, Ascoli Piceno; and to the Curator, Capitolo della Cattedrale di Pienza.

REFERENCES

1. For example, 'Item, unum dorsale de opere anglicano cum imagine Salvatoris et beate Virginis...' and 'Item, aliud repositorium de opere anglicano cum imagine Salvatoris...' from *Inv. du Trésor*, 38 and quoted in Christie (1938), 36.

2. Fitch (1976). For mention of Rose, wife of John de Bureford see below p. 136.

3. *Plea and Memoranda Rolls*, 107 and quoted in Christie (1938), 36.

4. Christie (1938), 45–51 and pls I–III.

5. As may be seen in the Inventory of Christ Church, Canterbury of about the time of the Metropolitan Visitation of 1634: 'On the Cathedral-Altar-Glory Cloth... That Glory which is the shame of their Cathedral is made of very rich Imbroydery of Gold and Silver...' and the document of 14 June 1645 which shows the fate of the altar cloth: 'Receipt by Richard Culmer of £8.11s. 2d from Sir Robert Hartley, being the procedes of the burning of the embroidery called the Glory, belonging to the High Altar of Canterbury Cathedral...' from Legge and St John Hope (1902), 247 and its addenda opposite 1.

6. Copes were often stored in quadrant-shaped chests — two of which are preserved in York Minster (illustrated in Christie (1938), pl. LX) necessitating the vestment being folded in half; this led to much wear along the centre back. The copes in Saint Maximin and the Abegg-Stiftung Bern, Riggisberg have both had worn sections cut away; the former has just been stitched together (Christie (1938), pl. LX), and the latter has had its front edges joined.

7. This happened to the Chichester-Constable chasuble in New York (King (1963), 39 and pl. 16) and also to the Clare Chasuble in the Victoria and Albert Museum (673 — 1864) (King (1963), 19 and pl. 2); both were cut down from a bell-shape at some date, to form a modern design.

8.   Christie (1938), 3; King (1963), 5.

9.   'Eisdemque diebus, dominus Papa videns in aliquorum Anglicorum ornamentis ecclesiasticis, utpote in capis choralibus et infulis, aurifrisia concuspiscibilia, interrogavit ubinam ficta fuissent. Cui resposum est; "In Anglia." At ipse; "Vere hortus noster deliciarum est Anglia. Vere puteus inexhaustus est; et ubi multa abundant, de multis multa possunt extorqueri." Unde idem dominus Papa, concupiscentia illectus oculorum, literas suas bullatas sacras misit ad omnes fere Cisterciensis ordinis abbates in Anglia commorantes, quorum orationibus se nuper in capitulo Cisterciensi commendaverat, ut ipsi aurifrisia, ac si pro nihilo ipsa possent adquirere, mittere non differrent praeelecta, ad planetas et capas suas chorales adornadas. Quod mercennariis Londoniae qui ea venalia habebant non displicuit, ad placitum vendentibus; unde multi manifestam avaritiam Romana ecclesiae detestabantur.' *Chron. Maj.*, IV, 1240–4, 547. Translation from Christie (1938), 2.

10. Fitch (1976), 289.

11. *Letterbook B*, f. LXXX, 35 Edward I, translated in Riley (1868), 60 and cited in Christie (1938), 35 and Fitch (1976), 292.

12. Fitch (1976), 288–90.

13. *Golden Legend*, IV, 40, 41.

14. Issue Roll Easter 10 Edward II in *Pell Records*, 133.

15. King (1963), 32. (The orphrey shown on the watercolour drawing is somewhat later than the cope itself.)

16. *Plea and Memoranda Rolls*, 107: referred to in Christie (1938), 36.

17. *Letterbook H*, f. CXXXVIII, 5 Richard II, 8 January 1382, translated in Riley (1868), 455.

18. Christie (1938), 54ff. and pls VIII and IX: King (1963), 13.

19. Erdington Abbey, Birmingham: illustrated in Zarnecki *et al.* (1984), no. 490.

20. King (1963), 21. Similar designs were to be seen on other vestments. For example, on a chasuble at St Paul's, London: 'Item, casula de radice Jesse, quam dedit Rex Henricus, preciosa, breudata cum stellis et lunis et dorsali cum ymagine crucis, XVI lapidibus insertis, et deficiunt duo lapides' from an inventory of 1295 in Dugdale (1818), 323; and also on a cope at Christ Church, Canterbury: 'Capa W. de Middleton Norwicensis Episcopi, de rubeo Samicto brudata cum Jesse' from an inventory of 1315 in Legge and St John Hope (1902), 56.

21. Victoria and Albert Museum (175—1889).

22. King (1963), 21.

23. Victoria and Albert Museum (T256—1967). For this chasuble see King (1968), 59–64.

24. King (1963), 57.

25. King (1963), 58.

26. King (1963), 58.

27. Chandler and King (1960), 20–3, and pls I–IV.

28. Ibid., pls I and II.

29. Ibid., pls III and IV.

Some New Types of Late Medieval Tombs in the London Area

By Bridget Cherry

The fragmentary and much restored Perpendicular monuments which can be found in a few City churches and in a number of the parish churches scattered around the Greater London suburbs might seem to be an unpromising subject for research. Much greater attention has been given to their predecessors of the 13th and 14th centuries, particularly to the famous group in Westminster Abbey, and to the few more exceptional early 16th-century essays in the Renaissance style.

The 15th- and early 16th-century tombs which are the subject of this paper represent only a fragment of what once existed. The London friaries were exceptionally rich in monuments, as the accounts given by Stow make clear. In the case of Greyfriars, for example, his list of eminent people buried in the church runs to several pages, and includes members of the Royal family, nobles, bishops, knights and gentlemen:

All these and five times so many more have been buried there, whose monuments are wholly defaced; for there were nine tombs of alabaster and marble environ'd with strikes of iron in the choir, and one tomb in the body of the church also coped with iron, all pulled down, beside seven score gravestones of marble, all sold for £50 or thereabouts, by Sir Martin Bowes, goldsmith and alderman of London.[1]

Yet a centre of the importance of London should not be ignored if one is trying to gain some impression both of the tastes and attitudes of the patrons, and of the standards of monumental craftsmanship in the century before the Reformation. Enough survives to give some indication of the development of a number of types of monument. It is indeed the nature of some of these types that may account for their neglect. Many Perpendicular monuments are primarily architectural, and do not have sculptured effigies. They were often conceived as architectural frames for brasses, but relatively few of these brasses have survived the recurrent depredations and modernisations to which London churches were later subjected. Such tombs therefore may have little appeal to those whose chief interest is in the depiction of the deceased. But to concentrate solely on the effigy, whether in stone or brass, can be restricting. Unlike many tombs of earlier centuries, the late medieval monument was often a complex creation in many materials, of which the tomb chest and the effigy (if it existed) were only a part, and needs to be studied as a whole if its nature is to be fully understood.

THE SCREENED ENCLOSURE

One of the most distinctive attributes of many late medieval tombs is the private screened enclosure which marks out the area around the tomb. Chantry chapels were not a new idea in the 15th century, but it is during this period that their design and decoration are closely related to the tomb itself. The tomb could be made the centrepiece of such an enclosure, or could form a part of the screen dividing the chapel from the main body of the church, giving the opportunity for a more public display. Either solution provided scope for a complex iconography reflecting the patron's particular interests.

Two important survivals in London from the earlier 15th century illustrate these two types. The cage-tomb is exemplified by the chantry chapel of Henry V at Westminster

Abbey, planned when Henry made his will in 1415, but not completed until after 1439.[2] Although the siting of the tomb follows the tradition of the earlier royal tombs ranged around the shrine of King Edward, it departs from them in being set within its own enclosure, and in being a unique two-storey structure with an upper chapel whose outer walls and reredos provide ample scope for an elaborate programme of sculpture. This royal endorsement of the cage-tomb must have helped to promote the popularity of the type, even though it was to have no immediate royal successors. No further kings were buried at Westminster until Henry VII, whose chapel could be described as the *nec plus ultra* of the tomb within its own sculptured enclosure.

THE SCREEN-TOMB: THE MONUMENT OF JOHN HOLAND

The example of the screen-tomb is the less well-known monument to John Holand, third Duke of Exeter, who died in 1447 (Pl. XLA). This was formerly in the chancel of the Hospital of St Katharine-by-the-Tower. When this was destroyed in the 1820s for the new docks, after considerable protest from antiquarians, the tomb was preserved, and together with some other furnishings moved to the new church provided for the hospital in Regent's Park. In 1951, when St Katharine's Regent's Park became the Danish Church, the tomb was shifted again, to the chapel of St Peter ad Vincula within the precincts of the Tower of London, its present resting place. It now stands against a wall, but was originally a screen-tomb, with a doorway to its west which opened into a chapel north of the chancel, as is clear both from 18th-century plans and views of the interior of St Katharine's and from the fact that there is carving on the back of the canopy which would have faced into the chapel.[3]

John Holand (the second to bear the name) was a nephew of Henry IV, a military commander under both Henry IV and V, Constable of the Tower, member of the Privy Council, and a very wealthy man.[4] He died in 1447, but the monument was erected during his lifetime, probably before his second marriage in 1433, as the heraldry within the canopy above the feet of the effigies commemorates only Holand and his first wife Anne Stafford, who died in 1432. However, the tomb contains three alabaster effigies, that of Holand, and two more or less identical ladies. One of these must be Anne Stafford. The second has been identified as either his sister Constance or his third wife, both of whom are referred to in Holand's will, in which he specifies that he is to be buried in a chapel within the church of St Katharine's 'atte north ende of the high auter, in a tombe that is ordeyned for me, wt Anne my first wyff, and wt my sister Custaunce, and wt my wyff Anne that now is'.[5] This does not entirely elucidate the identity of the third effigy, as the will could be interpreted as intending only a common burial in the vault beneath, but it seems most likely that the second lady is intended to be Anne Montague, Holand's third wife, who died in 1457. Her will specifies that she was to be buried with her husband,[6] and her arms are painted on one of the shields held by the two angels carved between the cusps of the canopy arch. This may well have been an afterthought, together with the third effigy, for both the cramped positions of the three effigies upon the tomb chest and the arrangement of the shields above the effigies strongly suggest the tomb was originally intended for only two figures.

As one might expect from Holand's importance, this is an exceptional monument, and of great interest as the sole survivor of the major 15th-century royal and aristocratic memorials that once existed in and around the City of London. Although the alabaster effigies are not of the finest quality, the richly carved canopy recalls the tradition of the grandest 14th-century tombs, such as the Percy tomb at Beverley, but with up-to-date architectural motifs of the second quarter of the 15th century. The most striking of these is the use of the cusped and sub-cusped four-centred arch in place of the older form of the ogee arch or triplet of gabled arches. This is an early example of a type of tomb canopy that became extremely popular in the later 15th and early 16th centuries. The four-centred arch appears around the same time in the less elaborate screen-tomb of Lord Bouchier (died 1430) at Westminster Abbey.[7] But whereas the Bouchier tomb is primarily an exercise in heraldic display, the Holand tomb is remarkable for the quantity of its small-scale sculpture. The angular form of the canopy arch (a fashionable shape at this time), creates large spandrels on either side, which are filled by trumpeting angels. In addition there are censing angels between the cusps, angels with shields, and angels along the frieze above. The carving, now heavily whitewashed, is in suspiciously good condition and one suspects that some restoration may have taken place, either when the hospital buildings and church were repaired in 1800 and in 1820, or on the occasion of the move to Regent's Park. Ducarel found the effigies 'somewhat defaced' in 1782. Heads and hands of the effigies have certainly been restored; the same may be true of some of the smaller carvings.

Only part of the original sculptural scheme survives. The superstructure has only twelve empty niches, perhaps once filled by figures of the Apostles, which flank a central niche, now with a figure of St George,[8] but possibly intended for a figure of the Trinity, Christ in Majesty, or the Virgin. 18th-century drawings show niches with figures around the doorway beside the tomb which led into the Holand chapel. These were lost when the tomb was moved to Regent's Park. Carter's description of the chantry chapel (which survived the Reformation, and was later used as a vestry and then as chapter-house and Commissary's Court), mentions that 'an infinite number of small niches (statues destroyed) with a profusion of ornaments, fill every part of the work'.[9] This was clearly a tomb chapel with a complex iconographic programme, perhaps comparable in its richness to the surviving Beauchamp chapel at Warwick. A few hints remain on the tomb structure itself: on the lower part of the moulded edge of the tomb slab are a curious row of heads, and up the sides of the jambs are a series of lively carvings depicting a stag hunt, hare coursing, and groups of fox and geese, an idiosyncratic and presumably personal selection of subjects, possibly with some symbolic intention, for which no parallels are known on other tombs.[10]

OTHER SCREEN-TOMBS

While one cannot say for certain that the Holand tomb initiates this form of Perpendicular monument, the elaborate nature of its sculptural decoration suggests that it is one of the first designs of its type. It is noticeable that there is a general tendency when tomb designs are imitated for the sculptural ornament to become sparser and simpler. An especially close derivative of the Holand tomb is the canopy erected over the older late-13th-century effigy of Bishop Branscombe in Exeter Cathedral, described as new in 1443, which converted the monument into a screen-tomb between the Lady Chapel and St Gabriel's chapel. It not only has a cusped four-centred arch, but repeats the Holand tomb's motifs of censing and flying angels, although it has nothing similar to the genre sculpture of the jambs.[11]

A more basic reduction of the canopy type is the one at St Andrew Enfield, over the tomb of Joyce Tiptoft (died 1446). The heraldry of this canopy, a plain four-centred uncusped arch, with panelled soffit and spandrels simply decorated with foliage and shields, refers to Joyce Tiptoft's grandchildren, suggesting that the canopy is an addition of the early 16th century, possibly made to convert a simpler older monument into a grand screen-tomb between the chancel and the family chantry chapel to its north.[12] The tomb chest was also probably remade at this time: its design with shields in a series of lozenges is a slightly simpler version of the tomb chest shown on the well-known drawing of a royal tomb from the Royal Works. This project for Henry VI's tomb (intended at first for Windsor, then for Westminster, but never executed) illustrates how at the end of the century the four-centred canopy arch was still considered appropriate for the grandest of monuments, although its sculptured detail is restricted to foliage, shields and tracery; the inventive ingenuity of the designer is concentrated on the elaboration of the domed pinnacled niches adorning the superstructure.[13]

WALL MONUMENTS

A simpler version of the screen-tomb was the less space-consuming wall-monument with tomb chest and canopy, a compromise between the freestanding tomb, and the older tradition of the low 'founder's tomb' which forms part of the structure of the building. A favourite design for the canopy of this type of tomb throughout the 15th and into the early 16th century was the triplet of gabled arches divided by pinnacles, with the central arch springing from pendants. This type of canopy is found above the effigy of the celebrated court poet John Gower at St Mary Overie, (now Southwark Cathedral), a monument whose quality has been somewhat obscured by heavy restoration and overpainting (Fig. 1). This form of canopy must derive from the 13th- and 14th-century triple-gabled examples where the central gable rests on mullions, as in the cases of the Westminster tombs of Edmund Crouchback (1296) or John of Eltham (1334). The lost canopy of the latter is a closer source, as the three arches are of equal width.[14] With the elimination of the central mullions the effigy could be displayed to better advantage, and there was scope for the inclusion of details which must have been intended to be viewed by the onlooker, and in the case of the example at Southwark were very likely selected by Gower himself. The tomb may have been prepared before his death in 1408, for his will requested burial 'in loco ad hoc specialiter deputato'. His head rests on three books, his three major works: *Vox Clamantis*, *Speculum Meditantis* and *Confessio Amantis*. Painted beneath the canopy there were once three crowned allegorical female figures representing Charity, Mercy and Pity, with scrolls inscribed with French verses; there were also four Latin hexameters (attributed to Gower himself) on the theme of death and immortality.[15] The whole composition must have been intended as a didactic exposition on the theme of death and salvation by means of the three virtues depicted, a visual counterpart to Gower's moralising writing. The treatment of the tomb chest is conservative. It is decorated with panelled tracery (an echo of the tradition of weepers in niches), instead of the quatrefoils with shields which were becoming increasingly popular.

A triple canopy very similar in design to Gower's but used over a chest with quatrefoils, is employed for the commemorative tomb of Rahere, the Norman founder of the Hospital of St Bartholomew, Smithfield. The date of this is not recorded, although *c*. 1405 has been plausibly suggested, contemporary with the remodelling of the east end of the church.[16] As in the case of Gower's tomb, the monument is 'personalised'. Beside the effigy, and carved from the same block of stone, are two bedesmen holding books with quotations from Isaiah 'the Lord shall comfort Sion . . . and the desert shall rejoice and blossom as a rose' — no doubt intended as comment on the success of Rahere's foundation. A separate angel holds the arms of the priory. Rahere's tomb is in the place of honour on the north side of the sanctuary, as one might expect for a founder. It originally formed part of a canopied wall arcade, with two further arches to the east over a priest's doorway. These were removed in the 19th-century restoration, when the 12th-century apse was restored, and the floor lowered from its late medieval level, leaving the tomb on an uncomfortably high

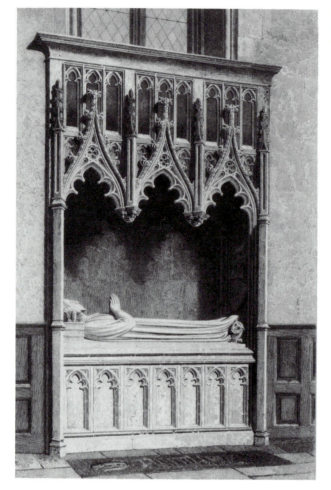

A similar arched canopy of around the same date is found over the tomb of Sir Bernard Brocas in Westminster Abbey, and the type continued to be popular in the later 15th century, as is shown by the monument of William Dudley, Bishop of Durham, at Westminster Abbey (1483), where the tomb chest has a brass instead of a stone effigy.[17] The type was also produced in Purbeck marble, as is illustrated by the tomb of Hugh Pemberton (1500) now at St Helen's Bishopsgate (Fig. 2).[18] This also had brasses instead of sculpture, but the arrangement here is rather different, for there were brasses on the back panel. The incorporation of mural brasses within an elaborate architectural framework became extremely popular in the later part of the 15th century, and can be seen as a further development of the desire to display the tomb to the onlooker, almost as if the monument were a stage set, which has already been noted in the case of the Gower tomb. It is perhaps not surprising that such arrangements are especially common in the case of tombs made entirely of Purbeck marble, as this was the usual material into which brasses were set.

Another specially lavish Purbeck marble tomb is that of Alderman John Croke in All Hallows by the Tower (1477) (Fig. 3).[19] This also had brasses on the back panel, from

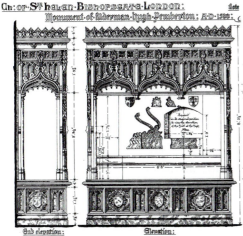

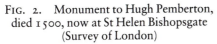

FIG. 2. Monument to Hugh Pemberton,
died 1500, now at St Helen Bishopsgate
(Survey of London)

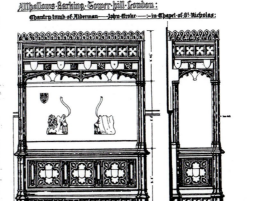

FIG. 3. Monument to John Croke, died
1477, All Hallows by the Tower (Survey of
London)

FIG. 4. Monument to Jane, Duchess of
Northumberland, All Saints Chelsea,
after a drawing (Survey of London)

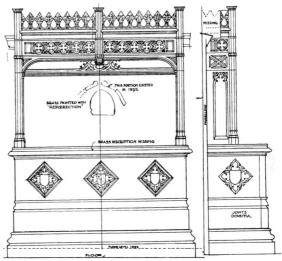

FIG. 5. Anonymous monument formerly in All
Hallows Barking (Survey of London)

which two groups of kneeling figures survive. The architectural detail is unusually rich, as
it is on the Pemberton tomb, unlike the more standard productions in Purbeck marble.
The two designs are not identical, but both tombs have chests with quatrefoils containing shields alternating with narrow niches, and a canopy with a miniature fan vault with
pendants. The Croke canopy departs from the triple-arched model, and has instead
a pair of very flat four-centred arches, and a frieze above with alternating fleurons and
shields.

A damaged Purbeck tomb in All Saints Chelsea, to Jane Guyldetord, wife of John Dudley, Duke of Northumberland, who died in 1555, shows how a similar type with panelled vaults and pendants and with brasses on the back panel, was still being produced in the middle of the 16th century. The tomb has been badly mutilated and has lost both its chest and the front of the canopy, but its original condition is recorded in two drawings reproduced by the Survey of London. These show a canopy with four hanging arches supported on two columns with reticulated decoration, and a small tomb chest, shorter than the canopy, decorated with shields in quatrefoils.[20] The 'Chaucer tomb' in Westminster Abbey is of exactly the same design, with a better preserved canopy. This monument was erected by Nicholas Brigham in 1556 after the original tomb had been destroyed; Lethaby suggested it could have been a reused tomb from a City church but its similarity to the contemporary Northumberland tomb indicates it is of the same date, and that the apparent discrepancy between canopy and tomb was deliberate. The design can perhaps be seen as a compressed chantry chapel, with space for the officiating priest at one end.[21]

PURBECK MARBLE TOMBS AND EASTER SEPULCHRES

The more common type of late medieval Purbeck tomb, widespread in the Home Counties, and very likely emanating from London workshops, is much plainer. The decoration of the tomb chest is restricted to incised diamonds with cusped quatrefoils and shields; the canopy is set back from the front of the chest, and has a single simple flattened arch with a frieze of quatrefoils or circles below cresting. Surviving examples in the London area are a tomb at St Mary Harefield, Middlesex, another in the church of Old St Pancras, Camden,[22] and the monument to Ann Packington in St Botolph Aldersgate in the City.[23] The first has later brasses of c. 1545 added to the back plate, the second has lost its brasses, but there are matrices indicating a Trinity and three groups of kneeling figures. The Packington monument is as late as 1563, with incised figures on the back panel imitating brasses. Another tomb of similar design existed in All Hallows Barking, until its destruction in World War II (Fig. 5).[24] It has been suggested that this could have been the tomb of Sir Robert Tate (died 1488) which was erected in the Lady Chapel which stood separately in the churchyard, but this is unproven, as no inscription remained when the tomb was recorded. The sole survival now is a brass plate from the back panel, rescued after the war, which depicts the Resurrection.[25] This strongly suggests that the tomb was of the type where an Easter Sepulchre was combined with a personal monument. Such structures were usually sited on the north side of the chancel, the traditional position for the Easter Sepulchre, although this does not appear to have been the position of this example. Back panels of such tombs sometimes included a depiction of the Resurrection flanked by kneeling figures of the donor and family, either in brass or carved in stone.[26]

The dates of such monuments are often difficult to establish if, as in this case, the identifying brasses with inscriptions and heraldry have disappeared, but there is evidence that this type of Easter Sepulchre already existed in the last quarter of the 15th century. A pertinent example is recorded at Stanwell, a village west of London (formerly in Middlesex, now Surrey). The will made in 1479 by Thomas Windsor, Lord of the manor, specified that he should be buried on the north side of the choir of his parish church, 'afore the ymage of our lady wher the sepultur of our Lord stondith wherupon I will that ther be made a playne tombe of marble of a competent hight to th'entent that yt may ber the blissid body of our Lord and the sepulture at the time of Estre to stand upon the same and with myne Armes and a scriptur convenient to be sett aboute the same tombe'.[27] The precise instructions suggest this may have been an early instance of a new practice. The monument is illustrated

FIG. 6.   Monument to Thomas Windsor,
died 1483, formerly in St Mary Stanwell
(*Gentleman's Magazine*, 1813)

FIG. 7.   Monument to Henry Colet, died
1505, St Dunstan Stepney, as it appeared in
the 18th century (*Gentleman's Magazine*,
1793)

in the volumes of the *Gentleman's Magazine* for 1793 and 1813 (Fig. 6). Although by then
the canopy had been mutilated, it is clear that its design was extremely close to the
anonymous monument in All Hallows Barking, with the same flattened arch below a row of
quatrefoils, broken by a central pendant, and even the same small motif of a diagonal cross
above the tracery panel on the exterior of the end wall. Matrices for brasses on the back
panel are clearly visible.[28] The tomb chest is plain apart from an end panel with quatrefoils;
this panel appears to be of a more elaborate design than the incised lozenges of the All
Hallows tomb. Windsor died in 1483 and his will was proved two years later. His tomb is
interesting not only as an early well-documented case of the Easter Sepulchre combined
with a personal monument, but as an early dated example of what became one of the most
popular designs produced by the Purbeck marblers.

A grander surviving example of an Easter Sepulchre is the tomb of Henry Colet, mercer,
Lord Mayor, and father of Dean Colet, at St Dunstan's Stepney (1505).[29] This is a large
monument on the north side of the chancel, with freestone canopy with panelled interior.
No evidence remains of any brasses. Its present appearance is somewhat suspect. Strype
records that the tomb was 'refreshed' by the Company of Mercers in 1605, and repaired
again in 1697, while the *Gentleman's Magazine* of 1793 reports a further restoration 'ten
years ago' and illustrates the tomb with a classical cornice (Fig. 7).[30] It seems therefore that
the straight top to the canopy with little cusped arches (not paralleled by any known
contemporary canopies) is not the original design.

THE 'LONDON EASTER SEPULCHRE'

Frequently the Easter Sepulchre-cum-tomb was a smaller structure, not more than six feet
long. The absence of recumbent effigies made a full-length tomb unnecessary, and such

FIG. 8.   Monument to Sir Richard and Jane
Rokeby, died 1523, formerly in the Savoy
Hospital (J. T. Smith, Antiquities of London
and Environs, 1791–1800)

FIG. 9.   Monument to Thomas More,
All Saints Chelsea, erected 1532
(Faulkner 1829)

compact structures must have been a boon in the crowded City churches. There is a notable group of monuments of this type in and around London, dating from the first third of the 16th century, which are based on the same architectural pattern, and which probably came from the same workshop in the London area.[31] The common feature that identifies them is a free-stone canopy consisting of a four-centred arch with splayed reveals framing a back panel, and an elaborately carved vine-scroll frieze and shields above. Five examples are or were in Easter Sepulchre positions; the function of one of them, the tomb of Johane Alfrey at St Helen's Bishopsgate, is confirmed by her will.[32] Six other tombs based on the same pattern, but sited elsewhere in their churches, demonstrate the popularity of the type.[33] The details of the architectural design suggest a connection with the circle involved in the royal works in Windsor and London; a possible mason who could have been responsible was John Aylmer, who worked at St George's Windsor and at the Savoy hospital, where one of these tombs once existed (Fig. 8). He lived in Southwark, and both his will and inventory indicate that he was engaged in the production of monuments.[34]

Most of the tombs in this group were designed with brasses of kneeling figures on their back panels, although generally nothing but the matrices remain. They are a refinement of the Purbeck marble sepulchre-cum-tomb design, for the splayed reveals make the back panel more easily visible, and accentuate the tendency already noted of providing a display for the onlooker.

THE NEW ICONOGRAPHY

In this type of monument, whether Easter Sepulchre or simple tomb, one is dealing not just with the substitution of brasses for carved stone effigies, but with the replacement of the recumbent effigy by something quite different: portraits of the deceased and his or her family kneeling in prayer. There are plenty of earlier examples of full-length brasses on tomb chests, also occasional kneeling figures appearing as 15th-century floor brasses, but in England the combination of mural kneeling figures with a canopied tomb chest appears to be a development of the later 15th century. The kneeling figure witnessing the Resurrection was particularly appropriate for an Easter Sepulchre, but the idea is not restricted to such monuments and not even to wall-monuments. It sometimes occurs on freestanding full-size chest tombs, as in the case of the Purbeck monument to Sir William Say, of the early 16th century, at Broxbourne, Herts, which has, instead of effigies, an upright panel at the east end where matrices indicate there were kneeling figures and the Trinity.[35] The inclusion of kneeling figures on such tombs can be seen as a part of a wider movement toward the integration of sacred and secular subjects, in an endeavour to give greater actuality to the events of the Passion, and to stress the personal redemption of the individuals commemorated.

This new way of commemorating the deceased did not entirely oust the traditional full-scale tomb with lifesize recumbent effigies, which remained the accepted mode for tombs of outstanding importance. The type is represented in the City by the excellent monument to Sir John Crosby and his wife at St Helen's Bishopsgate (1476),[36] and at Westminster Abbey by the still more famous tomb of Henry VII, which despite its Italian workmanship is traditional in its composition.[37] However, the new iconography is sufficiently common in the London area in the late 15th and early 16th centuries to indicate a widespread preference. What were the reasons for its popularity, and from where did these ideas come? The desire to avoid the expense of a traditional recumbent effigy is hardly a sufficient explanation. The inspiration for a more theatrical display of figural subjects must ultimately be the new types of tomb which were being developed on the continent from the end of the 14th century, particularly those of the Avignon Popes, with their elaborate tiers of sculptured scenes and figures set against the wall behind the effigy.[38] The prominence given to kneeling figures in 15th-century French and Burgundian painting and sculpture is part of the same trend.[39] In England such ideas only gradually found favour. The kneeling donor figure is not uncommon in English stained glass of the 15th century, but its occurrence as a major element in sculptured monuments is exceptional, as on the grandiose tomb of Thomas, Lord Morley (died 1435), at Hingham, Norfolk, where conventional full-length brass effigies are supplemented by kneeling donor figures on the canopy.[40] It is only from the later 15th century that the idea was taken up widely, with the Purbeck marblers taking a leading role in its dissemination. The substitution of living figures for recumbent effigies of the dead may be derived more directly from French and Flemish wall-tombs with sculptured scenes, the equivalent in sculpture of the painting with donor figures. The loss of so many continental tombs makes comparisons difficult, but the French monuments of the 15th century recorded in the Gagnières collection of drawings include several which depart from the tomb with recumbent effigy, although this undoubtedly remains the dominant type. Some of these include donor figures, with saints or the Virgin, others have scenes of the Passion, for example two tombs at Rouen, both in Easter Sepulchre positions on the north side of the choir: number 999, Jean de Hangest (died 1409) at the church of the Celestins, where a tomb chest is shown with ogee-arched canopy, framing what appears to be a depiction of the Pietà, and the more certain entombment group shown in number 1135, the tomb of Robert Jolivet (died 1444), at Saint Michel de Rouen. This tomb has no donor or effigy, but an inscription to Jolivet is shown along the edge of the tomb chest.[41] The identification of a personal tomb with an Easter Sepulchre group is found again in the much more elaborate Entombment group at Solesmes, which has been identified from the seemingly deliberately cryptic inscriptions on the orphreys of the lifesize figures, as the tomb of Abel Rouault and his wife, completed in 1496.[42]

In England there is no evidence for a tradition of large and elaborate entombment groups of this type. The one partial exception is the remarkably fine 16th-century stone figure of the dead Christ which was found in 1954 in the ruins of the Mercers' chapel in the City, but this appears to have been without attendant figures.[43] Generally it was not the drama and pathos of the entombment that was depicted, but the more hopeful occasion of the resurrection, with the figure of Christ stepping from the tomb. In this respect the English late medieval Easter sepulchres continue an iconographic tradition established in the 14th century, but with the innovation of donor figures witnessing the scene, as in the continental examples.[44] This is not a type of monument that is exclusive to London: examples can be found in most counties, and there must be many more that have disappeared. However, the concentration of survivals in and around London, despite the unfavourable circumstances, does indicate that this was a particularly popular type of memorial in the capital, and perhaps something of a speciality of the London workshops. The choice of the iconography, however, was a matter for the patron; one reason for the continuing popularity of the Easter Sepulchre in the 1520s among both clergy and laymen may be that such monuments indicate a deliberate effort to stress traditional doctrine and liturgy in explicit visual form in the face of growing criticism of the Church's practices.

THE 'LITTLE MONUMENT'

It is interesting that several of the earlier examples of the London Easter Sepulchre design with the splayed reveals are associated with men connected with leading ecclesiastics: Hugh Peyntwyn (died 1504) and Henry Mompesson (died 1509), who are both buried at St Mary Lambeth and both worked for Archbishop Warham, and Christopher Urswyck, rector of St John Hackney, a more notable figure, a former Dean of Windsor and friend not only of Warham but of Erasmus, John Colet and Sir Thomas More (Pl. XLB).[45] This connection with leading members of the 'reforming establishment' leads to a consideration of two monuments whose humble nature is in even starker contrast to the significance of the persons they commemorated. Of the first, the earliest monument to John Colet, Dean of St Paul's, we know very little. He died in 1519, and his will stated that he was to be buried in the cathedral 'nigh unto the image of St Wilgefort where I made a lytel monument'. A letter from Erasmus confirms that he was buried on the south side of the choir 'in humili sepulchro quod in eum usum iam ante annos aliquot deligerat, inscriptione addita Joan. Col.'.[46] It seems possible that this exceptionally minimal inscription had an influence on Urswyck, for his Easter Sepulchre, unusually, has nothing on the back plate except his name, motto, and the date 1519, two years before his death, but the same year as the death of Colet. Urswyck's more conventional floor brass was perhaps put down only after his death. In the case of Colet, it is clear that others did not consider his humble monument appropriate, and not long afterwards the Mercers' Company had it replaced by a more elaborate one, incorporating a bust (probably by Torregiano) and a cadaver.[47]

Colet's low tomb could have resembled the one which was erected by Sir Thomas More in 1532, on the south side of the chancel of his parish church of All Saints Chelsea, after the death of his father and his first wife, and immediately after his resignation as Chancellor.[48] It consists of a canopy with four-centered arch, which, unusually, rests only on a low plinth, without a tomb chest. The present monument is not the original one, but a conscientious facsimile made in 1833, as is shown by the engraving in Faulkner's *History of Chelsea*, made before it was replaced (Fig. 9). The inscription had been recut already in the 17th century.[49] This inscription, unlike the one on Colet's tomb, is of exceptional length, giving in addition to the celebrated Latin verse mentioning his two wives, a carefully considered account of More's career, a precocious forerunner of the long epitaphs on tombs of later centuries. More was sufficiently concerned about this epitaph to send a copy of it in a letter to Erasmus in 1533. More had resigned over his support of the independence of the Church courts against the Commons 'Supplication Against the Ordinaries', and it seems likely that the epitaph was intended as a kind of public apology for his life, at a time when his political career appeared to be over.[50] Traditional in its architectural form, innovative in its inscription, radical in its lowly nature, More's tomb in its humble way can be seen as a reflection of the complex nature of the man himself, eager to assimilate the new learning of Colet and Erasmus, but a defender of the power of the established Church, although uninterested in traditional forms of popular piety.[51] More and Colet's tombs must surely have been intended as deliberate demonstrations against pompous burial ceremonies, elaborate monuments and attendant chantry arrangements in private chapels. They may have been modest, but they were not stereotyped productions ordered casually from a monumental mason, and the striking contrast in the approach to their inscriptions is revealing evidence of the different characters of the two men. One should however be wary of making too simplistic an equation between traditional architectural forms and defence of the old order: it is worth recalling that in contrast to the conventional Perpendicular ornament on More's tomb, the capitals of the responds to the south chapel at Chelsea, which bear More's arms and the date 1528, are one of the first examples in England of the use of Renaissance forms for architectural detail.[52] Yet it is telling that More chose to set up his tomb not in the family chapel but in the chancel.

As far as one can judge from the 19th-century copy, the Perpendicular canopy of More's tomb was competent but not particularly original in its details. It has the feature of traceried panelling, cusped top and bottom, around the soffit of the arch, a widespread 16th-century motif, but does not have the splayed reveals of the 'London design'. A closer stylistic comparison is with a canopy arch of similar proportions which belongs to the Easter Sepulchre tomb of Gregory Lovell (died 1545), at St Peter and St Paul, Harlington (Pl. XLc).[53]

This is a curious structure, which before the 19th-century restoration of the church consisted of a plain tomb chest with brasses, with the small, ill-fitting, canopy upon it, standing on the north side of the chancel, as is shown in a painting reproduced in Wilson's history of Harlington.[54] During the restoration the two parts were separated, and it was discovered that the brasses were palimpsests. It seems very possible that not only the brasses but the whole structure was cobbled together from reused material, perhaps spoil from a monastic house.[55] The quality of the carving on the canopy is exceptionally high, with a delicate vine scroll surmounted by cresting in the form of repeated IHS monograms. But the most unusual feature is a small shafted and arched recess at the back. This has been explained as a receptacle for the Sacrament during the Holy Week ceremonies, but if this was its function, it is odd that the recess is not paralleled in any other known Easter Sepulchres of this period. There is no trace of a door, so it could not have been used as an aumbry. Whatever the original liturgical function, once incorporated in the Lovell tomb it seems likely that the canopy functioned as an Easter Sepulchre, and is of interest in showing that the tradition still flourished in the 1540s.[56]

CONCLUSION

Antiquarian records and fragmentary remains, both of the ubiquitous quatrefoiled tomb chest and of brasses which may once have had architectural surrounds, hint at the huge quantity of late medieval monuments which have disappeared or of which one knows tantalizingly little.[57] From the survivals, it is clear that some London tombs are not of inspiring quality, and have helped to give the late medieval monument a poor reputation as being repetitive and mass produced. Many monuments were repeats of standard designs, but there was sufficient variety of these to suit a wide range of purses and tastes. The quality of the best work could be extremely high, as is shown by the Holand tomb, and this is true also of work on a small scale, such as the delicately carved Peyntwyn Easter Sepulchre at Lambeth, or the canopy at Harlington, and also by the best of the tombs in Purbeck marble.

But artistic merit and evidence for workshop connections are not the only reasons why London tombs are interesting. Their form and iconography are also revealing. Some common themes can be traced which, although found in late medieval tombs elsewhere, seem to be particularly pronounced in the examples discussed above. One of these is an increasing tendency for the tombs to be designed for display. The screen-tomb, where the effigy is visible from outside as well as from within the chantry chapel, the disappearance of the impediment of central mullions from the canopied tomb and, in the most extreme form, the use of a pictorial vertical image in place of the recumbent effigy are all different manifestations of this principle. In these later monuments, the emphasis on the person commemorated as alive, often shown together with his or her family, and in close association with images of the saints, the Trinity, or the Resurrected Saviour, is a striking departure from the traditional formal representation of the lifeless body upon the tomb chest. The theme of personal resurrection is at its most explicit in the tombs which also funtioned as Easter Sepulchres. 'Ego resurgam et in carne meo videbo Jesum / Deum Salvatorem meum' is the start of an inscription recorded on the anonymous tomb with the resurrection brass at All Hallows Barking.[58] This attitude can be seen as the direct antithesis to the more exceptional late medieval tomb which stresses mortality by showing the decaying cadaver,[59] for both types are concerned not with the moment of death but with what happens afterwards. Placed in a sanctified position in the chancel, and forming a centre of liturgical activity, the Easter Sepulchre tomb can also be seen as an alternative to the divisive tradition of the separate chantry chapel, and in this respect is related to the deliberately unassuming monuments put up by Colet and More.

The monuments discussed above all made use of the traditional late Gothic vocabulary of architectural detail, and suggest that the existence of foreign craftsmen working in England at first had little effect on the conservative traditons of the London tomb-makers. Only in the Purbeck monuments of the 1550s does one begin to find some new motifs, such as the reticulated columns (which had appeared earlier on the choir stalls in Henry VII's chapel). By then monuments existed in England which were fully in the Renaissance spirit, but an examination of these and their influence lies outside the scope of this paper.

REFERENCES

1. Stow (1912), 283–8. Many tombs in other churches mentioned by Stow, which are now lost, survived into the early 18th century, see especially Strype's edition of Stow (1720), which includes the churches of the villages around London.
2. St John Hope (1913–4), 129–86; Colvin and Brown (1963), 488–90.
3. For description, plan and views of the tomb in its original position see Nicholls (1824). This reproduces views published in Ducarel's account in *Bib. Top. Brit.* v. For a description of the tomb when at Regent's Park see RCHM *London*, II, 88–9, and more fully, *SLond*, XIX, part 2, 110, pls 65–8 and frontispiece.

4. For Holand's career see *Compl. Peerage*, V, 205–11.
5. Nicholls (1780), 282 ff., also quoted in Nicholls (1824), 5–7.
6. *Compl. Peerage*, V, 211.
7. For the tomb of Lewis Robessart, Lord Bourchier see RCHM *London*, I, 37, pls 62, 65.
8. 18th-century views show all the upper niches empty.
9. J. Carter, quoted in Nicholls (1824), 16.
10. Varty (1967), 82, interprets these depictions of fox and geese (the fox seizing the goose, followed by the goose capturing and hanging the fox) as a gloss on the theme of the Wheel of Fortune; this does not however explain the presence of the more conventional hunting scenes.
11. For discussion of the Branscombe canopy and the related tomb of Bishop Stafford at Exeter Cathedral, see Cherry (forthcoming).
12. RCHM *Middlesex*, 21, pl. 58. The heraldry is described in *Mon. Sepul.*, 5, 136.
13. Colvin (1975), III, 211, pl. 15. The traceried lozenge diaper pattern found on the tomb chest of the royal design was widely imitated. See e.g. the monument attributed to Sir Richard Ryther (d. 1491), at Ryther, Yorkshire West Riding, discussed in Routh and Knowles (1981).
14. The two canopies are illustrated in Crossley (1921), 54, 57.
15. The tomb is illustrated in Blore (1826). Blore was responsible for moving the tomb from the nave to the south transept in 1832, when the old paintwork was stripped off and renewed by Willement. The paintings of the Virtues, which had been replaced by copies on canvas, probably during a restoration in 1798, were removed, and the French verses repainted on inscribed scrolls. These disappeared when the monument was moved back into the restored nave in 1894. See Dollman (1881), 37, 47; Thompson (1910), 201–19, which gives the verses and excerpts from Gower's will. For the modern repainting see Friends of Southwark (1958).
16. RCHM *London*, IV, 127, pls 70, 173. See Webb (1821), I, 70–5, for an account of the monument and its restorations. The pinnacles and other details were restored in Coade stone in 1815; this was replaced in the restoration of 1867. *Vet. Mon.*, II, pl. XXXVI, shows the canopied front extending further east with a total of six arches.
17. RCHM *London*, I, 40, 43, pls 69, 80.
18. *SLond.*, IX, part 1, 38, 63, pls 77, 78. This tomb was brought from St Martin Outwich when that church was demolished in 1874.
19. *SLond.*, XII, part 2, 71, 77, pls 84–6.
20. RCHM *London*, II, 10, pl. 15; *SLond.*, VII, part 3, 36–8, pls 61–6.
21. RCHM *London*, I, 51a, pl. 95; Lethaby (1925), 287–8. Tombs with chests shorter than the canopy occur elsewhere, see e.g. the monument to Sir John Spencer, d. 1522, at Great Brington, Northamptonshire.
22. RCHM *Middlesex*, 54, 53; *SLond.*, XIX, part 2, 82, pl. 41.
23. RCHM *London*, IV, 3. The will of Ann Packington, quoted in Heales (1869), 308, makes it clear that she wanted a tomb in the tradition of the Easter Sepulchre monuments discussed below. It was to be sited 'at thende of the highe aulter wheras the sepulture was used moste commonly to stande, if the roome and place maie be suffered'.
24. *SLond.*, XII, 71–2, 87, pls 101, 105, 106.
25. The brass is illustrated in Blewett (n.d.) 17 and Owen Evans (1969), 89.
26. For examples in brass see Owen Evans (1969), 88. For Easter sepulchres generally, Heales (1869), 263–308; Sheingorn (1987).
27. Heales (1865–9), 105; the will is quoted in full on pp. 120–1.
28. *Gentleman's Magazine*, vol. 63, part 2, 1793, fig. 3 facing p. 993; vol. 82, part 2, 1812, fig. facing page 121, illustrates the same tomb, but wrongly states it is at Harlington.
29. RCHM *London*, V, 70, pl. 127.
30. Stow (1720), 86; *Gentleman's Magazine*, 63, 179, Part 2, 712–3.
31. For further discussion of this group see Cherry (1984), 86–94.
32. PRO Prob. 11/22, 38–9; quoted in *SLond.*, IX, 55.
33. The other tombs in this group (in Greater London unless otherwise specified) which are or were in Easter Sepulchre postions are at St John Hackney, St Mary Lambeth, St Mary Norwood, at Otford, Kent, and at the Savoy Chapel (destroyed); the examples in other positions are a second tomb at St Mary Lambeth, and tombs at All Saints Edmonton, St Mary Beddington, St John Croydon, St Mary Stone, Kent. For further details see Cherry (1984).
34. Harvey (1984), 11.
35. RCHM *Hertfordshire*, 72.
36. *SLond.*, IX, part 1, 70; RCHM *London*, IV, 23, pls 70–2.
37. RCHM *London*, I, 59 ff., pls 106–27.
38. Baron (1979), 169–86. *Sculp. fun. à Avignon*.

39. For the growing popularity of kneeling figures on French tombs see Mâle (1908), 467–8. Kneeling figures are also found on a few 15th-century French brasses, see Cameron (1970), 34 (Bishop Avantage, Amiens, 1456); 35 (Canon Faulcquier, Dargnies, 1433); 38 (John Mouey and wife, Paris, Musèe de Cluny 1453). Wall brasses with religious scenes were known in England by the mid-15th century. The will of John Mollesley, drover (d. 1444/5), specified a brass with the Trinity and saints, to be placed on the exterior wall of the chapel of St Stephen, St Sepulchre Holborn. See Bradford (1940), 179. I am grateful to Nicholas Rogers for this reference.
40. Prior and Gardner (1912), 456–7, fig. 529.
41. Adhémar (1974), 178; idem. (1976), 11.
42. Tonellier (1962), 318–38; idem. (1963), 22–40.
43. Cook and Evans(1954), 168–80.
44. For English Sepulchres in the 14th century see Sekules (1986), 118–31. The tradition is continued by the carved 16th-century Renaissance tombs of Sussex and Hampshire see Shilliam (1986), ch. iv.
45. Cherry (1984), 90–1. On Urswyck's intellectual interests see Trapp (1987); on his relationship with Colet, Gleason (1989), 55–7.
46. For the history of Colet's monuments see Grossman (1950), 202–36.
47. Illustrated in Grossman (1950), fig. 54c.
48. RCHM *London*, II, 9–10.
49. Faulkner (1829), 206–7.
50. On the epitaph see Faulkner (1829); also Marius (1985), 376, 442–3.
51. Marius (1985), 296–7.
52. Summerson (1977), 31, fig. 6.
53. RCHM *Middlesex*, 59, pl. 141.
54. Wilson (1926), 26–33.
55. On the brasses see Page Phillips (1980), 1, 47. One fragment probably came from St John of Jerusalem, Clerkenwell.
56. For instances of Easter Sepulchre practices continuing in the 1540s see Heales (1869), 306–8.
57. For example: one would like to know more about the tomb at St John's Hackney of Sir John Heron, (d. 1525). A fragment of a quatrefoiled tomb chest with the Heron arms is shown in the 18th-century view of the interior of the church (Pl. XLb), and is shown in more detail in *Misc. Gen. et Her.*, N.S. 1. (I am grateful to Dr Maurice Howard for this reference). Heron was lord of the manor at Hackney; his son Giles married a daughter of Sir Thomas More. The Heron arms appeared on the rebuilt church in which Urswyck placed his Easter Sepulchre. Likewise, for different reasons, another tantalising survival is the brass to the important royal mason Henry Redman, at St Lawrence, New Brentford, which one suspects must have had an architectural frame. He died in 1528, and his will stated he should be buried on the north side of the choir 'where the vestry would be made'. (Harvey (1984), 248.) The tomb could have been an Easter Sepulchre; perhaps it is of significance that his widow, who died in 1531, left 'a fine shete wt a sym of venyce gold and sylke' for the Easter Sepulchre. (Harvey (1987), 7.)
58. See n. 24 above.
59. There are few extant examples of London cadaver tombs of this period; one is in St Mary Overie Southwark, identity unknown; another is the figure surviving from a larger monument to William Weston, the last Prior of St John of Jerusalem, Clerkenwell, who died in 1540. The rush mat below the cadaver suggests this was a tomb of Franco-Flemish type.

ABBREVIATIONS AND SHORTENED TITLES

AASB	*Architectural Association Sketchbooks*
Acta Sanct.	*Acta Sanctorum*
Age of Chivalry	*The Age of Chivalry: Art in Plantagenet England 1200–1400*, ed. J. Alexander and P. Binski (Royal Academy, London 1987)
Ann. Bermund.	'Annales de Bermundeseia', ed. H. R. Luard, in *Annales Monastici*, III (RS 36, London 1866)
Ann. Lond.	'Annales Londonienses', ed. W. Stubbs, in *Chronicles of the Reigns of Edward I and Edward II* (RS 76, London 1882)
Archaeol. J.	*Archaeological Journal*
A-S Chron.	*The Anglo-Saxon Chronicle*, ed. D. Whitlock *et al.* (London 1961)
Assize of Nuisance	*London Assize of Nuisance, 1301–1431*, ed. H. M. Chew and W. Kellaway (Lond. RS 10, London 1973)
BAA CT	*British Archaeological Association Conference Transactions*
BAR	*British Archaeological Reports*
B/E	N. Pevsner, *et al.*, ed., *The Buildings of England* (Harmondsworth various dates)
Bib. Top. Brit.	*Bibliotheca Topographica Britannica*, ed. John Nicholls (London 1782)
BM Cat. Mss Adds.	(British Museum) *Catalogue of Additions to the Manuscripts, 1926–1930* (London 1959)
BM Cat. Mss Cott.	*A Catalogue of the Manuscripts in the Cottonian Library, deposited in the British Museum* (London 1802)
BOMPT	Book of Orders of Parliament of the Middle Temple, Middle Temple Library
Bull. Mon.	*Bulletin Monumental*
CA	*Congrès Archéologique de France*
Cal. Inquis. Misc.	*Calendar of Inquisitions Miscellaneous* 7 vols (London 1916–68)
Cat. Mss Univ. Camb.	*A Catalogue of the Manuscripts Preserved in the Library of the University of Cambridge*, I (Cambridge 1856), III (Cambridge 1858)
CBA	Council for British Archaeology
Chron. Maj.	*Matthaei Parisienis, monachi sancti Albani, chronica majora*, ed. H. R. Luard, 7 vols (RS 57, London 1872–83)
Chrons Edward I and Edward II	*Chronicles of the Reigns of Edward I and Edward II*, ed. W. Stubbs (RS 76, London 1882–3)
CL	Conway Library
CLRO	Corporation of London Records Office
Compl. Peerage	G. E. Cockayne, *The Complete Peerage*, ed. V. Gibbs *et al.*, 12 vols (London 1910–59)
Corinti	*Firenze antica nei desegni di Corinto Corinti* (Istituto Geographico Militare, Florence 1976)
Councils and Eccles. Docs.	*Councils and Ecclesiastical Documents*, III, ed. A. W. Haddan and W. Stubbs (Oxford 1871)
DB	*Domesday Book seu Liber Censualis* (London 1783)

De Ant. Leg. Lib.	*De Antiquis Legibus Liber*, ed. T. Stapleton (Camden Society original series 34, London 1846)
De Gestis Pontificum	William of Malmesbury, *De Gestis Pontificum Anglorum*, ed. N. E. S. A. Hamilton (RS 52, London 1870)
De Gestis Regum	William of Malmesbury, *De Gestis Regum*, ed. W. Stubbs (RS 90, London 1887–9)
EHR	*English Historical Review*
Florence	*Florence of Worcester, Chronicon ex Chronicis*, ed. B. Thorpe (London 1848–9)
Foliot Letters	*Letters and Charters of Gilbert Foliot*, ed. A. Morey and C. N. L. Brooke (Cambridge 1967)
Foxe Acts	*The Acts and Monuments of John Foxe*, ed. S. R. Cattley, 8 vols (London 1837–41)
GBA	*Gazette des Beaux Arts*
Golden Legend	Jacobus de Voragine, *The Golden Legend*, Englished by William Caxton, ed. F. S. Ellis (London 1900)
HBMC	Historic Buildings and Monuments Commission
Henry III: Letters	*Royal and other letters illustrative of the reign of Henry III*, ed. W. W. Shirley (RS 27, London 1862)
Henry VIII: Letters	*Letters and Papers . . . of Henry VIII*, ed. J. S. Brewer *et al.*, 21 vols plus Addenda (London 1864–1932)
HMSO	Her Majesty's Stationery Office
Huntingdon	Henry of Huntingdon, *Historia Anglorum*, ed. T. Arnold (RS 74, London 1879)
Husting, Wills	*Calendar of Wills Proved and Enrolled in the Court of Husting, London, A.D. 1258–A.D. 1688, part 1 (A.D. 1258–A.D. 1358)*, ed. R. R. Sharpe (London 1889)
Inv. du Trésor	*Inventaire du Trésor du Saint Siège sous Boniface VIII (1295)*, ed. E. Moliner (Paris 1888)
JBAA	*Journal of the British Archaeological Association*
JSAH	*Journal of the Society of Architectural Historians*
JWCI	*Journal of the Warburg and Courtauld Institutes*
Island of England	*A relation of the island of England*, ed. C. A. Sneyd (Camden Society original series 37, London 1847)
ITBTO	Inner Temple Bench Table Orders
ITL MISC.	Inner Temple Library Miscellanae xx
Letter-Book B	*Calendar of Letter-Books . . . of the City of London: Letter-Book B*, ed. R. R. Sharpe (London 1900)
Letter-Book H	*Calendar of Letter-Books . . . of the City of London: Letter-Book H*, ed. R. R. Sharpe (London 1907)
Lib. Alb.	*Liber Albus*, ed. H. T. Riley in *Munimenta Gildhallae Londoniensis*, I and III (RS 12, London 1859–62)
Lib. Cust.	*Liber Custumarum*, ed. H. T. Riley in *Munimenta Gildhallae Londoniensis*, II (RS 12, London 1860)
LMAS	London and Middlesex Archaeological Society
Lond. Arch.	*The London Archaeologist*

London Eyre	*The London Eyre of 1244*, ed. H. M. Chew and M. Weinbaum (Lond. RS 6, London 1970)
Lond. RS	London Record Society
Lond. TR	*London Topographical Record*
Lond. TS	London Topographical Society
Magnum Rot. Scacc.	*Magnum Rotulum Scaccarii*, ed. J. Hunter (London 1833)
Med. House Fittings	*Medieval House Fittings*, Department of Urban Archaeology, Museum of London, Medieval small finds from excavations in London series (in preparation)
Memorials	*Memorials of London and London Life in the XIIIth, XIVth and XVth Centuries*, ed. H. T. Riley (London 1868)
Misc. Gen. et Her.	*Miscellanea Genealogica et Heraldica*
Mon. Sepul.	Gough, R., *Monumenta Sepulchura*, 2 vols (London 1786, 96)
MTMP	Middle Temple Minutes of Proceedings, Middle Temple Library
NMR	National Monuments Record
Novae Narrat.	*Novae Narrationes*, ed. E. Shanks (Selden Society 80, London 1963)
Orderic	*The Ecclesiastical History of Orderic Vitalis*, ed. M. Chibnall (Oxford 1969–)
Pell Records	*Pell Records extracted and translated from the original*, ed. F. Devon (London 1837)
Pepys	*The Diary of Samuel Pepys*, ed. R. Latham and W. Matthews, 11 vols (London 1970–83)
PL	Migne, *Patrologia Latina*
Plea and Memoranda Rolls	Calendar of *Plea and Memoranda Rolls Preserved among the archives of the Corporation of the City of London at the Guildhall, 1364–1381*, ed. A. H. Thomas (1929)
PRO	Public Record Office
Proc. Soc. Ants.	*Proceedings of the Society of Antiquaries*
RCHM	Royal Commission on Historical Monuments
RCHM *Hertfordshire*	RCHM *Hertfordshire* (London 1910)
RCHM *London*, I	RCHM *London, I, Westminster Abbey* (London 1924)
RCHM *London*, II	RCHM *London, II, West London* (London 1935)
RCHM *London*, IV	RCHM *London, IV, The City* (London 1929)
RCHM *London*, V	RCHM *London, V, East London* (London 1930)
RCHM *Middlesex*	RCHM *Middlesex* (London 1937)
Regesta I	*Regesta Regum Anglo-Normannorum, I*, ed. H. W. C. Davis (Oxford 1913)
Reports and Opinions	*Reports and Opinions of Architects and Surveyors regarding the Condition and Renovation of the Temple Church, 1842–1927*, Middle Temple Library
Report on the Temple Church	*Report on the Temple Church sent by the surveyors of the Inner and Middle Temples*, Middle Temple Library
Rot. Hund.	*Rotuli Hundredorum* (Record Commission, London 1812)
RS	Rolls Series

L*

St Mary at Hill: Medieval records	*The Medieval records of a London City church (St Mary at Hill)* A.D. *1420–1559*, ed. H. Littlehales (Early English Text Soc., London 1904)
St Paul's Charters	*Early Charters of St Paul's*, ed. M. Gibbs (Camden Soc., 3rd ser., LVIII, London 1939)
St Paul's Chron.	*Short Chronicles of St Paul's*, in *Documents illustrating the History of St Paul's Cathedral*, ed. W. S. Simpson (Camden Soc., new ser., XXVI, London 1880)
St Paul's Docs	*Documents Illustrating the History of Old St Paul's Cathedral*, ed. W. S. Simpson (Camden Soc., new ser., XXVI, London 1880)
Sculp. fun. à Avignon	*Sculpture funeraire à Avignon au temps des Papes* (Musée du Petit Palais, Avignon 1979)
SESML	The Social and Economic Survey of Medieval London
SLond., VII	*Survey of London*, VII, *Chelsea* (London 1921)
SLond., IX	*Survey of London*, IX, *St Helen's Bishopgate* (London 1924)
SLond., XI	*Survey of London*, XI, *Crosby Place* (London 1907)
SLond., XII	*Survey of London*, XII, *All Hallow's Barking* (London 1929)
SLond., XIX	*Survey of London*, XIX, *St Pancras* (London 1938)
Soc.	Society
SyAS	Surrey Archaeological Society
Tacitus	P. Cornelius Tacitus, *Annals*, ed. H. Furneaux (Oxford 1891)
Text. Roff.	Textus Roffensis, ed. T. Hearne (Oxford 1720)
Trans.	Transactions
Trans. LMAS	*Transactions of the London and Middlesex Archaeological Society*
VCH	Victoria History of the Counties of England
VCH *London*, I	*Victoria County History of the Counties of England: London, vol. I*, ed. W. Page (London 1909)
Vet. Mon.	F. Nash, *Vetusta Monumenta Quae ad Rerum Britannicarum*, Society of Antiquaries V (London 1818)
Westminster Charters	*Westminster Abbey Charters, 1066–c. 1214*, ed. E. Mason (Lond. RS 25, London 1988)
Wren Drawings	C. Wren, Pre-Fire Design drawings for Old St Paul's Cathedral, Codrington Library, All Souls College, Oxford
Wrens. Soc. *St Paul's*	Wren Society: *I. St Paul's Cathedral. Original Wren Drawings from the Collection of All Soul's College, Oxford*, ed. A. T. Bolton and H. D. Hendry (Oxford 1924)

REFERENCES

ADAMS (1983) B. Adams, *London Illustrated, 1604–1851* (London 1983)

ADBURGHAM (1981) A. Adburgham, *Shops and Shopping, 1800–1914*, 2nd edition (London 1981)

ADDISON (1843) C. G. Addison, *The Temple Church* (London 1843)

ADHÉMAR (1974, 1976) J. Adhémar, 'Les Tombeaux de la Collection Gaignières', *GBA*, LXXXIV (1974), 5–192, LXXXVIII (1976), 3–128

ALEXANDER (1974) J. J. G. Alexander, 'English early fourteenth-century illumination: recent acquisitions', *Bodleian Library Record*, IX (1974), 72–80

ALEXANDER AND TEMPLE (1985) J. J. G. Alexander and E. Temple, *Illuminated Manuscripts in Oxford College Libraries, The University Archives and The Taylor Institution* (Oxford 1985)

ALLEN (1827) T. Allen, *History of London* (London 1827).

ANGLO (1969) S. Anglo, *Spectacle, Pageantry and Early Tudor Policy* (London 1969)

ARCHER *et al.* (1988) I. Archer, C. Barron, and V. Harding, *Hugh Alley's caveat: the Markets of London in 1598* (Lond. TS no. 137, London 1988)

BALESTRACCI AND PICCINNI (1977) D. Balestracci and G. Piccinni, *Siena nel Trecento: Assotto urbano e strutture edilizie* (Florence 1977)

BARKER AND JACKSON (1974, 1983) F. Barker and P. Jackson, *London: 2000 Years of a City and Its People* (London 1974, 1983)

BARLOW (1979) F. Barlow, *The English Church 1066–1154* (London 1979)

BARLOW *et al.* (1976) F. Barlow, M. Biddle, O. von Feilitzen and D. J. Keene, *Winchester in the Early Middle Ages: an edition and discussion of the Winton Domesday* (Winchester Studies 1, Oxford 1976)

BARON (1979) F. Baron, 'Collèges apostoliques et Couronnement de la Vièrge dans la Sculpture avignonnaise des XIVe et XVe Siècles', *La Revue du Louvre*, 3 (1979), 169–86

BARRON (1974) C. Barron, *The Medieval Guildhall of London* (London 1974)

BATESON (1902) M. Bateson, 'A London municipal collection of the reign of John', *EHR* 17 (1902), 480–511, 707–30

BAYLIS (1893) T. H. Baylis, *The Temple Church and the Chapel of St Anne* (London 1893)

BEARD AND COWAN (1988) D. Beard and C. Cowan, 'Excavations at 15–23 Southwark Street', *Lond. Arch.*, V, no. 14 (1988), 375–81

BENNETT (1982) A. Bennett, review of L. F. Sandler, *The Peterborough Psalter in Brussels*, in *Art Bulletin*, LXIV (1982), 502–8

—— (1985) A. Bennett, 'A Late Thirteenth-Century Psalter-Hours from London', in *England in the Thirteenth Century, Proceedings of the 1984 Harlaxton Symposium*, ed. W. M. Ormrod (Harlaxton 1985), 15–30

BIDDLE (1984) M. Biddle, 'London on the Strand', *Popular Archaeology*, VI, no. 1 (1984)

—— *et al.* (1973) M. Biddle, D. Hudson, C. Heighway, *The Future of London's Past* (London 1973)

BILLINGS (1838) R. W. Billings, *Architectural Illustrations and Account of the Temple Church, London* (London 1838)

BIRD *et al.* (1978)   J. Bird *et al.* (eds), *Southwark Excavations, 1972–1974* (LMAS and SyAS Joint Publication No. 1, London 1978)

BLEWETT (n.d.)   P. Blewett, *All Hallows by the Tower of London* (Pitkin Pictorials, n.d.)

BLORE (1826)   E. Blore, *The Monumental Remains of Eminent Persons, comprising the Sepulchral Antiquities of Great Britain* (London 1826)

BOCK (1962)   H. Bock, *Der Decorated Style* (Heidelberg 1962)

BOND (1840)   E. A. Bond, 'Extracts from the Liberate Rolls, relative to loans supplied by Italian Merchants to the kings of England, in the 13th and 14th centuries: with an introductory memoir', *Archaeologia*, XXVIII (1840), 207–326

—— (1863)   E. A. Bond, 'Description of an Illuminated Latin Psalter, formerly in the Library founded by Archbishop Tenison in the Parish of St Martin in the Fields, London', *The Fine Arts Quarterly Review*, I (1863), 77–96

—— (1906)   F. Bond, *Gothic Architecture in England* (London 1906)

—— (1913)   F. Bond, *An Introduction to English Church Architecture*, 2 vols (London 1913)

BONY (1979)   J. Bony, *The English Decorated Style* (Oxford 1979)

—— (1983)   J. Bony, *French Gothic Architecture of the 12th and 13th Centuries* (Berkeley 1983)

BOSWORTH AND TOLLER (1898)   J. Bosworth and T. N. Toller, *An Anglo-Saxon Dictionary* (Oxford 1898)

BRADFORD (1940)   C. A. Bradford, 'Fresh Facts from Wills', *Trans. LMAS*, No. 8 (1940)

BRADLEY (1982)   R. Bradley, 'The destruction of wealth in later prehistory', *Man*, 17 (1982), 108–22

BRAKSPEAR (1912–3)   H. Brakspear, 'Malmesbury Abbey', *Archaeologia*, LXIV (1912–3), 399–436

BRANNER (1965)   R. Branner, *St Louis and the Court Style in Gothic Architecture* (London 1965)

—— (1977)   R. Branner, *Manuscript Painting in Paris during the reign of St Louis, a study of styles* (Berkeley and Los Angeles, 1977)

BREWER (1962)   *Old London Illustrated: Drawings by H. W. Brewer*, 9th edition (A Builder Book, London 1962)

BRIEGER (1957)   P. Brieger, *English Art 1216–1307* (Oxford 1957)

BRITTON (1811)   J. Britton, *Facts and Observations relating to the Temple Church and the Monuments contained in it* (London 1811)

BROOKE AND KEIR (1975)   C. N. L. Brooke and G. Keir, *London 800–1216* (London 1975)

BROWN (1982)   D. B. Brown (ed.), *Ashmolean Museum Oxford: Catalogue of the Collection of Drawings*, IV (Oxford 1982)

BROWN (1979)   R. A. Brown, 'Some observations on the Tower of London', *Archaeol. J.*, CXXXVI (1979), 99–108

BURGE (1843)   W. Burge, *The Temple Church: An Account of its Restoration and Repairs* (London 1843)

CAMERON (1970)   H. K. Cameron, *A List of Monumental Brasses on the Continent of Europe* (London 1970)

CAMILLE (1988a)   M. Camille, 'Visualising in the Vernacular: a New Cycle of Early Fourteenth-Century Bible Illustrations', *The Burlington Magazine*, CXXX (1988), 97–106

—— (1988b)   M. Camille, review of *Artistes, Artisans et production artistique au Moyen Age: Vol. I. Les hommes*, in *The Burlington Magazine*, CXXX (1988), 143–4

CAPGRAVE (1901)   J. Capgrave, *Nova Legenda Anglie*, ed. C. Horstman (Oxford 1901)

CARTER (1808)   J. Carter, *The Gentleman's Magazine* (November 1808), 999

CATTO (1981)   J. Catto, 'Andrew Horn: law and history in fourteenth-century England', in *The Writing of History in the Middle Ages: Essays Presented to Richard William Southern*, ed. R. H. C. Davis and J. M. Wallace-Hadrill (Oxford 1981), 367–91

CHANDLER AND KING (1960)   M. Chandler and D. King, 'Two Charters and Seal-bags of 12 Edward II', *Guildhall Miscellany*, II (1960), 20–3

CHERRY (1984)   B. Cherry, 'An early 16th-century London tomb design', *Architectural History*, 27 (1984), 86–94

—— (forthcoming)   B. Cherry, 'Flying Angels and Bishops' Tombs, a Fifteenth Century Conundrum', in *Art and Architecture at Exeter*, BAA CT (forthcoming)

CHRIST (1947)   Y. Christ, *Églises Parisiennes Actuelles et Disparues* (Paris 1947)

CHRISTIE (1938)   A. G. I. Christie, *English Medieval Embroidery* (London 1938)

CLAPHAM (1932)   A. W. Clapham, 'Proceedings at Meetings: Crowland Abbey', *Archaeol. J.*, LXXXIX (1932), 349–51

—— (1934)   A. W. Clapham, *English Romanesque Architecture after the Conquest* (Oxford 1934)

CLAPHAM AND GODFREY (1913)   A. W. Clapham and W. H. Godfrey, *Some Famous buildings and their story* (London 1913)

CLARK (1981)   P. Clark, 'Introduction', in *Country Towns in pre-industrial England*, ed. P. Clark (Leicester 1981)

CLERET (1941)   J. Cleret, 'La corporation des merciers de Paris des origines à la fin du XVIème siècle', *École Nationale des Chartes: Positions des Thèses* (Paris 1941), 31–8

CLUTTERBUCK (1815)   R. Clutterbuck, *History and Antiquities of the County of Hertfordshire* (London 1815)

COCKERELL (1900)   S. C. Cockerell, 'An Engraving of London in 1510', *Lond. TR*, I (1900)

—— (1907)   S. C. Cockerell, *The Gorleston Psalter* (London 1907)

COCKERELL AND PLUMMER (1969)   S. C. Cockerell and J. Plummer, *Old Testament Miniatures: a medieval picture book with 283 paintings from the Creation of the Story of David* (New York and London 1969)

COLDSTREAM (1976)   N. Coldstream, 'English Decorated Shrine Bases', *JBAA*, new ser., CXXIX (1976), 15–34

—— (1979)   N. Coldstream, 'Ely Cathedral: the Fourteenth-Century Work', *Medieval Art and Architecture at Ely Cathedral, BAA CT*, II (1979)

—— (1980)   N. Coldstream, 'York Minster and the Decorated Style in Yorkshire: Architectural Reaction to York in the first half of the 14th Century', *Yorkshire Archaeological Journal*, 52 (1980), 89–110

—— (1985)   N. Coldstream, 'The Lady Chapel at Ely: its Place in English Decorated Style', *Reading Medieval Studies*, XI (1985), 1–30

COLVIN (1975)   H. M. Colvin (ed.), *The History of the King's Works*, III (London 1975)

—— (1978)   H. Colvin, *A Biographical Dictionary of British Architects 1600–1840* (London 1978)

COLVIN AND BROWN (1963)
H. M. Colvin and R. A. Brown, *History of the King's Works: The Middle Ages*, 2 vols (London 1963)

COOK (1955)
G. H. Cook, *Old St. Paul's Cathedral: A Lost Glory of Medieval London* (London 1955)

COOK AND EVANS (1954)
N. Cook and J. Evans, 'A Statue of Christ from the Ruins of the Mercer's Hall', *Archaeol J.*, CXI (1954), 168–80

CORFIELD (1972)
P. Corfield, 'A provincial capital in the late seventeenth century', in *Crisis and order in English Towns, 1500–1700*, ed., P. Clark and P. Slack (London 1972)

CORFIELD (1982)
P. J. Corfield, *The Impact of English Towns 1700–1800* (Oxford 1982)

COULTON (1914–15)
G. G. Coulton, 'Medieval Graffiti, especially in the Eastern Counties', *Proceedings of the Cambridge Antiquarian Society*, XIX (1914–15), 53–62

COWAN (1951)
J. D. Cowan, 'The Earliest Bronze Swords in Britain and their Origins on the Continent of Europe', *Proceedings of the Prehistoric Society*, XVII (1951), 195–213

——(1967)
J. D. Cowan, 'The Hallstatt Sword of Bronze: on the Continent and in Britain', *Proceedings of the Prehistoric Society*, XXXIII (1967), 377–454

COWGILL *et al.* (1987)
J. Cowgill, M. de Neergaard and N. Griffiths, *Knives and Scabbards* (Medieval Finds from Excavations in London 1, London 1987)

CROSSLEY (1921)
F. H. Crossley, *English Church Monuments 1150–1550* (London 1921)

CURNOW (1978)
P. E. Curnow, 'The Bloody Tower' in *The Tower of London: its Buildings and Institutions*, ed. J. Charlton (London 1978)

DALE (1932–4)
M. K. Dale, 'The London silkwomen of the fifteenth century', *Economic History Review*, 1st ser., 4 (1932–4), 324–35

DAVIS (1966)
D. Davis, *A History of Shopping* (London 1966)

DELAISSÉ (1967)
L. M. J. Delaissé, 'Towards a History for the Mediaeval Book', *Divinitas*, XI (1967), 423–35

DENNISON (1986a)
L. Dennison, 'An illuminator of the Queen Mary Psalter Group: the Ancient 6 Master', *The Antiquaries Journal*, LXVI, pt. 2 (1986), 287–314

——(1986b)
L. Dennison, '"The Fitzwarin Psalter and its Allies": a Reappraisal', *England in the Fourteenth Century, Proceedings of the 1985 Harlaxton Symposium*, ed. W. M. Ormrod (Woodbridge 1986), 42–66

——(1988)
L. Dennison, 'The Stylistic Sources, Dating and Development of the Bohun Workshop, *ca* 1340–1400', unpublished Ph.D. thesis, University of London (1988)

DENSEM AND SEELEY (1982)
R. Densem and D. Seeley, 'Excavation at Rectory Grove Clapham, 1980–81', *Lond. Arch.*, IV, no. 7 (1982), 177–84

DICKINS (1967)
B. Dickins, 'Historical Graffiti at Ashwell, Hertfordshire', in V. Pritchard, *English Medieval Graffiti* (Cambridge 1967), 181–3

DIMOCK (1900)
A. Dimock, *The Cathedral Church of St Paul*, 2nd edition, rev. (Bells Cathedral's Series, London 1900)

DOLLMAN (1881)
F. T. Dollman, *The Priory of St Marie Overie Southwark* (London 1881)

DOVE (1967)
W. Dove, 'The Temple Church and its Restoration', *Trans. LMAS* (1967), 164–72

DRAPER (1979)
P. Draper, 'Bishop Northwold and the Cult of Saint Etheldreda', *Medieval Art and Architecture at Ely Cathedral*, BAA CT, II (1979), 8–27

DUGDALE (1658)   W. Dugdale, *The History of St Paul's Cathedral in London* (London 1658)

——(1673)   W. Dugdale, *Monasticon Anglicanum* (London 1673)

——(1716)   W. Dugdale, *The History of St Paul's Cathedral in London*, 2nd edition (London 1716)

——(1818)   W. Dugdale, *The History of St Paul's Cathedral in London* (London 1818)

DYSON (1980)   T. Dyson, 'London and Southwark in the Seventh Century and Later', *Trans. LMAS*, 31 (1980)

——(1982)   T. Dyson, 'Documentary Survey', in *Milne and Milne* (1982), 4–9

DYSON AND SCHOFIELD (1981)   T. Dyson and J. Schofield, 'Excavations in the City of London: Second Interim Report, 1974–1978', *Trans. LMAS*, 32 (1981), 24–81

EKWALL (1947)   E. Ekwall, *Early London Personal Names* (Lund 1947)

——(1951)   E. Ekwall, *Two Early London Subsidy Rolls* (Lund 1951)

——(1965)   E. Ekwall, *Street-names of the City of London*, corrected edition (Oxford 1965)

ESSEX AND SMIRKE (1845)   W. Essex and S. Smirke, *The Architectural Embellishments and Painted Glass of the Temple Church, London* (London 1845)

EVANS (1966)   J. Evans, ed., *The Flowering of the Middle Ages* (London 1966)

FAIRWEATHER (1926–8)   F. H. Fairweather, 'The Priory of St Mary and All Saints, Westacre, and Excavations Upon its Site', *Norfolk Archaeology*, XXIII (1926–8), 359–94

——(1937)   F. H. Fairweather, 'Colne Priory, Essex, and the Burials of the Earls of Oxford', *Archaeologia*, LXXXVII (1937), 279–86

FAULKNER (1829)   T. Faulkner, *An historical and topographical history of Chelsea and its environs* (London 1829)

FINCH (1935)   R. H. C. Finch, 'Old St Paul's; a Reconstruction', *The Builder*, 148 (19 and 26 April 1935), 728–30, 772–3 and 778–9

FISHER (1981)   J. Fisher, *A Collection of Early Maps of London, 1553–1667* (Lympne Castle [Kent] 1981)

FITCH (1976)   M. Fitch, 'The London Makers of Opus Anglicanum', *Trans. LMAS*, new ser., 27 (1976), 288–96

FITZGERALD-LOMBARD (1981)   C. Fitzgerald-Lombard, *A Guide to the Church of St Gregory the Great, Downside Abbey* (Stratton-on-the-Fosse 1981)

FRIENDS OF SOUTHWARK (1958)   Friends of Southwark Cathedral, Occasional Paper no. 1, *The tomb of John Gower* (London 1958)

GARDAM (1983)   C. M. L. Gardam, 'The Temple Church in the 12th Century', unpublished M.Phil. thesis, University of London (1983)

GEM (1980)   R. D. H. Gem, 'The Romanesque rebuilding of Westminster Abbey', *Proc. Battle Conference* (Anglo-Norman Studies), III (1980), 33–60

——(1982)   R. D. H. Gem, 'The significance of the 11th-century rebuilding of Christ Church and St Augustine's, Canterbury, in the development of Romanesque architecture', *BAA CT*, V, Canterbury (1982), 1–45

——(1983)   R. D. H. Gem, 'The Romanesque cathedral of Winchester: patron and design in the 11th century', *BAA CT*, VI, Winchester (1983), 1–12

——(1984)   R. D. H. Gem, 'L'architecture pré-romane et romane en Angleterre', *Bull. Mon.*, CXLII (1984), 233–72

—— (1986)   R. D. H. Gem, 'The bishop's chapel at Hereford: the roles of patron and craftsman', in *Art and Patronage in the English Romanesque*, ed. S. Macready and H. Thompson, Society of Antiquaries, Occasional Papers, VIII (1986), 87–96

—— (1987)   R. D. H. Gem, 'Canterbury and the cushion capital', in *Romanesque and Gothic Essays for George Zarnecki*, ed. N. Stratford (Woodbridge 1987), 85–92

GIRARDON AND HEATHCOTE (1988)   S. Girardon and J. Heathcote, 'Excavation Round-up 1987: pt 2, London Boroughs', *Lond. Arch.*, V, no. 15 (1988), 410–15

GLEASON (1989)   J. B. Gleason, *John Colet* (London 1989)

GODEFROY (1884)   F. Godefroy, *Dictionaire de l'ancienne langue française* 10 vols (Paris 1880–1902)

GODFREY (1953)   W. H. Godfrey, 'Recent Discoveries at the Temple, London, and Notes on the Topography of the Site', *Archaeologia*, XCV (1953)

—— (1955)   W. H. Godfrey, 'The Temple Church, London — Treatment of the Exterior of the Round Church', typescript in Middle Temple Library (1955)

GODWIN (1838)   G. Godwin, *Churches of London* (London 1838)

GOTCH (1928)   J. A. Gotch, *Inigo Jones* (New York 1928)

GRAHAM (1926)   R. Graham, 'The priory of La Charité sur Loire and the monastery of Bermondsey', *JBAA*, 2nd ser., XXXII (1926), 157–84

—— (1945–7)   R. Graham, 'An appeal about 1175 for the building fund of St Paul's Cathedral', *JBAA*, 3rd ser., X (1945–7), 73–6

GRAY (1985)   D. Gray, ed., *The Oxford Book of Late Medieval Verse and Prose* (Oxford 1985)

GRIMES (1968)   W. F. Grimes, *The Excavation of Roman and Medieval London* (London 1968)

GROSSMAN (1950)   F. Grossman, 'Holbein, Torregiano, and some portraits of Dean Colet', *JWCI*, 13 (1950), 202–36

GUISEPPI (1920)   M. S. Guiseppi, 'The Wardrobe and Household Accounts of Bogo de Clare', *Archaeologia*, 70 (1920), 1–56

HAMMERSON (1975)   M. Hammerson, 'Excavations on the site of Arundel House in the Strand, WC2, in 1972', *Trans. LMAS*, 26 (1975), 209–51

HANWORTH (1987)   R. Hanworth, 'The Iron Age in Surrey', in *The Archaeology of Surrey to 1540*, ed. J. and D. G. Bird (London 1987)

HARBEN (1918)   H. A. Harben, *A Dictionary of London* (London 1918)

HARDING (1980)   V. Harding, 'The Two Coldharbours of the City of London', *Lond. TR*, 24 (1980)

HARTLEY AND ELLIOT (1925)   D. Hartley and M. M. Elliot, *The Life and Work of the people of England: The Sixteenth Century* (London 1925)

—— (1928)   D. Hartley and M. M. Elliot, *The Life and Work of the people of England: The Seventeenth Century* (London 1928)

HARVEY (1954)   J. Harvey, *English Medieval Architects* (London 1954)

—— (1961)   J. H. Harvey, 'The Origin of the Perpendicular Style', *Studies in Building History*, ed. E. M. Jope (London 1961), 134–65

—— (1974)   J. H. Harvey, *The Cathedrals of England and Wales* (London 1974)

—— (1977)   J. H. Harvey, 'The Architectural History from 1291 to 1558', in *History of York Minster*, ed. G. E. Aylmer and R. G. Cant (Oxford 1977), 149–92

—— (1978)   J. H. Harvey, *The Perpendicular Style, 1330–1455* (London 1978)

—— (1982)   J. H. Harvey, 'The Building of Wells Cathedral, I: 1175–1307', in *Wells Cathedral, A History*, ed. L. S. Colchester (West Compton House [nr Shepton Mallet] 1982), 52–75

—— (1984)   J. H. Harvey, *English Mediaeval Architects: a Biographical Dictionary down to 1550*, revised edition (Gloucester 1984)

—— (1987)   J. H. Harvey, *Supplement to the Revised Edition of English Mediaeval Architects* (Hulverstone Manor [Isle of Wight], 1987)

HASTINGS (1955)   M. Hastings, *St Stephens Chapel and its place in the Development of the Perpendicular Style in England* (Cambridge 1955)

HATTON (1708)   E. Hatton, *A New View of London* (London 1708)

HEALES (1865–9)   A. Heales, 'The Church of Stanwell and its Monuments', *Trans. LMAS*, III (1865–9), 105–302

—— (1869)   A. Heales, 'Easter Sepulchres, their object, nature and history', *Archaeologia*, XLII (1869), 263–308

HEBDITCH (1973)   M. Hebditch, *Archaeology in the City of London — an Opportunity* (London 1973)

HENDERSON (1937)   A. E. Henderson, *Saint Paul's Cathedral Then and Now* (London 1937)

HERD (1956)   C. O. Herd, *Notes on the Restoration of the Temple Church (1185–1240)* (London 1956)

HILL (1976)   D. Hill, 'London Bridge: a Reasonable Doubt', *Trans. LMAS*, 27 (1976)

HILL *et al.* (1980)   C. Hill, M. Millet, T. Blagg and T. Dyson (eds), *The Roman Riverside Wall and Monumental Arch in London* (LMAS Special Paper no. 3, London 1980)

HIND (1922)   A. M. Hind, *Wenceslaus Hollar and his Views of London and Windsor in the Seventeenth Century* (London 1922)

—— (1952)   A. M. Hind, *Engraving in England in the Sixteenth and Seventeenth Centuries: The Tudor period* (Cambridge 1952)

—— (1955)   A. M. Hind, *Engraving in England in the Sixteenth and Seventeenth Centuries: The Reign of James I* (Cambridge 1955)

HOBLEY (1985)   B. Hobley, *Roman and Saxon London — A Reappraisal* (1985)

—— (forthcoming)   B. Hobley, 'Lundenwic and Lundenburh: two cities rediscovered', in *The Rebirth of Towns in the west A.D. 700–1050*, ed. R. Hodges and B. Hobley, CBA research Report 68 (forthcoming)

HOBLEY AND LAMBERT (1971)   B. Hobley and M. W. Lambert, 'Excavations at the Cathedral and Benedictine Priory of St Mary, Coventry', *Birmingham and Warwickshire Archaeological Society Transactions (for 1967–70)*, LXXXIV (1971), 45–139

HOBLEY AND SCHOFIELD (1977)   B. Hobley and J. Schofield, 'Excavations in the City of London, 1974–5: First Interim Report', *Antiquaries Journal*, 57 (1977), 31–66

HOME (1931)   G. Home. *Old London Bridge* (1931)

HONEYBOURNE (1965)   M. B. Honeybourne, 'The Reconstructed Map of London under Richard II', *Lond. TR* 22 (1965), 29–76

HORSMAN *et al.* (1988) V. Horsman, G. Milne, C. Milne, *Aspects of Saxo-Norman London I: Building and property development*, LMAS Special Paper (1988)

JAMES (1921a) M. R. James, *A Peterborough Psalter and Bestiary of the Fourteenth Century* (Oxford 1921)

—— (1921b) M. R. James, *Illustrations of the Book of Genesis* (Roxburghe Club 1921)

JANSEN (1979) V. Jansen, 'Superposed Wall Passages and the Triforium Elevation of St Werburg's, Chester', *Society of Architectural Historians (US) Journal*, XXXVIII (3), 223–43

KEENE (1985a) D. Keene, *Survey of Medieval Winchester*, Winchester Studies 2, 2 vols (Oxford 1985)

—— (1985b) D. Keene, *Cheapside before the Great Fire* (London 1985)

—— (1987) D. Keene, 'The Walbrook Study: a summary report' (typescript at Institute of Historical Research 1987)

—— (1988) D. Keene, 'Interim report on the study of the Bank of England Area' (typescript at Institute of Historical Research 1988)

KEENE AND HARDING (1987) D. Keene and V. Harding, *Historical Gazeteer of London before the Great Fire: Part 1, Cheapside* (Cambridge 1987)

KENT (1978) J. Kent, 'The London Area in the Late Iron Age: an Interpretation of the Earliest Coins', in *Collectanea Londoniensia*, ed. J. Bird, H. Chapman and J. Clark (LMAS Special Paper no. 2, London 1978)

KER (1954) N. R. Ker, 'Liber Custumarum, and other Manuscripts formerly at the Guildhall', *The Guildhall Miscellany*, III (1954), 37–45

—— (1969) N. R. Ker, *Medieval Manuscripts in British Libraries*, I, London (Oxford 1969)

—— (1977) N. R. Ker, *Medieval Manuscripts in British Libraries*, II, Abbotsford–Keele (London 1977)

KIDSON *et al.* (1979) P. Kidson *et al.*, A History of English Architecture, 2nd edition (Harmondsworth 1979)

KING (1963) D. King, *Opus Anglicanum*, Exhibition Catalogue (London 1963)

—— (1968) D. King, 'A Relic of "Noble Erpinham"', *Victoria and Albert Museum Bulletin* (1968), 59–64

KINGSFORD (1915) C. L. Kingsford, *The Grey Friars of London* (Aberdeen 1915)

—— (1916, 1917, 1920) C. L. Kingsford, 'Historical Notes on Medieval London Houses', *Lond. TR* 10 (1916), 44–144; 11 (1917), 28–81; 12 (1920), 1–66

KURMANN (1971) P. Kurmann, *La cathédrale Saint-Etienne de Meaux* (Paris 1971)

LACEY (1985) K. E. Lacey, 'Women and work in fourteenth- and fifteenth-century London', in *Women and work in pre-industrial Britain*, ed. L. Duffin and L. Charles (London 1985), 24–82

LANG (1956) J. Lang, *Rebuilding St Paul's after the Great Fire of London* (London 1956)

LASKO AND MORGAN (1973) P. Lasko and N. J. Morgan, *Medieval Art in East Anglia 1300–1520* (London 1973)

LEES-MILNE (1953) J. Lees-Milne, *The Age of Inigo Jones* (London 1953)

LEGGE AND ST JOHN HOPE (1902) J. Wickham Legge and W. H. St John Hope, *Inventories of Christ Church Canterbury* (London 1902)

LEGUAY (1984)   J.-P. Leguay, *La rue au Moyen Age* (Rennes 1984)

LETHABY (1925)   W. R. Lethaby, *Westminster Abbey Re-examined* (London 1925)

—— (1930)   W. R. Lethaby, 'Old St Paul's', *The Builder*, 138 (Jan.-June 1930),
                         671–3, 862–4, 1091–3; 139 (July–Dec, 1930), 24–6, 193–5, 234–6,
                         393–5, 613–5, 791–3, 1005–7, 1088–90

LEWER (1968–9)   D. Lewer, 'Restoration and the Temple Church', *Trans. Ancient Monu-
                         ments Soc.*, new ser., XVI (London 1968–9), 23–31

—— (1971)   D. Lewer, *The Temple Church* (London 1971)

LONGLEY AND NEEDHAM   D. Longley and S. Needham, *Runnymede Bridge, 1976: Excavations on
   (1980a)   the Site of a Late Bronze Age Settlement*, SyAS Research vol. 6 (1980)

—— (1980b)   D. Longley and S. Needham, 'Runnymede Bridge, Egham' in *Settlement
                         and Society in the British Later Bronze Age*, ed. J. Barrett and R. Bradley,
                         BAR no. 83 (1980), 397–436

LONGMAN (1873)   W. Longman, *A History of the Three Cathedrals Dedicated to St Paul*
                         (London 1873)

LOOMIS (1942)   L. H. Loomis, 'The Auchinleck Manuscript and a Possible London
                         Workshop of 1330–40', *Publications of the Modern Language Associa-
                         tion of America*, LVII (1942), 595–627

MÂLE (1908)   E. Mâle, *L'art religieux de la fin du moyen age en France* (Paris 1908)

MALONEY (1980)   J. Maloney, 'The Discovery of Bastion 4A in the City of London and its
                         implications', *Trans. LMAS*, 31 (1980), 68–76

MARIUS (1985)   R. Marius, *Thomas More* (London 1985)

MARKS AND MORGAN   R. Marks and N. Morgan, *The Golden Age of English Manuscript
   (1981)   Painting 1200–1500* (London 1981)

MARSDEN (1980)   P. Marsden, *Roman London* (London 1980)

MARTIN (1926)   A. R. Martin, 'Topography of the Cluniac Abbey of St Saviour at
                         Bermondsey', *JBAA*, 2nd ser., XXXII (1926), 192–228

McALEER (1984)   J. P. McAleer, *The Romanesque church façade in Britain*, Ph.D. thesis,
                         University of London (1963); Garland Press, Outstanding theses from
                         the Courtauld Institute of Art (New York 1984)

MERRIFIELD (1962)   R. Merrifield, 'Coins from the Bed of the Walbrook and their Signifi-
                         cance', *Antiquaries Journal*, XLII (1962), 38–52

—— (1965)   R. Merrifield, *The Roman City of London* (London 1965)

—— (1969)   R. Merrifield, *Roman London* (London 1969)

—— (1975)   R. Merrifield, *The Archaeology of London* (London 1975)

—— (1983)   R. Merrifield, *London, City of the Romans* (London 1983)

—— (1987)   R. Merrifield, *The Archaeology of Ritual and Magic* (London 1987)

MERRIMAN (1987)   N. Merriman, 'A Prehistory for Central London?', *Lond. Arch.*, V, no. 12
                         (1987), 318 ff

MICHAEL (1981)   M. A. Michael, 'The Harnhulle Psalter-Hours: an Early Fourteenth-
                         Century English Illuminated Manuscript at Downside Abbey', *JBAA*,
                         CXXXIV (1981), 81–99

—— (1988)   M. A. Michael, 'Oxford, Cambridge and London: towards a Theory for
                         "grouping" Gothic Manuscripts', *The Burlington Magazine*, CXXX
                         (1988), 107–15

MILLAR (1928)   E. G. Millar, *English Illuminated Manuscripts of the XIVth and XVth Centuries* (Paris 1928)

—— (1932)   E. G. Millar, *The Luttrell Psalter* (London 1932)

MILNE (1985)   G. Milne, *The Port of Roman London* (1985)

MILNE AND MILNE (1982)   G. Milne and C. Milne, *Medieval waterfront development at Trig Lane, London* (LMAS Special Paper no. 5, London 1982)

MILSOM (1981)   S. F. C. Milsom, *Historical Foundations of the Common Law*, 2nd edition (London 1981)

MORDAUNT CROOK (1965) J. Mordaunt Crook, 'The Restoration of the Temple Church: Ecclesiology and Recrimination', *JSAH* (British) VIII (1965), 39–51

MORGAN (1982)   N. Morgan, *Early Gothic Manuscripts [I], 1190–1250* (A Survey of Manuscripts Illuminated in the British Isles, IV) (London 1982)

MORRIS (1972)   R. K. Morris, 'Decorated Architecture in Herefordshire; Sources, Workshops and Influence', unpublished Ph.D. thesis, 3 vols, University of London (1972)

—— (1974)   R. K. Morris, 'The Remodelling of the Hereford Aisles', *JBAA*, 3rd ser., XXXVIII (1974), 21–39

—— (1978/9)   R. K. Morris, 'The Development of Later Gothic Mouldings in England *c.*1250–1400', *Architectural History*, 21 (1978), 18–57; 22 (1979), 1–48

—— (1984)   R. K. Morris, 'The Architectural History of Wells Cathedral', *Trans. of the Ancient Monuments Soc.*, new ser., 28 (1984), 194–207

—— (1985)   R. K. Morris, 'Ballflower Work in Gloucester and its Vicinity', *Medieval Art and Architecture at Gloucester and Tewkesbury*, BAA CT, VII (1985), 99–115

MUI AND MUI (1989)   H.-C. and L. H. Mui, *Shops and shopkeeping in eighteenth-century England* (London 1989)

NEEDHAM (1987)   S. Needham, 'The Bronze age' in *The Archaeology of Surrey to 1540*, ed. J. and D. G. Bird (London 1987), 116–23

NICHOLLS (1780)   J. B. Nicholls, *Royal Wills* (London 1780)

—— (1824)   J. B. Nicholls, *Account of the Royal Hospital and Collegiate Church of Saint Katharine near the Tower of London* (London 1824)

NORMAN (1907)   P. Norman, *S.Lond. XI, Crosby Place* (London 1907)

O'CONNELL (1986)   M. O'Connell, *Petters Sports Field, Egham*, SyAS Research vol. 10 (1986)

OSWALD (1958)   A. Oswald, 'The Temple Church Restored', *Country Life*, CXXIV (1958), 1104

OVERALL (1871)   W. H. Overall, *The Accounts of the Churchwardens of St Michael, Cornhill, 1456–1608* (London, privately printed, 1871)

—— (1873–6)   W. H. Overall, 'The Early Maps of London, and more especially as to the map attributed to Ralph Agas', *Proc. Soc. Ants.*, 2nd ser., VI (1873–6), 81–99

—— (1874)   W. H. Overall, *Civitas Londinum. Ralph Agas. A Survey of the Cities of London and Westminster ... in the Reign of Queen Elizabeth* (London 1874)

OWEN EVANS (1969)   M. F. Owen Evans, 'The Resurrection on Brasses', *Trans. Monumental Brass Soc.*, II (1969), 88–101

PÄCHT (1943)　　　　　O. Pächt, 'A Giottesque episode in English mediaeval art', *JWCI*, VI (1943), 51–70

PÄCHT AND ALEXANDER (1973)　　　O. Pächt and J. J. G. Alexander, *Illuminated Manuscripts in the Bodleian Library, Oxford*, III (Oxford 1973)

PAGE (1898)　　　　　W. Page, 'On some recent discoveries in the Abbey Church of St Alban', *Archaeologia*, LVI (1898), 21–6

PAGE PHILLIPS (1980)　J. Page Phillips, *Palimpsests, the backs of monumental brasses* (London 1980)

PARNELL (1977)　　　G. Parnell, 'Excavations at the Tower of London, 1976–7', *Lond. Arch.*, III, no. 4 (1977)

—— (1978)　　　　　G. Parnell, 'An earlier Roman Riverside Wall at the Tower of London', *Lond. Arch.*, III, no. 7 (1978)

PEERS (1917)　　　　C. R. Peers, *St Botolph's Priory, Colchester, Essex* (HMSO, London 1917)

PENROSE (1883)　　　F. C. Penrose, 'On the Recent Discoveries of Portions of Old St Paul's Cathedral', *Archaeologia*, XLVIII (1883), 381–92

PHILIPPE (1905)　　　A. Philippe, 'L'église de la Charité sur Loire', *Bull. Mon.*, LXIX (1905), 469–500

PHILLIPS (1985)　　　D. Phillips, *The Cathedral of Archbishop Thomas of Bayeux at York* (Excavations at York Minster 1967–1973, I, London 1985)

PLUCKNETT (1954)　　T. F. T. Plucknett, *The Medieval Bailiff* (London 1954)

PRÉ (1961)　　　　　M. Pré, 'Le château de Laval', *CA*, Maine (1961), 353–72

PRIESTLY AND CORFIELD (1982)　U. Priestly and P. Corfield, 'Rooms and room use in Norwich housing, 1580–1730', *Post-Medieval Archaeology*, 16 (1982)

PRIOR AND GARDNER (1912)　E. S. Prior and A. Gardner, *Medieval Figure Sculpture in England* (Cambridge 1912)

RAIMES (1938)　　　A. L. Raimes, 'The Family of Reymes of Wherstead in Suffolk', *Proceedings of the Suffolk Institute of Archaeology*, XXIII, pt. 2 (1938), 89–115

REDDAWAY (1963)　　T. F. Reddaway, 'Elizabethan London — Goldsmiths' row in Cheapside, 1558–1645', *The Guildhall Miscellany* 2.5 (October 1963), 181–206

RENIMEL (1976)　　　S. Renimel, 'L'établissement clunisien primitif de la Charité sur Loire', *Bull. Mon.*, CXXXIV (1976), 167–229

RICHARDSON (1982)　B. Richardson, 'Excavation Round-Up 1981', *Lond. Arch.*, IV, no. 6 (1982)

RICKERT (1965)　　　M. Rickert, *Painting in Britain: The Middle Ages* (Harmondsworth 1965)

RILEY (1868)　　　　H. T. Riley, *Memorials of London* (London 1868)

ROUTH AND KNOWLES (1981)　P. Routh and R. Knowles, *A Ryther Legacy: the monuments assessed* (Wakefield 1981)

ST AUBYN (1864)　　J. P. St Aubyn, 'An Account of the Repairs at the Temple Church', *Trans. Royal Institute of British Architects* (1864), 153–5

ST JOHN HOPE (1914)　W. H. St John Hope, 'The Funeral Monument and Chantry Chapel of King Henry V in Westminster Abbey', *Archaeologia*, 65 (1914), 129–86

—— (1919)　　　　　W. H. St John Hope, *Cowdray and Easebourne Priory in the County of Sussex* (London 1919)

SALZMAN (1952)　　　L. F. Salzman, *Building in England down to 1540: a Documentary History* (Oxford 1952)

—— (1968)   L. F. Salzman, *Building in England down to 1540: a Documentary History*, reprinted (Oxford 1968)

SANDLER (1974)   L. F. Sandler, *The Peterborough Psalter in Brussels and Other Fenland Manuscripts* (London 1974)

—— (1976)   L. F. Sandler, 'An Early Fourteenth-Century English Breviary at Longleat', *JWCI*, XXXIX (1976), 1–20

—— (1986)   L. F. Sandler, *A Survey of Manuscripts Illuminated in the British Isles*, 5 (in 2 vols), *Gothic Manuscripts, 1285–1385* (Oxford 1986)

SCHARF (1865)   G. Scharf, *A Catalogue of the Pictures Belonging to the Society of Antiquaries, London* (London 1865)

SCHOFIELD (1977)   J. Schofield, 'New Fresh Wharf: 3, the medieval buildings', *Lond. Arch.*, III (1977), 66–73

—— (1981)   J. A. Schofield, 'Medieval Water-front buildings in the City of London', in *Waterfront Archaeology in Britain and Northern Europe*, ed. G. Milne and B. Hobley, CBA Research Report no. 41 (London 1981)

—— (1984)   J. Schofield, *The building of London from the Conquest to the Great Fire* (London 1984)

—— (1987)   J. Schofield, *The London Surveys of Ralph Treswell* (Lond. TS no. 135, London 1987)

—— (in prep.)   J. Schofield, 'Holy Trinity Priory, Aldgate, and the Dissolution in London' (in preparation)

SCHOFIELD AND DYSON (1980)   J. Schofield and T. Dyson, eds, *Archaeology of the City of London* (London 1980)

SCHOFIELD *et al.* (in prep.)   J. Schofield *et al.*, 'Medieval Waterfront Tenements in London' (in preparation)

SCHOFIELD AND ALLEN (in prep.)   J. Schofield and P. Allen, *Medieval building and property development in the area of Cheapside, London* (in preparation)

SCHOLZ (1961)   B. W. Scholz, 'The Canonisation of Edward the Confessor', *Speculum*, XXXVI (1961), 38–60

SCOULOUDI (1953)   I. Scouloudi, *Panoramic Views of London, 1600–1666, with some later adaptations: An annotated list* (Corporation of London, 1953; unpublished copy in Guildhall Library)

SEKULES (1986)   V. Sekules, 'The Tomb of Christ at Lincoln and the Development of the Sacrament Shrine: Easter Sepulchres Reconsidered', *Medieval Art and Architecture at Lincoln, BAA CT* (1986), 118–31

SHARPE (1848)   E. Sharpe, *Supplement to 'Architectural Parallels'* (London 1848)

SHEINGORN (1987)   P. Sheingorn, *The Easter Sepulchre in England* (Kalamazoo 1987)

SHELDON (1981)   H. Sheldon, 'London and south-east Britain', in *The Roman West in the Third Century*, ed. A. King and M. Henig, *BAR* International Series 109 (1981) 363–82

SHELDON AND TYERS (1983)   H. Sheldon and I. Tyers, 'Recent dendro-chronological work in Southwark and its implications', *Lond. Arch.*. IV, no. 13 (1983), 355–61

SHERLOCK (1978)   D. Sherlock, *Medieval Drawings and Writings in Ashwell Church, Hertfordshire* (Ashwell 1978)

SHILLIAM (1986)   N. J. Shilliam, 'Foreign Influences on, and Innovation in English Tomb Sculpture in the First Half of the Sixteenth Century', unpublished Ph.D. (Warwick 1986)

SIMPSON (1881a)   W. S. Simpson, *Chapters in the History of Old St Paul's Cathedral* (London 1881)

—— (1881b)   W. S. Simpson, 'Some Early Drawings of Old St Paul's', *JBAA*, XXXVII (1881), 123–34

—— (1905)   W. S. Simpson, 'The Bishop of London's Palace near St Paul's. Its Early History', *Trans. LMAS*, new ser., I (1905), 13–47

SMITH (1859)   C. R. Smith, *Illustrations of Roman London* (London 1859)

SPEED (1611–2)   J. Speed, *Theatre of the Empire of Great Britaine* (London 1611–2)

STENNING (1985)   D. F. Stenning, 'Timber-framed shops, 1300–1600: comparative plans', *Vernacular Architecture* 16 (1985)

STOW (1598)   J. Stow, *A Survey of London* (London 1598)

—— (1603)   J. Stow, *A Survey of London* (London 1603)

—— (1615)   J. Stow, *Annals* (London 1615)

—— (1720)   J. Stow, *A Survey of the Cities of London and Westminster*, ed. J. Strype (London 1720)

—— (1754)   J. Stow, *A New View of London*, ed. J. Strype (London 1754)

—— (1912)   J. Stow, *Survey of London* (Everyman edition, London 1912)

—— (1955)   J. Stow, *Survey of London*, ed. H. B. Wheatley, revised edition, based on Stow (1603) (London 1955)

—— (1971)   J. Stow, *A Survey of London*, reprinted from the text of 1603, ed. C. L. Kingsford, 2 vols, reprinted (Oxford 1971)

STRIK (1982)   H. J. A. Strik, 'Remains of the Lanfranc Building', *BAA CT*, V, Canterbury (1982), 20–5

SUMMERSON (1953)   J. Summerson, *Architecture in Britain: 1530–1830* (London 1953)

—— (1966)   J. Summerson, *Inigo Jones* (Harmondsworth 1966)

—— (1977)   J. Summerson, *Architecture in Britain: 1530–1830*, 6th edition (London 1977)

THOMPSON (1949)   A. H. Thompson, *Lindisfarne Priory, Northumberland* (HMSO, London 1949)

—— (1973)   A. H. Thompson, *Netley Abbey*, revised edition (HMSO, London 1973)

THOMPSON (1910)   W. Thompson, *Southwark Cathedral* (London 1910)

TICKNER (1919)   T. F. Tickner, 'The Cathedral and Priory of St Mary of Coventry and an Approximate Restoration of the Plan of the Church', *JBAA*, new ser., XXV (1919), 24–38

TODD (1812)   H. J. Todd, *Catalogue of the Archiepiscopal Manuscripts in the Library at Lambeth Palace* (London 1812)

TONELLIER (1962, 1963) C. Tonellier, 'Les Broderies à Alphabet et la Mise en Tombeau de Solesmes', *Bull. Mon.*, CXX (1962), 318–38; CXI (1963), 22–40

TRAPP (1987)   J. B. Trapp, 'Christopher Urswyck and his books, the reading of Henry VII's almoner', *Renaissance Studies*, I, no. 1 (1987), 48–70

UNWIN (1925)   G. Unwin, *The Gilds and Companies of London*, 2nd edition (London 1925)

VARTY (1967)   K. Varty, *Reynard the Fox* (London 1967)

VAUGHAN (1958)   R. Vaughan, *Matthew Paris*, Cambridge Studies in Medieval Life and Thought, new ser., VI (Cambridge 1958)

VERDIER *et al.* (1972)   P. Verdier, P. Brieger, M. Farquhar-Montpetit, *Art and the Courts: France and England from 1259 to 1328*, 2 vols (Ottawa 1972)

VINCE (1984)   A. Vince, 'The Aldwych: Mid-Saxon London Discovered?', *Current Archaeology*, VIII, no. 10 (1984)

WARNER (1901)   G. F. Warner, *Illuminated Manuscripts in the British Museum: Miniatures, Borders, and Initials*, 3rd ser. (London 1901)

—— (1912)   G. F. Warner, *Queen Mary's Psalter* (London 1912)

WARNER AND GILSON (1921)   G. F. Warner and J. P. Gilson, *Catalogue of Western manuscripts in the Old Royal and King's Collections*, 4 vols (London 1921)

WATSON (1979)   A. G. Watson, *Catalogue of Dated and Datable Manuscripts c.700–1600 in the British Library* (London 1979)

WEBB (1821)   E. A. Webb, *The Records of St Bartholomew, Smithfield* (London 1821)

WEBB (1956)   G. Webb, *Architecture in Britain: the Middle Ages* (Harmondsworth 1956)

WHYTEHEAD AND BLACKMORE (1983)   R. Whytehead and L. Blackmore, 'Excavations at Tottenham Court, 250 Euston Road, NW1', *Trans. LMAS*, 34 (1983)

WILKINSON (1816)   R. Wilkinson, *Londina Illustrata, Graphic and historic memorials of monasteries, churches, chapels ... in the cities and suburbs of London and Westminster* (London 1816)

WILLIAMSON (1983)   P. Williamson, 'Catalogue of Romanesque Sculpture in the Victoria and Albert Museum' (London 1983)

—— (1985)   P. Williamson, 'The West Doorway of the Temple Church, London', *Burlington Magazine*, CXXVII (October 1985), 716

WILSON (1976)   C. Wilson, 'The Original Design of the City of London Guildhall', *JBAA*, 129 (1976), 1–14

—— (1980)   C. Wilson, 'The Origins of the Perpendicular Style and its Development to *c.* 1360', unpublished Ph.D. thesis, University of London (1980)

—— (1987)   C. Wilson, 'The English Response to French Gothic Architecture *c.* 1200–1350', in *Age of Chivalry*

WILSON *et al.* (1986)   C. Wilson, P. Tudor-Craig, J. Physick, R. Gem, *Westminster Abbey* (New Bell's Cathedral Guide, London 1986)

WILSON (1926)   H. Wilson, *Eight hundred years of Harlington parish church in the County of Middlesex* (London 1926)

WOOD (1965)   M. Wood, *The English Mediaeval House* (London 1965)

WOODHOUSE (1909)   F. W. Woodhouse, *The Churches of Coventry* (London 1909)

ZARNECKI (1975)   G. Zarnecki, 'The West Doorway of the Temple Church in London', *Beiträge zur Kunst des Mittelalters, Festschrift für Hans Wentzel zum 60 Geburtstag* (Berlin 1975), 246–53

ZARNECKI *et al.* (1984)   G. Zarnecki *et al.*, *English Romanesque Art 1066–1200* (Arts Council of Great Britain, London 1984)

THE PLATES

DRAWN AND ETCHED BY J.T. SMITH. DOMESTIC ARCHITECTURE. DRAWN IN JULY 1796

HOUSES ON THE SOUTH SIDE OF LEADENHALL STREET.

PUBLISHED SEPT.ᵗ 15, 1814 BY J.T. SMITH, Nº 18, Gᵗ MAY'S BUILDINGS ST MARTIN'S LANE.

I. Houses on the south side of Leadenhall Street, drawn in 1796 by J. T. Smith. The house on the right is exceptional among those drawn by antiquaries for showing features probably of pre-Reformation date

Museum of London

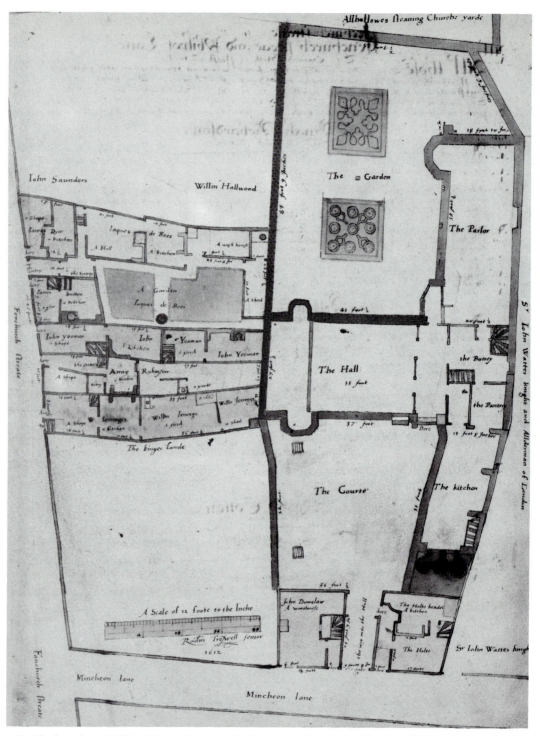

II. Clothworkers' Hall in Mincing Lane, and adjacent housing at 46–8 Fenchurch Street, surveyed in 1612 by Ralph Treswell; from the planbook of the Clothworkers' Company. Among many interesting features this plan is the earliest known to the writer to show a London garden in detail
By kind permission of The Clothworkers' Company

IIIA. (above) Eastern undercroft of
Guildhall, *c.* 1430
Museum of London

IIIB. (left) Undercroft of Gisors'
(Gerard's) Hall, Basing Lane, *c.* 1290,
drawn by C. Whichelo in 1810
Museum of London

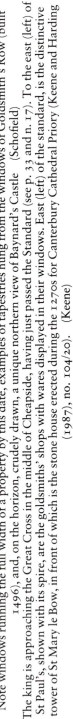

IV. Cheapside in 1547 during the Coronation procession of King Edward VI. From an 18th-century copy (belonging to the Society of Antiquaries of London) of a contemporary wall painting, now destroyed, at Cowdray Park.

Note windows running the full width of a property by this date, examples of tapestries hung from the windows of Goldsmith's Row (built 1496), and, on the horizon, crudely drawn, a unique northern view of Baynard's Castle (Schofield)

The king is approaching the Great Cross in the middle of Cheapside, having just passed the Standard (see p. 33 and n. 17). To the east (left) of St Paul's, shown with its spire, are the goldsmiths' shops with wares displayed in their windows. East (left) of the standard, is the distinctive tower of St Mary le Bow, in front of which is the stone house erected during the 1270s for Canterbury Cathedral Priory (Keene and Harding (1987), no. 104/20).   (Keene)

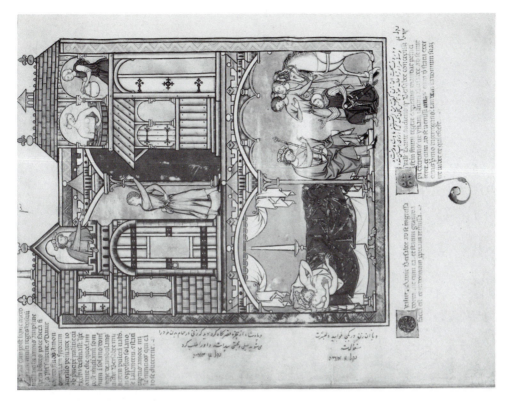

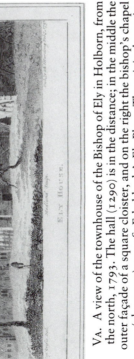

Vᴀ. A view of the townhouse of the Bishop of Ely in Holborn, from the north, 1793. The hall (1290) is in the distance; in the middle the outer façade of a square cloister, and on the right the bishop's chapel (also 1290), now St Etheldreda's Ely Place. The original exterior decoration of the chapel and its corner pinnacles (since removed) are shown

Courtauld Institute of Art

Vʙ. (right) King David sees Bathsheba from across the street. From a Parisian, or possibly English, illumination of the mid-13th century (see pp. 36, 41 and n. 40). Bathsheba is shown bathing in the upper room of a house of distinctly lower status than the king's. Downstairs is a shop with shuttered windows, a pentice, and a narrow door. New York, Pierpont Morgan Library, MS 638, f. 41v

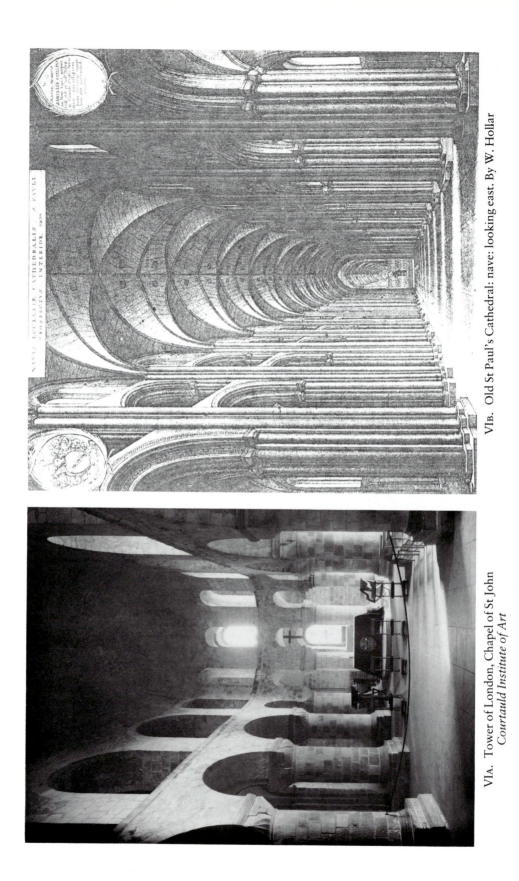

VIB. Old St Paul's Cathedral: nave: looking east. By W. Hollar

VIA. Tower of London, Chapel of St John
Courtauld Institute of Art

VII. Old St Paul's Cathedral, east side of crossing and transepts: Dugdale (1716)

VIIIA. St Mary le Bow, crypt: central vessel
Courtauld Institute of Art

VIIIB. St Mary le Bow, crypt: south aisle
Courtauld Institute of Art

IXA. Wenceslaus Hollar, View of Old St Paul's from the south-west, *c.* 1658, engraving, from
Wm Dugdale, *The History of St. Paul's Cathedral in London* (London 1658), 167
Photo Courtauld Institute, B53/624

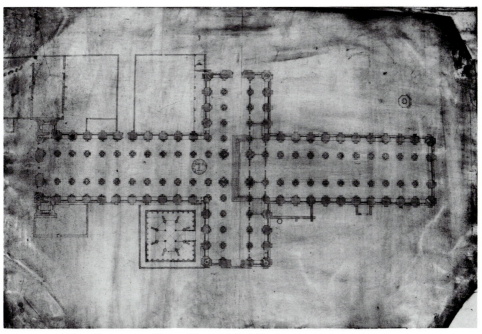

IXB. Christopher Wren, Plan of Old St Paul's, *c.* 1661/3–6, drawing.
Codrington Library, All Souls College, Oxford
Photo Courtauld Institute, B73/131

XA. Anonymous, 'A prospect of parte of ye citye of London . . .', *c.* 1561–94, engraving, detail. Society of Antiquaries, London
Photo Courtauld Institute, 278/6(3)

XB. Anonymous, '*Civitas Londinum*', *c.* 1561/2–70, woodcut, detail. Guildhall Library, London
Photo Guildhall Library

XC. John Gipkyn, Old St Paul's viewed from the North-east ('The Bishop of London [Dr John King] Preaching at St Paul's Cross before the King, Queen and Prince Charles'), 1616, panel painting. Society of Antiquaries, London
Photo Courtauld Institute, 293/39(7)

XD. Claes Jansz Visscher, Long View of London from the South, 1616, engraving, detail. British Museum, London
Photo British Museum, PS 058983

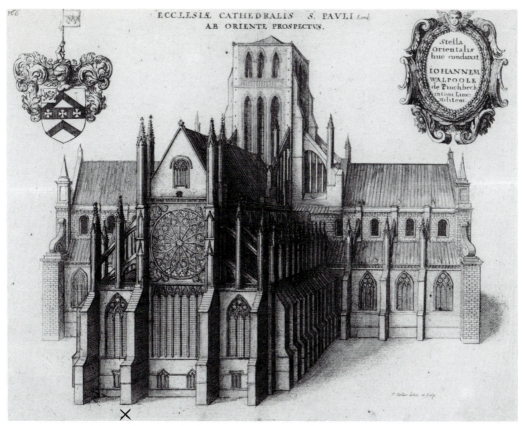

XIA. Old St Paul's Cathedral, eastern arm, exterior from east: Dugdale (1716), detail

XIB. Old St Paul's Cathedral, eastern arm, exterior from north: Dugdale (1716)

XIIA. Old St Paul's Cathedral, crypt of St Faith, interior looking east: Dugdale (1716)

XIIB. Old St Paul's Cathedral, eastern arm, interior looking east: Dugdale (1716), detail

GUIL. WALTER
primogenitus Guil.
Walter de Saresden
in agro Oxon:
Baronetti
P.

Ecclesiæ Paulinæ moles sacra
Pietatis avitæ documentum,
Senio, et sacrilego ruitura.
Sequioris seculi opprobrium
Tantum Religio potuit

ORIENTALIS PARTIS ECCL: CATH: S: PAVLI PROSPECTVS INTERIOR

XIII. Old St Paul's Cathedral, sanctuary and Lady Chapel, interior looking east: Dugdale (1716)

XIVA. Old St Paul's Cathedral, eastern arm, north aisle bay 7, tomb of Bishop Chishull:
Dugdale (1716)

XIVB. Old St Paul's Cathedral, eastern arm, south aisle bay 3, tombs of Bishops
Wengham and Fauconberg: Dugdale (1716)

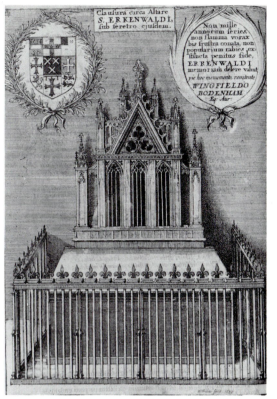

XVA. Old St Paul's Cathedral, eastern arm, north arcade bay 8, tomb of Bishop Roger Niger: Dugdale (1716)

XVB. Old St Paul's Cathedral, shrine of St Erkenwald: Dugdale (1716)

XVC. Old St Paul's Cathedral, eastern arm, north aisle bay 10, tombs of the Saxon Kings: Dugdale (1716)

XVI. Old St Paul's Cathedral, Wren's Pre-Fire design, section drawing, bays 7, 8, 9: Codrington
Library, All Souls College, Oxford, Wren drawings, Vol. II, No. 7
Reproduced by permission of the Warden and Fellows of All Souls College, Oxford

XVIIA. Old St Paul's Cathedral, former crypt of St Faith's, south-east respond, capitals

XVIIB. Old St Paul's Cathedral, former crypt of St Faith's, south-east respond, bases

XVIIc. Netley Abbey (Hampshire), processional door from cloister, detail

XVIIIA. Old St Paul's Cathedral, arch stone:
(Warwick Mouldings Archive OSP1003)
Cathedral Library

XVIIIB. (top right) Old St Paul's Cathedral, window
tracery stone, major mullion profile: (Warwick
Mouldings Archive OSP1007)
Cathedral Library

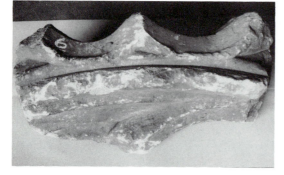

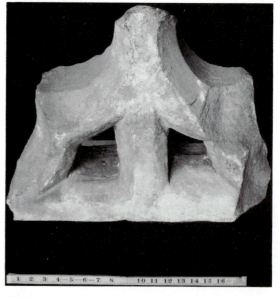

XVIIIc. Old St Paul's Cathedral, window tracery
stone, minor mullion profile: (Warwick Mouldings
Archive OSP1006) Cathedral Library

XVIIID. Old St Paul's Cathedral, openwork parapet
stone: (Warwick Mouldings Archive OSP1026)
Cathedral Library

XIX. Temple Church: details of capitals, bases and mouldings. Drawing by F. Nash at Society of Antiquaries, Red Portfolio London 4, VII

XXA. Temple Church: west portal. Drawing by
F. Nash at Society of Antiquaries,
Red Portfolio London 4, V

XXB. Temple Church; nave aisle elevation.
Drawing by F. Nash at Society of Antiquaries,
Red Portfolio London 4, II

XXC. Temple Church: south side. Crowle-Pennant
Collection of Drawings, volume 6, no. 191
© RCHM

XXD. Temple Church from the south:
engraving (1770) of a drawing of 1671
© RCHM

XXIA. Temple Church: watercolour, 1862. J. W. Archer, volume 9, no. 8
© *RCHM*

XXIB. Temple Church from the south, 1792.
Crowle-Pennant Collection of Drawings,
volume 6, no. 187, by Thomas Malton
© *RCHM*

XXIC. Temple Church: watercolour,
1862. J. W. Archer, volume 9, no. 4
© *RCHM*

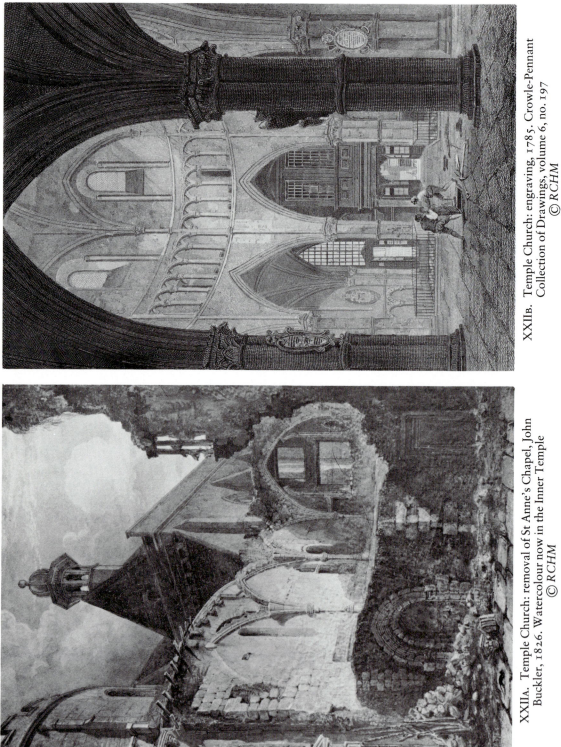

XXIIB. Temple Church: engraving, 1785, Crowle-Pennant Collection of Drawings, volume 6, no. 197
© RCHM

XXIIA. Temple Church: removal of St Anne's Chapel, John Buckler, 1826. Watercolour now in the Inner Temple
© RCHM

XXIIIB. Temple Church: south side
Courtauld Institute of Art

XXIIIA. Temple Church: interior: nave aisle, east bays, looking
east into choir
Courtauld Institute of Art

XXIVA. Temple Church: north-east capitals of porch responds

XXIVB. Temple Church: north-west capitals of porch responds

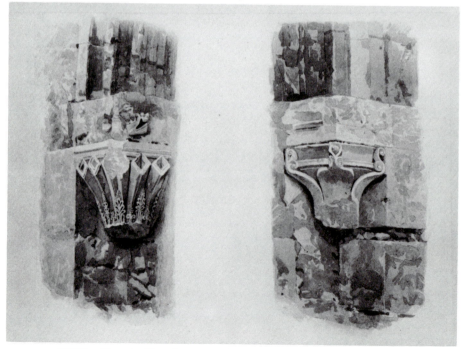

XXIVc. Temple Church: watercolour, capitals of church porch, 1874.
J. W. Archer, volume 9, no. 7
© *RCHM*

XXVa. Temple Church: watercolour, west window, 1874. J. W. Archer, volume 9, no. 5
© RCHM

XXVb. Temple Church: north-east nave window
Courtauld Institute of Art

XXVc. Temple Church: view from the north-west, pre-dating the Blitz
© RCHM

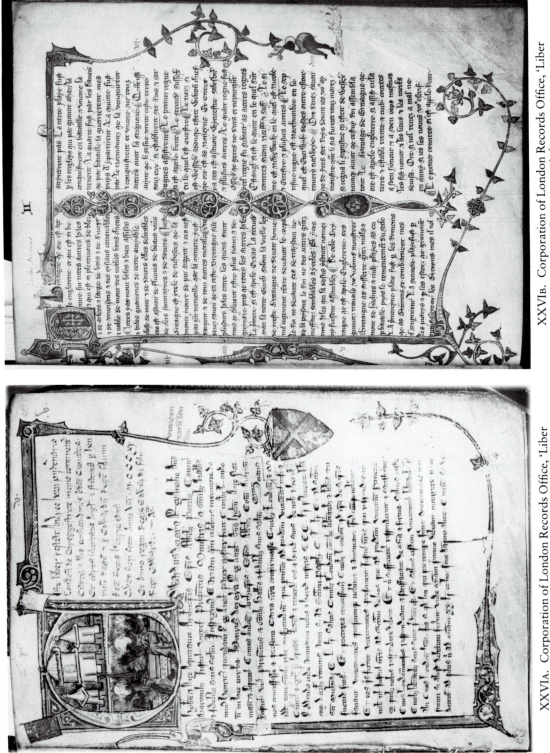

XXVIB. Corporation of London Records Office, 'Liber
Custumarum', f. 1
By permission of The Corporation of London Records Office

XXVIA. Corporation of London Records Office, 'Liber
Horn', f. 206
By permission of The Corporation of London Records Office

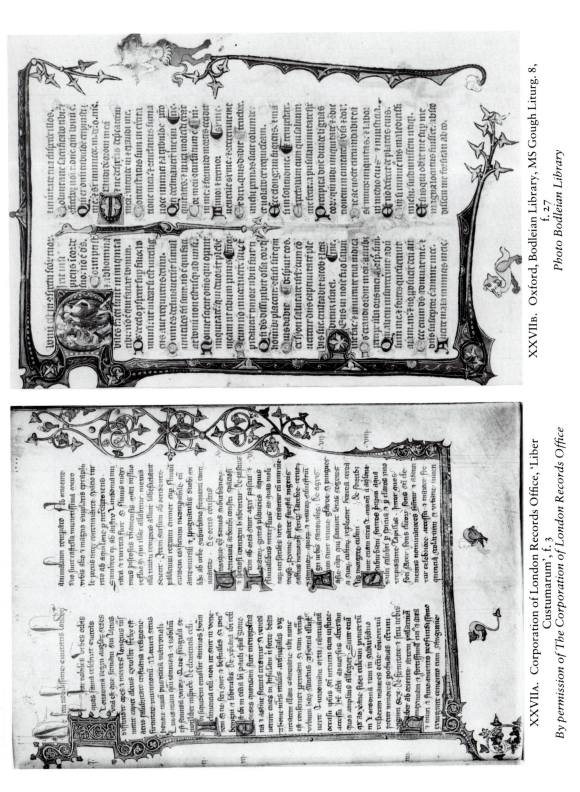

XXVIIA. Corporation of London Records Office, 'Liber Custumarum', f. 3
By permission of The Corporation of London Records Office

XXVIIB. Oxford, Bodleian Library, MS Gough Liturg. 8, f. 27
Photo Bodleian Library

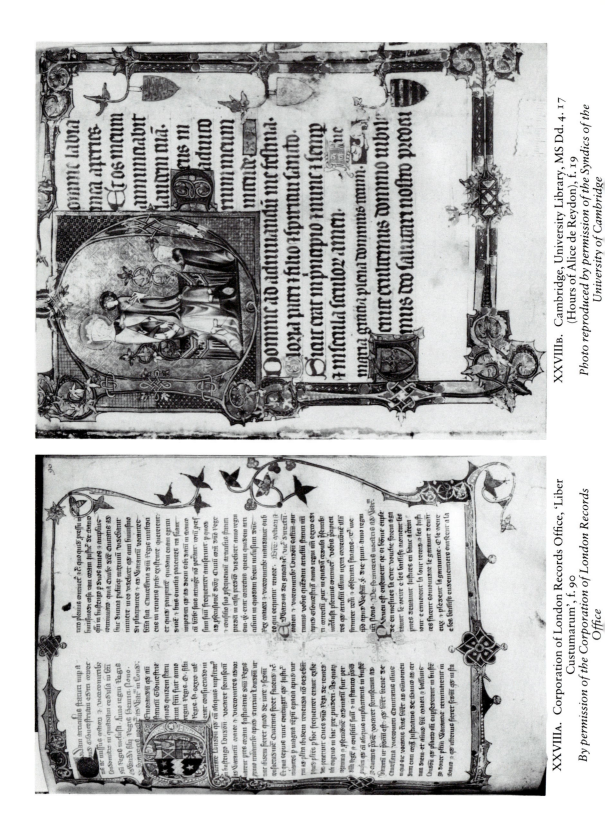

XXVIIIA. Corporation of London Records Office, 'Liber
Custumarum', f. 90
By permission of the Corporation of London Records
Office

XXVIIIB. Cambridge, University Library, MS Dd. 4. 17
(Hours of Alice de Reydon), f. 19
Photo reproduced by permission of the Syndics of the
University of Cambridge

XXIXb. London, British Library, Add. MS 49622 (Gorleston Psalter), f. 35
Conway Library and British Library

XXIXa. London, British Library, Arundel MS 83, part I (Howard Psalter), f. 47
Conway Library and British Library

XXXA. Cambridge, Corpus Christi
College, MS 53 (Peterborough Psalter and
Bestiary), f. 7v
*Photo reproduced courtesy of the Master
and Fellows of Corpus Christi, Cambridge*

XXXB. Cambridge, University Library, MS
Dd. 4. 17 (Hours of Alice de Reydon), f. 5v
*Photo reproduced by permission of the Syndics of the
University of Cambridge*

XXXC. (left) London, British Library, Add. MS
24686 (Alfonso Psalter), f. 2
Photo Conway Library and British Library

XXXD. (above) London, British Library, Cotton
Claudius MS D.II (part of 'Liber Custumarum'), f. 76
(detail)
Photo British Library

XXXIA.   Corporation of London Records Office, 'Liber Custumarum', ff. 184v–185
By permission of The Corporation of London Records Office

XXXIB.   Oxford, Oriel College, MS. 46 (part of 'Liber Custumarum'), ff. 115v–116
Photo Bodleian Library

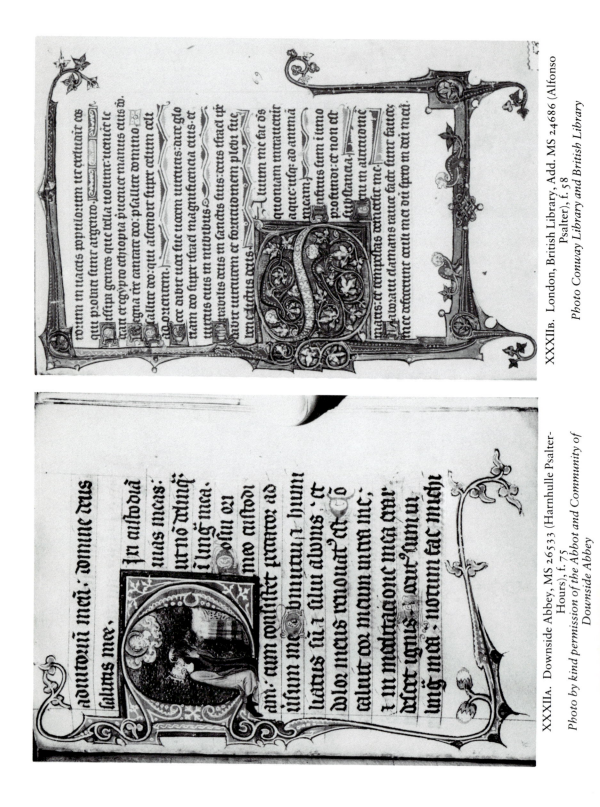

XXXIIB. London, British Library, Add. MS 24686 (Alfonso Psalter), f. 58
Photo Conway Library and British Library

XXXIIA. Downside Abbey, MS 26533 (Harnhulle Psalter-Hours), f. 75
Photo by kind permission of the Abbot and Community of Downside Abbey

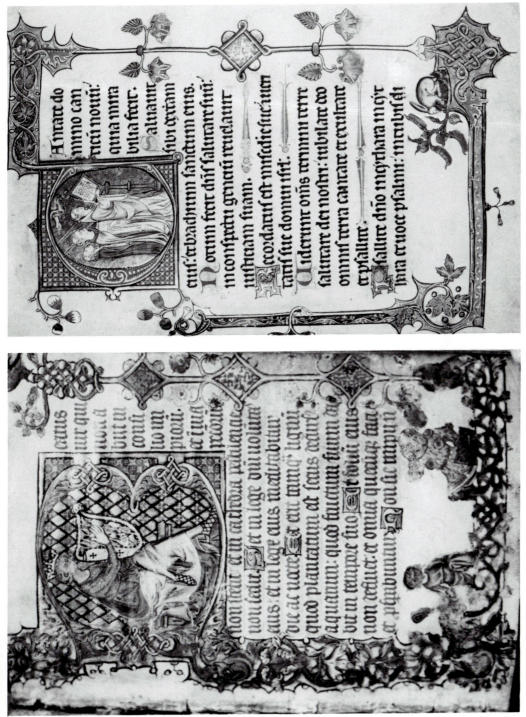

XXXIIIA. London, Dr Williams's Library, MS Ancient 6
(Psalter), f. 20
Photo by kind permission of the Dr Williams's Trust

XXXIIIB. Longleat House, Wiltshire, Library of the
Marquess of Bath (Longleat Psalter), f. 126
*Photo Copyright Conway Library; reproduced by
permission of the Marquess of Bath, Longleat House,
Warminster, Wilts.*

XXXIVA. Cambridge, University Library, MS
Dd. 4. 17 (Hours of Alice de Reydon), f. 6
*Photo reproduced by permission of the Syndics of
the University of Cambridge*

XXXIVB. London, British Library,
Royal MS 2. B. vii (Queen Mary's
Psalter), f. 85
Photo British Library

XXXIVC. Corporation of London Records
Office, 'Liber Horn' (binding *c.* 1320)
*By permission of The Corporation of
London Records Office*

XXXIVD. Corporation of London Records
Office, 'Liber Albus', f. 16 (detail)
*By permission of The Corporation of London
Records Office*

XXXVA. London, British Library, Royal MS 2. B. vii (Queen Mary's Psalter), f. 74 (detail)
Photo British Library

XXXVB. Corporation of London Records Office, 'Liber Horn', f. 174 (detail)
By permission of The Corporation of London Records Office

XXXVIIA. Corporation of London Records Office, 'Liber Horn', f. 41
By permission of The Corporation of London Records Office

XXXVIIB. Corporation of London Records Office, 'Liber Horn', f. 41v (detail)
By permission of the Corporation of London Records Office

XXXVIIIA. Corporation of London Records Office, 'Liber Horn', f. 46
By permission of The Corporation of London Records Office

XXXVIIIB. Corporation of London Records Office, 'Liber Horn', f. 160v
By permission of The Corporation of London Records Office

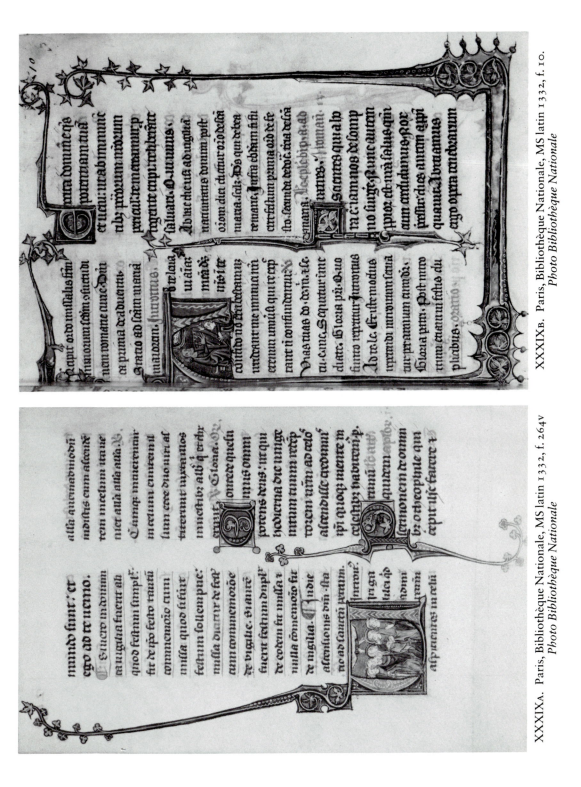

XXXIXA. Paris, Bibliothèque Nationale, MS latin 1332, f. 264v
Photo Bibliothèque Nationale

XXXIXB. Paris, Bibliothèque Nationale, MS latin 1332, f. 10.
Photo Bibliothèque Nationale

XLA. (above, left) Monument to John Holand, Duke of Exeter, probably erected *c.* 1432, now in St Peter ad Vincula, Tower of London
Courtauld Institute

XLB. (above) Interior of St John Hackney in the later 18th century, showing the Easter Sepulchre erected by Christopher Urswyck, 1519, and a fragment of the monument to Sir John Heron, died 1525
London Borough of Hackney Archives

XLC. (left) Upper part of the Easter Sepulchre monument to Gregory Lovell, died 1545, at St Peter and St Paul, Harlington
RCHM